Lecture Notes in Computer Scienc

T0238506

Commenced Publication in 1973
Founding and Former Series Editors:
Gerhard Goos, Juris Hartmanis, and Jan van Leeuwen

Hana Kubátová   Christian Hochberger
Martin Daněk   Bernhard Sick (Eds.)

Architecture of Computing Systems – ARCS 2013

26th International Conference
Prague, Czech Republic, February 19-22, 2013
Proceedings

 Springer

Volume Editors

Hana Kubátová
Czech Technical University
Thákurova 9
160 00 Prague 6, Czech Republic
E-mail: kubatova@fit.cvut.cz

Christian Hochberger
Technische Universität Darmstadt
Merckstraße 25
64283 Darmstadt, Germany
E-mail: hochberger@rs.tu-darmstadt.de

Martin Daněk
Institute of Information Theory and Automation
Pod Vodárenskou věží 4
18208 Prague 8, Czech Republic
E-mail: danek@utia.cas.cz

Bernhard Sick
Universität Kassel
Wilhelmshöher Allee 73
34121 Kassel, Germany
E-mail: bsick@uni-kassel.de

ISSN 0302-9743   e-ISSN 1611-3349
ISBN 978-3-642-36423-5   e-ISBN 978-3-642-36424-2
DOI 10.1007/978-3-642-36424-2
Springer Heidelberg Dordrecht London New York

Library of Congress Control Number: 2013930452

CR Subject Classification (1998): C.2, C.5.3, D.4, D.2.11, H.3.5, H.4, H.5.4

Typesetting: Camera-ready by author, data conversion by Scientific Publishing Services, Chennai, India

Printed on acid-free paper

Springer is part of Springer Science+Business Media (www.springer.com)

Preface

The *Architecture of Computing Systems (ARCS)* series of conferences has a long tradition of reporting high-quality results in computer architecture research and closely related fields. ARCS represents a dynamic, evolving community that closely follows new research trends and also defines new research areas such as the field of organic computing. Over the years, ARCS has evolved from a small national event to an important international forum. The 26th ARCS, with a special focus on application acceleration, was hosted by the renowned Czech Technical University in Prague, one of the oldest technical universities in the world, in one of the most beautiful European cities.

ARCS 2013 attracted 73 submissions coming from 26 countries spread over all but one inhabited continent. Of those, 29 were accepted for presentation at the conference and have been published in this book. We would like to acknowledge the efforts of all researchers who submitted their work to ARCS 2013, even though many papers could not be be included in the final program due to the packed conference schedule.

We would like to express our gratitude to all those who made this ARCS possible. This includes the Chairs, the members of the Steering Committee (GI/ITG Fachausschuss ARCS), the members of the Technical Program Committee, the additional reviewers, and in particular the authors that submitted their work to ARCS 2013. We would also like to thank all our sponsors and supporters. Finally, we wish to express our appreciation to Petr Fišer, for the web support, and André Gensler, for typesetting the proceedings.

We hope you enjoyed ARCS 2013.

December 2012

Hana Kubátová
Christian Hochberger
Martin Daněk
Bernhard Sick

Organization

Organizing Committee

General Chair

Hana Kubátová   CTU in Prague, Czech Republic
Christian Hochberger   TU Dresden, Germany

PC Chairs

Martin Daněk   UTIA AV CR, Czech Republic
Bernhard Sick   University of Kassel, Germany

Workshop and Tutorial Chair

Mladen Berekovic   TU Braunschweig, Germany

Publicity Chairs

Josef Hlaváč   CTU in Prague, Czech Republic
Dietmar Fey   University of Erlangen-Nürnberg, Germany

Conference Web Chairs

Petr Fišer   CTU in Prague, Czech Republic
Martin Chloupek   CTU in Prague, Czech Republic

Industry Liaison

Robert Lórencz   CTU in Prague, Czech Republic

Local Organization

Rudolf Kinc   AMCA, Czech Republic
Eva Uhrová (Finance)   AMCA, Czech Republic

Program Committee

Michael Beigl	Karlsruhe Institute of Technology, Germany
Mladen Berekovic	TU Braunschweig, Germany
Koen Bertels	Technical University of Delft, The Netherlands
Jürgen Brehm	University of Hanover, Germany
Uwe Brinkschulte	University of Frankfurt, Germany
Philip Brisk	University of California, USA
Jiannong Cao	Hong Kong Polytechnic University, Hong Kong
Joao Cardoso	University of Porto, Portugal
Luigi Carro	Universidade Federal do Rio Grande do Sul, Brazil
Martin Daněk	Akademie věd České Republiky, Czech Republic
Koen De Bosschere	Ghent University, Belgium
Oliver Diessel	University of New South Wales, Australia
Nikitas Dimopoulos	University of Victoria, Canada
Ahmed El-Mahdy	E-JUST, Egypt
Fabrizio Ferrandi	Politecnico di Milano, Italy
Alois Ferscha	University of Linz, Austria
Petr Fišer	Czech Technical University in Prague, Czech Republic
Pierfrancesco Foglia	Università di Pisa, Italy
William Fornaciari	Politecnico di Milano, Italy
Björn Franke	University of Edinburgh, UK
Roberto Giorgi	University of Siena, Italy
Daniel Gracia-Pérez	CEA, France
Jan Haase	Technical University Vienna, Austria
Jörg Henkel	Karlsruhe Institute of Technology, Germany
Andreas Herkersdorf	Technical University of Munich, Germany
Christian Hochberger	TU Dresden, Germany
Michael Hübner	University of Bochum, Germany
Murali Jayapala	IMEC, Belgium
Gert Jervan	University of Tallinn, Estonia
Ben Juurlink	TU Berlin, Germany
Wolfgang Karl	Karlsruhe Institute of Technology, Germany
Andreas Koch	TU Darmstadt, Germany
Jan Kořenek	Brno University of Technology, Czech Republic
Hana Kubátová	Czech Technical University in Prague, Czech Republic

Olaf Landsiedel	KTH Stockholm, Sweden
Róbert Lórencz	Czech Technical University in Prague, Czech Republic
Paul Lukowicz	DFKI and University of Kaiserslautern, Germany
Erik Mähle	University of Lübeck, Germany
Christian Müller-Schloer	Leibniz Universität Hannover, Germany
Alex Orailoglu	UC San Diego, USA
Francois Pacull	Commissariat à l'énergie atomique, France
Raphael Poss	University of Amsterdam, The Netherlands
Kay Römer	ETH Zürich, Switzerland
Pascal Sainrat	Université de Toulouse, France
Silvia Santini	ETH Zürich, Switzerland
Toshinori Sato	Fukuoka University, Japan
Jan Schmidt	Czech Technical University in Prague, Czech Republic
Martin Schulz	Lawerence Livermore National Laboratory, Canada
Karsten Schwan	Georgia Institute of Technology, USA
Lukáš Sekanina	Czech Technical University in Prague, Czech Republic
Bernhard Sick	University of Kassel, Germany
Cristina Silvano	Politecnico di Milano, Italy
Leonel Sousa	TU Lisboa, Portugal
Rainer Spallek	TU Dresden, Germany
Olaf Spinczyk	TU Dortmund, Germany
Benno Stabernack	Fraunhofer HHI, Germany
Walter Stechele	TU München, Germany
Jarmo Takala	Tampere University of Technology, Finland
Djamshid Tavanagraian	Universität Rostock, Germany
Jürgen Teich	Universität Erlangen, Germany
Pedro Trancoso	University of Cyprus, Cyprus
Theo Ungerer	University of Augsburg, Germany
Hans Vandierendonck	Queens University Belfast, UK
Stéphane Vialle	Supelec, France
Lucian Vintan	University of Sibiu, Romania
Klaus Waldschmidt	Universität Frankfurt, Germany
Stephan Wong	Delft University of Technology, The Netherlands

Additional Referees

F. Terraneo	T. Schuster	J. Wenninger
N. Moser	R. Pujari	J. Paul
Y. Chaaban	R. Paseman	G. Mariani

G. Nazar

R. Seedorf

C. Kang

T. Preußer

R. Backasch

J. Lucas

A. Ilic

I. Zgeras

M. Kicherer

L. Kuan

G. Thomas

H. Amrouch

M. Solinas

F. Miller

J. Matousek

M. Pacher

M. Kohlik

M. Gunia

M. Raitza

J. Mische

L. Cassano

S. Roloff

J. Mottin

C. Li

S. Lal

H. Mushtaq

D. Matos

B. Motruk

A. Brandon

S. Campanelli

M. Zabel

I. Koutras

F. Stock

S. Boppu

F. Nowak

V. Lari

S. Schlingmann

F. Nadeem

G. Hempel

A. Garbade

T. Wink

J. Sykora

G. Bournoutian

A. Portero

S. Metzlaff

B. Thielmann

S. Wildermann

F. Kluge

A. Ostadzadeh

G. Gabrielli

S. Xydis

F. Anjam

R. Ferreira

A. Barenghi

F. Hameed

T. Martinek

S. Mühlbach

Z. Vasicek

S. Michalik

M. Kajan

B. Schmidt

M. Vogt

S. Niemann

We also thank all additional referees whose names are unknown to the Executive Committee.

Table of Contents

An Unstructured Termination Detection Algorithm Using Gossip in Cloud Computing Environments[*]

JongBeom Lim[1], Kwang-Sik Chung[2], Joon-Min Gil[3], TaeWeon Suh[1], and HeonChang Yu[1],[**]

[1] Department of Computer Science Education, Korea University, Seoul, Korea
{jblim,suhtw,yuhc}@korea.ac.kr
[2] Department of Computer Science, Korea National Open University, Seoul, Korea
kchung0825@knou.ac.kr
[3] School of Computer & Information Communications Engineering,
Catholic University of Daegu, Daegu, Korea
jmgil@cu.ac.kr

Abstract. Determining termination in dynamic environments is hard due to node joining and leaving. In previous studies on termination detection, some structures, such as spanning tree or computational tree, are used. In this work, we present an unstructured termination detection algorithm, which uses a gossip based scheme to cope with scalability and fault-tolerance issues. This approach allows the algorithm not to maintain specific structures even when nodes join and leave during runtime. These dynamic behaviors are prevalent in cloud computing environments and little attention has been paid by existing approaches. To measure the complexity of our proposed algorithm, a new metric, *self-centered message complexity* is used. Our evaluation over scalable settings shows that an unstructured approach has a significant merit to solve scalability and fault-tolerance problems with lower message complexity over existing algorithms.

Keywords: Termination detection, Unstructured algorithm, Gossip, Cloud computing.

1 Introduction

In the termination detection problem, a set of nodes in the system collectively execute a distributed computation and the purpose of termination detection algorithms is to safely detect the termination of the distributed computation, whereupon the next distributed computation can progress. Determining whether a distributed computation has terminated or not is a non-trivial task because no

---

[*] This work was supported by the National Research Foundation of Korea (NRF) grant funded by the Korea goverment (MEST) (No. 2012046684).
[**] Corresponding author.

C. Hochberger et al. (Eds.): ARCS 2013, LNCS 7767, pp. 1–12, 2013.

node has complete knowledge of the global state, and there is no notion of global time or global memory. Each node only knows its own local state and local time, and communication among nodes can be done only by passing messages.

Termination detection problem has been extensively studied for static distributed systems where all of the nodes are stationary in terms of node joining and leaving from the beginning to the end (e.g., [1], [2], [3], [4], [5] and [6]). One of the systems where termination detection algorithms can be used is the cloud computing system in which constituent nodes can easily join and leave with dynamic behavior due to loosely-coupled environments. However, although numerous research efforts for the termination detection problem in recent years mainly focus on reducing message complexity, little attention has been paid to the aforementioned dynamic behavior. Most of the studies assumed that the system is static without considering node failures and joining which are vital aspects in cloud computing environments and should not be dismissed.

Recently, gossip-based algorithms have received much attention due to its inherent scalable and fault-tolerant properties which offer additional benefits in distributed systems [7]. Correctness of a gossip-based protocol is presented in [8] and [9]. In gossip-based algorithms, each node maintains some number of neighbors called a *PartialView*. With this PartialView, at each cycle (round), every node in the system selects f (fanout) number of nodes at random and then communicates using one of the following ways: 1) Push, 2) Pull, and 3) Push-pull mode. Gossip-based algorithms guarantee message delivery to all nodes with high probability and their variation can be found in [10], [11], [12], [13], [14] and [15]. Applications of gossip-based algorithms include message dissemination, failure detection services, data aggregation etc.

In this paper, we present an unstructured termination detection algorithm based on the gossip-based algorithm. Having PartialView in the gossip-based algorithm is the essential key to solve the scalability issue. In other words, each node does not have to maintain all the nodes in the system, but the small number of nodes. Furthermore, in structured termination detection algorithms (using spanning tree or computational tree), reconstruction of the structure of algorithms is required when node joining and leaving occur. Otherwise, detecting the termination of a distributed computation is virtually impossible since node connection has not established or has broken.

The rest of the paper is organized as follows. We present the system model and formally describe the termination detection problem in Section 2. Section 3 provides our gossip-based termination detection algorithm. Experimental results for the algorithm and their interpretation are given in Section 4; this section also analyzes the message complexity. Finally, Section 5 gives our conclusions.

2   Model and Problem Specifications

2.1   System Model

We assume that the cloud computing infrastructure consists of numerous nodes of resources, and individual nodes perform arbitrary programs to achieve a common goal. Because of the absence of shared memory, each process or node should communicate with other nodes only by passing messages through a set of channels. In addition, we assume that all channels are reliable but are not restricted to FIFO (first-in, first-out). The message delay is bounded. There is no global clock. However, we assume that each node synchronizes its time by gossiping with other nodes. This approach has been justified by [16]. Furthermore, the communication model is asynchronous.

2.2   Model and Problem Specifications

Termination detection is a fundamental problem in distributed systems; it is not an exception in cloud computing systems. The importance of determining termination derives from the observation that some nodes may execute several sub-problems, and in some cases, there are precedence dependencies among them. Because there is no shared memory, message passing is the only way to deal with the termination detection problem satisfying following properties:

- **Safety:** If the termination detection algorithm announces termination, then the underlying computation has indeed terminated.
- **Liveness:** If termination holds in the underlying computation, then eventually the termination detection algorithm announces termination and henceforth termination is not revoked.
- **Non-Interference:** The termination detection algorithm must not influence the underlying computation.

The definition of termination detection is as follows: Let $P_i(t)$ denote the state (active or passive) of process P_i at time t and $C_{i,j}(t)$ denote the number of messages in transit in the channel at time t from P_i to P_j. A distributed computation is said to be terminated at time t if and only if:

$$(\forall_i :: P_i(t) = passive) \land (\forall_{i,j} :: C_{i,j}(t) = null) \qquad (1)$$

2.3   Performance Metrics

Traditionally, the following metric has been used to measure the performance of termination detection algorithms:

- **Message complexity:** The number of messages required to detect the termination.

In addition to the message complexity, we propose a new metric called *self-centered message complexity*. Self-centered message complexity counts the number of messages required to detect the termination from a requester point of view rather than from the whole nodes in the system. Self-centered message can be defined as follows:

- **Self-centered message complexity:** The number of messages required to detect the termination from a requester point of view.

It is believed that this is more flexible and simpler metric to measure the structured and unstructured termination detection algorithms because some algorithms are not always intuitive and observable from a high-level domain.

3   Unstructured Termination Detection Algorithm

In this section, we first review the basic gossip-based protocol based on [17] to describe our gossip-based termination detection algorithm. The termination detection algorithm proposed in this section can be viewed as an extension of the gossip-based algorithm to support the termination detection functionality.

3.1   Basic Idea

In the gossip-based algorithm, there are two different kinds of threads in each node: active and passive. At each cycle (round), an active thread selects a neighbor at random and sends a message. The active thread then waits for the message from the receiver. Upon receiving the message from the neighbor, the active thread updates its local state with the received message and its previous information. A passive thread waits for messages from active threads and replies to the senders. Afterwards, the passive thread updates its local state with the received message from the sender accordingly.

A simple way to solve the termination detection problem is to use distributed snapshots (e.g., [3]). If a consistent snapshot of a distributed computation is taken after the distributed computation has terminated, the snapshot will capture the termination of the computation. However, the algorithm that uses distributed snapshots broadcasts to all other nodes when a process goes passive; this involves a large number of request messages. Furthermore, detecting whether all the other processes have taken a snapshot is not a trivial job even though all of processes are passive and taken a snapshot.

Hence, we take the distributed approach with the gossip-based algorithm. To let a process decide whether all of the nodes are passive and distributed computation has terminated, we use a piggy-backing mechanism by which a node adds additional information of neighbors to the message during gossiping. By using the piggy-backing mechanism, any node wishing to detect termination can eventually detect whether distributed computation is terminated or not.

In the previous researches using the distributed approach, however, they assumed that the number of nodes is static. Few studies have focused on the dynamic behavior such as adding and removing nodes while request operations are ongoing, which is that we want to deal with.

3.2   Details of Termination Detection Algorithm

The unstructured termination detection algorithm using the gossip-based approach is summarized in Algorithm 1. We explain only our extensions to the gossip algorithm. We assume that each process has a unique identifier, which

---

Algorithm 1. Unstructured termination detection algorithm for P_i

---

1 **begin** initialization
2     $\mathsf{State}_i[j] = passive$, where $\forall_j \in \{1 \ldots n\}$;
3   isActive$= false$;

4 **begin** at each cycle
5   **begin** upon sending <basicMessage> to P_j
6         $\mathsf{State}_i[j].state = \mathsf{State}_j[j].state = active$;
7         $\mathsf{State}_i[j].timestamp = \mathsf{State}_j[j].timestamp = LC_{current}$;
8   **call** updateStatesArray ();

9   **begin** upon receiving <basicMessage> from P_j
10         $\mathsf{State}_i[j].state = \mathsf{State}_j[j].state = active$;
11         $\mathsf{State}_i[j].timestamp = \mathsf{State}_j[j].timestamp = LC_{current}$;
12   **call** updateStatesArray ();
13   **call** checkTermination ();

14 **begin** upon local computation is completed
15     $\mathsf{State}_i[i].state = passive$;
16     $\mathsf{State}_i[i].timestamp = LC_{current}$;

17 **function** updateStatesArray ()
18   **foreach** *elements in* $\mathsf{State}_i[k]$ *and* $\mathsf{State}_j[k]$ **do**
19   **if** $\mathsf{State}_i[k].timestamp < \mathsf{State}_j[k].timestamp$ **then**
20             $\mathsf{State}_i[k].state = \mathsf{State}_j[k].state$;
21             $\mathsf{State}_i[k].timestamp = \mathsf{State}_j[k].timestamp$;
22   **else**
23             $\mathsf{State}_j[k].state = \mathsf{State}_i[k].state$;
24             $\mathsf{State}_j[k].timestamp = \mathsf{State}_i[k].timestamp$;

25 **function** checkTermination ()
26   isActive $= false$;
27   **foreach** *element in* $\mathsf{State}_i[k]$ **do**
28   isActive $|= \mathsf{State}_i[k].state$;
29   **if** isActive $== false$ **then**
30   Termination is detected;
31   **else**
32   Termination is not detected;

---

is indexed by from 1 to n, where n is the number of processes (nodes) in the system. Henceforth, the terms a node and a process are used interchangeably.

Each process P_i maintains the following data structure:

- $\mathsf{State}_i[1:n]$: An array of states for P_i. This data structure consists of two components for each array element: *state* and *timestamp*. State value can be active or passive, and timestamp value is logical clock (LC) at which state value is updated.

Algorithm 2. Extended algorithm for Alg. 1

```
1 begin at each cycle
2 │   begin upon sending <basicMessage> to P_j
3 │   │   timestamp = LC_current;
4 │   └   BasicMsgSet_i = BasicMsgSet_i ∪ (j, timestamp);

5 function updateStatesArray ()
6 │   if BasicMsgSet_i ≠ null ∨ BasicMsgSet_j ≠ null then
7 │   │   foreach elements in State_i[k] and State_j[k] do
8 │   │   │   if State_i[k].timestamp < timestamp∨ State_j[k].timestamp <
      │   │   │   timestamp then
9 │   │   │   │   // where timestamp∈ (k, timestamp) in BasicMsgSet_i ∪
      │   │   │   │      BasicMsgSet_j
10│   │   │   │   State_i[k].state = State_j[k].state = active;
11│   │   │   └   State_i[k].timestamp = State_j[k].timestamp = timestamp;
```

We describe our extensions as follows:

1. If P_i selects P_j during gossiping the following states are performed:
   (a) When P_i sends a basic message to P_j, State array is updated as follows:
      i. jth elements (i.e., state and timestamp) of array of both processes are updated with active and $LC_{current}$.
   (b) When P_j sends a basic message to P_i, State array is updated as follows:
      i. ith elements (i.e., state and timestamp) of array of both processes are updated with active and $LC_{current}$.
   (c) Each element of State$[k]$ of both processes, where $\forall k \in \{1 \ldots n\}$, is updated with the one whose timestamp value is fresher.
2. When local computation is completed, State values are updated as follows:
   (a) State$_i[i]$.state and State$_i[i]$.timestamp are updated with passive and $LC_{current}$, respectively.
3. In order to decide whether local computation of whole processes is completed, following states are performed:
   (a) State array is checked:
      i. If State$_i[k]$.state $==$ passive, where $\forall k \in \{1 \ldots n\}$, then it concludes that termination is detected.
      ii. Otherwise, it concludes that termination is not detected and local computation of some processes is ongoing.

Obviously, Algorithm 1 works correctly if computation is distributed at the initial stage and no further basic messages are sent out. However, when basic messages are sent at arbitrary time, then the algorithm could violate the safety property. For instance, let P_i be an initiator, and P_j's state is active and other nodes' state are passive. If P_j sends a basic message (immediately before P_j changes its state from active to passive) to P_k whose state is passive and then P_j selects P_i as a gossip target, then P_i could announce termination without knowing P_k's state is active.

To enable our algorithm working safely, we introduce the modified algorithm. Algorithm 2 shows only the added procedures from Algorithm 1. When P_i sends a basic message to P_j, $(j, \texttt{timestamp})$ is added to BasicMsgSet$_i$, where $\texttt{timestamp}$ is the time the basic message is sent out. Then, P_i sets State$_i[j].state$ to active and State$_i[j].timestamp$ to the time the basic message is sent out.

In the $\texttt{updateStatesArray}$ procedure, if BasicMsgSet$_i$ or BasicMsgSet$_j$ is not *null*, and timestamp value of k's element of State arrays is less than that of $(k, \texttt{timestamp})$, where $(k, \texttt{timestamp}) \in$ BasicMsgSet$_i$ $\cup$ BasicMsgSet$_j$, then k's elements of State arrays are updated with active and timestamp that are in BasicMsgSet. Thus, even if a process sends a basic message at arbitrary time, our algorithm can safely announce the termination.

4 Experimental Evaluation

In this section, we evaluate our unstructured termination detection algorithm compared with the broadcast algorithm and the tree-based algorithm. Due to restriction of node scalability on physical machines, we used the PeerSim simulator [18], which supports extreme scalability and dynamicity of nodes. Furthermore, message complexity is compared to show the efficiency of our unstructured termination detection algorithm with existing algorithms. For simplicity, we assume that every node completed its local computation before a request for the termination detection is initiated.

4.1 Experimental Setup and Methodology

Table 1 summarizes our experimental setup parameters. We assume that a request for termination detection is initiated before cycles begin. We set the size of PartialView to 20, which is 0.2% of the number of nodes. Because of the nature of dynamism of cloud computing environments, some nodes may join and leave at any time. Thus, we consider the following scenarios:

1. Nodes are static: nodes does not fail and join during runtime.
2. Nodes join during execution: some numbers of nodes are added during gossip cycle 1 through 10.
3. Nodes leave during execution: some numbers of nodes are removed during gossip cycle 1 through 10.

4.2 PartialView Size and the Requisite Number of Cycles

We first evaluate the impact of the size of PartialView on the requisite number of cycles. Figure 1(a) and 1(b) show the results for the requisite number of cycles to detect termination with varying the size of PartialView from 5 to 30 for 10^4 nodes, and with varying the number of nodes from 10^2 to $10^{4.5}$ with 20 of PartialView size.

Table 1. Experimental Setup Parameters

Parameter	Value
The number of nodes	10,000
Fanout	1
The size of PartialView	20
Cycles for node joining and leaving	1 through 10
The number of nodes that join at a cycle	500
The number of nodes that leave at a cycle	100

We have confirmed that the impact of the size of PartialView is unpredictable because the gossip algorithm relies ôn random samples. Notice that in Figure 1(b), the requisite number of cycles grows linearly as the total number of nodes increases exponentially. In Figure 1(c) shows the fraction data of the requester's State array whose state value is passive. At the early cycles, the fraction data increase slowly, but increase sharply at later cycles.

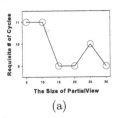 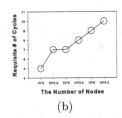 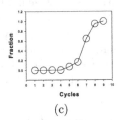

(a)   (b)   (c)

Fig. 1. The requisite numbers of cycles to detect termination and its fraction data. The number of nodes is set to 10^4 in (a) and (c). The size of PartialView is set to 20 in (b) and (c).

4.3   Impact on Node Joining

To show the impact of node joining during a request to detect termination is in progress, we compared with existing algorithms, that is, the broadcast algorithm and tree-based algorithm. Because of node joining, the broadcast algorithm and the tree-based algorithm should re-initiate the request to detect termination. In the broadcast algorithm, the requester sends a request message to all nodes. After that, some nodes may join. In this case, the requester should receive acknowledges from all the nodes. Therefore, the broadcast algorithm should re-initiate the request to safely announce the termination. The tree-based algorithm also requires the re-initiation because it is possible that a node joins with an active state. In this case, the tree-based algorithm involves two steps: 1) rebuild a computational tree, and 2) re-initiate the request.

On the other hand, the unstructured algorithm does not require re-initiating the request due to its inherent property. In our scenario such that some nodes are joined at cycle 1 through 10, the number of trial for the termination detection is 11, 11 and 1 for the broadcast algorithm, the tree-based algorithm, and the unstructured algorithm, respectively. Hence, the requisite number of cycles to detect termination is 11 for the broadcast algorithm and tree-based algorithm. However, in the unstructured algorithm, it requires 13 cycles to detect termination because information about newly joined nodes should also be taken into account (see Figure 2(a)).

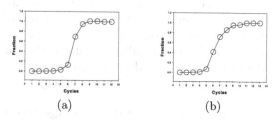

(a)   (b)

Fig. 2. Fraction data for the node joining scenario (a) and leaving scenario (b)

4.4   Impact on Node Leaving

Like the node joining scenario, we compared three algorithms to see the impact of node leaving. As in the node joining scenario, if some nodes leave due to failure or unavailability, the broadcast algorithm and the tree-based algorithm should re-initiate the request to detect termination. Thus, the requisite number of cycles is 11 for the two algorithms.

For the unstructured algorithm, the requisite number of cycles is 12 and its fraction data are shown in Figure 2(b). The curve of the graph is changing uncertainly. This phenomenon can be explained from two extreme points of view. First, because some nodes leave from the system, the requester only needs to know information about nodes that alive. Therefore, the fraction data may increase sharply. The other extreme is that when nodes contact a node that has failed frequently, the requisite number of cycles may get delayed and the fraction data may increase slowly.

4.5   Message Complexity

We analyze the message complexity of our unstructured algorithm compared with the broadcast algorithm and the tree-based algorithm. Obviously, message complexity of the broadcast algorithm is $2 \cdot (n-1)$, $n-1$ for request messages and $n-1$ for acknowledge messages, where n is the number of nodes. For the tree-based algorithm, message complexity is $2t$, t for request messages and t for acknowledge messages, where t is the number of tasks distributed. In the worst case, message complexity of the tree-based algorithm is equivalent to the broadcast algorithm.

On the other hand, the message complexity of the unstructured algorithm is cn, where c is the requisite number of cycles, and n is the number of nodes. However, the message complexity of the unstructured algorithm amortized by a cycle is n. The rationale of amortizing it by a cycle is that cycles of the gossip algorithm may become infinite periodic events when we use it as, for example, a failure detection service, and that the amortized message complexity is more intuitive regarding the gossip algorithm because c will vary each run due to random uncertainty. Figure 3(a) shows the comparison of the message complexity for the static scenario.

When we analyze the self-centered message complexity, we count the messages from a requester point of view. In other words, in the unstructured algorithm, each node sees 2 messages on average because at each cycle a node selects a neighbor as a gossip target (if fanout is set to 1) and the probability of being selected as a gossip target from other nodes at a cycle is 1. Specifically, $P_s = v/n \cdot 1/v \cdot n = 1$, where v is the size of PartialView and n is the number of nodes. For the tree-based algorithm, we assume that each node sends e basic messages, where e is the base of natural logarithm. Thus the height of the tree-based algorithm is $ln(n)$.

The self-centered message complexity of the three algorithms for the static scenario is shown in Figure 3(b). Because the requester of the broadcast algorithm sees the whole $2 \cdot (n-1)$ messages, the self-centered message complexity of the broadcast algorithm is huge enough to offset the other two algorithms' data. Therefore, the two algorithms' data is shown in Figure 3(c) separately. Besides the broadcast algorithm, the requester of the tree-based algorithm sees $2e$ messages, whereas the requester of the unstructured algorithm sees 2 messages on average at each cycle.

Figure 4(a) shows the message complexity of the three algorithms for each scenario. Note that data in Figure 4(a) are used at which until the requisite number of cycles is reached. Apart from the static scenario, the unstructured algorithm has a lower message complexity than other algorithms. Figure 4(b) shows the fraction data for the number of times that is selected from other nodes. The expectation of being selected from other nodes is 1 because $\sum_{i=1}^{n} i \times \frac{s_i}{n} = 1$, where s_i is the number of nodes selected i times, and n is the number of nodes.

Finally, Figure 4(c), 4(d) show the self-centered message complexity for each scenario. As in Figure 4(a), data for the self-centered message complexity is used at which until the requisite number of cycles is reached. The broadcast algorithm always has higher self-centered message complexity than that of the two algorithms. When we compare the tree-based algorithm and the unstructured algorithm, the phenomenon is similar to that appeared in Figure 4(a). In the static scenario, the tree-based algorithm has lower complexity but higher complexity in node joining and leaving scenarios than the unstructured algorithm.

Besides message complexity, we analyze the algorithmic properties of the three algorithms with respect to maintenance cost, re-initiating, and fault-tolerance as shown in Table 2. The tree-based algorithm is required to maintain the computational tree when node joining and leaving occur as well as when sending a basic message. The unstructured algorithm does not require re-initiating the request due to node joining and leaving but others do. In this regard, the unstructured algorithm is also fault-tolerant.

Table 2. Comparison of algorithms with respect to maintenance cost, re-initiating, and fault-tolerance

Algorithm	Maintenance cost	Re-initiating due to joins and leave	Fault tolerance
Broadcast	No	Required	No
Tree	Required	Required	No
Unstructured	No	No	Yes

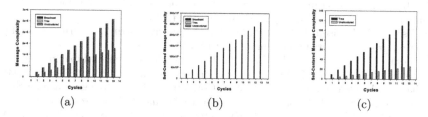

(a)   (b)   (c)

Fig. 3. Comparison of self-centered message complexity of algorithms for the static scenario

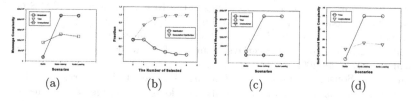

(a)   (b)   (c)   (d)

Fig. 4. Comparison of message complexity for each scenario (a) and the fraction data for the number of times selected from other nodes (b), and self-centered message complexity for each scenario (c) and (d)

5   Conclusion

In this work, we presented a termination detection algorithm using a gossip-based approach to cope with scalability and fault tolerance issues. A cloud environment, in which the behavior of their constituting nodes is dynamic (i.e., a node may join and leave at any time), is an example to which our algorithm can be applied. Furthermore, our gossip-based termination detection algorithm could be embedded seamlessly into other existing gossip-based algorithms. In other words, if a gossip-based algorithm is implemented for the failure detection service, then the termination detection algorithm proposed in our work can be embedded into the existing gossip-based algorithm. A self-centered message complexity allows us to measure the distribution of messages of in the system. The self-centered message complexity of our proposed termination detection algorithm shows that messages are diffused among nodes almost evenly without a bottleneck.

References

1. Dijkstra, E.W., Scholten, C.S.: Termination detection for diffusing computations. Inf. Proc. Letters 11(1), 1–4 (1980)
2. Mattern, F.: Algorithms for distributed termination detection. Distributed Computing 2(3), 161–175 (1987)
3. Huang, S.T.: Termination detection by using distributed snapshots. Inf. Process. Lett. 32(3), 113–120 (1989)
4. Mahapatra, N.R., Dutt, S.: An efficient delay-optimal distributed termination detection algorithm. J. Parallel Distrib. Comput. 67(10), 1047–1066 (2007)
5. Mittal, N., Venkatesan, S., Peri, S.: A family of optimal termination detection algorithms. Distributed Computing 20, 141–162 (2007)
6. Livesey, M., Morrison, R., Munro, D.: The doomsday distributed termination detection protocol. Distributed Computing 19, 419–431 (2007)
7. Ganesh, A., Kermarrec, A.M., Massoulie, L.: Peer-to-peer membership management for gossip-based protocols. IEEE Transactions on Computers 52(2), 139–149 (2003)
8. Allavena, A., Demers, A., Hopcroft, J.E.: Correctness of a gossip based membership protocol. In: Proceedings of the Twenty-Fourth Annual ACM Symposium on Principles of Distributed Computing, PODC 2005, pp. 292–301. ACM, New York (2005)
9. Gurevich, M., Keidar, I.: Correctness of gossip-based membership under message loss. In: Proceedings of the 28th ACM Symposium on Principles of Distributed Computing, PODC 2009, pp. 151–160. ACM, New York (2009)
10. Ganesh, A.J., Kermarrec, A.M., Massoulié, L.: Hiscamp: self-organizing hierarchical membership protocol. In: Proceedings of the 10th Workshop on ACM SIGOPS European Workshop, EW 10, pp. 133–139. ACM, New York (2002)
11. Voulgaris, S., Gavidia, D., Steen, M.: Cyclon: Inexpensive membership management for unstructured p2p overlays. Journal of Network and Systems Management 13, 197–217 (2005)
12. Matos, M., Sousa, A., Pereira, J., Oliveira, R., Deliot, E., Murray, P.: CLON: Overlay Networks and Gossip Protocols for Cloud Environments. In: Meersman, R., Dillon, T., Herrero, P. (eds.) OTM 2009, Part I. LNCS, vol. 5870, pp. 549–566. Springer, Heidelberg (2009)
13. Jelasity, M., Montresor, A., Babaoglu, O.: T-man: Gossip-based fast overlay topology construction. Comput. Netw. 53(13), 2321–2339 (2009)
14. Lim, J.B., Lee, J.H., Chin, S.H., Yu, H.C.: Group-Based Gossip Multicast Protocol for Efficient and Fault Tolerant Message Dissemination in Clouds. In: Riekki, J., Ylianttila, M., Guo, M. (eds.) GPC 2011. LNCS, vol. 6646, pp. 13–22. Springer, Heidelberg (2011)
15. Lim, J., Chung, K.-S., Chin, S.-H., Yu, H.-C.: A Gossip-Based Mutual Exclusion Algorithm for Cloud Environments. In: Li, R., Cao, J., Bourgeois, J. (eds.) GPC 2012. LNCS, vol. 7296, pp. 31–45. Springer, Heidelberg (2012)
16. Iwanicki, K., van Steen, M., Voulgaris, S.: Gossip-Based Clock Synchronization for Large Decentralized Systems. In: Keller, A., Martin-Flatin, J.-P. (eds.) SelfMan 2006. LNCS, vol. 3996, pp. 28–42. Springer, Heidelberg (2006)
17. Jelasity, M., Guerraoui, R., Kermarrec, A.-M., van Steen, M.: The Peer Sampling Service: Experimental Evaluation of Unstructured Gossip-Based Implementations. In: Jacobsen, H.-A. (ed.) Middleware 2004. LNCS, vol. 3231, pp. 79–98. Springer, Heidelberg (2004)
18. Montresor, A., Jelasity, M.: Peersim: A scalable p2p simulator. In: IEEE Ninth International Conference on Peer-to-Peer Computing, P2P 2009, pp. 99–100 (September 2009)

Power Monitoring for Mixed-Criticality on a Many-Core Platform

Boris Motruk[1], Jonas Diemer[1], Rainer Buchty[2], and Mladen Berekovic[2]

[1] Institute of Computer and Network Engineering
[2] Chair for Chip Design for Embedded Computing
Technische Universität Braunschweig, Germany
{motruk,diemer}@ida.ing.tu-bs.de,
{buchty,berekovic}@c3e.cs.tu-bs.de

Abstract. Mixed-critical applications on a many-core platform have to be sufficiently independent to be certified separately. This does not only include independence in terms of time and space, but also in terms of power consumption as the available energy for a many-core system has to be shared by all running applications. Increased power consumption of one application may reduce the available energy for other applications or the reliability and lifetime of the complete chip. This paper presents a monitoring and control mechanism based on event-driven power estimation to isolate dynamic power consumption of mixed-critical applications running on a many-core platform. Isolating dynamic power consumption significantly reduces safety requirements for lower critical applications and therefore overall certification costs, making many-core systems more attractive for safety-critical applications.

Keywords: embedded systems, dependability, energy, fault-tolerance, isolation, many-core, mixed-criticality, monitoring, multi-core, power.

1 Introduction

Time and space partitioning are mandatory for fault containment in safety-critical systems [14]. Power is another resource that has to be shared among individual applications running on the same platform. Increased power consumption of one application could negatively influence other applications of other or the same criticality. Power can be described by a dynamic and a static part. The static part is mainly due to leakage, and the dynamic part can further be divided into switching power and short-circuit power:

$$P = P_{dyn} + P_{sta} = P_{swi} + P_{sc} + P_{leak} \ . \tag{1}$$

Switching power has the largest share of power consumption in CMOS circuits and can be expressed by

$$P_{swi} = \alpha C_L V^2 f \ , \tag{2}$$

where V is the supply voltage, C_L are parasitic capacitances that are charged and discharged with frequency f when the corresponding component is active [7]. The

C. Hochberger et al. (Eds.): ARCS 2013, LNCS 7767, pp. 13–24, 2013.
© Springer-Verlag Berlin Heidelberg 2013

switching activity α is highly dependent on the running applications and their input data [18]. Therefore, the amount of dynamic power consumption cannot be guaranteed in case of unspecified or faulty behavior of running applications.

A chip's overall power budget is defined at design time based on packaging and cooling, battery capacity (if applicable), and environmental conditions. Meeting this budget is especially important for battery-powered devices [18] as increased power consumption of one application would reduce the available energy for all other running applications. Moreover, high local power consumption could lead to hotspots influencing neighboring components, or may reduce the entire chip's lifetime and reliability [21]. Detecting over consuming applications potentially endangering safe execution of other applications requires monitoring of dynamic power consumption for each application and region separately. As the internal logic of most silicon devices is supplied by a single or few external voltage sources, it is only possible to physically measure the power consumption of the whole internal logic and not of individual regions. Even systems like Intel's Single Chip Cloud Computer (SCC) that provide several voltage islands only allow measuring the accumulated supply current, and herewith power consumption, of all cores [15]. Moreover, it is impossible to identify the originator (application) of the consumed energy in a shared component [3], which is important to avoid thermal hazards. This makes physical measurements inapplicable to isolate dynamic power consumption of different applications at run time.

Isolation of dynamic power consumption of all individual applications is especially important for devices implementing functions of different criticality (mixed-criticality). The generic standard *IEC 61508* [1] defines four discrete criticality levels. Each level specifies requirements to be fulfilled to reduce the residual risk. If multiple functions of different criticality are implemented on the same platform without proper isolation, all have to fulfill the highest level's requirements [1]. This significantly increases certification cost for non- or low-critical applications if implemented on a shared platform together with high-critical applications. Mechanisms for time and space separation are available in most embedded systems including our platform [17], but to the best of our knowledge, this work is the first that concentrates on dynamic power isolation of mixed-critical applications on a shared platform.

The main contributions of this paper are: (1) We introduce a power analysis method for embedded systems based on an existing performance analysis method. (2) We develop a fast and lightweight monitoring and control mechanism for dynamic power consumption of individual mixed-critical applications on a single platform. (3) We implement and evaluate our mechanism on a many-core platform hosting several mixed-critical applications and show its effectiveness in case of failure of one of the running applications.

Starting with background information and related work in Section 2, we introduce our power model and analysis method in Section 3. In Section 4, we shortly explain our many-core platform and introduce its monitoring and control mechanisms. We present experiments showing the effectiveness of our approach in Section 5 before concluding in Section 6.

2   Background and Related Work

The last decade saw much work on run-time power monitoring using performance monitoring counters (PMC). PMCs are available in various processors for performance measurement, but have successfully been used for power estimation. Bellosa et al. [4] discovered a strong correlation between system performance events, like floating-point operations or cache misses, and required energy. The dynamic power consumption of a system with n PMCs can then be described by multiplying the performance counter readings PMC_i with the corresponding energy per performance event e_i divided by the sampling interval t_{sample},

$$P_{dyn} = \frac{\sum_{i=1}^{n}(PMC_i \cdot e_i)}{t_{sample}} . \tag{3}$$

The authors of [4] used microbenchmarks exclusively triggering single performance events with variable sleep intervals, e.g., floating point operations, while measuring the system's power consumption. They found a linear correlation between sleep intervals in the microbenchmarks and consumed energy. Thus, the energy consumption per performance event could be computed using linear regression technique. Bhattacharjee et al. [6] used gate-level simulations of their system instead of live measurements for event characterization. They used a power analysis tool to calculate component-wise power consumption using the system's switching activity gathered during simulation of their microbenchmarks.

To be able to estimate power consumption by counting events, power models of all components in the system are required. These power models assign one or more activating events and the corresponding consumed energy to a component or to a group of components. The number and kind of events determine the power monitoring's overhead and accuracy. Existing solutions range from very few existing counters available in standard CPUs for performance measurement [11] to counters for almost every gate activity [10]. The authors of [18] and [6] added additional counters dedicated to collect power events to existing processors. State-of-the-art microprocessors, like Intel's Sandy Bridge microprocessor [19], implement a digital power meter based on dedicated counters to track activity of the main building blocks but without allowing to identify the originator of power consumption in shared components, e.g., memories or graphics processor.

Since PMCs are not dedicated to power monitoring, additional effort must be made to extract power information from them. It is especially complicated to estimate power consumption of components outside the processor. For example, cache misses counted by PMCs are used to estimate memory activity [11]. The authors of [8] connected a monitoring unit to the system bus to estimate power consumption in memory devices based on bus traffic. Their approach could also be used for systems-on-chip (SoC) based on existing IPs without any counters that could or should be used for power monitoring. For safety-critical applications, it is even desirable not to use available counters or to add counters to existing IPs to separate monitor and monitored function [1]. In this case, power consumed in these IP cores can be modeled from their external behavior by monitoring transactions on the local busses or transactions sent over a network-on-chip (NoC). We extend this approach to estimate and control the power consumption of a many-core system as described in Section 4.1.

The power information gathered by run-time power monitoring has been used for various applications, but to the best of our knowledge, has not been applied to isolate power consumption of mixed-critical applications on a shared platform. In [6], the monitored data is used for hardware-accelerated power emulation to reduce extensive simulation times for complex SoCs. Monitored data can also be used for application profiling [12], enabling software engineers to develop power-aware applications before the chip is produced. The authors of [5] applied power information emulated by the use of PMCs for energy accounting for virtual machines in server farms. There has been much work on power management based on run-time power information. In [22], dynamic voltage scaling, and in [4], energy-aware scheduling is applied. Associated problems of heat dissipation are modeled in [2]. Hazards arising in case of extensive power consumption or occurrence of hotspots are tackled in [6,16]. Tasks from overheated processors are migrated to cooler ones, or the system performance is degraded by the reduction of the frequency. Chung et al. [9] presented how activity counts translate to temperature and detected fine-grained hotspots based on PMCs, which could not be detected by the use of regular temperature sensors.

3 Power Model and Analysis

Our power analysis is based on the performance analysis described by Henia et al. [13]. They analyzed the system performance based on task execution times and task activating event functions $\eta_T^+(\Delta t)$ and $\eta_T^-(\Delta t)$. $\eta_T^+(\Delta t)$ specifies the maximum number of activating events for task T that can occur during any time interval of length Δt and $\eta_T^-(\Delta t)$ specifies the minimum number of events. Schliecker et al. [20] extended this model with the definition of the shared-resource request bound $\tilde{\eta}_{T \to S}^+(\Delta t)$ and the aggregate busy time. $\tilde{\eta}_{T \to S}^+(\Delta t)$ is the maximum number of requests that may be issued from a task T to a shared resource S within a time-window of size Δt and the aggregate busy time accumulates the product of the number of operations to a shared resource and the corresponding amount of time to be completed. For our power analysis, we replace the required amount of time per operation with the amount of energy per operation. The weights of these energy events can be gathered using microbenchmarks and linear regression technique [4,6,12]. Since we estimate power consumption from component's external interfaces and transactions sent over local busses and the NoC, energy weights that depend on the corresponding component's internal state or on past events are modeled with an energy interval. Following the notation introduced by Schliecker et al., $\tilde{e}_{T \to S}^+$ and $\tilde{e}_{T \to S}^-$ are the maximum and minimum energy required for a task T to access a resource S. For example, an event for a component in idle state may cost more energy because of a possible wake-up overhead. Another example is writing data to the same location in memory twice. Writing both times the same data would cost less energy than writing different data because reloading the capacitance of that memory location is not required. To be able to give power guarantees to different applications, we are mainly interested in safe upper bounds for power consumption of individual applications and energy density in components in close proximity. Therefore, we use the upper bounds $\tilde{e}^+_{T \to S}$ for our analysis and power/energy budget allocation.

From event functions and energy weights, the maximum dynamic energy consumed by the set of all running tasks $\mathbf{T}$ using the set of all available resources $\mathbf{S}$ in any time interval of length Δt is expressed by

$$E^+_{\mathbf{T} \to \mathbf{S}}(\Delta t) = \sum_{T_i \in \mathbf{T}} \left(\sum_{S_k \in \mathbf{S}} \tilde{\eta}^+_{T_i \to S_k}(\Delta t) \cdot \tilde{e}^+_{T_i \to S_k} \right) . \qquad (4)$$

The worst-case average dynamic power consumption of the analyzed system in any time interval of length Δt is then given by

$$P^+_{dyn}(\Delta t) = \frac{E^+_{\mathbf{T} \to \mathbf{S}}(\Delta t)}{\Delta t} . \qquad (5)$$

To detect a possible hotspot in a specific area on the die, the maximum possible power density for this area in any time interval of length Δt has to be calculated. Therefore, the subset $\mathbf{S}^* \subseteq \mathbf{S}$ of all resources in this area has to be used in Equation 5. Equation 5 can also be used to get the worst-case average dynamic power consumption per application. In this case, the subset of all tasks $\mathbf{T}^* \subseteq \mathbf{T}$ of the investigated application has to be entered into the equation.

From the overall power budget of the device and analyzed power requirements of all applications, power/energy budgets can be assigned to individual applications and regions. If, at run time, the number of energy events originated by a low-critical application differs from the one used for analysis, e.g., due to less strict safety requirements, power guarantees given to high-critical applications may not hold any longer. Therefore, we introduce a monitoring and control mechanism in Section 4.1 to limit the number of energy events per application to the number used during analysis. This requires the monitoring and control mechanism to be certified to the highest level of criticality but not the lower critical applications.

4 Architecture

Our *Integrated Dependable Architecture for Many-Cores (IDAMC)* [17] is a research vehicle for developing and evaluating methods and mechanisms for reduced certification cost for trusted multi-core platforms. It consists of nodes (N) connected by a network-on-chip. The number of nodes as well as the network topology is configurable. Fig. 1a shows 9 nodes connected by a 2D mesh network. Each node includes a router (R) and up to 4 tiles connected by network interfaces (NI). Tiles are based on Gaisler's *GRLIB* IP library including the open-source *LEON3* processor and various other IPs connected to local buses. Tiles are configurable as well and reach from simple processing or memory tiles, containing a

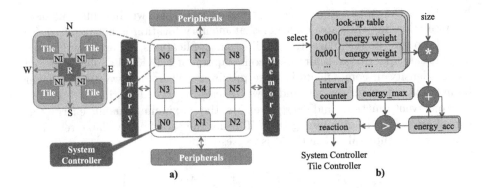

Fig. 1. System Overview and Power Monitoring

single core or memory controller respectively, to complete systems with multiple cores, peripherals and memory interfaces. One of the tiles acts as system controller, assigning resources to applications and supervising their safe execution. Mapping of physical memory interfaces and peripherals to local applications is done by address translation tables (ATT) in the network interfaces. The ATT translates local tile addresses to addresses in destination tiles and contains required routing information. The system controller can re-program the tables at run time. This enables replacing faulty peripherals or memory interfaces, and re-mapping of applications to other tiles without interaction or knowledge of the running application.

4.1 Power Monitoring and Control

Activity in local masters, and peripheral and memory usage in local and remote tiles cost energy. Energy consumption estimation is performed using event counters as described in Section 2. First, the local per-tile power consumption is monitored to detect hotspots caused by an application running locally or a remote application accessing a local resource. Second, the power consumption caused by every application is monitored separately even if power is consumed in another tile, e.g., shared memory. This way, the total available power budget, like any other shared resource, can be allocated to individual applications in the system. The collected power information is used to detect and prevent excessive dynamic power consumption of individual applications, assuring independence of the running applications, especially high-critical ones. We monitor and isolate power consumption in the network interfaces connecting the tiles and the rest of the system, separating monitor and monitored function [1]. Thus, only single applications or applications of same criticality should be mapped to the same processing tile representing an error containment zone.

Per-tile energy density is monitored by counting and weighting activity in local masters and slaves. Increased local dynamic power consumption could also be caused by a master in another tile sending an unexpectedly high number of requests to local slaves. For local power density monitoring it does not matter if the originator of local activity is an application running locally or on a core in another tile. The expected thermal emission based on the estimated energy density can be calculated using the approach presented by [21].

To monitor local power consumption within each tile, two of the look-up tables (LUT) shown in Fig. 1b are programmed with energy weights for activity in local masters and slaves. When an event is detected, the corresponding energy amount multiplied by access size (in words) is added to an energy accumulator (*energy_acc*). For increased accuracy, the local masters' table may include weights for different events per master, e.g., activity in floating-point units or co-processors. Our experiments presented in Section 5.2 showed that the difference in energy consumption of different operations within the *LEON3* core compared to such of remote memory accesses is negligible. Therefore, the LUTs for local masters contain a single (the largest) energy weight per master. The LUT entries for local masters are selected by signals extracted from the cores' debug interfaces. Similar to [8], the table for local slaves contains weights for local slave accesses. This table's entries are selected by slave select signals of the local bus.

Dynamic per-application energy consumption, monitored in the network interfaces, is calculated by accumulating and weighting all activity issued by the locally running application, no matter if consumed locally or outside the tile. For estimating a locally running application's power, energy consumed in local slaves is only accumulated if originated by a local master. Monitoring dynamic power consumption caused by a local application but consumed in other tiles is done by utilizing *IDAMC*'s ATTs: each activation selects a corresponding entry in the third LUT shown in Fig. 1b, containing required energy to access a module in the respective address range. The energy weights contain an entire request's consumed energy, including local busses and the NoC. Thus, the energy weights of two resources of same type may differ if located in tiles with different distances to the source tile.

To not only isolate applications on *IDAMC* in terms of time and space but also in terms of energy, energy budgets (*energy_max*) per time period have to be monitored for each tile and application individually, especially of low-critical applications to prevent any interference with high-critical ones. Two different energy accumulators and maximum energy values are implemented. One is required for power consumption (energy density) per tile independent of the originator, the other for power consumption per application including power consumed in other tiles and the NoC. Appropriate budgets are derived from analyzing the power requirements of all applications and the chip's overall power budget as described in Section 3. The system controller stores these upper bounds in the power monitoring and control modules in the network interfaces of all tiles. Moreover, an interval counter is programmed with the corresponding time period. When this counter elapses without any energy budget exceeding its maximum, the energy accumulators are reset. If one of the limits exceeds within the corresponding time period at run time due to a possible fault or unexpected input data, the following reactions can be taken: (1) A message can be sent to the system controller for further analysis, advanced reactions like remapping of applications, or simple error collection. (2) The tile can be paused until the end of the time period preventing further activity and herewith dynamic power consumption in the current time period. At the end of the time period, the application continues where it was stopped. (3) The tile can be reset to recover from a possible transient error. It is not restarted before the end of the selected time period; an immediate restart could lead to further dynamic power consumption. (4) The tile can be disabled, isolating a tile potentially containing a permanent defect.

The last three listed reactions could also be executed by the system controller after receiving a message. Due to network latency and overhead of software running on the system controller, this option's reaction time to prevent further dynamic power consumption of an application exceeding it budgets is much longer than a reaction executed directly by hardware in the NIs. Moreover, this time increases with the size of the system and is hard to predict. Therefore, a centralized solution can not be used to guarantee separation of applications of different criticality on a many-core platform.

Note that the implemented reactions do not target the optimization of power consumption of the running applications but only preventing a faulty (low-critical) application from negatively affecting a high-critical application running on another tile. Therefore, neither effects of the reactions on the locally running (faulty) application, nor other possible reactions, like power/clock gating or voltage/frequency scaling, are further investigated.

Our proposed dynamic power estimation and control mechanism is done in parallel with address translation or local slave access and hence does not add any latency. On detecting an exceeded power budget, a faulty application can be prevented from consuming further dynamic power without delay. This reaction time can be guaranteed and does not increase with a larger number of tiles. Our mechanism's area overhead depends on the number of events required for estimating power consumption of local masters and slaves, and distributed resources supported by the ATTs. An implementation of our mechanism supporting a single local master, 16 local slaves, and 32 distributed resources per tile increases area by around 2.4 %. Every additional event to be monitored increases only the memory requirements by 8 additional bits per energy weight. The amount of required logic stays constant also for a large number of monitored events.

5   Evaluation

We implemented an *IDAMC* baseline system on a *Virtex-6 LX760* FPGA to evaluate our proposed mechanism at minimal synthesis/simulation time. Since our distributed power monitoring and control mechanism does not require a central instance at run time [17], our setup's small number of tiles does not limit general applicability. The approach is also applicable for ASICs using a standard cell library similar to [6]. Our baseline system comprises 4 routers with a single connected tile each. Tile 0, the system controller, includes a debug interface, UART, timer unit, interrupt controller and $256\,kB$ on-chip memory. It

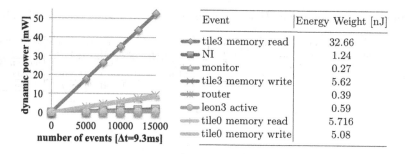

Event	Energy Weight [nJ]
tile3 memory read	32.66
NI	1.24
monitor	0.27
tile3 memory write	5.62
router	0.39
leon3 active	0.59
tile0 memory read	5.716
tile0 memory write	5.08

Fig. 2. Energy Weights

controls the other tiles and assigns resources to applications. Tile 1 and Tile 2 are memory-less processing tiles with a single core, 1 kB of data and instruction cache each, timer unit, and interrupt controller. Tile 3 contains 2 MB of on-chip memory shared by applications running on the processing tiles.

5.1 Event Characterization

We used microbenchmarks and linear regression technique as described in [4,6] for characterizing all events in local masters and slaves, and remote slaves with the largest impact on dynamic power consumption. These microbenchmarks consist of a variable number of operations exclusively triggering single or a small number of components. For example, we used microbenchmarks that write/read a different number of words to/from the shared memory in Tile 3 to get the energy per read/written word consumed in the network interfaces, the NoC's routers, and the on-chip memory. The overall switching activity of the placed and routed design gathered during simulating the individual microbenchmarks is fed into Xilinx' *XPower Analyzer* tool. With this method, we get component-wise power consumption for each microbenchmark as proposed by [6]. From power consumption of a specific microbenchmark and number and type of operations used in it, we calculate per-event energy (energy weight) using linear regression technique, similar to [12] and as shown in Fig. 2. Reading the large on-chip memory in Tile 3 consumes much more power than the different operations in the *LEON3* core. Therefore, we use a single energy weight (the largest measured) for all operations of the *LEON3* core with only a small impact on the overall accuracy. Systems with different components, memory or cache sizes require an additional one-time effort for event selection and characterization but no changes to the proposed methodology. Reading and writing the on-chip memory in Tile 3 includes the complete transfer's energy (2x NI, 1x monitor, 2x router). In larger systems, a single router's weight as in Fig. 2 can be used to calculate energy weights for memory accesses in tiles requiring a different number of hops in the NoC.

We evaluated the accuracy of our model while running more complex workloads based on the Dhrystone benchmark [23]. The error of estimated power consumption vs. real power consumption taken from post place-and-route

Table 1. Simulation results (Energy numbers based on $3.25ms$ sample interval)

App.	Criticality	Activation Interval	Run-time	Memory Acc. Reads	Writes	LEON3 (act. cycles)	Worst-case activation	Energy per interval	Worst-case Avg. Power
A1	high	$1.6\,ms$	$1.2\,ms$	3337	291	2625	$112.17\,\mu J$	$224.34\mu J$	$69.03\,mW$
A2	none/low	$2.4\,ms$	$720\,\mu s$	2107	180	1640	$70.73\,\mu J$	$141.46\mu J$	$43.53\,mW$
							Total	$365.80\,\mu J$	$112.56\,mW$

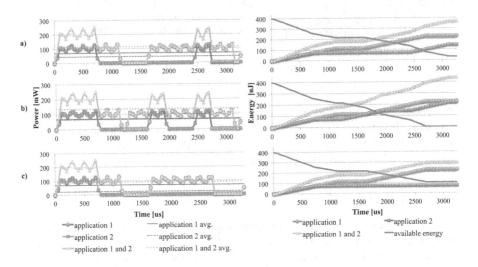

Fig. 3. Monitored Power/Energy

simulations was between $8\,\%$ and $23\,\%$, which can be improved by either monitoring more events or by a higher measurement resolution. In all cases, the estimation was higher than the actual consumption, which is required for a safe separation of power consumption of different applications.

5.2 Experiments

In our experiments, Tile 1 runs a high-critical application (A1) and Tile 2 a low- or non-critical one (A2), both based on the Dhrystone benchmark [23]. Tab. 1 shows the experimental setup with application properties acquired from simulation, and derived energy and power numbers based on Equations 4 and 5.

Fig. 3a shows energy and power consumption for both applications behaving as expected. If the low-critical A2 causes more power-sensitive events, e.g., due to a longer run time because of unexpected input data or due to more frequent activation (e.g., due to a timer error in Tile 2), energy and power requirements of A2 increase as shown in Fig. 3b. One further activation of A2 within $3.25\,ms$ leads to a worst-case energy consumption of $212.19\,\mu J$ and a corresponding dynamic power consumption of $65.29\,mW$ ($134.32\,mW$ for the entire system).

Let $400\,\mu J$ be the maximum available dynamic energy within $3.25\,ms$, only $175.66\,\mu J$ may be consumed by A2. In Fig. 3b, the available energy is already spent after $2.7\,ms$ due to A2's increased power consumption. This may prevent the high-critical A1 from successful completion. Fig. 3c shows the system's energy and power consumption running a faulty A2 with our monitoring and control mechanism being activated. A2 is disabled as soon as an increased energy consumption is detected by our mechanism (after $1.2\,ms$). Other options are pausing A2 until further activity is expected (after $1.6\,ms$) or allowing as much activity as long A2 consumes less energy than left by the high-critical A1 ($175.66\,\mu J$). Our mechanism reacts to increased energy consumption without any delay due to its implementation in hardware. In contrast, solutions based on interaction with a central controller require a worst-case energy margin that may be consumed by a faulty application during the time between detecting an increased energy consumption and the reaction to be completed. This time increases with larger systems, is hard to predict, and may lead to an overdimensioned system [17].

6   Conclusion

To the best of our knowledge, this paper is the first presenting a many-core platform isolating dynamic power consumption of mixed-critical applications. Our solution significantly decreases certification costs for safety-relevant embedded multi- and many-core systems by reducing safety requirements for low-critical applications. The per-application and per-region worst-case dynamic power consumption is first analyzed at design time, and then supervised at run time based on event-driven power estimation. The presented fast and lightweight monitoring and control mechanism is separated from the monitored function and does not require any changes to existing software or any special operating system. It is scalable and applicable to very large systems, due to it's decentralized nature, and does not impose any timing overhead. We implemented our system on an FPGA and demonstrated the effectiveness of our method running a high-critical and a (faulty) low-critical application.

Acknowledgment. This work has been funded by the *Bundesministerium für Bildung und Forschung* (BMBF), the *Deutsche Forschungsgemeinschaft* (DFG), and *Advanced Research & Technology for Embedded Intelligence and Systems* (ARTEMIS) within the project "RECOMP" (grant no. 01IS10001A / 100202).

References

1. Functional safety of electrical/electronic/programmable electronic safety-related systems. Int. Electrotechnical Commission (2010)
2. Atienza, D., Del Valle, P.G., Paci, G., Poletti, F., Benini, L., De Micheli, G., Mendias, J.M.: A Fast HW/SW FPGA-Based Thermal Emulation Framework for Multi-Processor System-on-Chip. In: Proc. 43rd Design Automation Conf. ACM (2006)
3. Bellosa, F.: The Case for Event-Driven Energy Accounting. Tech. rep., University of Erlangen, Department of Computer Science (2001)
4. Bellosa, F.: The Benefits of Event-Driven Energy Accounting in Power-Sensitive Systems. In: Proc. of the 9th ACM SIGOPS European Workshop (2000)

5. Bertran, R., Becerra, Y., Carrera, D., Beltran, V., Gonzalez, M., Martorell, X., Torres, J., Ayguade, E.: Accurate Energy Accounting for Shared Virtualized Environments using PMC-based Power Modeling Techniques. In: Int. Conf. on Grid Computing (2010)
6. Bhattacharjee, A., Contreras, G., Martonosi, M.: Full-System Chip Multiprocessor Power Evaluations Using FPGA-Based Emulation. In: ACM/IEEE Int. Symp. on Low Power Electronics and Design, ISLPED (2008)
7. Bhunia, S., Mukhopadhyay, S. (eds.): Low-Power Variation-Tolerant Design in Nanometer Silicon. Springer (2010)
8. Cho, Y., Kim, Y., Park, S., Chang, N.: System-Level Power Estimation using an On-Chip Bus Performance Monitoring Unit. In: IEEE/ACM Int. Conf. on Computer-Aided Design, ICCAD (2008)
9. Chung, S., Skadron, K.: Using On-Chip Event Counters For High-Resolution, Real-Time Temperature Measurement. In: The Tenth Intersociety Conf. on Thermal and Thermomechanical Phenomena in Electronics Systems. IEEE (2006)
10. Coburn, J., Ravi, S., Raghunathan, A.: Power Emulation: A New Paradigm for Power Estimation. In: Design Automation Conf. Proc. 42nd (2005)
11. Contreras, G., Martonosi, M.: Power Prediction for Intel XScale Processors Using Performance Monitoring Unit Events. In: Proc. of the Int. Symp. on Low Power Electronics and Design, ISLPED 2005. ACM (2005)
12. Genser, A., Bachmann, C., Haid, J., Steger, C., Weiss, R.: An Emulation-Based Real-Time Power Profiling Unit for Embedded Software. In: Int. Symp. on Systems, Architectures, Modeling, and Simulation, SAMOS 2009. IEEE (2009)
13. Henia, R., Hamann, A., Jersak, M., Racu, R., Richter, K., Ernst, R.: System level performance analysis - the SymTA/S approach. IEEE Computers and Digital Techniques (2005)
14. Hoyme, K., Driscoll, K.: Safebus [for avionics]. IEEE Aerospace and Electronic Systems Magazine (1993)
15. Intel Labs: The SccKit 1.4.0 User's Guide (2011)
16. Merkel, A., Bellosa, F.: Balancing Power Consumption in Multiprocessor Systems. In: Proc. of the 1st ACM SIGOPS/EuroSys Conf. on Computer Systems (2006)
17. Motruk, B., Diemer, J., Buchty, R., Ernst, R., Berekovic, M.: Idamc: A many-core platform with run-time monitoring for mixed-criticality. In: IEEE 14th International Symposium on High-Assurance Systems Engineering, HASE (2012)
18. Peddersen, J., Parameswaran, S.: Low-Impact Processor for Dynamic Runtime Power Management. IEEE Design Test of Computers (2008)
19. Rotem, E., Naveh, A., Rajwan, D., Ananthakrishnan, A., Weissmann, E.: Power-management architecture of the Intel microarchitecture code-named Sandy Bridge. IEEE Micro (2012)
20. Schliecker, S., Ernst, R.: Real-Time Performance Analysis of Multiprocessor Systems with Shared Memory. ACM Trans. Embed. Comput. Syst. (2010)
21. Skadron, K., Stan, M., Sankaranarayanan, K., Huang, W., Velusamy, S., Tarjan, D.: Temperature-aware microarchitecture: Modeling and implementation. ACM Transactions on Architecture and Code Optimization, TACO (2004)
22. Snowdon, D.C., Petters, S.M., Heiser, G.: Accurate On-line Prediction of Processor and Memory Energy Usage Under Voltage Scaling. In: Proc. of the 7th Int. Conf. on Embedded Software (2007)
23. Weicker, R.: Dhrystone: A Synthetic Systems Programming Benchmark. Communications of the ACM (1984)

On Confident Task-Accurate Performance Estimation

Yang Xu[1], Bo Wang[1], Rafael Rosales[2], Ralph Hasholzner[1], and Jürgen Teich[2]

[1] Intel Mobile Communications, Munich, Germany
{yang.a.xu,bo1.wang,ralph.hasholzner}@intel.com
[2] University of Erlangen-Nuremberg, Germany
{rafael.rosales,teich}@informatik.uni-erlangen.de

Abstract. Task-accurate performance estimation methods are widely applied for design space exploration at the Electronic System Level (ESL). These methods estimate performance by simulating task-level models annotated with nominal execution time. In early design phases, source code, which is necessary for generating accurate annotations, is usually not available. Instead, extrapolated values or even estimated values are used for performance estimation, which makes the results unreliable and may eventually cause performance violations if used to guide critical design decisions. In this paper, we propose a confident task-accurate performance estimation methodology that uses high-level information available in early design phases and provides confident estimation to guide design space exploration with respect to performance constraints.

1 Introduction

In modern System-on-Chip (SoC) design methodologies, performance together with other design constraints, e.g., power consumption and die size, are usually defined in very early design phases. Respecting these design constraints, the design space is explored to choose appropriate system architectures. Correct design decisions made in such early design phases are very important in avoiding significant modification efforts and cost in later phases. Therefore, early and confident performance estimations are required to guarantee the fulfillment of a set of performance constraints. Additionally, owing to the increasing complexity of modern SoCs, the design space becomes very huge. Thus, fast performance estimation methods are mandatory to allow efficient design space exploration.

1.1 Related Work

To achieve high efficiency during design space exploration, task-accurate performance estimation methods have been proposed [1–4]. In these methods, basic system operations, such as functions or communication transactions, are modeled as tasks whose timing information is back-annotated into the task models for fast performance simulation. Since the task is the finest granularity in such kind of method, it is called Task-Accurate Performance Estimation (TAPE). In [1],

C. Hochberger et al. (Eds.): ARCS 2013, LNCS 7767, pp. 25–37, 2013.
© Springer-Verlag Berlin Heidelberg 2013

the processing time of each task is modeled by annotating the delay budgets to the communication events. Then a so called virtual processing unit is introduced to capture the timing behavior of the system. Thanks to its XML-based performance model, the design space exploration is significantly accelerated. Similarly, in [2] [3], a Virtual Processing Component (VPC) approach is adopted. They differentiate themselves from [1] by applying an actor-oriented modeling approach, which strictly separates the functionalities and their underlying architecture to ease the exploration of different architecture options. A hybrid method is proposed in [4] where Worst-Case Execution Time (WCET) analysis is first executed and then the resulting WCET values are back-annotated into task models to simulate system performance. The dynamic effects at run-time, such as data dependencies, are also incorporated by using dynamic correction.

All of the above methods can provide performance estimation very efficiently. However, none of them can guarantee confident performance estimation because of the errors propagated form the annotation values. These errors are mainly caused by source code analysis and profiling. Even worse, in early design phases where source code is not yet available for generating annotation values, estimated timing information must be used as annotation values to estimate system performance. This will make the final result even more unreliable. Even though absolutely accurate estimation is not always required in early design phases since relatively accurate results can still help the designers differentiate different architecture options, confident performance estimation is still mandatory when critical design decisions or real-time constraints are involved. For example, given two baseband processor architectures $arch1$ and $arch2$, the TAPE methods can confirm that $arch1$ is faster than $arch2$ in processing Long Term Evolution (LTE) packets. But because of the unreliable performance estimation they cannot confirm whether these two architectures can finish the packet processing within 1 ms (real-time constraint of LTE) especially when the estimated time is too close to the real-time constraint. Therefore, it is highly desired to have a confident performance estimation method providing confidence information, i.e., the probability of an architecture meeting a specific performance constraint, given errors existed in the estimation results.

To incorporate uncertain objectives during design space exploration, the author in [5] proposes a Pareto-Front exploration method treating the objectives as random variables. There are also a few low-level methods proposed to estimate performance with confidence information [6–8]. In [6], the software behavior is modeled by a sequence of virtual instructions with each one representing a type of real instructions. Then linear regression method is used to determine a predictor equation, which estimates performance along with confidence levels. The drawback of this method is that the statistical predictor equation is only trained for a specific application population; whenever a new type of application is under evaluation, it needs a new dedicated equation. To overcome this limitation, the work in [7] proposes a trace-based estimation method. Instead of training a statistical equation for each application, it generates statistical model for each virtual instruction, which is consequently used to estimate the performance and its expected confidence intervals of a pre-generated instruction trace. Since the virtual instructions are fixed for a specific target processor, the statistical models can be reused for different applications. In the more recent work [8], the authors propose a method to build a statistical performance model for a processor by exploiting linear regression techniques. All these methods stay at lower level of abstraction. Therefore, they cannot solve the challenges of confident TAPE.

1.2 Challenges of Confident TAPE

Compared with instruction-level performance estimation, TAPE has the following advantages: 1) it is much more efficient during design space exploration thanks to its high level of abstraction; 2) it is more applicable than low-level methods in early design phases where only limited high-level information is available for use. However, these advantages also come with challenges:

Firstly, because of having a different abstraction level, TAPE cannot directly reuse the confidence level calculation methods used in the low-level confident performance estimation. One specific example is the trace-based approach proposed in [7]. In this approach, the confidence level can be easily calculated by traversing a pre-generated instruction trace and accumulating the mean and variance of execution time of each instruction. Unfortunately, such kind of approach cannot be applied by TAPE, even though a task trace can be easily generated, because the scheduling of tasks may be determined by the execution time of tasks; different execution time for the same task may lead to completely different task traces, as shown in Fig. 1. In this example, two tasks t_1 and t_2 are executed on two dedicated hardware accelerators, which are connected to a CPU whose scheduling algorithm is First Come First Served (FCFS). If the execution time of t_1 is shorter than t_2, as shown in Fig. 1 (2), the interrupt service routine 1 (isr_1) is scheduled after t_1 terminates; on the other hand, if the execution time of t_1 is longer than t_2, isr_2 is scheduled first instead (Fig. 1 (3)). If the execution time is modeled statistically to model the effect of errors, the scheduling of tasks becomes indeterministic and the trace-based approach is no longer valid. Therefore, in confident TAPE, the first challenge is how to incorporate the statistical aspect caused by the errors propgated from the annotation values.

Secondly, how to calculate the confidence level of parallel task execution is another challenge. This has not yet been addressed by the instruction-level methods

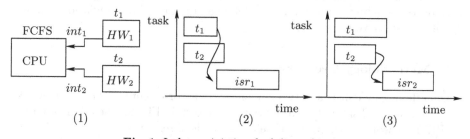

Fig. 1. Indeterministic scheduling of tasks

in [6–8] because they only focus on single processor systems. Although TAPE has been used to evaluate MPSoC systems [1] [3], it only handles deterministic simulation. On MPSoC, instead of having one task stream executing sequentially, the system has several task streams executing in parallel. The confidence level of the system performance cannot be easily calculated by simply accumulating the mean and variance of execution time as used in the instruction-level method [7] because of the overlap between parallel tasks.

Finally, in early design phases, the source code used to extract system behavior and timing information is usually not available. How to make use of the limited high-level information available in early design phases to provide confident performance estimation still remains a challenge.

In this paper, we propose a novel methodology that solves the challenges of confident TAPE. The contributions of this paper are:

1. Our method complements traditional TAPE methods by adding the capability to provide confidence information on meeting a performance constraint. This information can guide designers to explore architecture options with respect to real-time constraints.
2. The proposed methodology integrates an actor-oriented TAPE approach with a parallel Monte Carlo (MC) simulation method to form an efficient confident TAPE framework, which can not only easily incorporate the statistical aspect propagated from the errors of annotations but also naturally handle the confidence level calculation of parallel task execution.
3. Our method can be applied in very early design phases, even when no source code is available. It only relies on high-level information available in early design phases. And the results can be refined throughout the whole design phases when detailed information becomes available.

The rest of this paper is organized as follows: In Section 2 we will present our framework in details. Thereafter, we will present the experimental results in Section 3. Finally we will conclude this paper in Section 4.

2   Methodology

In this section, we will first illustrate an overview of our methodology. Then four different aspects of this methodology, namely, behavior modeling, architecture & resource modeling, performance modeling and parallel MC simulation, will be detailed, respectively.

2.1   Methodology Overview

Our methodology consists of two key parts: an actor-oriented TAPE framework and a parallel MC simulation framework, as shown in Fig. 2. The actor-oriented TAPE framework is composed of behavior models, resource models as well as a Mapping & Performance Annotation (MPA) file. The system functionalities are

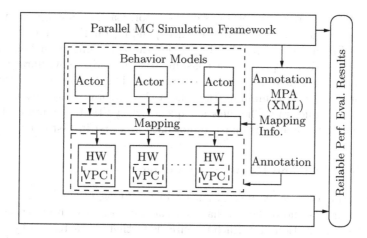

Fig. 2. Methodology overview

modeled by the behavior models as different actors. The benefit of this actor-oriented modeling is the strict separation between the system functionalities and the underlying architecture. This separation significantly eases the design space exploration by allowing modification of the mappings between functionalities and their corresponding hardware resources. All the mapping information is specified in the MPA file, which also specifies the characteristics of the hardware resources and execution time of each task. The execution time information is used by the VPC [2] associated to each hardware resource to simulate the performance of the whole system. All these models together form the kernel of the MC simulation, which subsequently generates confident performance estimation.

The reason why we prefer MC simulation to the statistical performance model approaches in [6–8] is that MC simulation can easily handle the indeterministic task scheduling challenge and it can also naturally solve the challenge of confidence level calculation of parallel task execution mentioned in Section 1. Additionally, in our methodology, the kernel of the MC simulation is the highly efficient TAPE, which can eventually compensate the drawback of MC simulation, i.e., relatively long simulation time.

2.2   Behavior Modeling

In our methodology, the functionalities executed on hardware components are modeled as a series of actors [9] [10]. The behaviors of the functionalities are defined in the specifications. Therefore, they can be extracted without having source code. Each actor is defined as a tuple $a = (P, F, S)$ containing a set of actor ports $P = I \cup O$ including input ports I and output ports O, the actor functionalities F and the firing FSM S. The actor ports P are used to pass and receive tokens from other actors for communication. Such kind of communication can only take place via dedicated channels, i.e., no implicit communication is allowed. The behavior of the actor is constructed by a set of actor functionalities

F, representing the atomic operations of the actor. Each atomic operation may correspond to a function or even a task, depending on the required level of abstraction. Finally, the firing FSM specifies the communication behavior of each actor, i.e., when to produce or consume tokens. A SystemC library [11] is used as our actor-oriented modeling infrastructure. This library provides special channels for inter-actor communication and a C++ syntax to specify the actor behavior in a unique way. Channels are queues with FIFO semantics allowing actors to read/write and consume/produce data in a first in first out discipline.

2.3 Architecture and Resource Modeling

A system architecture is modeled by a set of resources, e.g., processors, memories, interconnects and dedicated hardware accelerators, which are specified in the MPA file (annotation file). Each resource is further characterized by its performance attribute, including a *scheduler*, *frequency settings* and *transaction delay*. The *scheduler* is required to resolve the resource contention caused by multi-tasking on each resource. The *frequency settings* are introduced to model the effect of Dynamic Voltage & Frequency Scaling (DVFS), which is widely applied on modern SoCs for dynamic power management. Under each *frequency setting*, a *transaction delay* is defined to specify the latency of transferring one byte of data into or out of its corresponding resource running at that frequency.

```
<resources>
  <component name="CPU" scheduler="FCFS">
    <frequency="100 MHz">
    <transaction_delay value="10 ns" />
    <frequency="200 MHz">
    <transaction_delay value="5 ns" />
    <frequency="400 MHz">
      ......
  </component>
  <component name="DSP" scheduler="FCFS">
      ......
</resources>
```

Fig. 3. Example of an MPA file

Fig. 3 shows an example of an MPA file that specifies a SoC architecture and its resources. In the example, the CPU is configured with a FCFS scheduler and it supports three frequency settings. Each frequency setting has a transaction delay value associated to it where the value may be an existing measurement value, estimated value based on extrapolation, or a value from a data-sheet. The other system resources, such as the DSP, can be specified similarly.

The mappings between the behavior actors and resources are specified in the MPA file where timing information of actors is also specified. Fig. 4 shows a portion of an MPA file that specifies mappings. In this example, actor A1 is mapped to a CPU, which supports two frequency settings. The computation time of two functions, f1 and f2, is separately annotated for each frequency setting. Additionally, topology information is also defined here, from which we can see the CPU is connected to a memory via a crossbar (XBar). Thus, the communication overhead from the CPU to the memory can be calculated by summing up the transaction delays of CPU, XBar and Mem that are specified together with the resources.

```
<mappings>
    <mapping actor="A1" target="CPU">
        <delay frequency="400 MHz" name="f1" mean="10 us" sigma="1 us" dist_type="Gaussian"/>
        <delay frequency="400 MHz" name="f2" mean="20 us" sigma="2 us" dist_type="Gaussian"/>
        <delay frequency="200 MHz" name="f1" mean="20 us" sigma="2 us" dist_type="Gaussian"/>
        <delay frequency="200 MHz" name="f2" mean="40 us" sigma="4 us" dist_type="Gaussian"/>
        ...
    </mapping>
    ...
</mappings>
<topology>
    <route src="CPU" destination="Mem">
    <hop name="CPU"/>
    <hop name="XBar"/>
    <hop name="Mem"/>
    </route>
    ......
</topology>
```

Fig. 4. Example of mappings with an MPA file

2.4   Performance Modeling

In traditional TAPE, software profiling is used to obtain accurate annotation values, hence to guarantee accurate estimation result. However, in early design phases, there is no source code available for profiling. Instead, estimated execution time is usually used as annotation values, which will consequently result in significant estimation errors. Even though in some rare cases source code might be available for profiling, modeling the execution time as a constant value may still generate errors because data and architecture dependencies, such as cache misses, will eventually lead to variable execution time of tasks. Therefore, constant annotation values cannot guarantee confident performance estimation.

Conventionally, designers handle these estimation errors by using over-design, e.g., add margins or guardbands according to worst-case analysis or their experience, but without systematic analysis, which makes the late design changes after integration testing very likely. In our methodology, execution time of atomic operations is modeled as statistical variables with mean value, standard deviation (σ) and a specific distribution type, as shown in Fig. 4. These values are imported into the MC simulation framework to generate samples for each iteration. Within each MC iteration, deterministic TAPE is executed. Therefore, the indeterministic task scheduling challenge is solved. After all iterations are finished, the confidence level of performance estimation can be calculated by analyzing the performance samples. Thus, the challenge of calculating the confidence level of parallel task execution is also resolved. This framework allows to determine minimum margins and guardbands already during early design phases.

In early design phases, instead of exact execution time, high-level performance information, such as the mean value, σ and distribution type of execution time is usually available. They can be obtained either by analytical method, e.g., the datasheet analysis proposed in [6] or measurements from previous products or even the experience of the designers. Although some of these values may also be estimated, e.g., the σ, it can still provide more guidance to the designer than the mean-value or worst-case based methods by showing the confidence information as shown in the experimental results.

2.5   Parallel MC Simulation

In this section, we will introduce the parallel MC simulation framework used in our methodology. Although TAPE is far more efficient than the instruction-level estimation methods, as the kernel of the MC simulation, it may still cause relatively long runtime when the number of iterations is large. Therefore, we introduce a parallel MC simulation framework, which takes advantage of modern multiprocessing power on PCs, to accelerate the simulation.

It is straight forward to parallelize a MC simulation because there is no data dependencies between different iterations. The parallelization is done by splitting a normal sequential MC simulation into several sections and distributing them to available CPU cores. The whole process is summarized in Algorithm 1:

Algorithm 1. Parallel MC simulation

---

   input : MPA, number of cores ($\#cpu$), number of iterations ($\#i$)
   output: mean and standard deviation of performance estimation
1 generate_samples(MPA) ;
2 $N = \#i/\#cpu$;
3 **for** $cnt = 0 \rightarrow \#cpu - 1$ **do**
4    $offset = cnt * N$;
5   fork(MC(N, $offset$)) ;
6 **end**
7 wait_process(); ;
8 sample_analyze() ;

The input to the parallel MC simulation framework is the MPA file, the number of CPU cores used for simulation and the number of iterations to be executed. The framework first generates execution time samples for all tasks according to their statistical models specified in the MPA file. Then it calculates the corresponding iterations (N) for each parallel section. Thereafter, within each section, the framework will start a new MC simulation process and set its iteration and sample offset ($offset$) accordingly. The $offset$ indicates the starting point of samples for each section. These samples are used by the TAPE for deterministic

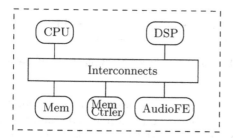

Fig. 5. Simplified platform architecture

performance simulation. Finally, after all MC simulation finished, all the estimation samples will be analyzed by the function sample_analyze() to calculate the mean value and standard deviation of the system performance.

3 Experimental Results

We applied the proposed methodology to a real world scenario, MP3 decoding time estimation, to evaluate its effectiveness. The framework is implemented with C++ and all the behavior models are written in SystemC in an actor-oriented style. The simulations are executed on a Linux machine with 4 GB RAM and a 3.4 GHz CPU, which has 4 cores and each core supports 2 threads executing in parallel. We first compared our method to TAPE with worst-case annotations to show its advantages during design space exploration. Then we carried out a case study to demonstrate the effectiveness of our confident TAPE, i.e., exploring architecture options with respect to real-time constraints.

3.1 Confident TAPE vs. Worst-Case TAPE

We modeled a simplified embedded platform which consists of one CPU, one DSP, memory subsystem, interconnections and a dedicated hardware, as illustrated in Fig. 5. The AudioFE (Audio Front End) is an analog hardware responsible for decoded data playback. The functionality of MP3 decoding is modeled as a data flow as shown in Fig. 6, which is composed of five actors, namely, source (Src), pre-processing (PrePro), decoding (Dec), post-processing (PostPro) and Playback (Play). The MP3 decoding time is defined as the time between the data streaming into the PrePro stage and leaving the PostPro stage. The functionality mappings and execution time are specified in Table 1. Since the Src models the data source, it has no real corresponding processing unit and its execution time is annotated as 0 us.

The mean execution time for each task is obtained from profiling results. In early design phases, it can also be estimated values. To model the errors contained in the annotation values, we set standard deviation (σ) associated to each execution time value as listed in Table 1. It stands for the percentage of

Fig. 6. Actor-based MP3 playback model

the nominal value. In this paper, we assume the distribution type is Gaussian for simplicity. If the distribution type is non-Gaussian, a non-linear transform [12] [13] can be applied to convert the variable to Gaussian. Based on these annotations, we executed our confident TAPE to estimate the time of decoding 2 KB MP3 data. Additionally, we also carried out one worst-case estimation, which takes $mean + 3\sigma$ as annotation value.

Table 1. State-of-the-art annotations

Task	Mapping	mean exe. T (us)	σ	dist_type
Src	-	0	0	-
PrePro	CPU	96.014	10%	Gaussian
Dec	CPU	221.205	16%	Gaussian
PostPro	DSP	646.793	20%	Gaussian
Play	AudioFE	20	0	-

Table 2. Annotations of architecture options

Task	Mapping		mean exe. T (us)		σ		dist_type
	cpu-dsp	all-cpu	cpu-dsp	all-cpu	cpu-dsp	all-cpu	
Src	-	-	0	0	0	0	-
PrePro	CPU	CPU	461.29	461.29	10%	10%	Gaussian
Dec	CPU	CPU	1061.78	1061.78	10%	10%	Gaussian
PostPro	DSP	CPU	3104.61	1809.41	10%	10%	Gaussian
Play	AudioFE	AudioFE	20	20	0	0	-

Fig. 7 shows the Cumulative Distribution Function (CDF) of decoding time generated by our confident TAPE, from which we can see that the mean execution time is 29 ms, which is the same with the one evaluated by the traditional TAPE method, but with small confidence level; the worst-case execution time is 40.29 ms, which has very high confidence level, but it is also too conservative. The confident estimation can be read from the CDF, which is around 35 ms. Therefore, we can conclude that in spite of unavoidable errors in annotation values, our method can still provide more confident and realistic estimation than mean-value or worst-case based methods.

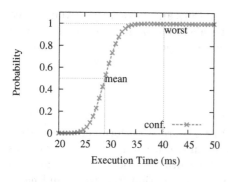

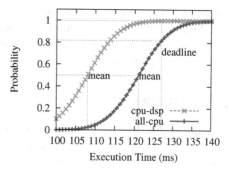

Fig. 7. CDF of decoding time   **Fig. 8.** CDFs of cpu-dsp and all-cpu

3.2   Case Study

In the following we will describe the case study to demonstrate the effectiveness of our method to explore different architectures with respect to real-time constraints. In this case study, we would like to reduce the cost of the platform in Fig. 5. One architecture option is to replace the processors with slower ones (5 times slower), noted as cpu-dsp. And another more aggressive option is to even get rid of the DSP by moving all functionalities to the CPU, noted as all-cpu. Before making these design decisions, we need to evaluate whether these new architectures will meet the performance constraint or not.

The performance constraint is defined as the real-time constraint of the MP3 data decoding, i.e., whether MP3 data decoding can be finished before a specific deadline. Assuming the sampling frequency is 44.1 KHz and the compression ration is $1 : 11$, for 2 KB MP3 data, the decoding must be finished within $(2048 \times 11)/4/44.1 = 127$ ms. The mappings and execution time of these new architectures are specified in Table 2. We assume 10% standard deviation for all execution time.

Fig. 8 illustrates the CDFs of the decoding time for both cpu-dsp architecture and all-cpu architecture. The mean decoding time of both architectures (108 ms, 121 ms) meets the real-time constraint (127 ms). However, the confidence information tells us that only the cpu-dsp architecture can meet the real-time constraint with 100% confidence while the all-cpu architecture can meet the deadline with about 80% confidence. Therefore, we can confirm that the cpu-dsp architecture can be applied to lower the cost and it would be very risky to use the all-cpu architecture. From this case study, we can conclude that applying traditional TAPE to guide critical design decisions may lead to performance constraint violation; in contrast our methodology can provide confident estimation result to explore architecture options with respect to real-time constraint.

We also measured the simulation speed of our framework executed with different parallelism degrees to evaluate the acceleration effect of our parallel MC simulation. We totally carried out four measurements, i.e., partitioning the simulation into 1, 2, 4 and 8 sections ($4 \times 2 = 8$ threads). For 10000 iterations, the corresponding simulation time is 775 s, 330 s, 189 s and 145 s, respectively. Based on these results we can conclude that our parallel MC simulation scales very well with the parallelism degrees and the simulation speed (145 s) is acceptable in early design phases.

4   Conclusions

In this paper, we propose a confident task-accurate performance estimation methodology used in early design phases to guide critical design decisions. This method integrates an actor-oriented task-accurate performance estimation method with an efficient parallel Monte Carlo simulation framework and naturally solves the indeterministic task scheduling issue and the challenge of confidence level calculation of parallel task execution. Experimental results show that our methodology can provide more confident performance estimation than the worst-case based method; and in early design phases it can be used to explore architecture options with respect to real-time constraint.

Acknowledgment. This work was supported in part by the Project PowerEval (funded by Bayerisches Wirtschafsministerium, support code IUK314/001).

References

1. Kempf, T., Doerper, M., Leupers, R., Ascheid, G., Meyr, H., Kogel, T., Vanthournout, B.: A Modular Simulation Framework for Spatial and Temporal Task Mapping onto Multi-Processor SoC Platforms. In: DATE, pp. 876–881 (2005)
2. Streubühr, M., Falk, J., Haubelt, C., Teich, J., Dorsch, R., Schlipf, T.: Task-Accurate Performance Modeling in SystemC for Real-Time Multi-Processor Architectures. In: DATE, pp. 480–481 (2006)
3. Streubühr, M., Gladigau, J., Haubelt, C., Teich, J.: Efficient Approximately-Timed Performance Modeling for Architectural Exploration of MPSoCs. In: Advances in Design Methods from Modeling Languages for Embedded Systems and SoC's, vol. 63, pp. 59–72 (2010)
4. Schnerr, J., Bringmann, O., Viehl, A., Rosenstiel, W.: High-performance timing simulation of embedded software. In: DAC, pp. 290–295 (2008)
5. Teich, J.: Pareto-Front Exploration with Uncertain Objectives. In: 1st International Conference on Evolutionary Multi-Criterion Optimization, March 7-9, pp. 314–328 (2001)
6. Giusto, P., Martin, G., Harcourt, E.: Reliable Estimation of Execution Time of Embedded Software. In: DATE, pp. 580–589 (2001)
7. Bjuréus, P., Jantsch, A.: Performance Analysis with Confidence Intervals for Embedded Software Processes. In: Proceedings of the 14th International Symposium on Systems Synthesis, pp. 45–50 (2001)
8. Lattuada, M., Ferrandi, F.: Performance Estimation of Embedded Software with Confidence Levels. In: ASP-DAC, pp. 573–578 (2012)
9. Lee, E., Neuendorffer, S., Wirthlin, M.: Actor-Oriented Design of Embedded Hardware and Software Systems. Journal of Circuits Systems and Computers 12(3), 231–260 (2003)

10. Lee, E.A., Neuendorffer, S.: Actor-Oriented Models for Codesign: Balancing Re-Use and Performance. In: Formal Methods and Models for System Design, pp. 33–56 (2004)
11. Falk, J., Haubelt, C., Teich, J.: Efficient Representation and Simulation of Model-Based Designs in System. In: Forum on Design Languages, pp. 129–134 (2006)
12. Li, X., Le, J., Pileggi, L.T.: Statistical performance modeling and optimization. Found. Trends Electron. Des. Autom. 1(4), 331–480 (2006)
13. Seber, G.: Multivariate Observations. Wiley Series (1984)

Iwazaru: The Byzantine Sequencer

Maciej Zbierski

Institute of Computer Science,
Warsaw University of Technology, Poland
m.zbierski@ii.pw.edu.pl

Abstract. In this article we present Iwazaru - a dedicated Byzantine fault-tolerant distributed sequencer that significantly outperforms similar solutions previously used for that purpose. The proposed protocol is designed for timed asynchronous systems, i.e. environments in which the response time is bounded by a known value. Using this assumption we were able to reduce the total number of required communication rounds by one. Additionally, although Iwazaru itself still requires $3f + 1$ replicas to tolerate f malicious parties, once the ordering is established no more than $2f + 1$ machines are required to execute the requests. The performance evaluation shows that in gracious executions Iwazaru can perform around 30% faster than Castro and Liskov's PBFT, which was previously used as an algorithm of choice for request ordering.

Keywords: Byzantine fault tolerance, distributed sequencer, dependability, state machine replication.

1   Introduction

Nowadays more and more business and home users rely on correctness and high availability of computer infrastructure. Consequently, simple hardware malfunction or software errors, if not properly counteracted, might lead to significant outages resulting for instance in financial loses or user frustration. Ensuring reliability is therefore an inherent part of the design of most modern computer systems.

Byzantine fault tolerance (BFT) is a powerful, yet still not very widely applied replication technique for providing availability against arbitrary (Byzantine) faults. This approach is usually divided into two phases: agreement and execution. In the agreement phase replicas decide on the order of incoming requests, and in the execution phase the requests are processed according to previously established sequence. In order to tolerate f faulty nodes, at least $3f + 1$ replicas are required to participate in the agreement phase. Once the ordering is known, however, only $2f + 1$ replicas are needed to execute them. While certain protocols (for instance [1, 14]) incorporate both these phases, the separation of agreement and execution is important for two main reasons. First of all, it allows to reduce the overall cost of the applied solution and secondly, it enables better resource utilization, as it is believed that the execution phase is far more expensive than the agreement [17].

C. Hochberger et al. (Eds.): ARCS 2013, LNCS 7767, pp. 38–49, 2013.

The algorithms previously applied in the agreement phase can be divided into two main categories. The first type uses a trusted component in the role of a sequencer. This technique has been described for instance in [2,3,15] and will not be further analysed in this article. The other, presented for instance in [18], applies another state-machine replication protocol to agree on the order of requests. While the efficiency of both methods is still a subject of discussions, the second approach is usually treated as more versatile, as it places lower requirements on system components.

To the best of our knowledge however, no dedicated distributed sequencer tolerating Byzantine faults has been previously proposed. Instead, existing protocols, not necessarily optimized for this purpose, have been used. For instance, Yin et al. have applied a modified version of PBFT [1] to agree on the ordering of requests [18]. Please note however that PBFT itself combines the agreement and execution, and requires three communication rounds even when no execution phase is required. Consequently, as the order imposed by PBFT needs to be afterwards relayed to execution replicas, this approach introduces a fourth communication round, one more than in PBFT or other traditional protocols [11,14].

In this article we contribute with a dedicated Byzantine fault-tolerant protocol for request ordering that can be applied in the agreement phase. We additionally show that it can be used to implement a Byzantine replication protocol consisting of three communication rounds, the same number as PBFT, at the same time allowing to reduce the number of machines executing the requests to $2f + 1$.

The article is constructed as follows. We start by presenting the model and the assumptions about the underlying distributed system in section 2. Section 3 presents the proposed sequencer protocol under the assumption that the reply is relayed directly to the client that has issued the request. We drop this assumption in section 4, where we use the proposed sequencer to build a Byzantine replication protocol for executing the requests. Section 5 evaluates the algorithm and discusses the obtained test results. Finally, we present the related work in section 6 and conclude in section 7.

2   System Model

It is widely known that no protocol can reach consensus in a completely asynchronous environment if at least one process can be faulty [7]. To circumvent this, it is usually assumed that the system run consists of sufficiently frequent intervals during which the system behaves synchronously. We have on the other hand decided to focus on a timed asynchronous model [4]. In such environment machines communicate asynchronously, but the maximum response time (including the reaction time and communication overhead) is finite and known. If the machine either stops responding or responds very slowly, due to for instance heavy workload, it is regarded as faulty. We believe that, as long as the timeouts are reasonably set, these conditions represent real-life distributed systems.

Let us call the attacker a party that is able to infiltrate all the components of our system and has the ability to alter the protocol execution on any replica.

Please note that this also includes any hardware or software failure. The attacker can perform his actions either by directly controlling the replica or by intercepting the messages in a communication channel between the machines. In the first case it can perform any arbitrary action at any point of the protocol. In the second case it can either prevent the replicas from receiving the transmitted messages or change their contents.

It is worth noting that the variety of actions the attacker can perform by intercepting the messages in the channel is a subset of all the actions that can be performed after gaining control over the sender of the message. Namely, removing a message in the channel is equivalent to a case when the sender does not produce a message at all. Similarly, changing the contents of a message corresponds to a situation where the originating replica creates an already altered version of the message. For simplicity we therefore assume that the attacker can only alter the protocol execution on any subset of replicas, while the channel remains fault-free. Consequently, the receiver will obtain exactly one copy of every sent message in a known, finite time. The latter can be ensured by the abovementioned assumption and the properties of the underlying communication protocol (such as TCP). We however keep in mind that gaining control over the communication channel is usually much simpler than over a replica.

Whenever the attacker has gained control over a replica or any communication channel originating from it, we say that this replica is faulty. The safety and liveness of our protocol are guaranteed as long as no more than $f = \lfloor \frac{n-1}{3} \rfloor$ machines are faulty, where n is the total number of nodes in the system.

The protocol uses signatures to verify contents of messages exchanged in the system. The primary signs the requests with newly assigned identifiers before they are passed to backups. Additionally, all nodes attach a signature to every message sent to the clients. Similarly to other Byzantine fault-tolerant protocols, we assume that the cryptographic techniques cannot be broken.

3   The Algorithm

The proposed algorithm takes advantage of the primary-backup replication. Exactly one machine in the system (denoted as primary) performs the role of a centralised sequencer, ordering the requests received from clients. The other nodes, or the backups, ensure that these assignments are correct. The general outline of the proposed protocol can be described as follows:

1. The client sends a request to the primary
2. The primary assigns a sequence number to the received request and sends it to backups
3. Backups try to prove that the primary is faulty. If they fail to do so, they sign the proposed identifier and send it to the client as soon as they process all the requests with lower sequence numbers
4. The client waits for at least $f + 1$ replies with the same identifier signed by different replicas. If it succeeds, the obtained identifier is treated as valid.

For now we assume that the replicas send the result directly to the client that has issued the request. In section 4 we will drop this assumption and consider a situation where the replicas forward their response to machines other than the client, such as execution nodes.

Following the well-known nomenclature of Castro and Liskov [1] we denote a view as the replica configuration distinguished by the current primary. View changes are performed whenever the backups determine that the primary is faulty. We introduce two data structures, queue and log, for storing requests on replicated machines. The queue holds the messages that are waiting for being sent to the client. The log on the other hand preserves the history of messages that have already been sent to the client in the current view.

The identifiers assigned by the primary are in a form $\langle v, c \rangle$, where v is the current view number and c is the next number in a sequence. For two identifiers id_1 and id_2 we say that $id_1 < id_2$ iff. $v_1 < v_2$ or $v_1 = v_2 \wedge c_1 < c_2$. Additionally, two identifiers are equal when both their compounds are the same.

3.1 The Client

Whenever a client c wishes to obtain a unique identifier for the payload p, it sends a $\langle REQ, c, p \rangle$ message to the primary. The protocol ensures that for some finite, yet unknown time two different requests $\langle REQ, c, p_1 \rangle$ and $\langle REQ, c, p_2 \rangle$ such that $p_1 = p_2$ result in obtaining the same identifier. If this behaviour is not desired, the payload p should be concatenated with a unique value, such as the current timestamp.

The replies sent to the client are in a form $\langle REP, v, r, h, i \rangle$, where v is the identifier of the current primary, r the identifier of the sender, h the hashed value of the corresponding payload and i is the assigned identifier. The hashed contents of the message are additionally signed by the replica r. For a given payload p, the client waits for messages with valid signatures and the same i value. If such messages are obtained from at least $f + 1$ different replicas, i is treated as a genuine identifier of payload p.

If the client does not receive these replies after some specified amount of time, it resends its original request to all the replicas. If the response for the given payload has been sent to the client before, replicas respond with a REP message along with the identifier assigned before. If the request from the client was already processed, but the response has not yet been generated, replicas simply ignore the received message. Finally, if replicas have not processed that request before, they relay it to the primary and wait either for an identifier to be assigned, or a timeout, after which they start the recovery protocol.

3.2 The Main Protocol

Upon the start of the service the replicas set the values of the current view number v and a counter value c to zero. Whenever the primary receives a request, it creates an identifier in a form of a tuple $id = \langle v, c \rangle$ and increments the c value. This identifier, along with the original request is then signed and sent to all the backups, which in turn forward it to all the other replicas (including the primary).

For a given request, the machines wait for at least $2f + 1$ messages from different replicas, which both contain the same identifier and are properly signed by the primary. If any replica fails to do so before the assigned timeout, it issues a view change request. Additionally, if a replica obtains two or more different assignments for the same payload, it attaches them as a proof to its request for a view change.

Whenever a machine successfully obtains the abovementioned messages, we say that the corresponding request is locally committed. The replica then checks if the newly committed request has left the system before, i.e. whether that replica has once sent it to the client. If that is the case, the result is resent to the client. Otherwise the committed request is inserted into the request queue, provided that the following are true:

a) Neither the queue nor log contains a message with a different identifier assigned to the considered payload
b) Neither the queue nor log contains a request with the same identifier as in the considered message, assigned to a different payload

If either of those requirements is not met, the replica triggers the view change protocol attaching both arguable requests.

A committed message is taken out from the queue and sent to the client as soon as all the messages with lower identifiers (even those that the replica might be unaware of) have also been sent. In other words, the message with identifier $id > 0$ is processed only when the message with $id' = id - 1$ has been sent and removed from the queue. Additionally, if a message is not removed from the queue before a timeout, the replica starts the recovery protocol. The pseudocode for the main protocol is presented as algorithm 1.

3.3   Recovery Protocol

Whenever a replica believes the primary is faulty, it broadcasts a view change request $\langle VCR, v, r, p \rangle$ to all other replicas, where v is the current view number, r is the reason and p is an optional proof. Upon retrieving such message, a replica checks whether, based on its own knowledge and the acquired proof, it can regard the primary as faulty. If the replica agrees and the view number specified in the request matches the current one, it sends a VC_PREP message to other machines; otherwise it performs no action.

When a replica receives at least $f + 1$ VC_PREP messages, it broadcasts VC_EXEC request, even though it might not agree that the primary is faulty. Finally, when a replica obtains at least $2f+1$ VC_EXEC messages, it changes the current view number, provided it is still in the same view that the one specified in the VC_EXEC message. Upon entering the new view, the replicas can erase the contents of their queues and logs, unless they might be required for further reference by other protocols.

Algorithm 1. The main protocol

---

1 **Upon** reception of m=$\langle REQ, c, p \rangle \wedge$ replica_is_primary
2   **if** $\neg$ *log.contains(m)* **then**
3   id $\leftarrow$ assign_identifier(m)
4   sign $\leftarrow$ create_signature(c,p)
5   broadcast($\langle PREPARE, id, c, p, sign \rangle$)
6   **else**
7   `// do nothing`

8 **Upon** reception of m=$\langle REQ, c, p \rangle \wedge$ replica_is_backup
9   **if** *log.contains(p)* **then**
10   send(c, log.get(p))
11   **else**
12   send(primary, m)
13   set_timeout(m)

14 **Upon** reception of m=$\langle PREPARE, id, c, p \rangle$
15   broadcast($\langle COMMIT, id, c, p, sign \rangle$)

16 **Upon** reception of m=$\langle COMMIT, id, c, p, sign \rangle$
17   **if** $\neg$ *verify_signature(c,p,sign)* **then**
18   `// ignore message`
19   **if** *log_or_queue.contains(id)* $\vee$ *log_or_queue.contains(p)* **then**
20         $id' \leftarrow$ log_or_queue.get(p)
21         $p' \leftarrow$ log_or_queue.get(id)
22   **if** $p' \neq p \vee id' \neq id$ **then**
23   `// different assignment in the past`
24   start_recovery_protocol()

25 **Upon** #m = $\langle COMMIT, id, c, p \rangle = 2f + 1$
26   **if** $\neg$*committed_locally(m)* **then**
27   commit_locally(m)
28   queue.insert(m)

29 **Upon** new message in queue
30   **while** *next_id = queue.front.id* **do**
31   m $\leftarrow$ queue.front
32   send(m.c, m.id)
33   queue.pop()
34   next_id++

35 **Upon** timeout on event e
36   start_recovery_protocol()

---

4   Cooperation with Execution Protocols

In the previous section we have described a simplified version of the protocol, where all replicas reply directly to the client that has issued the request. In this chapter we will drop this assumption and use the presented algorithm in cooperation with protocols executing the requests. For simplicity we will use a straightforward execution protocol that requires $2f + 1$ replicas, although, as mentioned earlier, Iwazaru can also be used with speculative solutions requiring only $f + 1$ machines. The modified outline of the protocol from section 3 is presented below.

1. The client sends a request to the primary
2. The primary assigns a sequence number to the received request and sends it to backups
3. Backups try to prove that the primary is faulty. If they fail to do so, they sign the proposed identifier and send it to the machine from execution cluster as soon as they process all the requests with lower sequence numbers
4. Upon receiving $2f + 1$ replies with the same identifier signed by different replicas, machines in the execution cluster add the request to their queues
5. Execution cluster replicas execute the job from their queue and send a reply to the client as soon as all the tasks with lower identifiers have been processed
6. The client waits for at least $f + 1$ replies containing the same result signed by different replicas. If it succeeds, the obtained result is treated as valid

In contrast to the protocol presented in the previous section, ordering messages between views is not straightforward, as in some cases the execution cluster might contain at least one replica that is unaware of some of the requests processed by the remaining nodes. Since the number of execution replicas is insufficient to reach a consensus, the ordering between the views needs to be implemented by the agreement cluster. The modified view change procedure is presented in the following chapter.

4.1   The Modified Recovery Protocol

The recovery procedure is the same as in section 3.3 up to the point when a valid replica receives at least $f + 1$ VC_PREP messages. At that stage, regardless of its beliefs about the state of the primary, the replica creates a $\langle QUERY\_M, v, l \rangle$ message, where v is the current view number and l is an excerpt from its log. The data in l contains all the assignments of identifiers between a certain value called a milestone and the greatest identifier known by that replica. We will present a broader definition of a milestone and describe how they are created at the end of this chapter.

After relaying the message, replicas set theirs timers. Adjusting the timeout is feasible, since the maximum reaction time of a node is known due to our assumption about the timed asynchronous model. Replicas then wait either for a reply from *all* the machines or for a timeout to occur. After that it can be said, that every node has received a reply from all valid replicas. Each machine then established the highest identifier confirmed by at least $f + 1$ replicas, i.e. performs a search for such identifier M that:

$$\forall i \leq M \ \#confirmed(i) \geq f + 1 \ \land \ \#confirmed(M + 1) \leq f$$

In other words, M represents the last message that could have been executed by at least one replica from the execution cluster. Once the decision is made, replicas increment their view number and relay the responsibilities of a primary to the next machine. Additionally, each node sends a confirmation of a view change along with M to the machines from the execution cluster.

The replicas in the execution cluster continue to execute requests from their queues and switch to the new view as soon as the request with identifier M is processed. If any replica is unable to proceed due to absence of a request in its queue, it queries the remaining machines from the execution cluster and waits for a response from at least $f + 1$ nodes.

The process of creating the list of the assignments known to the replica can be very time-consuming, especially if the view change has not been performed for quite a long time. In order to minimize the time required for this operation we have introduced a concept of milestones. A milestone represents a certain identifier that has been confirmed by at least $2f + 1$ replicas. Since a prerequisite for a request to be processed by a valid node is that all the messages with lower identifiers have also been processed, the M value cannot be less than the identifier of a milestone.

Replicas from the execution cluster periodically create a new milestone after executing a batch of requests. Whenever a node decides to do so, it sends a message to every replica in the agreement cluster. Upon receiving $f + 1$ propositions, replicas move the current milestone to the new position.

5   Performance and Evaluation

In order to evaluate our approach we have performed a series of comparison test between Iwazaru and PBFT, which has previously been used as an algorithm for request ordering [18]. As described before, Iwazaru requires one communication round less than PBFT while introducing only minor additional workload in remaining rounds. The expected theoretical speedup as compared to PBFT is therefore around 33%.

To verify this estimation we have implemented and executed simplified versions of both algorithms, focusing only on gracious executions, i.e. executions during which the primary is correct. The parts of both protocols responsible for changing a faulty primary have not been implemented, as they base on different assumptions and are therefore beyond comparison. In normal conditions the recovery protocol of Iwazaru may be several times slower, depending on the imposed timeouts and the distance from the last milestone. This however does not limit the practicality of our approach, since as long as the timeouts are properly adjusted, primary faults should be rather rare. The overhead introduced by the

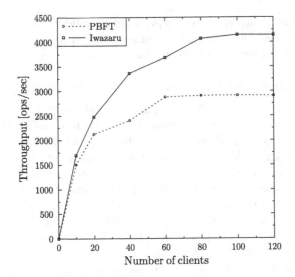

Fig. 1. Throughput of PBFT and Iwazaru in systems tolerating $f = 1$ faults.

view changes should therefore be balanced by the gain obtained from correct protocol runs.

The simulations were performed on an 8 core server equipped with 64GB RAM. In each run of the experiment a certain number of clients simultaneously issued requests to both protocols. The duration of an experiment spans between the first issued request and the point where the last client receives at least $f + 1$ identical identifiers. The throughput of an algorithm is represented by the mean number of assigned identifiers per second achieved throughout the duration of the simulation.

Figure 1 presents the throughput achieved for both algorithms in a system configured for tolerating a single faulty node. As the number of clients increases, Iwazaru scales better than PBFT. In its peak performance Iwazaru has proved to perform a little less than 30% faster than PBFT, as compared to theoretical 33%. The difference between both values can be justified by additional actions that are undertaken by Iwazaru. These include for instance setting timeouts on the request queue and executing additional references to log. In general however, the achieved result is very close to our theoretical predictions.

Fault scalability of both algorithms for a constant number of clients is presented in figure 2. In comparison to a system with $f = 1$, the introduction of additional three nodes has halved the throughput of both protocols. This trend also holds as the number of tolerated faults increases. An interesting observation is that, apart from the case when $f = 1$, the throughput of Iwazaru tolerating $f + 1$ faults is very close to PBFT tolerating f faults.

Although increasing the number of tolerated faults significantly reduces obtained throughput regardless of the algorithm, Iwazaru has generally demonstrated better fault scalability. While, as presented earlier, for $f = 1$ Iwazaru

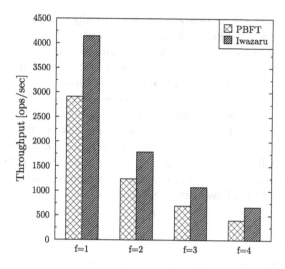

Fig. 2. Fault scalability of PBFT and Iwazaru with 100 clients

has performed around 30% faster than PBFT, with introducing more nodes to the system we have observed an increase of this value to around 40%.

The experimental results have therefore confirmed our expectations. Using Iwazaru as a distributed sequencer rather than PBFT can significantly improve performance of the whole system. Consequently, a replication algorithm based on Iwazaru, despite introducing an additional communication round, can be almost as fast as PBFT itself, while at the same time allowing for reduction in the number of machines performing the requests.

6 Related Work

The problem of Byzantine agreement was originally presented by Lamport, Shostak and Pease [12]. Early BFT solutions were either synchronous or introduced an overhead too high for practical applications [9,13]. PBFT by Castro and Liskov [1] is considered to be the first practical asynchronous Byzantine replication algorithm and is treated as a baseline ever since.

Throughout the years various approaches to reduce the throughput and cost of Byzantine fault-tolerant replicated systems have been presented. Kotla et. al. [11] proposed to parallelize the execution of incoming requests, as long as their order was insignificant. Speculative execution was also analysed, on both server [10] and client side [16].

Yin et. al. [18] proposed the separation of agreement and execution using a slightly modified version of PBFT in the role of a sequencer. Subsequently, trusted components became a commonly used alternative to distributed sequencers. This method is represented for instance by TTCB [3], A2M [2] and

MinBFT [15]. Trusted subsystems are however usually either very costly to implement or introduce a major performance bottleneck. CheapBFT [8] tries to approach this problem by using FPGA-based trusted component.

Another implication of separating agreement and execution is the possible reduction in the number of machines required to perform the requests. While originally at least $2f + 1$ nodes are needed, several protocols require only $f + 1$ machines during gracious executions. SPARE [6] and ZZ [17] rely on virtualization and are able to activate up to f additional replicas when faults are detected or suspected. ODRC [5] proposes a different approach by using surplus replicas to execute requests in parallel, as long as they operate on disjoint parts of the internal state. Finally, it is worth noting that Iwazaru can be adopted to work with the majority of the abovementioned protocols.

7   Conclusion

In this article we have presented Iwazaru - a distributed Byzantine fault-tolerant sequencer that can be applied in the agreement phase of the majority of contemporary state machine replication protocols. By assuming timed asynchronous model for the underlying distributed system we were able to reduce the number of communication steps required to agree on the order of the incoming requests.

Our tests have demonstrated that under normal execution Iwazaru significantly outperforms distributed sequencer used by Yin et. al. [18]. By applying it into a replication algorithm separating agreement from execution we were able to obtain a solution only several percent slower than PBFT itself, while at the same time allowing for a significant reduction in number of machines executing the requests.

We believe that timed asynchronous model, if correctly configured, is appropriate for the majority of modern distributed systems. In the future we plan to focus on optimizing the execution algorithm and deploying an Iwazaru-based protocol in wide area networks.

References

1. Castro, M., Liskov, B.: Practical Byzantine fault tolerance. In: Proceedings of the Third Symposium on Operating Systems Design and Implementation, OSDI 1999, pp. 173–186. USENIX Association, Berkeley (1999)
2. Chun, B.-G., Maniatis, P., Shenker, S., Kubiatowicz, J.: Attested append-only memory: Making adversaries stick to their word. In: Proceedings of the 21st Symposium on Operating Systems Principles (2007)
3. Correia, M., Neves, N.F., Veríssimo, P.: How to tolerate half less one Byzantine nodes in practical distributed systems. In: Proceedings of the 23rd IEEE Symposium on Reliable Distributed Systems, pp. 174–183 (October 2004)
4. Cristian, F., Fetzer, C.: The timed asynchronous distributed system model. IEEE Transactions on Parallel and Distributed Systems 10, 642–657 (1999)
5. Distler, T., Kapitza, R.: Increasing performance in Byzantine fault-tolerant systems with on-demand replica consistency. In: Proceedings of the EuroSys 2011 Conference (EuroSys 2011), pp. 91–105 (2011)

6. Distler, T., Kapitza, R., Popov, I., Reiser, H.P., Schröder-Preikschat, W.: SPARE: Replicas on hold. In: Proceedings of the 18th Network and Distributed System Security Symposium (NDSS 2011), pp. 407–420 (2011)
7. Fischer, M.J., Lynch, N.A., Paterson, M.S.: Impossibility of distributed consensus with one faulty process. Technical report, Cambridge, MA, USA (1982)
8. Kapitza, R., Behl, J., Cachin, C., Distler, T., Kuhnle, S., Mohammadi, S.V., Schröder-Preikschat, W., Stengel, K.: CheapBFT: Resource-efficient Byzantine fault tolerance. In: Proceedings of the EuroSys 2012 Conference (EuroSys 2012), pp. 295–308 (2012)
9. Kihlstrom, K.P., Moser, L.E., Melliar-Smith, P.M.: The SecureRing protocols for securing group communication. In: Hawaii International Conference on System Sciences, pp. 317–326 (1998)
10. Kotla, R., Clement, A., Wong, E., Alvisi, L., Dahlin, M.: Zyzzyva: Speculative Byzantine fault tolerance. In: Symposium on Operating Systems Principles (2007)
11. Kotla, R., Dahlin, M.: High throughput Byzantine fault tolerance. In: Proceedings of the 2004 Conference on Dependable Systems and Networks, pp. 575–584 (2004)
12. Lamport, L., Shostak, R., Pease, M.: The Byzantine generals problem. ACM Transactions on Programming Languages and Systems 4, 382–401 (1982)
13. Reiter, M.K.: The Rampart Toolkit for Building High-Integrity Services. In: Birman, K.P., Mattern, F., Schiper, A. (eds.) Dagstuhl Seminar 1994. LNCS, vol. 938, pp. 99–110. Springer, Heidelberg (1995)
14. Rodrigues, R., Castro, M., Liskov, B.: BASE: using abstraction to improve fault tolerance. In: Proceedings of the 18th Symposium on Operating Systems Principles, pp. 15–28. ACM Press (2001)
15. Veronese, G.S., Correia, M., Bessani, A.N., Lung, L.C., Verissimo, P.: Efficient Byzantine fault tolerance. IEEE Transactions on Computers 99(prePrints) (2011)
16. Wester, B., Cowling, J., Nightingale, E.B., Chen, P.M., Flinn, J., Liskov, B.: Tolerating latency in replicated state machines through client speculation. In: Proceedings of the 6th USENIX Symposium on Networked Systems Design and Implementation, pp. 245–260. USENIX Association, Berkeley (2009)
17. Wood, T., Singh, R., Venkataramani, A., Shenoy, P., Cecchet, E.: Zz and the art of practical bft execution. In: Proceedings of the Sixth Conference on Computer Systems, EuroSys 2011, pp. 123–138 (2011)
18. Yin, J., Martin, J.-P., Venkataramani, A., Alvisi, L., Dahlin, M.: Separating agreement from execution for byzantine fault tolerant services. In: Proceedings of the Nineteenth ACM Symposium on Operating Systems Principles, pp. 253–267. ACM Press (2003)

Exploiting Thermal Coupling Information in MPSoC Dynamic Thermal Management

Simone Corbetta and William Fornaciari

Politecnico di Milano – Dipartimento di Elettronica e Informazione
Via Ponzio 34/5 – 20133 Milano, Italy
{scorbetta,fornacia}@elet.polimi.it

Abstract. Temperature profile optimization is one of the most relevant and challenging problems in modern multi-core architectures. Several Dynamic Thermal Management approaches have been proposed in literature, and run-time policies have been designed to direct the allocation of tasks according to temperature constraints. Thermal coupling is recognized to have a role of paramount importance in determining the thermal envelope of the processor, nevertheless several works in literature do not take directly into account this aspect while determining the status of the system at run-time. Without this information, the DTM design is not able to fully redistribute the roles that each core have on the system-level temperature, thus neglecting important information for temperature-constrained workload allocation.

Purpose of this work is to provide a novel *mechanism* to better support DTM policies, focusing on the estimation of the impact of thermal coupling in determining the appropriate status from a thermal stand-point. The presented approach is based on two stages: off-line characterization of the target architecture estimates thermal coupling coefficients, that will be used at run-time for proper DTM decisions.

1   Introduction

Microelectronics integration density is limited by the reliability of the circuits. Increasing power consumption of VLSI circuits causes thermal effects to become one of the most important concerns for circuit reliability. Experimental results show that more than 50% of integrated circuit failures are due to thermal issues [1]. In addition, it has been demonstrated that temperature spatial gradients have negative effect on the performance of the circuit [2]. Temperature profile optimization for reliable system design has become of paramount importance, and several Dynamic Thermal Management (DTM) approaches have been proposed in literature. The purpose of DTM is to control the varying temperature profile to optimize a given objective function: for instance, in reliable systems, the optimization goal is generally the maximum operating temperature or the maximum variability of the temperature (in time) compared to the average chip temperature. All these aspects require an accurate estimation of the status, from a thermal view-point, of the processor. With multi-core technology gaining further attention, this aspect is of paramount relevance since the problem of estimation is just a fraction of the DTM process, but the benefits of a good DTM are entirely based on the

C. Hochberger et al. (Eds.): ARCS 2013, LNCS 7767, pp. 50–61, 2013.
© Springer-Verlag Berlin Heidelberg 2013

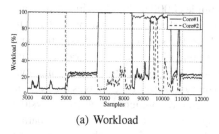

(a) Workload

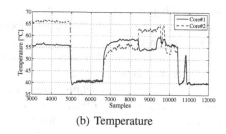

(b) Temperature

Fig. 1. Thermal coupling effects on a dual-core architecture, showing (a) workload and (b) temperature of both cores

estimation process itself. For this reason, it is belief of the authors that an accurate estimation methodology should be employed. The main important aspects of the proposed methodology are to be searched in the role that thermal coupling has on the temperature distribution in a chip [3].

1.1 Motivation Example

This research work faces the problem of an appropriate dynamic thermal management support for multi-core processors, that focuses on the role of thermal coupling in the estimation process. The proposed work aims at the definition of a *mechanism* supporting DTM policies, while the definition of an appropriate *policy* is part of on-going research. The proposed novel methodology accounts for two important aspects: the coupling between pairs of cores, and the transient profile to reach steady-state temperature values. The importance of these two aspects will be discussed in this section, and a brief overview of the problem will be proposed from a formal stand-point.

In single-core processors the operating temperature is a function of the only core operating point: frequency, supply voltage and the load impacting on the switching activity of the core circuitry. In this context, temperature is mainly due to the self-heating process, since power consumption leads to thermal energy dissipation. Thermal management in this scenario is rather trivial, since control points converge into the processor itself. Nevertheless, this is not the case with multi-core architectures. Assume a double-core architecture with asymmetric load, i.e. each core is loaded with applications that are different from a power requirements view-point, and suppose to sample the temperature of each core once every τ time units. Then, consider the temperature profile as a function of the workload in each processor. Figure 1 reports the temperature profile and the workload of an Intel©Core™2 Duo processor; temperature values are sampled once every second using appropriate standard interfaces available in the GNU/Linux operating system. Two main aspects are clear from this scenario. The first one is on the effect of cores proximity on the temperature distribution inside the package: even though Core#1 is low loaded (under 10% on average) in the first period from sample 3000 to sample 5000, it actually *does* consume a non negligible portion of static power due to the temperature induced by the activity of Core#2. As a matter of fact, the operating temperature of Core#1 is 55°C in this time period, while its lowest value is around

40°C as it happens in the time frame between samples 5000 and 6500. This means that an inactive core should be actually subject to power/performance decisions, and also to reliability concerns, since it plays a relevant role in the system power dissipation and thermal envelope. Another important aspect is the one of transients. The rate at which a core heats up depends on several factors, both local (i.e., proper to the core) and non-local (i.e., induced by neighbor cores). The proximity to active cores makes the average cores temperature higher than in the case of isolated environments or when the system is entirely in low activity, also due to the package resistance and capacitance charac-teristics to spread thermal energy. Furthermore, the rate speed at which a core heats up is a function of the difference between the steady-state and the actual temperatures [4], the physical parameters determined by the architecture and fabrication of the chip, the workload of that core and of the neighbor ones, and power consumption.

1.2 Novel Contributions

By exploiting the current temperature readings, the temperature history and appropriate thermal status information, purpose of our research work is giving a major source of information to the system-wide thermal management subsystem to control temperature envelope and to prolong device lifetime. The proposed approach tries to convey raw information and power/performance metrics to give a more accurate overview of the system status from a temperature view-point, considering the direct effects of thermal coupling and core-to-core proximity. To this extent, we define a methodology to esti-mate the status, from a thermal view point, of each core in a multi-core processor. We developed a two-stages methodology, where accurate thermal coupling information is collected once off-line, properly stressing the target architecture, and used at run-time to take appropriate power/thermal management optimizations. The novel contributions of this work can be summarized as follows: (i) a novel *mechanism* for supporting Dy-namic Thermal Management is proposed, focusing on the role of thermal coupling in specifying the status of each core; (ii) a novel system-wide metric is proposed, through an appropriate formal model; (iii) a two-stage estimation methodology has been devel-oped, general enough to be virtually employed in any multi-core architecture.

The remainder of the paper is organized as follows. The metric will be presented in a formal way in Section 2: the analytical expressions raising the metric will be presented, and the methodology to estimate the coupling coefficients in the target architecture will be also discussed. Experimental results are then given in Section 3. Related works on the topic are given in Section 4, while conclusions are drawn in Section 5.

2 Definition of a Thermal Status Metric

The proposed methodology is based on the novel concept of *thermal status* (or *status*), combining power, performance and temperature metrics; the logic that glues together these aspects resides in the thermal coupling. It is meant to be employed on-line and to give a comprehensive status of the processor to support dynamic thermal management policy selection.

2.1 Neighbor-Aware Thermal Status

As sketched in Section 1, in multi-core architectures the temperature reached by a core is a function of local and non-local contributions. In particular, the heat associated to a core j is a function of two different sources. A *generative* one accounts for the dynamic power consumption according to its activity; this is independent on the floorplan, but impacts cores in the proximity. Also, an *exchange* contribution takes into account coupling effects among cores that reside in the neighborhood, and it is proportional to the physical distance between cores. This last term models the spatial aspect of thermal heat diffusion. With these definitions, the generative contribution can be mapped to the power consumption profile of the generic core j, while the exchange contribution accounts for thermal proximity. We define the generative contribution $g_j(t)$ of core j at sample time t in Equation 1, through a function of the operating point tuple $\mathcal{O}_j(t) = \langle V_j(t), f_j(t), w_j(t), T_j(t) \rangle$, with $V_j(t)$ being the supply voltage applied to that core, $f_j(t)$ its operating frequency, $w_j(t)$ its average load and $T_j(t)$ its operating temperature. Notice that $V_j(t)$ and $f_j(t)$ can change dynamically according to the presence of a power management framework. To simplify the on-line estimation process, their values are defined relative to the maximum (architecture dependent) voltage V_{MAX} and frequency f_{MAX}. The additive term takes into account temperature-dependent leakage effects. The values ξ_{dyn} and ξ_{st} are used to weight the dynamic and static power contributions; their typical values are set according to reflect scaled technologies [5], e.g. $\langle \xi_{dyn}, \xi_{st} \rangle = \langle 0.65, 0.35 \rangle$.

$$g_j(t) = \xi_{dyn} \cdot \left(\left(\frac{V_j(t)}{V_{MAX}} \right)^2 \frac{f_j(t)}{f_{MAX}} w_j(t) \right) + \xi_{st} \cdot exp\left\{ -1/T_j(t) \right\} \qquad (1)$$

Equation 1 provides a perspective with respect to local information on the cores, i.e. its validity is confined to the generic core j. In order to account for the heat conduction between adjacent cores, we apply the generative contribution definition to each core k in the neighborhood set N_j of core j, as given in Equation 2. The second contribution from $s_j(t)$ is due to neighbors activity. θ_{jk} represents the thermal coupling factor that holds between cores j and k. The generative value is then further weighted through an index $\alpha_j(t)$ accounting for aging aspects. The value of α changes over time as a consequence of temperature-accelerated reliability concerns, for instance considering the impact of Negative Bias Temperature Instability (NBTI) on the performance of the device [6]. In this work, we assume it constant ($\alpha_j = 1$) for simplicity.

$$s_j(t) = \alpha_j(t) \cdot g_j(t) + \sum_{k \in N_j} \theta_{jk} \cdot \alpha_k(t) \cdot g_k(t) \qquad (2)$$

$$\Lambda = \frac{s_1 T_1 + s_2 T_2 + \cdots + s_N T_N}{T_1 + T_2 + \cdots + T_N} = \frac{1}{N T_p} \sum_{j=1}^{N} s_j T_j \qquad (3)$$

The definition of thermal status given in Equation 2 provides local as well as coupling information, but focuses on a per-core perspective and does not provide a system-wide perspective. A system-wide thermal status metric Λ is defined in Equation 3, where N

is the number of cores [1]. The system-wide perspective is a weighted sum of the thermal status of each core in the processor and weights are determined by the local temperature values T_j; in this way, it jointly exploits local and package (average) temperature as well as thermal status information. The expression at the denominator equals N times the average temperature T_p in the processor.

2.2 Proactive Thermal Status

The model given in Equation 3 allows us to capture the heat-up rate of the system, in terms of perturbations of the (local) thermal status of each core. In general, considering the thermal coupling effects exploited in the model of Equation 2, a perturbation of the local thermal status s_j will have direct effects on the thermal status s_k in the neighborhood set N_j, by means of thermal coupling phenomenon. From a system-wide perspective, on the other hand, a perturbation of the (local) thermal status of each core will have additive effects on the value of Λ. According to Equation 3, these effects will be a function of the local temperature values with respect to the system's average temperature. This aspect ranks the cores according to their role in determining the system temperature: the higher the core-to-package ratio T_j/T_p, the higher the role of core j in determining temperature T_p; this can be due for instance to the different power/performance profile of core j, or to coupling contributions. To formalize the effects on the system-wide metric Λ by means of local perturbations, we have to consider the total derivative of Λ with respect to the perturbation s_j in the vector $\underline{S} = [s_1 s_2 ... s_N]$. Equation 4 reports the analytical expression of the derivative. By definition, we have to take care of three quantities: the partial effects on Λ of an increase in s_j; the partial effects on Λ due to an increase in s_k, for each k in the neighborhood set N_j, and the mutual effects of s_j and s_k.

$$\frac{\mathrm{d}\Lambda}{\mathrm{d}s_j} = \frac{\partial \Lambda}{\partial s_j} + \sum_{k \neq j} \frac{\partial \Lambda}{\partial s_k} \frac{\mathrm{d}s_k}{\mathrm{d}s_j} = \frac{T_j}{N\,T_p} + \sum_{k \neq j} \frac{T_k}{N\,T_p} \theta_{jk} \qquad (4)$$

The first term $\partial \Lambda/\partial s_j$ defines the effect on Λ of an increase in the value of thermal status s_j; according to Equation 3 this derivative equals $T_j/(N\,T_p)$: an increase in the local status has an impact on the system-wide perspective that is a function of the relative temperature with respect to the system average temperature. The summation term extends the derivative to the adjacent cores; the first factor of the summation has the same meaning as the previous one but focuses on adjacent cores. As a second factor, the effects of considering the ratio of the differentials $\mathrm{d}s_k$ and $\mathrm{d}s_j$ from two cores k and j, models the mutual influence that a change in thermal status s_j has on the adjacent ones; the ratio $\mathrm{d}s_k/\mathrm{d}s_j$ can thus be understood to be the thermal coupling factor θ_{jk} from Equation 2. The values assumed by these coefficients are estimated through an appropriate methodology, discussed later on in Section 2.3. Hence, the model in Equation 4 is a suitable tool to keep track of the dynamic behavior of the system in response to an evolution of the thermal status of each core, and to assess the mutual influence of thermal status between pairs of cores as the system evolves. The only relationship

---

[1] From now on, the notation will be simplified avoiding the use of time variable t.

modeled in Equation 4 is the one between status s_j and Λ and nothing is said about the relationship between a change in g_j and Λ, necessary to estimate the effects of local power/performance requirements on system-wide metrics. Similar to what has been done in Equation 4, we can compute the effect of a perturbation of the self-heating contribution on Λ. In this case, however, additional care must be taken: s_j is a function of g_j, such that Λ is a compound function of s_j and g_j and $\Lambda = f(s_j \circ g_j) = f(s_j(g_j))$; as a consequence the impact on Λ of g_j is not directly exploited, but should pass through the analysis of the impact on s_j; last, the mutual influence between $\mathrm{d}g_j$ and $\mathrm{d}g_k$ is to be considered null, by definition of the self-heating contribution in Equation 2. The total derivative is reported in Equation 5.

$$
\frac{\mathrm{d}\Lambda}{\mathrm{d}g_j} = \frac{\mathrm{d}\Lambda}{\mathrm{d}s_j} \cdot \frac{\mathrm{d}s_j}{\mathrm{d}g_j} = \left(\frac{\partial \Lambda}{\partial s_j} + \sum_{k \neq j} \frac{\partial \Lambda}{\partial s_k} \cdot \frac{\mathrm{d}s_k}{\mathrm{d}s_j} \right) \cdot \left(\frac{\partial s_j}{\partial g_j} + \sum_{k \neq j} \frac{\partial s_j}{\partial g_k} \cdot \frac{\mathrm{d}g_k}{\mathrm{d}g_j} \right) \tag{5}
$$

Locally, we can compute the impact on the thermal status by an increase in the generative contribution in three generic cases: (a) when an increase in the core activity does not modify the operating point; (b) is in the opposite direction, in which the only operating point is changed; (c) refers to the mixed change in the activity and operating point. The common contribution in cases (a), (b) and (c) relies on the sole ξ_{dyn} factor, determining the impact of dynamic power contribution as a function of the power/performance point of core j. Last, the ratio between the two differentials $\mathrm{d}g_k$ and $\mathrm{d}g_j$ is null by definition.

2.3 Coupling Coefficients Estimation

The proposed estimation methodology accounts for the contribution given by the different subsystems composing the reference SoC architecture (e.g., the coupling contribution due to hardware blocks different from the cores). Also, it can be employed on different architectures, thus developing as a general methodology. The interest on this last aspect increases with the increasing availability of multi-core architectures in different domains, pushing researchers to find a suitable methodology to easily adapt their thermal-aware designs and thermal management solutions in a broad range of platforms and operating environments. The proposed approach accounts for the availability of on-chip resources and on-board cooling facilities (e.g., fans or fan less, heat sinks dimension and geometries...), through *direct* temperature observation and platform characterization at warm-up periods. The proposed methodology is divided into three steps. The generic mapping specification M is used to load the multi-core architecture to cover a broad range of allocation patterns: each pattern specifies which core will be assigned work to, and which load. For each mapping M, temperature values are sampled from each core until the steady-state temperature of the system is reached. Once the temperature vector T is known, coupling factor θ is estimated for that particular configuration, and for each core pairs. The flow ensures that different load levels are allocated to each core in the system; this is driven by the rationale that the effective thermal coupling coefficient is a function of the status of each core, in terms of power consumption, and it is not dependent on the sole floorplan. To estimate the coupling coefficients, we run a predefined set of typical applications with the objective to heat-up the processors in a controlled environment. Denoting with X the set of active processors, and with Y the available CPU activity, the mapping should cover a proper subset of $X \times Y$. Temperature profiles are used for computing the thermal coupling coefficients θ_{jk} between cores j and k as $\theta_{jk} = \left(T_j - T_k^{(q)} \right) / T_k^{(q)}$, where T_j is the maximum temperature reached by core j in a particular configuration $\langle x, y \rangle \in X \times Y$, while $T_k^{(q)}$ is the quiet-state temperature of core k, i.e. its temperature when the system is idle (for simplicity, this equals ambient temperature). The output of the second stage is a multi-dimensional matrix summarizing the thermal coupling phenomena at different configurations. Each entry defines the coupling factor as a function of the workload, and can be hard-coded in the DTM policy.

3 Results

We conducted several experiments on representative Intel©i7 820QM quad-core processor, featuring 4 physical on-chip cores supporting up to 8 threads, operating at a maximum frequency of 1.73GHz and fabrication node 45nm; the processor is design to support a Thermal Design Power of 45W. We used different real-life applications, ranging from scientific to multimedia workloads. Since the aspect of interest resides in the coupling phenomenon without any specific relationship with the application running on each core, we will not go through any workload characterization: from our perspective the heating process is the most important feature, independently on the application of interest. Data related to temperature, frequency and workload is taken during execution of mixed applications. Results here are grouped into different sections. Section 3.1 shows the difference of estimation in two cases: with and without the support of the thermal coupling contribution from Equation 2. Section 3.2 shows the results obtained from the estimation of thermal coupling with the methodology proposed in Section 2.3, considering quad-core processors. Finally, Section 3.3 gives an overview of the estimation process overhead as a function of the history window depth.

3.1 The Impact of Thermal Coupling

There is a slightly different estimate in the proposed model with respect to neglecting coupling contributions. Such difference can be as high as as 30% in some cases. This difference is shown in Figure 2(a), highlighting the influence of operating temperature on the estimation. The top-most figure reports the thermal status estimate with and without considering the thermal-coupling contributions (respectively, Floorplan-aware and Classical scenarios); such difference demonstrates that without considering coupling contribution θ, there will be an underestimation, and this underestimation being as much as 65%. This will generally influence DTM decisions, since policies are biased to the information provided about the system from a thermal view-point. The bottom-part of the figure, on the other hand, shows the relative error (with its moving-average) superimposed to the normalized temperature profile. In this case, the error is higher when average temperature is lower; this empirical observation of our model is in concordance with reality, since at higher temperatures the impact of coupling decreases due to the

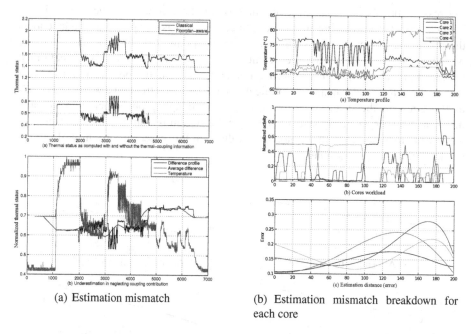

(a) Estimation mismatch

(b) Estimation mismatch breakdown for each core

Fig. 2. Estimation mismatch and error profile in a quad-core processor, as a function of the operating temperature and workload

fact that the neighborhood average temperature tend to saturate. For completeness, Figure 2(b) reports the absolute difference for each core considering a specified time span of 200 samples, as a function of the activity and temperature of each core. The difference in a quad-core processor can reach up to 65%, while experimental results (not reported for lack in space) on dual-core processors show the difference is below 50%. Similar conclusions as for the previous case can thus be drawn.

3.2 Thermal Coupling Coefficients

The results in this section show how to determine quantitative values for the $\theta_{j,k}$ coefficients from Equation 2, varying with the dynamic power and performance state of the processor. To simplify the characterization process, we consider the temperature ranges of each core as a function of the workload associated to each core, rather than as a function of the effective power consumption. The advantage of this approach is in the simplified estimation process, although its validity is bound to a particular power management policy. In this perspective, we conducted several experiments with different allocation patterns: we then discretized the available workload in steps of 25%, using tools available in GNU/Linux operating system. In order to find the values in the multidimensional matrix, an exhaustive set of tests should be performed covering all possible allocation patterns. Due to lack in space, only a selected subset of representative tests will be reported. Notice that we are not interested in selecting a specific benchmark to stress the processor, because we are interested in heating-up the processors without being aware of the executing application, since the focus is on application-independent thermal management. Figure 3 shows how the coupling coefficient varies effectively with the load; the values of the coefficients are reported normalized with respect to the maximum. Figure 3 highlights a varying trend, relying upon the core's activity. The fact that all the cores' coefficients asymptotically reach the same trend line while load tends to 100% reveals the steady-state nature of thermal coupling phenomenon, as already mentioned earlier: at steady-state temperature the system is stable, influence decreases and the coefficients reach their maximum values. In this case, the system will remain stable until it changes its state.

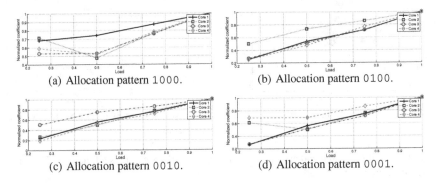

(a) Allocation pattern 1000.　　　　(b) Allocation pattern 0100.

(c) Allocation pattern 0010.　　　　(d) Allocation pattern 0001.

Fig. 3. Thermal coupling coefficients trend, as a function of the load of the active core when a single core is active, for different allocation patterns

The same experiments have been conducted while loading more than one core in the processor; the procedure has been exhaustively repeated for every allocation pattern. Figure 4 reports the coefficients for one single allocation pattern, for lack in space. The surface shows the influence of cores activity on each core in the architecture (active or idle). The values plotted on the surface are normalized to their maximum values. As already sketched in the previous results, the coefficients have much higher variance at lower temperatures (represented by lower cores' activity).

We can also capture additional relevant aspects in the thermal coupling phenomenon. The thermal coupling coefficient is monotonically non-decreasing for a given mixed workload. The first difference we encounter in the quad-core case is a steady-state flat region early toward higher values of the cores activity; this aspect was not experienced in the dual-core case, and it might be associated to the allocation pattern and to the relevant differences in the architecture design and floorplan (however, at the same technology node). Furthermore, the coupling trend is in general a function of the allocation pattern. Even though this dependence is weak at higher cores' activity, it is quite relevant when the cores are loaded weakly: this is clear if we compare the trend for Core#2 in the two allocation patterns.

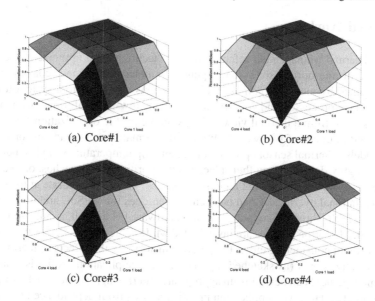

(a) Core#1   (b) Core#2

(c) Core#3   (d) Core#4

Fig. 4. Thermal coupling trend of each core, as a function of the CPU activity of the active cores. Cores are reported in order (Core#1 on the extreme left and Core#4 on the extreme right). Data are reported for allocation patterns `1001`.

Notice that the aforementioned aspects are in line with the concept of thermal impedance in chip packages. Indeed, for a given package, the thermal impedance is reported to be a function of both the duty cycle and the duration of the (equivalent) power consumption pulse. To the best of our knowledge, this is the first time a concept like this is employed in multi-core architectures to characterize the thermal behavior of the SoC importance of thermal coupling in future technology nodes and multi-core architectures, we can envision that in perspective a coupling pre-characterization of commercial multi-core processors will be integrated in the processor data sheet.

3.3 Estimation Overhead

The estimation process reported in Section 2 and Section 2.3 has been completely developed under a GNU/Linux operating system, based on the `lm-sensors` interface to retrieve low-level information from the hardware architecture (e.g., temperature samples, workload activity, frequency and supply voltage values). The framework has been developed entirely as user-space, using `gcc` compiler version 4.4.3. Slow-down estimates as a function of the history depth have been proven to be in the order of a few milliseconds, making it suitable for real deployment. Furthermore, the performance requirements have been shown to be independent on the history depth: the bottleneck is given by the communication overhead in retrieving values from the `lm-sensors` API, since the framework has been entirely developed in user-space.

4   Related Works

Dynamic Thermal Management refers to a set of techniques to optimize the temperature profile of microprocessor systems, generally under performance constraints [7]. DTM is defined by means of *policies* taking decisions according to a system-level or local view of the processor, and *mechanisms* supplying low-level information on the status of the system from a thermal view-point. Runtime profile optimization can usually be performed in either of two ways [8]: through thermal sensors readings, or solving formal models. Thermal sensors provide direct on-chip temperature samples, but these values are highly dependent on their placement; algorithmic approaches, on the other hand, are based on solving formal models at runtime, generally accurate at the cost of high computational overhead. Load balancing techniques for MPSoC architectures can benefit from multi-threaded support from the hardware [9] as well as multi-processor support [10]. Migration policies are investigated while achieving processor throughput, however without considering either temperature history nor the effects of thermal coupling on inactive cores (as sketched in Section 1). If application profile is available, thermal management can benefit from appropriate ordering approaches, such as the one presented in [11]. However, application profiling suffers from dependence of mapping policies. Off-line profiling is used also in other predictive approaches [12]. Temperature history and workload are weighted in [13] to predict future operating temperature of the processor. However, the authors do not consider the effects of cores proximity in determining the thermal status of active and inactive cores.

5   Conclusions

This paper presented a novel methodology to *support* Dynamic Thermal Management in complex MPSoC architectures, in which the thermal requirements are limiting the integration capability as well as the efficiency of optimization policies. Since thermal coupling phenomena are a major source of challenge, and proactive approaches are preferred in reliability-aware designs, the proposed methodology focuses on a coupling-driven estimation of the effects of self-heating contributions on system-wide thermal status metrics. The proposed methodology is able to avoid underestimations in predicting the thermal status. Indeed, even a typical difference of $20 \div 30\%$ in the local status estimation process has a negative impact on the system-wide perspective. Our approach is able to provide a better estimation support, employing architecture-dependent information on the dynamic behavior of heat exchange among the different subsystems in the processor. Such support is of paramount importance in DTM to dynamically reveal the evolution of the system from a temperature stand-point. The proposed approach presents a *mechanism*, rather than a policy, to support DTM decisions. The overhead is kept low thanks to a double-phase approach: off-line pre-characterization of the target architecture (e.g., at bootstrap time) collects sensible information that will be conveniently used at run-time for proper DTM decisions. Experimental results have been collected on real commercial processors, and temperature values reflect the real usage of the system, with typical workloads from different scenarios.

Acknowledgments. This research work is partially supported by the EU-funded 2 PARMA FP7 research project (http://www.2parma.eu/) focusing on resources management techniques and methodologies in multi-core and many-core architectures.

References

1. Lasance, C.J.M.: Thermally driven reliability issues in microelectronic systems: status-quo and challenges. Microelectronics Reliability 43(12), 1969–1974 (2003)
2. Ajami, A., Banerjee, K., Pedram, M.: Modeling and analysis of nonuniform substrate temperature effects on global ULSI interconnects. IEEE Transactions on Computer-Aided Design of Integrated Circuits and Systems 24(6), 849–861 (2005)
3. Janicki, M., Collet, J.H., Louri, A., Napieralski, A.: Hot spots and core-to-core thermal coupling in future multi-core architectures. In: 2010 26th Annual IEEE Semiconductor Thermal Measurement and Management Symposium (SEMI-THERM), pp. 205–210. IEEE (2010)
4. Incropera, F.P., DeWitt, D.P., Bergman, T.L., Lavine, A.S.: Fundamentals of heat and mass transfer. Wiley (2007)
5. International Technology Roadmap for Semiconductor, Design chapter (2010), http://www.itrs.net/
6. Alam, M., Kang, K., Paul, B., Roy, K.: Reliability- and process-variation aware design of vlsi circuits. In: 14th International Symposium on the Physical and Failure Analysis of Integrated Circuits, IPFA 2007, pp. 17–25 (July 2007)
7. Brooks, D., Martonosi, M.: Dynamic Thermal Management for High-Performance Microprocessors. In: 17th International Symposium on High Performance Computer Architecture, HPCA 2001 (2001)
8. Siozios, K., Rodopoulos, D., Soudris, D.: Quick_hotspot: A software supported methodology for supporting run-time thermal analysis at mpsoc designs. In: 23rd International Conference on Architecture of Computing Systems, ARCS 2011 (2011)
9. Gomaa, M., Powell, M., Vijaykumar, T.: Heat-and-run: leveraging smt and cmp to manage power density through the operating system. In: Proceedings of the 11th International Conference on Architectural Support for Programming Languages and Operating Systems, ASPLOS-XI, pp. 260–270. ACM, New York (2004)
10. Donald, J., Martonosi, M.: Techniques for Multicore Thermal Management: Classification and New Exploration. In: 33rd International Symposium on Computer Architecture, ISCA 2006 (2006)
11. Yang, J., Zhou, X., Chrobak, M., Zhang, Y., Jin, L.: Dynamic thermal management through task scheduling. In: IEEE International Symposium on Performance Analysis of Systems and Software, ISPASS 2008, pp. 191–201 (April 2008)
12. Srinivasan, J., Adve, S.V.: Predictive dynamic thermal management for multimedia applications. In: Proceedings of the 17th Annual International Conference on Supercomputing, ICS 2003 (2003)
13. Yeo, I., Liu, C.C., Kim, E.J.: Predictive dynamic thermal management for multicore systems. In: Proceedings of the 45th Annual Design Automation Conference, DAC 2008, pp. 734–739. ACM, New York (2008)

A Multi-core Memory Organization
for 3-D DRAM as Main Memory

Jared Sherman[1], Krishna Kavi[1], Brandon Potter[1], and Mike Ignatowski[2]

[1] University of North Texas, Denton, Texas, USA
{JaredSherman,BrandonPotter}@my.unt.edu, Krishna.Kavi@unt.edu
[2] Advanced Micro Devices, Austin, Texas USA
Mike.Ignatowski@amd.com

Abstract. There is a growing interest in using 3-D DRAM structures and non-volatile memories such as Phase Change Memories (PCM) to both improve access latencies and reduce energy consumption in multi-core systems. These new memory technologies present both opportunities and challenges to computer systems design.

In this paper we address how such memories should be organized to fully benefit from these technologies. We propose to keep 3-D DRAMs as main memory systems, but use non-volatile memories as backing store. In this connection, we view DRAM based main-memory both as a cache memory and as main memory. The cache like addressing allows for fast address translation and better memory allocation among multiple processes. We explore a set of wide-ranging design parameters for page sizes, sub-page sizes, TLB sizes, and sizes of write-buffers.

Keywords: 3-D stacked DRAM, non-volatile memories, phase-change memories, virtual memory management, set-associative indexing.

1 Introduction

An emerging DRAM technology, die-stacked DRAM (3-D DRAM), reduces access latencies for large amounts of memory due to its integration with the processor. In the near term, die-stacking may be used as a large last-level cache [1], however as capacity increases it may be an attractive option to use as a system's main memory. We also consider the use of non-volatile solid-state memories, such as phase-change memory (PCM), to replace the disk drive of a traditional computer.

A system where 3-D DRAM is main memory and PCM is the backing store could have significant overall performance benefits due to their improved latencies, however it would be necessary to rethink memory organizations for such a system. For example, 4K or 8K bytes (pages) are used as the units of transfer between DRAM and disks because of large disk latencies. Should we continue to transfer such large amounts of data when the PCM latencies are much smaller? Another issue to consider is the cost of context switches on page faults when the access latencies to PCM are in the same range as the access latencies to DRAM.

C. Hochberger et al. (Eds.): ARCS 2013, LNCS 7767, pp. 62–73, 2013.

Current systems use hierarchical page tables for virtual to physical address translation. With 64-bit virtual addresses, systems need to look up multiple levels of page tables to translate a virtual address into a physical address and the traversal can be relatively slow [2]. If address translation latencies can be minimized, context switches on page faults may be unnecessary. We explore changes to virtual memory management and structure of pages to improve address translation and minimize OS kernel intervention on page faults. When using 3-D DRAMs and PCMs, TLB performance becomes even more critical since delays in address translation can undercut the performance advantages. We attempt to increase TLB performance using large page sizes, say 32KB, 64KB pages, but still transfer only small amounts of data between DRAM and PCM via subpages. An additional challenge is the limited write-endurance of non-volatile memories. We address this by tailoring CMM parameters to consider write-back and using a victim buffer.

This paper makes the following contributions:

- Evaluates new memory organizations for 3-D DRAM as main memory and non-volatile PCM as secondary memory.
- Evaluates treating 3-D DRAM as both main memory and cache for the purpose of speeding up virtual to physical address translation.
- Evaluates the use of large pages with subpages to benefit from small access latencies to PCM, while improving the utilization of TLB and page tables.

Previously we explored our ideas in a single-core environment using Sparc (Serengeti) architecture [3]. In this paper we explore our ideas for multicore systems using x86-64 architecture running Ubuntu.

The remainder of this paper is organized as follows. Section 2 contains our approach to memory organization. Section 3 describes our experimental setup and Section 4 includes results and analysis of the experimental data. Section 5 details future work. Section 6 describes research that is closely related to our work. Section 7 concludes with ending remarks.

2   Memory Organization

Given the physical proximity to the processor, as well as the low access latencies, the 3-D DRAM memory is viewed both as a cache and a primary memory of a computing system. We utilize cache-like addressing using set-associative indexing schemes with main memory. For this reason, we call our main memory a Cache-Main Memory (CMM). Additional design details about our memory architecture and necessary hardware structures can be found in [3].

2.1   Virtual-Physical Address Translation

Our design relies on both page tables and cache-like indexing for addressing DRAM entries. In conventional main memories, virtual addresses are mapped to physical addresses (DRAM frames) using hierarchical page tables. Typically, a virtual address is divided into several parts where each part indexes into a

Fig. 1. Page Table Bit Divisions

different page table, and the page table entries provide addresses of the next level page table.

Some of the page tables can be eliminated if we use a portion of the virtual address as a set index, similar to addressing a set-associative cache. For example, the *efg* portion of the virtual address can be used as a set index into DRAM (see Figure 1). This idea can be viewed in one of two different ways. We can view this as using very large pages, thus *efg* along with page offset will become the offset into a very large page. Or we can also view this as using very large segments with pages, and *efg* constitutes the address of a segment. By using a set-associative index for the segment, we imply associating a working set of DRAM pages with a segment, and the pages within that segment compete for DRAM pages within the working set. The address of the working set for a segment is given by page tables identified by the higher order bits of the virtual address (*abcd* in Figure 1).

This allows us to satisfy the need for physical addresses (e.g., to eliminate address aliases for common or shared pages), but also speeds up address translation. Furthermore, it allows higher memory levels (L1, L2, and Last Level Caches) to use virtual address indexing. This approach is similar in principle to page coloring [4]. By using large segments with reasonably sized pages, we maintain fine-grained protection at page level. We still use a translation look-aside buffer (TLB) that speeds up address translation.

Page Structure. The CMM consists of large pages which are divided into subpages. Large pages are used to reduce the number of TLB entries while subpages allow us to transfer small chunks of data between DRAM and backing store. It will be necessary to keep track of valid and dirty subpages within a page. A subpage bitmap can be used to track valid and dirty status of subpages within a page.

Page Lookup. Pages are located in the CMM using the virtual address, in combination with an address space identifier (ASID). In addition to using set-associative mapping of addresses to CMM pages, we use a specialized TLB-like structure to accelerate this process. Our TLB is fully-associative and contains a small number of entries. In addition, it also contains the subpage bitmaps for its resident pages which may be rapidly accessed to determine a hit or miss. A page may still reside within the CMM even if there is no TLB entry for the page. In such cases, the CMM Tag Structure is searched using set-associative indexing. Bitmaps are not stored with tags but stored in the CMM page itself as header information. Only the actual CMM pages reside in the 3-D DRAM layers. The other structures can reside in the memory controller or MMU, possibly on the same layer as the processing cores.

Table 1. Benchmark mixes. Total (MB) represents the combined working set size of all applications in a given mix.

Mix	Bench1	Bench2	Bench3	Bench4	Total (MB)
Small1	Gobmk	Hmmer	H264Ref	Gromacs	41.7
Small2	Gamess	Sphinx3	Tonto	Namd	27.6
Medium1	Sjeng	Libquantum	Leslie3d	Astar	191.6
Medium2	Omnetpp	Astar	Calculix	Gcc	139.9
Large1	Milc	Wrf	Zeusmp	Soplex	865.9
Large2	Zeusmp	Leslie3d	Gcc	CactusADM	718.3
VeryLarge1	GemsFDTD	Mcf	Bwaves	CactusADM	2262.2
VeryLarge2	Mcf	Zeusmp	Milc	Bwaves	1656.0

3 Experimental Setup

We use Simics [5], a robust full-system simulator. Simics includes a timing module called G-Cache to gather cycle-accurate timing data. We modified G-Cache in order to simulate our 3-D DRAM CMM system. The target platform we use Ubuntu 8.04 running on a x86-64 Hammer processor running at 3GHz. We evaluate our design using mixes of SPEC CPU2006 benchmarks which are shown in Table 1, which are comparable to those of [6].

Each mix contains four benchmarks. Though we ran simulations for 2, 4 and 8 cores, due to space restrictions and the similarity of results we only include 4-core results here. Processes are statically bound to a core so we could more easily track how many instructions each benchmark executed. We are currently investigating the use of better process tracking so that benchmarks can be tracked regardless of the core on which it is scheduled.

Benchmark mixes are grouped by working set sizes, a measure of how much (total) memory is being actively used by an application. This is different from the amount of address space the OS has reserved for an application and resident set size which is how much physical memory an application uses. Working set size has been often considered by researchers looking at cache misses, TLB misses and page faults, and the working set sizes we use were determined by [7]. We felt that grouping our benchmarks by this measure would allow us to see how different applications with similar working set sizes might operate in our CMM design, and also see how benchmarks with small to very large working sets perform. We set the CMM size to 256 MB, so that we may be able to see the effects of heavy workloads up to ten times greater than the size of CMM. In time, 3-D DRAM modules will be able to store 8 to 32 GB and perhaps more, and we are confident that the trends which we report here will scale appropriately for larger CMMs.

Latencies and other fixed L1, L2 and CMM parameters used in our study are the same as reported previously in [3], except that here we are dealing with multiple cores and we use 32 KB L1s and 256KB L2s per core. These sizes are chosen to be representative of current L1 and L2 caches, and these values are fixed throughout our experiments. Design parameters we varied in experiments will be explained in the following section. The caches and CMM are warmed for 300 million user-level transactions to core-0, after which simulation data is gathered for all cores during the time taken for 500 million benchmark instructions executed by core-0. Several parameters are explored here including number of memory banks, associativity, TLB size, page size, subpage size, number of subpages to pre-fetch and size of victim buffers.

4   Results and Analysis

In this section we detail the results of our experiments. The most common metrics used for comparing different design parameters are *relative IPC* and relative amount of data copied back. IPC, or instructions per cycle, is a measure of how many instructions are executed per clock cycle, and data copied back measures the amount of data that is written back from CMM to PCM backing store. The graphs that follow, unless otherwise specified, use relative numbers ranging between 0 and 1, and display the IPC relative to the best IPC possible in that experiment. This is intended to provide a clearer picture (as one can view the range of performance possible for different values of the design parameter explored), than using raw numbers, since we use a wide ranging workloads.

Page Size. Larger pages are beneficial in that TLB and page tables can be smaller, while having small subpages grants us the ability to have smaller, quicker transfers between CMM and PCM, eliminating the excessive CPU stalls on a page/subpage miss. Page size affects the number of CMM entries and larger pages may cause more conflicts for (fewer) CMM entries.

We explored page sizes between 4KB and 2MB. In terms of IPC, Figure 2(a) shows that pages between 4KB to 64KB show minor performance changes, with a marginal peak at 32KB. IPC declines sharply after 128KB, particularly for benchmarks with large working sets; a result of having fewer pages that can reside in memory at any given time. Further, Figure 2(b) shows a general trend where page size increases leads to an increase in write-backs. Smaller benchmark mixes display more sensitivity to page size variation, and a linear increase in the amount of data written back with page sizes. *Of particular interest, for small working sets, CMM is not fully utilized and thus in case of 4KB pages, no data is written back, because page conflicts are eliminated.* However such page sizes require very large TLBs, thus we believe a 32KB page provides a reasonable trade-off between the amount of data written back and the cost of memory structures (e.g., TLB).

Subpage Size. When using larger pages (32KB), since the new technologies present very low data transfer latencies, we explore the use of subpages within a page as the unit of data transferred between DRAM and backing store (i.e., PCM). Subpage size is an important consideration in our design in both hardware cost and performance benefits. Hardware cost will increase as subpages get smaller because subpages must be tracked by a bitmap. Here we fix the page size at 32KB.

Figures 3(a) and 3(b) display the relative values for IPC and amount of data written back to PCM respectively for different subpage sizes. In most cases, IPC tends to peak at 512 or 1024 byte subpages, with the very large working

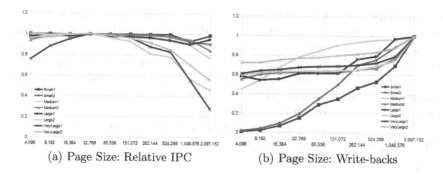

(a) Page Size: Relative IPC   (b) Page Size: Write-backs

Fig. 2. Page Size: subfigures (a) and (b) use a 0 to 1 relative scale. 4KB to 2MB pages are evaluated. Subpage size is set at 512 bytes.

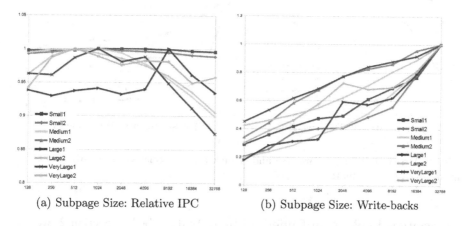

(a) Subpage Size: Relative IPC   (b) Subpage Size: Write-backs

Fig. 3. Subpage Size: subfigures (a) and (b) use a 0 to 1 relative scale. Subpage sizes from 128B-32KB. Simulated page size is 32KB, therefore 32KB subpage effectively represents no subpages.

set benchmark mixes displaying the most volatility when moving outside that range. The small working set mixes appear somewhat impervious to subpage size variations due to very few page faults and underutilization of CMM as discussed previously.

For write-backs, subpage size is easily the most important parameter to consider. As can be seen from Figure 3(b), all workloads display nearly a linear relationship between subpage size and amount of data copied back to PCM. On average, a 32KB page with 32KB subpages writes back 3 times more data to PCM as a 32KB page with 128 byte subpages. This is expected since we only write back dirty subpages to PCM. Taking all things into consideration, we would conservatively recommend a 512 byte subpage size.

Associativity. As described in Section 2, we use both page tables and set-associative style indexing to address the CMM. In this section we describe the effect of associativity within our CMM. Figure 4(a) shows that increasing associativity appears to improve IPC. Performance gains are due to reduced conflict misses as associativity increases. Beyond 8-way, however, performance gains are negligible. This phenomenon has been reported for very large caches, and our findings here corroborate previous studies [8].

Figure 4(b) shows that conflict reduction in CMM due to increased associativity can significantly reduce the amount of data copied back, but insignificant savings are achieved beyond 8-way.

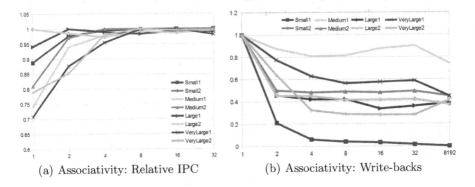

(a) Associativity: Relative IPC   (b) Associativity: Write-backs

Fig. 4. Associativity: subfigures (a) and (b) use a 0 to 1 relative scale. Associativities from 1 to 32 are evaluated.

Translation Look-aside Buffers (TLB). As described in Section 2, we use TLBs to speedup address translation and verify if the requested subpage is currently available in CMM using subpage bitmaps stored in TLB. Our TLB is a fully-associative cache of CMM page addresses and bitmaps for current pages tracked in TLB. We evaluated the performance impacts of using different sizes for TLBs from 128 entries to 32,768 (which represents one entry in TLB for each of CMM page).

We felt that TLB hit rate was the best basis for comparison. It can be clearly seen from Figure 5(a) that hit rate appears to max out at 1024 to 2048 entries, depending on the benchmark. Since the TLB contains a mapping between virtual-physical addresses, the number of TLB entries can be considered in terms of total coverage of CMM, representing the percentage of total CMM pages for which the physical address and bit map can be stored in TLB at any given time. Our experiments indicate that a 3% to 6% coverage is sufficient for TLB sizes. Even at these coverages, a TLB for 32GB CMM will be very large, and it may be necessary to use set-associative TLBs instead of fully associative TLBs. It should be noted, however, TLB's will be even larger when using 4K or 8K pages.

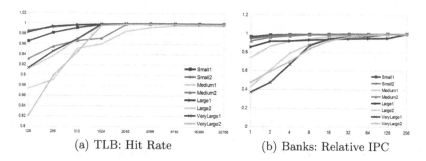

(a) TLB: Hit Rate   (b) Banks: Relative IPC

Fig. 5. TLB: (a) shows actual hit rates for varying TLB sizes. Sizes from 128 to 32,768 entries are explored. In these simulations CMM has a fixed size of 256MB and 32KB pages, which give 32,768 total pages that may reside in CMM, and therefore that many pages may be addressed by the TLB.
Banks: (b) shows relative IPC for varying bank sizes. Comparison on a 0 to 1 relative scale. 3-D DRAM with 1 to 256 banks are evaluated.

Pre-fetch. Pre-fetching has been shown to be very effective in reducing cache miss rates, however it can also substantially increase memory traffic [9][10]. At the CMM to PCM level, we expect less contention than at the L1 or L2 cache level. Therefore, we may direct the memory controller to use idle CMM cycles to pre-fetch additional subpages from backing store on a memory request. Pre-fetch may occasionally delay requests for new pages or subpages, since the current pre-fetched subpage must complete before a new request can be issued.

We explored pre-fetch policies of zero (no pre-fetch), up to 64 which is the total number of subpages in a page (with 32KB pages and 512 byte subpages). Figure 6(a) shows that the reduction in miss rates as a result of the spatial locality of pre-fetched pages account for a greater performance increase than the performance loss attributable to delaying demand fetches. However for large working set benchmark mix Large1, the applications exhibit poorer spatial localities and thus pre-fetching can actually be detrimental to performance.

Figure 6(b) and Figure 6(c) display subpage usage and efficiency respectively. Usage is a generally increasing trend because as more subpages are pre-fetched, more of those subpages are used, generating fewer demand requests. Efficiency is the percentage of prefetched subpages that were actually used. It declines as more subpages are prefetched. While we did not explicitly perform energy consumption calculations here, this figure captures the essence of energy efficiency of pre-fetching as unused subpage contribute to wasted power. Our results indicate that pre-fetching just one subpage provides the best tradeoff. We plan to extend these studies by using adaptive pre-fetching techniques similar to those proposed in [11].

Victim Buffer. Victim caches [12] have traditionally been used to decrease conflict misses in low associativity caches. We adapt this concept to alleviate the conflict misses in CMM, causing write-back to PCM. Our victim buffer can also be viewed similar to DRAM caches or write buffers used in [13][14].

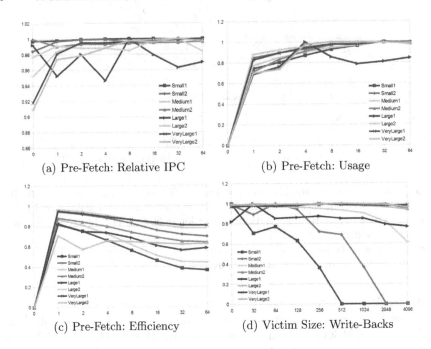

(a) Pre-Fetch: Relative IPC   (b) Pre-Fetch: Usage

(c) Pre-Fetch: Efficiency   (d) Victim Size: Write-Backs

Fig. 6. Pre-Fetch: (a) and (b) use a 0 to 1 relative scale. For (a), the X-axis represents the maximum number of subsequent subpages to be pre-fetched. Data simulates a CMM using 32KB pages with 512 byte subpages. For (b), a 1 would represent the pre-fetch policy had the most used subpages among all policies for a given benchmark. (c) shows the percentage of used subpages for a given prefetch policy where a 1 would mean every pre-fetched subpage was used.
Victim Cache: (d) displays write-back data for varying victim cache sizes. Comparison on a 0 to 1 relative scale. Victim cache sizes from 32 to 4,096 entries are explored along with having no victim cache at all (0). Page size is fixed at 32KB.

Figure 6(d) shows that data copied back becomes zero for smaller benchmarks as victim size is increased. Here the CMM, along with the victim buffer, is able to contain the entire address space of the benchmarks. However, data copied back for larger workloads is largely unaffected by victim buffer size. Much larger victim buffer sizes may have reduced write-backs even for large benchmarks, but this will add to the cost of the hardware.

Banks. Large 3-D DRAM are designed using multiple banks, each with a dedicated connection to the common bus. We assign addresses to different banks statically and simulate contention to banks.

Demand requests may interrupt pre-fetches and copybacks to the same bank, after the currently transferring subpage has finished, but may not interfere with copybacks or pre-fetches to different banks. Thus multiple prefetches and copybacks may occur simultaneously. A new demand request to a bank must wait for prior demand requests to finish. We explore the impact on performance by varying the number of banks.

Figure 5(b) shows that increasing the number of banks provides an IPC boost. However, the figure also shows diminishing returns beyond 16 or 32 banks. We feel that this behavior is due to our use of (mostly) virtual addresses to DRAM and our static assignment of addresses to banks. This means that most applications's addresses map to very few banks. However, with larger benchmarks, more cores, the virtual to physical address translation, and more dynamic distribution of addresses to banks would lead to better utilization of banks and scalable performance improvements with more banks. We will explore these issues in our future work.

5   Future Work

We are currently exploring in detail the implications of our ideas in terms of changes needed with OS virtual memory management. We will evaluate the advantages of our virtual memory management in the context of benchmarks with very large working sets, in order to fully exercise memory systems with 8GB-32GB. For this purpose, we will use server class and cloud application suites. We are currently working on models to evaluate energy consumed by applications when using our designs.

In the interest of further reducing the amount of data copied back, we will explore ideas (described in Section 6) such as eliminating dead writes, partial or delayed writes, flip-writes and other techniques that rely on compiler analysis.

6   Related Work

The ideas presented in Qureshi, et. al [14] are closely related. In that work, they explored the use of PCM as primary memory in place of DRAM. They compare the use of conventional organizations using very large DRAM systems (4GB-32GB), consider the merits of PCM vs DRAM, and subsequently examine a hybrid configuration that uses a 1GB DRAM as a cache to 32GB PCM. The purpose of their DRAM cache is to minimize writes to PCM. Their studies show that a hybrid configuration is a fair trade-off between scalability and latency. Our approach differs from this study as we use DRAM as primary memory and PCM as secondary memory, replacing magnetic disk drives.

The study by Lee, et. al [13] is similar to that of Qureshi [14], in that they also use PCM as a replacement to DRAM as the main memory system. Like Qureshi, Lee, et. al use DRAM based buffers between LLC and PCM, however Lee studies the use of multiple DRAM buffers instead of a single DRAM based cache. As an example, the authors show improved write endurance using four 512-byte buffers instead of using a single 2048-byte buffer. For our own purposes, we view the use of multiple buffers as an associative DRAM cache. Lee also investigates another technique for reducing writes, called partial writes or delayed writes. This compares data evicted from caches with the contents of PCM row buffers and writes only the data that is actually modified (it is possible for modified data to return to its original value). The study explores different granularities for these comparisons and, as expected, finer granularity leads to fewer bytes being written back.

Other studies have explored techniques to minimize write-backs. Cho, et al [15], writes either a modified, i.e. dirty, value or its complement, depending on the number of bits that will be written back. More recently, Bock, et al [16], explore how to eliminate writing modified data that is no longer useful. Useless data stems from freed objects, such as heap deallocations, and from popping stack frames which make previously stacked data inaccessible. We refer to these as dead writes.

Techniques such as these, including delayed writes [13], flip writes [15], and dead write elimination [16] are complimentary to our efforts. We explore them as a part of our on-going research.

Page coloring, Kessler, et. al [4], is similar to our page indexing schemes. Page coloring speeds up the virtual-physical address translations such that there are negligible differences between the virtual and physical addresses for large caches.

7   Conclusion

In this paper we investigated the use of 3-D DRAM as main memory and phase-change memory (PCM) as secondary memory. These technologies hold significant promise in reducing memory access latencies. PCM devices can also reduce the amount of energy consumed. However, data stored in non-volatile devices such as PCM can only be modified a limited number of times. Thus, it becomes critical to minimize the amount of data modified or copied back to such devices.

Our goal in this work is to study how to benefit from the faster accesses to 3-D DRAM and PCM devices. For this purpose, we describe a new memory organization that views DRAM both as a conventional main memory and a cache: the cache view allows us to use set-associative addresses to locate data in DRAM, while the memory view allows us to permit the use of traditional virtual memory management using page tables, eliminating aliases resulting from virtual addresses and enforcing protection at page level. Our approach can significantly eliminate the need for page table walks and context switches on page faults. We investigated the use of large pages with subpages, where the unit of transfer is a subpage between 3-D DRAM and PCM devices.

We reported the results of our experimental evaluation of a wide range of design parameters for page sizes, subpage sizes, TLB sizes, set-associativities, victim cache sizes, number of subpages to pre-fetch, in a multi-core environment. We reported our analyses, indicating preferred values for configuration parameters. With the right parameter choices, we show that a Cache-Main Memory organization, implemented in future technologies, can outperform contemporary DRAM memory configurations.

Acknowledgements. This project is supported in part by the NSF Net-Centric Industry/University Cooperative Research Center and a unrestricted research grant from the Advanced Micro Devices.

References

1. Loh, G.H., Hill, M.D.: Efficiently enabling conventional block sizes for very large die-stacked dram caches. Micro, 454–464 (2011)
2. Barr, T.W., Cox, A.L., Rixner, S.: Translation caching: skip, don't walk (the page table). SIGARCH Comput. Archit. News 38(3), 48–59 (2010)
3. Fawibe, A., Sherman, J., Kavi, K., Ignatowski, M., Mayhew, D.: New Memory Organizations for 3D DRAM and PCMs. In: Herkersdorf, A., Römer, K., Brinkschulte, U. (eds.) ARCS 2012. LNCS, vol. 7179, pp. 200–211. Springer, Heidelberg (2012)
4. Kessler, R.E., Hill, M.D.: Page placement algorithms for large real-indexed caches. ACM Trans. Comput. Syst. 10, 338–359 (1992)
5. Magnusson, P.S., Christensson, M., Eskilson, J., Forsgren, D., Hållberg, G., Högberg, J., Larsson, F., Moestedt, A., Werner, B.: Simics: A full system simulation platform. Computer 35(2), 50–58 (2002)
6. Loh, G.: 3d-stacked memory architectures for multi-core processors. In: 35th International Symposium on Computer Architecture, ISCA 2008, pp. 453–464 (June 2008)
7. Gove, D.: Cpu2006 working set size. SIGARCH Comput. Archit. News 35(1), 90–96 (2007)
8. Dube, P., Zhang, L., Daly, D., Bivens, A.: Performance of large low-associativity caches. SIGMETRICS Perform. Eval. Rev. 37(4), 11–18 (2010)
9. Callahan, D., Kennedy, K., Porterfield, A.: Software prefetching. In: Proceedings of the Fourth International Conference on Architectural Support for Programming Languages and Operating Systems, ASPLOS-IV, pp. 40–52. ACM, New York (1991)
10. Porterfield, A.K.: Software methods for improvement of cache performance on supercomputer applications. PhD thesis, Rice University, Houston, TX, USA (1989) AAI9012855
11. Ebrahimi, E., Lee, C.J., Mutlu, O., Patt, Y.N.: Prefetch-aware shared resource management for multi-core systems. SIGARCH Comput. Archit. News 39(3), 141–152 (2011)
12. Jouppi, N.P.: Improving direct-mapped cache performance by the addition of a small fully-associative cache and prefetch buffers. In: Proceedings of the 17th Annual International Symposium on Computer Architecture, ISCA 1990, pp. 364–373. ACM, New York (1990)
13. Lee, B.C., Ipek, E., Mutlu, O., Burger, D.: Architecting phase change memory as a scalable dram alternative. SIGARCH Comput. Archit. News 37(3), 2–13 (2009)
14. Qureshi, M.K., Srinivasan, V., Rivers, J.A.: Scalable high performance main memory system using phase-change memory technology. In: Proceedings of the 36th Annual International Symposium on Computer Architecture, ISCA 2009, pp. 24–33. ACM, New York (2009)
15. Cho, S., Lee, H.: Flip-n-write: A simple deterministic technique to improve pram write performance, energy and endurance. In: 42nd Annual IEEE/ACM International Symposium on Microarchitecture, MICRO-42, pp. 347–357 (December 2009)
16. Bock, S., Childers, B., Melhem, R., Mossé, D., Zhang, Y.: Analyzing the impact of useless write-backs on the endurance and energy consumption of pcm main memory. In: 2011 IEEE International Symposium on Performance Analysis of Systems and Software (ISPASS), pp. 56–65 (April 2011)

Synthetic Aperture Radar Data Processing on an FPGA Multi-core System

Pascal Schleuniger[1], Anders Kusk[2], Jørgen Dall[2], and Sven Karlsson[1]

[1] DTU Informatics
Technical University of Denmark
{pass,ska}@imm.dtu.dk
[2] DTU Space
Technical University of Denmark
{ak,jd}@space.dtu.dk

Abstract. Synthetic aperture radar, *SAR*, is a high resolution imaging radar. The direct back-projection algorithm allows for a precise SAR output image reconstruction and can compensate for deviations in the flight track of airborne radars. Often graphic processing units, GPUs are used for data processing as the back-projection algorithm is computationally expensive and highly parallel. However, GPUs may not be an appropriate solution for applications with strictly constrained space and power requirements.

In this paper, we describe how we map a SAR direct back-projection application to a multi-core system on an FPGA. The fabric consisting of 64 processor cores and 2D mesh interconnect utilizes 60% of the hardware resources of a Xilinx Virtex-7 device with 550 thousand logic cells and consumes about 10 watt. We apply software pipelining to hide memory latency and reduce the hardware footprint by 14%. We show that the system provides real-time processing of a SAR application that maps a 3000m wide area with a resolution of 2x2 meters.

Keywords: Synthetic aperture radar, multi-core, network-on-chip, FPGA.

1   Introduction

Synthetic aperture radar, *SAR*, is a form of imaging radar that provides high quality mapping independent of light and weather conditions. SAR is used across a wide range of scientific and military applications including environmental monitoring, earth-resource mapping, surveillance, and reconnaissance. The principle of SAR operation is that a radar antenna is attached to an aircraft or spacecraft. The antenna transmits electromagnetic pulses and records their echoes.

An output image is reconstructed from echoed data that is interpreted as a set of projections. The direct back-projection algorithm provides a precise output image reconstruction and can compensate for deviations in the flight track. A very high number of operations is required to reconstruct the output image because each pixel contains data of hundreds of projections.

C. Hochberger et al. (Eds.): ARCS 2013, LNCS 7767, pp. 74–85, 2013.

Therefore, graphic processing units, GPUs, are often used for this type of SAR data processing. However, for applications with strict space and power requirements GPUs may not be an appropriate solution. For example, small unmanned aircraft systems may want to use the direct back-projection algorithm to compensate for deviations in the flight track but do not provide space and power for a computing system with a high performance GPU.

In this paper, we describe how we map a specific SAR data processing application to a multi-core system on an FPGA. We design a scalable multi-core system consisting of Tinuso processor cores [10] and a 2D mesh interconnect. We evaluate the system by simulating data processing of the airborne POLARIS SAR [5]. This radar is currently used in the evaluation process of the European Space Agency's, *ESA*, BIOMASS candidate mission [6]. This mission aims for a P-band SAR satellite that provides global scale estimates for forest biomass.

To the best of our knowledge, we are the first ones using a multi-core on an FPGA for SAR data processing with direct back-projection algorithm. The proposed system provides a number of advantages including system integration, power, scalability, customization, and the use of industrial and space grade components. As the power efficiency and logic capacity of FPGAs increases, they become an attractive technology for use in low-volume, large-scale systems. For example, Xilinx's Virtex-7 family comes with devices up to two million logic cells. These devices allow for combining the processing power of hundreds of processor cores on a single FPGA. Moreover, the same device can also host the digital front-end used for SAR signal processing. FPGAs provide flexible I/O that allows for connecting a multitude of data links and memory units to a single device. We propose and advocate for a multi-core system because it raises the abstraction level for the application programmer without facing the current performance drawbacks of high-level synthesis [9]. The proposed system provides the ability for customizations at all levels. For example, it is possible to add processor cores, define special instructions, and change the interconnect link-width. FPGAs are available in industrial and space grade, which permits the use in rough environments and in space.

We make the following contributions:

- We design a scalable multi-core system consisting of Tinuso processor cores and a high throughput, low latency network-on-chip, *NoC*,
- We demonstrate that we can integrate 64 processor cores on a single FPGA and clock the system at 300MHz on a Xilinx Virtex-7 device.
- We evaluate the system by simulating the POLARIS SAR application that is based on direct back-projection. We achieve real-time data processing for a 3000m wide area with a resolution of 2x2 meters. The multi-core fabric consisting of 64 processor cores and 2D mesh network-on-chip utilizes 60% of the hardware resources of a Xilinx Virtex-7 device with 550 thousand logic cells and consumes about 10 watt.
- We apply software pipelining by distributing subtasks to dedicated processing elements. This hides memory latency and reduces the hardware resources by 14%.

2   Synthetic Aperture Radar Application

Synthetic aperture radar is a form of imaging radar that is operated from a moving platform, typically an aircraft or satellite. SAR provides high quality radar mapping independent of light and weather conditions. Therefore, SAR is an attractive choice for a broad range of scientific and military applications, such as environmental monitoring, earth-resource mapping, surveillance and reconnaissance. The principle of SAR operation is that a radar antenna is attached to an aircraft or spacecraft and alternately transmits an electromagnetic pulse and receives echoes. As the radar moves along the track it records its exact position, the energy level, and round trip delay of the received echoes. Signal and data processing is then applied to reconstruct an image of the scanned terrain.

The term synthetic aperture radar derives to the fact that a moving antenna effectively acts as a much larger antenna that can more accurately resolve distances in the flight direction. It is therefore possible to obtain radar maps with a resolution of up to decimeters from very large distances. Often frequency-domain algorithms are used for SAR image reconstruction [1]. These algorithms are based on the fast Fourier transform, *FFT*, technique and are computationally efficient to implement. A limitation of these algorithms is the high sensitivity to non-linear deviations in the flight track. Direct back-projection is a time-domain algorithm that can adapt to a general geometry of the synthetic aperture and therefore compensate for deviations in the flight track. The received echo of each transmitted radar pulse is stored in a one-dimensional array, called range line or projection. It represents the reflected energy and propagation delay of all points on the ground swath illuminated by this pulse. To reconstruct a projection image, for each projected pixel all range lines must be considered that possibly contain an echo from the corresponding point in the scene. The energy contribution of each range line for each pixel is computed and coherently accumulated. At the most, all range lines on the length of the synthetic aperture, L, are required to compute an output pixel. As the resolution of a SAR image depends on the length of the synthetic aperture, hundreds up to thousands of range lines contribute to a single output pixel.

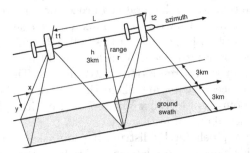

Fig. 1. SAR system overview

ALGORITHM 1. Pseudo code for SAR data processing with direct back-projection

---

> **for** *each pixel* **do**
>> **for** *each range line* **do**
>>> calculate round-trip delay and fetch data samples from memory
>>> reconstruct echo signal and interpolate the energy contribution
>>> do amplitude weighting and phase correction
>>> accumulate energy contributions of each range line
>> **end**
> **end**

In this case study we consider SAR data processing for the POLARIS system. The radar operates at 435 MHz with a pulse bandwidth of 85 MHz, which allows for a range resolution of 2 meters. The radar is mounted on an airplane that flies at an altitude of 3000m. Real-time data processing must be provided for a 3000m wide ground swath as shown in Figure 1. Due to the relatively low radar frequency and small antenna, we get a long synthetic aperture of 700 up to 1100 meters depending on the slant range. We assume an oversampling ratio of 1.25 and consider 50 range lines per second to avoid aliasing. Hence, for each pixel we need to calculate the energy components of 437 up to 688 range lines. 1500 Pixels in range dimension are required to map a 3000m wide ground swath with a resolution of 2 meters. Given a flight speed of 80 m/s, we need to compute 60'000 pixels per second to provide real-time processing. We use a direct back-projection algorithm for image reconstruction.

The first step of Algorithm 1 is to calculate the round trip delay of the transmitted signal. This corresponds to a signals traveling time from the antenna to a point on the ground swath and back to the receiver. The round trip delay specifies which data samples of a range line need to be fetched from memory. In the second step, data samples are interpolated to reconstructs the echo signal of the point on the ground swath. We decided for the *sinc* function interpolation because it shows a very low interpolation error and is well suited for image projection applications [7]. Each interpolation considers 8 data samples to provide sufficient accuracy. The next step of the algorithm applies phase correction and amplitude weighting. For this computation, we use *sine* and *cosine* functions to extract the phase and amplitude information of the interpolated IQ signal. A Hamming window function is used for weighting the amplitude. The result of this operation represents the energy component of a point on the ground swath in one range line. Finally, we coherently accumulate the energy components of all range lines, within the synthetic aperture, to determine the value of the pixel. This SAR data processing application provides a high degree of parallelism for reconstructing the output image. To optimize application performance, we exploit parallelism at task-level. We define a task as the computation of a single output pixel. As there is a memory operation in the time-critical path of the algorithm, the performance greatly depends on memory latency.

We evaluate two implementations of the application. The first implementation assumes a low memory latency and simultaneously executes the algorithm on a number of parallel processing elements. We call this homogeneous SAR. The second implementation applies software pipelining to hide memory latency. The algorithm is split up in three sub-tasks that run on individual processing elements as shown in Figure 2. The first sub-task calculates the round trip delay for each range line and thereby determines which data samples need to be fetched from memory. These samples are then forwarded directly to the processor that runs the second sub-task, which includes interpolation. The interpolated values are then sent to the core that runs the third sub-task. Hence, this implementation is less sensitive to memory latency because the processing element that sends the memory request does not need to wait on the data samples.

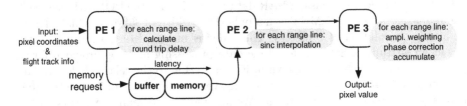

Fig. 2. Software pipelined SAR data processing application

3   System Architecture

We aim for a system as shown in Figure 3 to integrate SAR signal and data processing. Signal processing is done partially in an analogue front-end where the received echo is mixed down to base-band, IQ de-modulated, and A/D converted. The digital front-end is used for filtering and data preprocessing. Preprocessed data is then stored in off-chip memory. The SAR data processing application is mapped to a number of parallel processing elements that communicate over an interconnect with a memory controller. This application involves a high number of integer and floating-point operations. Therefore, synthesizable processor cores are well suited to implement the processing elements. To support efficient communication between processing elements, we use a message passing communication scheme and design a 2D mesh interconnect.

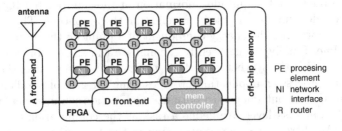

Fig. 3. Block diagram of a SAR signal and data processing system

3.1   Processing Element

We decided to use instances of the Tinuso processor architecture as processing elements. Tinuso is a three operand, load-store architecture with a fixed instruction word length of 32-bits. The current implementation has a super-pipelined, single issue, in-order pipeline that is optimized for a high instruction throughput when implemented on an FPGA. The pipeline is fully exposed to software where all types of hazards need to be considered. The architecture supports predicated execution to reduce the branch penalty. Tinuso is a lightweight architecture with a small instruction set that can easily be extended. Given the high instruction throughput, the small hardware footprint, and the ability to extend the design, Tinuso is an attractive choice for our multi-core system. However, we need to do a number of application specific modifications and extensions such as adding a floating point unit, $sinc$, sine, Hamming window functions and enable message passing communication.

We use the Xilinx floating-point core to implement a single precision FPU with the following operations: addition, subtraction, multiplication, division, and square root. Implementing mathematical functions on an FPGA is a trade-off between accuracy, clock speed and utilized resources. We have decided to use a lookup-table to implement $sinc$, sine, and Hamming window functions. The block RAM size in Xilinx Virtex-6 FPGAs is 36 kilobits, which allows for a lookup-table with 1024 data words. We analyzed the algorithm to limit the range of the functions that are placed in the lookup-tables and thereby reach sufficient accuracy.

Tinuso's network interface supports message passing communication to support efficient communication between processing elements. To keep the hardware footprint low, we only implement functionality strictly required by the application. The network interface contains a small FIFO buffer for outgoing messages. The processor core is writing to that FIFO and triggers a message transfer. The current Tinuso implementation utilizes first level instruction and data caches. Data caching functionality is not used for this case study application. Therefore, we disable the dirty-bit in the data cache to prevent the cache controller to write data back to main memory. The state machine in the network interface places the incoming data packets directly in the data cache. An identifier in the packet header specifies where data is placed. Once the complete incoming package is written to the data cache, a status register is set. The processor core is polling this status register to check whether a packet has arrived or not.

3.2   Network-on-Chip

The interconnection network plays a vital role in the performance of applications with a high communication to computation ratio. Therefore, we implement a high throughput, low latency network-on-chip that matches the requirements of the SAR data processing application. The network is deadlock free because SAR real-time processing cannot accept any deadlock situations, that require a system restart.

We implement a wormhole-switched router with five bidirectional ports for a 2D mesh interconnect. The router consists of crossbar, switch arbiter, slack buffers, output registers, and a control unit implemented as a finite state machine, *FSM*. When a header flit arrives at an input port its destination information is decoded. Following the routing scheme an output port is selected. We decided for XY routing scheme as it is deterministic, deadlock-free and very simple to implement. The control logic checks whether the desired port is available or not. If more than one flit arrive at the same time and want to use same output resource, the arbiter decides which is to succeed. If the desired output port is available and the header flit got the permission from the arbiter it is stored in the output register. In cases where the desired output port is not available or the arbiter prioritizes another package the flit is stored in slack buffers and the back-pressure signal is set. This back-pressure signal will then propagates upstream to pause the transmission until the desired output port is available. We use back-pressure flow-control and implement only one pipeline stage per router to reach a lowest possible latency of one cycle per hop.

We optimized the routers for a high clock frequency because the NoC operates in the same clock domain as the processing elements. We identified the time-critical path of the design in the decoder and arbitration logic of the router. Hence we use a fast, fixed priority arbitration scheme where priorities are given in a clockwise manner. The decode logic needs to extract the destination address of a packet and apply the XY routing scheme to determine to which output port the flit is forwarded. Lu et. al. use auxiliary routing information in the header flit to simplify the decode logic [8]. We use 8 bits of the 32 bit header flit for auxiliary routing information to avoid costly comparisons with carry chains in the decode logic. The simplified decode logic enables a very high system clock frequency of 300Mhz on a Xilinx Virtex device and a maximum link bandwidth of 9.6 Gbit/s.

4   Hardware Organization

We have now introduced processing elements, interconnect, and described how to map the application to hardware. At this point, we do not yet know how many parallel processing elements to employ in the final system. Therefore, we measure the scalability of the SAR data processing algorithm. In a massively parallel system memory access bandwidth is typically the limiting factor. We measure the scalability by running a number of parallel instances of the algorithm and record the total performance of the system. We use a network with 25 nodes whereas one node is used for the memory controller. We run a set of experiments where we populate 1 up to 24 nodes with processor cores.

All memory requests go to a memory controller that is connected to a corner node of the interconnect. As our implementation is sensitive to memory latency, we simulate a memory controller using fast synchronous SRAM. We argue for such a design as in recent years quad data rate SRAMS, *QDR*, started to penetrate the market. In QDR, data transfers use both rising and falling clock edges.

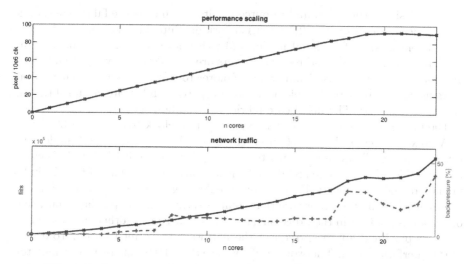

Fig. 4. Performance scaling and network traffic of the SAR application

For example, data can be read on the rising clock edge while writing is done on the falling clock edge. This allows for simultaneous read and write burst accesses. This is an important feature for SAR data processing because it allows for storing incoming data in real-time.

The upper part of Figure 4 shows the performance of the system for variable number of parallel instances. For this test setup, we define performance as the number of pixels calculated per 1 million clock cycles, whereas each pixel includes data of 500 range lines. We observe an almost linear performance increase until a system size of 19 processor cores. We measure an evenly distributed workload among the processing elements. The lower part of Figure 4 shows the number of flits in the network and the percentage of flits that are blocked due to back-pressure signaling. We observe a significant increase in blocked flits when 18 processor cores run the application in parallel.

To provide data processing in real-time we need to compute 60'000 pixels per second. Hence, we need to scale up the system. One of the advantages of FPGAs is the flexible I/O capabilities that allows for connecting a multitude of memory blocks to a single device. We decided for a multi-core system consisting of 4 memory controllers and 64 processor cores to provide sufficient computing power for the case study application.

5   Results

We evaluate the proposed multi-core system by running the SAR data processing application. First, we derive the system's maximum clock frequency and the required hardware resources for various FPGA families. Second, we evaluate the processing performance, network traffic, and application mapping.

Table 1 shows the speed and resource results of a multi-core fabric consisting of 64 processor cores and a 2D mesh network-on-chip. The memory controllers are implemented as functional models only, therefore they are not included in these results. The speed and resource results are based on Xilinx ISE 13.4 "place and route" report. We use Xilinx SmartXplorer to run multiple implementation flows using varying sets of implementation properties and strategies until timing closure is achieved. The multi-core fabric utilizes about 60% of an FPGA with 550'000 logic cells. We measure a maximal system clock frequency of 300 MHz on Virtex-7 device of the fastest speed grade. The homogeneous SAR implementation requires all processor cores to be equipped with full FPU and function lookup-tables. The pipelined SAR implementation allows for simplifying the individual processing elements. For example, the floating-point square root operation is only used in the processor core that computes the round trip delay. Thus, this operation is omitted in the processing elements that run the other sub-tasks.The software pipelined approach reduces the hardware footprint by 14%. To evaluate the performance and network traffic we use the VHDL open-source simulator GHDL. The memory controllers are integrated in a test bench that simulates synchronous SRAM memory and are connected to regular network nodes. As they receive a memory request message, memory address and destination node are decoded. Then, the desired data is fetched from memory and sent to the destination node. We assign a fixed latency of 5 clock cycles to this memory model. We used assembly language programming to optimize instruction scheduling. To speed up the application, we store pre-computed constants, packet headers, and intermediate results in registers. This allows for computing the energy content for one pixel of one range line in 350 clock cycles.

Table 1. Overview of clock frequency (a) and hardware resource usage (b)

(a)			(b)	
FPGA family Grade F.max			**Homogeneous SAR**	
Xilinx Virtex 7 -3	300 Mhz		200k Regs	209k LUTs
Xilinx Virtex 7 -2	260 Mhz		896 RAMB18E1	256 DSP48E1s
Xilinx Virtex 6 -2	250 Mhz		**Pipelined SAR**	
			190k Regs	167k LUTs
			600 RAMB18E1	240 DSP48E1s

Figure 5 illustrates the network traffic that includes memory requests, processor intercommunication, and communication with the host. Light colors in graph indicate high network traffic. We obtain this data by counting the number of flits in the network while we run the application. We extend the router ports with counters to record the network traffic. When the GHDL simulation has completed these counter values are stored in a file. We then use MATLAB to plot the data of the hardware simulation. We observe the highest traffic in the

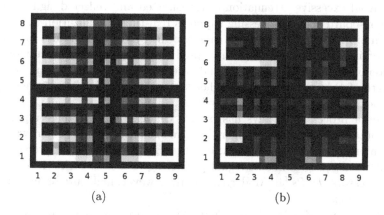

Fig. 5. Network traffic of homogeneous implementation (a) and software pipelined implementation (b) on a system with 8 x 9 network nodes

corners of the system where the memory controllers are located. It is also visible that the network traffic in the pipelined SAR application strongly depends on the mapping of the processing elements. According to Section 2, we provide real-time data processing for this case study application when we are able to calculate 60'000 pixels per second. Each pixel has to consider 437 up to 688 range lines depending on the length of the synthetic aperture. We measure an execution time of 905 ms to compute 60'000 pixels using the pipelined SAR application on a Virtex-7 device of a medium speed grade. The Xilinx Pocket Power Estimator computes a power dissipation of about 10 watts for the complete multi-core fabric.

6 Related Work

EMISAR is an airborne SAR developed at the Danish Technical University, DTU, which provides a resolution of 2x2m [2]. It was mainly used for research in remote-sensing techniques and to collect high-quality SAR data. A high frequency of up to 5.3 GHz and a relatively large antenna lead to a quite short aperture length which limits the number of echoes that need to be considered to compute a pixel of the output image. Real-time data processing is possible of a single channel [4]. This was mainly used to check the data acquisition. An offline system then did the high-quality processing of the data that was stored on HDDT tapes. Both the real-time and the offline processing system are based on the range-Doppler algorithm [11], as the relative bandwidth is so small that the back-projection algorithm is not required.

POLARIS is an ice sounding radar developed at DTU [5]. It was initially built to assess the potential and feasibility of a space-based P-band ice sounding mission. It operates in the P-band at 435MHz. A radar with a low frequency is used to avoid excessive attenuation of transmitted and reflected signals in the ice. The on-board signal processing supports real-time visualization at a coarse resolution only. This is sufficient to calibrate the system. Final data processing is done offline. POLARIS is currently used as a SAR system to support the evaluation of the ESA's BIOMASS candidate Earth Explorer mission. The long wavelength of P-band SAR has a higher saturation threshold to biomass than radars operating in a higher frequency band.

SAR data processing always has been a challenge due to huge input data and computationally expensive algorithms. In the past, dedicated hardware and large computing clusters were used, e.g. the EMISAR real-time processor includes about 20 programmable signal processing elements, each with 8 digital signal processors, *DSPs* [4]. Modern systems, however, make use of accelerators of various forms.

FPGA accelerated SAR data processing has been proposed previously by Cordes et. al. [3]. They use system with a host machine and an FPGA accelerator. The host machine provides the FPGA with preprocessed data and application specific information at run-time. The back-projection algorithm is then implemented on the FPGA to calculate the pixel values of the output image. However, their system is very different from our proposed approach. While our multi-core system consists of generic processing elements and interconnect, they use dedicated hardware blocks only. We use *sinc* interpolation to get a better estimate of the energy contribution of each echo, which is not done in their system. Finally, they use fixed-point arithmetic while we do all data processing in floating-point arithmetic.

7   Conclusions

We described how to map a SAR data processing application on a multi-core on an FPGA. We implemented a multi-core system consisting of 64 Tinuso processor cores and a high throughput, low latency network-on-chip. The multi-core fabric consisting of 64 processor elements and 2D mesh interconnect utilizes about 60% of the hardware resources of a Xilinx Virtex-7 device with 550 thousand logic cells and consumes about 10 watt.

We show that real-time data processing for the POLARIS SAR can be done on a multi-core system on an FPGA. FPGAs are often used to implement the digital front-end of radar systems. Hence, it is possible to combine SAR signal and data processing in a single device. The use of synthesizable processor cores raises the abstraction level for the application programmer. This is of particular interest when the application needs to adapt quickly to flight and scene properties. We conclude that multi-core systems on FPGA are an attractive choice for application with strictly constrained space and power budgets.

Acknowledgment. The research leading to these results has received funding from the ARTEMIS Joint Undertaking under grant agreement number 100230 and from the national programmes / funding authorities.

References

1. Carrara, W., Goodman, R., Majewski, R.: Spotlight synthetic aperture radar: Signal processing algorithms. Artech House (1995)
2. Christensen, E., Skou, N., Dall, J., Woelders, K., Jorgensen, J., Granholm, J., Madsen, S.: EMISAR: an absolutely calibrated polarimetric l- and c-band SAR 36, 1852–1865 (1998)
3. Cordes, B., Leeser, M.: Parallel backprojection: A case study in high-performance reconfigurable computing. In: Proceedings of the 14th IEEE Symposium on Field-Programmable Custom Computing Machines, FCCM 2006, pp. 205–216 (2009)
4. Dall, J., Joergensen, J., Christensen, E., Madsen, S.: Real-time processor for the danish airborne SAR. IEE Proceedings-F 139, 115–121 (1992)
5. Dall, J., Kristensen, S., Krozer, V., Hernandez, C., Vidkjr, J., Kusk, A., Balling, J., Skou, N., Sbjrg, S., Christensen, E.: ESA's polarimetric airborne radar ice sounder (POLARIS): design and first results. Journal on Radar, Sonar Navigation, IET 4, 488–496 (2010)
6. ESA: Measuring forest biomass from space - esa campaign tests biomass mission (2012), www.esa.int/esaLP/SEMFCJ9RR1F_index_0.html (retrieved on June 5, 2012)
7. Lehmann, T., Goenner, C., Spitzer, K.: Survey: Interpolation methods in medical image processing. IEEE Journal on Transactions on Medical Imaging 18, 1049–1075 (1999)
8. Lu, Y., McCanny, J., Sezer, S.: Generic low-latency noc router architecture for FPGA computing systems. In: Proceedings of the 21th International Conference on Field Programmable Logic and Applications, FPL 2011, pp. 82–89 (2011)
9. Papakonstantinou, A., Liang, Y., Stratton, J., Gururaj, K., Chen, D., Hwu, W., Cong, J.: Multilevel granularity parallelism synthesis on fpgas. In: Proceedings of the 19th IEEE Symposium on Field-Programmable Custom Computing Machines, FCCM 2011, pp. 178–185 (2011)
10. Schleuniger, P., McKee, S.A., Karlsson, S.: Design Principles for Synthesizable Processor Cores. In: Herkersdorf, A., Römer, K., Brinkschulte, U. (eds.) ARCS 2012. LNCS, vol. 7179, pp. 111–122. Springer, Heidelberg (2012)
11. Wu, C., Liu, K., Jin, M.: Modeling and a correlation algorithm for spaceborne sar signals. IEEE Journal on Transactions on Aerospace and Electronic Systems AES-18, 563–575 (1982)

Virtual Register Renaming

Mageda Sharafeddine[1], Haitham Akkary[1], and Doug Carmean[2]

[1] Electrical and Computer Engineering Department
American University of Beirut, Lebanon
{mas117,ha95}@aub.edu.lb
[2] Intel Corporation
Hillsboro, Oregon, USA
douglas.m.carmean@intel.com

Abstract. This paper presents a novel high performance substrate for building energy-efficient out-of-order superscalar cores. The architecture does not require a reorder buffer or physical registers for register renaming and instruction retirement. Instead, it uses a large number of virtual register IDs for register renaming, a physical register file of the same size as the logical register file, and checkpoints to bulk retire instructions and to recover from exceptions and branch mispredictions. By eliminating physical register renaming and the reorder buffer, the architecture not only eliminates complex power hungry hardware structures, but also reduces reorder buffer capacity stalls when execution encounters long delays from data cache misses, thus improving performance. The paper presents performance and power evaluation of this new architecture using Spec 2006 benchmarks. The performance data was collected using an x86 ASIM-based performance simulator from Intel Labs. The data shows that the new architecture improves performance of a 2-wide out-of-order x86 processor core by an average of 4.2%, while saving 43% of the energy consumption of the reorder buffer and retirement register file functional block.

Keywords: Superscalar Processors, Checkpoint Processors, Register Renaming.

1   Introduction

In conventional superscalar processors, a large physical register file is necessary for exposing large amount of instruction level parallelism [21]. By allocating a separate physical register for each instruction that writes a logical register, a feature known as register renaming, write-after-write and write-after-read register dependences are eliminated. This allows the processor to execute instructions in any order, limited only by true data dependences and readiness of input operands. Physical registers are either organized as data fields within an instruction reorder buffer, or as a separate physical register file of size larger than the number of logical registers [12].

Regardless of whether the physical registers used for register renaming are implemented as data registers within the reorder buffer or as separate physical register file, the reorder buffer in conventional superscalar processors provides key

C. Hochberger et al. (Eds.): ARCS 2013, LNCS 7767, pp. 86–97, 2013.

mechanisms for maintaining correct sequential program execution [20]. Even though register renaming allows the processor core to schedule instructions for execution out of program order, the reorder buffer reorders the execution results, thus updating (i.e. committing or retiring) register and memory state in the original program order, as needed in case of an interrupt or mispredicted branch event. In addition to the in-order retirement mechanism, the reorder buffer provides the mechanisms necessary to reclaim dead physical registers that have been read by all instructions that need their values, and for restoring the correct non-speculative register renaming map table to resume execution properly upon recovery from a branch misprediction event [1].

Although the reorder buffer has become a central structure in superscalar processors, researchers have shown that in-order retirement of instructions and the associated reorder buffer mechanisms limit performance, especially as the size of the reorder buffer increases to exploit more instruction level parallelism [1][2][3]. As a higher performance alternative to reorder buffers, Checkpoint Processing and Recovery architectures (CPR) were proposed for building scalable large instruction window processors [1]. CPR replaces in-order retirement and its associated branch recovery mechanisms with checkpoint recovery and bulk retirement of instructions. CPR also decouples physical register reclamation from retirement by using read counters and remapped flags [18] to identify and reclaim unneeded physical registers.

Despite the advantages that CPR provides by eliminating the reorder buffer and its sequential mechanisms, it introduces its own unique complexities. The CPR architecture studied in [1][3] requires too many checkpoints and too many counters. Specifically, CPR used eight mapping table checkpoints with flash copy support, eight instruction execution counters to manage bulk commit and checkpoint allocation and reclamation, register read counters and remapped flags, one per physical register, augmented with a free list array to track physical registers usage and reclamation.

The complexity of CPR was justified as a more efficient alternative to reorder buffers for scaling the instruction window on high performance superscalar cores. However, its complexity makes CPR unsuitable for energy-efficient small core architectures that target low power ultra-mobile devices (e.g. smart phones, tablets, etc...).

In this work, we propose and evaluate a novel checkpoint architecture that uses virtual register renaming (VRR). Our VRR architecture features a specialized "logical" register file, with in-cell fast checkpoint copy and restore. VRR completely eliminates the reorder buffer used in conventional out-of-order cores as well as CPR physical register file with its complex free list, register reclamation counters and remapped flags circuits. Moreover, VRR uses a special mechanism in the logical register file to fuse checkpoint contexts in one cycle, allowing checkpoints to be reclaimed out-of-order. This increases the checkpoint hardware utilization significantly and reduces the number of checkpoints needed for performance in comparison to CPR.

The rest of the paper is organized as follows. Section 2 describes in detail the virtual register renaming core architecture (VRR) and the register file checkpoint and context fusion algorithms. In section 3, we discuss our performance simulation methodology and benchmarks, and present performance and power results. Section 4 examines related work. The paper finally concludes in section 5.

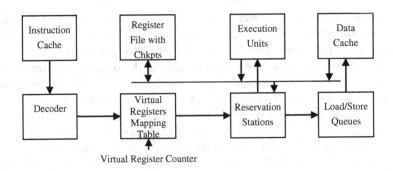

Fig. 1. VRR Architecture Block Diagram

2   Virtual Register Renaming Architecture

Figure 1 shows a block diagram of the VRR core architecture. An instruction in VRR goes through the typical processing steps of a conventional superscalar processor. These instruction processing steps include fetch, decode, rename, register operands read, schedule, execute, writeback and retire. VRR uses Tomasulo's algorithm [23] and performs equivalent processing steps to Intel P6 architecture [19], but has key distinguishing features and differences, as shown in Figure 1. First, VRR performs register renaming using virtual register IDs generated by a counter. These IDs are not mapped to any fixed storage locations in the core. Second, VRR does not have a reorder buffer or physical register file. Instead, it uses a logical register file with in-cell checkpoints. Third, VRR, like other CPR architectures, performs bulk commit of instructions using checkpoint counters and handles mispredicted branches and exceptions by rolling back execution to the last safe checkpoint.

We next discuss how each instruction executes as it advances through the pipeline stages. Depending on the core circuit implementation and the degree of pipelining, each one of the processing steps described next may correspond to one or more clock cycles.

2.1   VRR Instruction Processing Pipeline

Instruction Fetch and Decode Stages
These are the conventional fetch and decode stages. These stages include the L1 instruction cache, the ITLB, the branch predictor, the decoder and microcode sequencer units.

Rename and Allocate Stage
In this stage, VRR assigns to every instruction a unique virtual register ID (VID) generated by a virtual ID counter. Instructions receive VIDs in program order and the VID value of an instruction precisely indicates its order relative to other instructions. Moreover, if the instruction has a logical destination register, its VID is written into

the register mapping table entry corresponding to its logical destination. At the same time, the instruction reads from the mapping table the VID entries corresponding to its logical source registers.

The mapping table has the same number of entries as the number of logical registers defined by the VRR core instruction set architecture (ISA). Therefore, each entry in the table contains at any given time the VID of the last renamed instruction in the program that has as register destination the entry's corresponding logical register.

Any buffer entries needed by an instruction (e.g., reservation station, load queue, store queue) are allocated in this stage. If any needed buffer is full, the pipeline stalls until an entry becomes available.

Register File Access and RS Write Stage

In this stage, each instruction that has a destination register writes its VID in the logical register destination entry and clears the entry valid bit to 0, indicating that the destination register will be written at a later time. The valid bit of the instruction destination register is later set to 1 when the instruction writes back its result to the register file.

The instruction also reads its source registers with their valid bits. The source operands and their valid bits are subsequently written in the reservation station allocated for the instruction. Since instructions carry any valid source operands with them into the reservation stations, they do not need to access the register file again when they are scheduled and dispatched later for execution. In the case when source operands are not valid, i.e. have not been computed and written back into the register file, they are grabbed by the instruction reservation station from the bypass network during writeback.

RS Ready Stage

VRR has data-capture reservation stations, as in Tomasulo's algorithm [23] and Intel P6 architecture [19]. In this stage, a RS with an instruction that does not have a valid source operand will use the VID of the source operand to detect when the source operand value is being written back and to capture it from the write back bus.

RS Schedule and Dispatch Stage

In this this stage, an instruction that have all source "valid" bits set to 1 gets dispatched to an execution unit of its class with its operands. When an instruction is dispatched to execution, its reservation station is immediately freed to be made available for another instruction.

Execution Stage

Instructions are executed in this stage. Execution latency could be one or more cycles, depending on the type of instruction. In the first execution cycle the register destination VID is read from the register file, to be used later during the writeback stage as explained in the next paragraph.

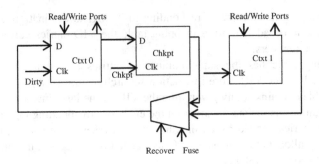

Fig. 2. VRR Register File Cell with Two Contexts and One Checkpoint

Writeback Stage

After an instruction executes, it broadcasts back its result data along with its VID on the write back bus to all reservation stations. If the VID matches any RS source operand VID, the data is grabbed by the RS. The data is also written into the destination register entry in the register file and the valid bit in the entry is set to 1, but only if the write back data VID matches the destination register file entry VID.

Commit Stage

VRR does not commit instructions one at a time as in reorder buffer architectures. Instead, it bulk commits groups of contiguous instructions. VRR tracks execution of instructions within a group using counters. When every instruction in a group executes (possibly out of order) without encountering an exception or mispredicted branch, VRR uses a flash copy (shift operation within the register file) to commit all the result registers instantaneously.

We next describe the VRR logical register file and its checkpoint copy and context fusion mechanisms.

2.2   VRR Register File

The logical register file is the central component in the VRR architecture. It replaces the reorder buffer and the physical register file of conventional superscalar cores.

Figure 2 shows a diagram of VRR register file cell with one checkpoint store, two work contexts and in-cell flash copy logic to support taking a checkpoint, restoring a checkpoint, and fusing the two contexts. The two context bits are connected to the register file read and write ports, while the checkpoint storage bit is not ported. Although not explicitly shown in Figure 2, the read and write ports are common to the two context bits. An instruction can read or write one of the context bits based on operand context ID assigned at rename. Finally, there are two copies of the logical register mapping table in the renaming block, one for each context. In one cycle, context 0 register mappings can be flash copied into context 1 mapping table.

Figure 3 shows a state machine diagram that represents the state and state transitions of VRR register file and the actions taken on these transitions. Events causing state transitions are annotated using regular font, and actions taken on a transition are annotated with bold font. We next discuss these events and the corresponding actions that are taken.

2.3   Creating and Committing Register Checkpoints

Program execution starts in context 0. Both the checkpoint storage and context 0 initially contain the startup state of the program, as defined by the ISA.

A checkpoint of the register state by definition corresponds to the precise execution state at some point in the program. The checkpoint bit ("Chkpt" latch in Figure 2) always contains the last committed, precise register state. VRR uses this checkpoint for handling exceptions and interrupts.

Notice that because only an instruction with a matching VID to that stored in the register file entry is allowed to write the register, and because a logical register entry always has its last assigned virtual mapping, a context in our VRR architecture is basically a "future file" for a contiguous group of instructions. If a checkpoint is desired at the end of a group of instructions, a possible implementation is to stall the execution of instructions located after the desired checkpoint until all the instructions in the group execute and write back their results. When all instructions in the group before the desired checkpoint complete, the future file becomes the precise state. Stalling the execution pipeline to create a checkpoint is not a good option however because of impact to performance.

To create a checkpoint without stalling and hurting performance, VRR provides two register work contexts. When VRR determines that a new checkpoint should be created, e.g. periodically every "n" instructions or when a low confidence branch [14] is decoded, VRR performs a flash copy of context 0 register mapping table to context 1 and continues renaming and execution of the instructions following the desired checkpoint using context 1. Therefore, instructions after the desired checkpoint do not disturb context 0 register state. After enough time elapses, all instructions before the checkpoint (context 0 instructions) finish execution leaving in context 0 the desired precise checkpoint state. At this point, indicated by the state of context 0 counter, context 0 bit is committed to the checkpoint bit to use for exception handling.

Notice that between the time context 1 is spawned and the time context 0 is committed, both contexts are active with their instructions executing concurrently in the pipeline. VRR identifies to which context an instruction belongs using a context ID assigned at the rename stage and carried with every instruction.

2.4   Recovering from Mispredicted Branches

VRR uses the two contexts for recovering from branch mispredictions by simply discarding the work context (or contexts) of the mispredicted branch and all instructions after the mispredicton. In other words, if a mispredicted branch is in context 0, all instructions belonging to both contexts are flushed and execution restarts from the checkpoint. If a mispredicted branch is in context 1, context 1 instructions are flushed and execution restarts from the beginning of context 1, after flash copying, again, context 0 register mappings to context 1 in the rename table.

2.5   Context Fusion

It was necessary for CPR performance [1] to have checkpoints created as close as possible to mispredicted branches in order to reduce the amount of rollback execution on branch recovery. Previous CPR architectures used eight checkpoints, low confidence branch estimation and limited maximum distance between checkpoints to minimize performance loss from rollbacks. CPR reclaims checkpoints in program order through bulk commit of all instructions in the oldest checkpoint when they complete execution. Therefore, a long latency instruction such as cache load miss that goes to DRAM can stall checkpoint reclamation in CPR, thus creating the need for larger number of checkpoints.

In contrast, VRR uses a new effective mechanism to improve checkpoint utilization and reduce rollback overhead after branch mispredictions, thus minimizing the number of needed contexts without hurting performance. Like CPR, VRR bulk commits context 0 (which is always the oldest context) into the checkpoint storage once all context 0 instructions execute. Moreover, VRR reclaims context 1 once it detects using a branch counter that all branches in context 1 are correctly predicted, even if other instructions in contexts 0 or 1 have not completed. We call this mechanism context fusion. VRR literally fuses context 0 and context 1 together into a new context 0 with a larger number of instructions, leaving context 1 available for a new checkpoint.

Figure 2 shows the context fusion logic within the register file cell. Context 0 bit can be updated with an input from a 2-to-1 multiplexer. The multiplexer selects between the checkpoint storage bit in case of execution roll back to the checkpoint (e.g. for handling interrupts or exceptions), or context 1 bit when fusing the contexts. However, there is an important difference between the two cases. When restoring the checkpoint, all registers are copied from the checkpoint storage into context 0. When fusing the contexts, only registers that have been actually written in context 1 are copied into context 0. A dirty bit within each context 1 register gates the clock to context 0 latch, thus enabling the copy only if the register has been written.

On fusing the two contexts, VRR globally clear all context IDs in the RS, load queue and store queue entries, thus moving all these entries to context 0.

Tying Some Architecture Loose Ends Together

We complete the description of the VRR architecture with a few important details.

1. Stores from a checkpoint are issued to the data cache only after the checkpoint is committed. When a checkpoint is flushed due to branch misprediction or exception, all stores belonging to the checkpoint are cleared.
2. The virtual ID counter is finite in size and cannot be allowed to overflow for correctness reason. VRR architecture opportunistically resets the VID counter whenever it can, e.g. when the pipeline is flushed to recover from a mispredicted branch.

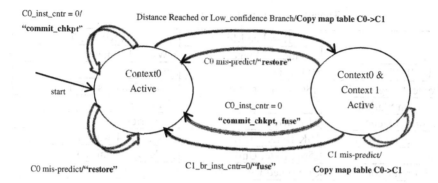

Fig. 3. State diagram for VRR Register File

When such opportunity does not arise before the counter overflows, VRR forces a pipeline flush. We have used a 10 bit VID counter in our simulations without seeing noticeable performance degradation from these forced pipeline flushes.

3. To ensure forward progress, a new checkpoint is taken immediately at the second instruction after execution restart from a checkpoint. This ensures that at least the first instruction after roll back always executes and commits.

4. After an exception, execution rolls back to the last committed checkpoint. VRR then switches to a special non-speculative in-order execution mode until the exception instruction is reached, leaving in the register file the precise state needed to take the exception. This mode can be implemented by allowing only one instruction at a time into the RS buffer using the allocate stage pipeline stall mechanism.

5. VRR attempts to create a checkpoint every 16 instructions, if possible. When both contexts are active, VRR keeps executing instructions beyond the checkpoint distance of 16 and then places the next checkpoint as soon as a context becomes free.

3   Performance Results and Analysis

3.1   Simulation Methodology

We used Spec 2006 benchmarks and a detailed ASIM-based performance simulator [7] from Intel labs to evaluate VRR performance relative to a 2-wide, out-of-order, X86 baseline core. The performance simulation model accounted for user as well as operating system code. Table 1 shows the baseline core configuration that we used, which represents a small core that is appropriate for power constrained computing devices. The VRR core model used a logical register file with two contexts and one checkpoint as described earlier. Other than not having a reorder buffer, the VRR core branch predictor, caches, pipeline and buffer configurations were identical to the baseline core configurations. We collected performance data using representative simulation samples from Spec 2006 benchmarks, after skipping an initial execution phase to warm-up the branch predictor and the instruction and data caches.

Table 1. Simulated Machine Configurations

	Baseline Model	VRR Model
Pipeline	2-Wide, 13 Stages	2-Wide, 13 Stages
Reorder Buffer	80 Entries	None
Retirement Register File	X86 Register File	2 X86 Contexts + Checkpoint
Reservation Stations	32 Entries	32 Entries
Load/Store Queue	24 Entries	24 Entries
L1 ICache, L1 DCache	16K Byte, 4-way	16K Byte, 4-way
L2 Cache	256K Byte, Unified	256K Byte, Unified
Branch Prediction	Combined Bimod-gshare	Combined Bimod-gshare

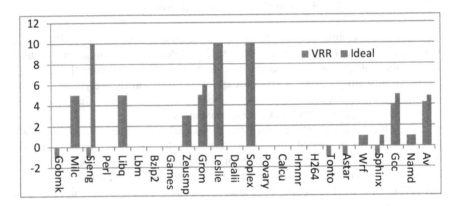

Fig. 4. VRR and Ideal VRR % Speedup over Baseline

3.2   Performance Analysis

Figure 3 shows the speedup percentage of VRR and an ideal VRR relative to the reorder buffer baseline for each of our benchmarks as well as the average (Av). The average includes two other benchmarks, Mcf and Bwaves, not shown in the graph. Mcf and Bwaves see 24% and 46% performance improvement from VRR respectively. We do not show them in the graph to minimize the y-axis range for readability. Ideal VRR uses an Oracle simulation mode to place the checkpoints exactly at mispredicted branches. It avoids having to undo and then redo some correctly predicted instructions during rollback to checkpoints when recovering from mispredicted branches, and thus captures the performance impact of having a small number of contexts.

VRR achieves an average speedup of 4.2% over baseline, which is very close to the best case performance improvement of 4.8% with ideal VRR. Notice that all benchmarks benefit from VRR except for Gobmk, Sjeng, Tonto and Astar, which suffer a very small slowdown (1%) due to very high branch misprediction rates and significant rollback execution from checkpoints. Since in our study we did not use branch confidence to improve checkpoint placement as suggested in previous CPR work, it may be possible to eliminate this observed slowdown by using a better branch predictor and low confidence branch estimation to select the checkpoints placement.

Many benchmarks show significant speedup with VRR. The variation in performance between benchmarks is due to the variation in cache misses and branch misprediction rates. VRR benefit is higher with higher cache miss rates since it has no reorder buffer and therefore does not encounter rename/allocate stage stalls resulting from the reorder buffer becoming full when long latency cache misses stall the in-order retirement. VRR performance also benefits from lower branch misprediction rates and the consequent reduction in checkpoint rollback execution.

3.3   Power Analysis

We used a power model derived from the performance model logic activity counters, and circuit simulation of the reorder buffer and register files structures of the baseline and VRR architectures. Notice that VRR energy savings come from completely eliminating the reorder buffer and the energy it consumes during register operands read and write activity as well as the energy it consumes to read out results and then write them in the retirement register file during the commit pipeline stage.

Our model shows that the reorder buffer consumes about 6% of total baseline core power or about 53% of the combined reorder buffer and retirement register file unit. However, the overall VRR core power saving is only 2% due to overhead. This VRR overhead includes additional complexity in the register file (1%), additional complexity in the register rename table (0.5%) and overhead execution from rollback to checkpoints to recover from branch mispredictions (2.5%). Accounting for the increased complexity in the VRR register file, the energy consumption saving from eliminating the reorder buffer is about 43% of the total reorder buffer and retirement register file of the baseline core.

Finally, notice that VRR does not achieve any performance improvement over CPR [3], since both eliminate the reorder buffer bottleneck created by in-order retirement of instructions and its associated mechanisms. However, VRR has a significant power benefit over CPR, especially on small cores. CPR requires multiple checkpoints (8 checkpoints were used in [3]) and a large physical register file to support these checkpoints. CPR also has significant overhead from the free list, register read counters and increased complexity in the rename table to support a larger number of checkpoints than VRR. We have estimated that VRR on a 2-wide out-of-order core has more than 10% core power advantage over 2-wide CPR.

4   Related Work

Tomasulo [23] proposed an algorithm for eliminating write-after-write and write-after-read register dependences and executing instructions out of order using reservation stations. Tomasulo's algorithm did not provide precise state for handling exceptions. In addition, it did not perform speculative execution and therefore did not require precise state for recovering from branch mispredictions.

Checkpoints in processors are used to repair architectural state to a known, precise previous state. The use of checkpoints for recovering from branch mispredictions and exceptions in out-of-order processors was first proposed by Hwu and Patt [13]. The Pentium 4 used a retirement register alias table to track register mappings [12] while the MIPS R10000 [24] and Alpha 21264 [16] used checkpoints to recover register rename mappings. All the above designs used physical registers for register renaming.

Architectures that use checkpoints with physical register files for recovery and for scaling the instruction execution window to help tolerate cache misses include Virtual ROBs [6], Cherry [17], Checkpoint Processing and Recovery [1][3], Continual Flow Pipelines [10][11][15][22] and Out of Order Commit Processors [5].

Gonzalez et al. [8][9] proposed using virtual registers to shorten the lifetime of physical registers. The idea was to use virtual-physical registers to delay the allocation of physical registers from the time instructions are renamed until instructions execute and produce results that need the physical registers. Until the physical destination registers are allocated at execution time, virtual registers are used for register renaming. Kilo instruction processors [4] also used virtual renaming and ephemeral registers to do late allocation of physical registers. In contrast to virtual-physical registers and ephemeral registers, VRR does not require physical registers for any allocation of execution results to physical registers.

5 Conclusion

This paper introduces an out-of-order virtual register renaming architecture that outperforms a conventional core of equally sized scheduling window by an average of 4.2%, while reducing the energy consumed in the reorder buffer and register file by 43% and the overall core energy by 2%. VRR achieves this speedup by eliminating the use of reorder buffer or physical registers for register renaming, thus improving energy efficiency as well. The performance and simple hardware advantages of VRR makes the architecture an interesting design option for power constrained computing devices, such as cores for ultra-mobile computing.

Acknowledgements. This work has been supported by a research grant from Intel Corporation.

References

1. Akkary, H., Rajwar, R., Srinivasan, S.: Checkpoint processing and recovery: towards scalable large instruction window processors. In: Proceedings of MICRO 2003 (2003)
2. Akkary, H., Rajwar, R., Srinivasan, S.: Checkpoint processing and recovery: an efficient, scalable alternative to reorder buffers. IEEE MICRO 23(6), 11–19 (2003)
3. Akkary, H., Rajwar, R., Srinivasan, S.: An analysis of a resource efficient checkpoint architecture. ACM Transactions on Architecture and Code Optimization 1(4), 418–444 (2004)

4. Cristal, A., Santana, O.J., Valero, M., Martinez, J.F.: Toward kilo-instruction processors. ACM Transactions on Architecture and Code Optimization 1(4), 389–417 (2004)
5. Cristal, A., Ortega, D., Llosa, J., Valero, M.: Out-of-order commit processors. In: Proceedings of HPCA 2004 (2004)
6. Cristal, A., Valero, M., Llosa, J., Gonzalez, A.: Large virtual ROBs by processor checkpointing. Tech. Report, UPC-DAC-2002-39, Department of Computer Science, Barcelona, Spain (July 2002)
7. Emer, J., Ahuja, P., Borch, E., Klauser, A., Luk, C.-K., Manne, S., Mukherjee, S.S., Patil, H., Wallace, S., Binkert, N., Espasa, R., Juan, T.: ASIM: A performance model framework. IEEE Computer 35(2), 68–76 (2002)
8. Gonzalez, A., Gonzalez, J., Valero, M.: Virtual-physical registers. In: Proceedings of HPCA 1998 (1998)
9. Gonzalez, A., Valero, M., Gonzalez, J., Monreal, T.: Virtual registers. In: Proceedings of HPCA 1997 (1997)
10. Hilton, A., Nagarakatte, S., Roth, A.: Tolerating all-level cache misses in in-order processors. In: Proceedings of HPCA 2009 (2009)
11. Hilton, A., Roth, A.: BOLT: energy-efficient out-of-order latency tolerant execution. In: Proceedings of HPCA 2010 (2010)
12. Hinton, G., Sager, D., Upton, M., Boggs, D., Carmean, D., Kyker, A., Roussel, P.: The microarchitecture of the Pentium 4 processor. Intel Technology Journal 5(4) (February 2001)
13. Hwu, W.W., Patt, Y.N.: Checkpoint repair for out-of-order execution machines. In: Proceedings of ISCA 1987 (1987)
14. Jacobsen, E., Rotenberg, E., Smith, J.E.: Assigning confidence to conditional branch predictions. In: Proceedings of MICRO 1996 (1996)
15. Jothi, K., Akkary, H., Sharafeddine, M.: Simultaneous continual flow pipeline architecture. In: Proceedings of ICCD 2011 (2011)
16. Leibholz, D., Razdan, R.: The Alpha 21264: a 500 MHz out-of-order execution microprocessor. In: Proceedings of the 42nd IEEE Computer Society International Conference (COMPCON), pp. 28–36 (February 1997)
17. Martinez, J.F., Renau, J., Huang, M.C., Prvulovic, M., Torrellas, J.: Cherry: checkpoint early resource recycling in out-of-order Microprocessors. In: Proc. of MICRO 2002 (2002)
18. Moudgill, M., Pingali, K., Vassiliadis, S.: Register renaming and dynamic speculation: an alternative approach. In: Proceedings of MICRO 1993 (1993)
19. Papworth, D.B.: Tuning the Pentium Pro microarchitecture. IEEE MICRO 16(2), 8–15 (1996)
20. Smith, J.E., Pleszkun, A.R.: Implementation of precise interrupts in pipelined processors. In: Proceedings of ISCA 1985 (1985)
21. Smith, J.E., Sohi, G.S.: The microarchitecture of superscalar processors. Proceedings of the IEEE 83(12), 1609–1624 (1995)
22. Srinivasan, S.T., Rajwar, R., Akkary, H., Gandhi, A., Upton, M.: Continual flow pipelines. In: ASPLOS-11 (October 2004)
23. Tomasulo, R.M.: An efficient algorithm for exploiting multiple arithmetic Units. IBM Journal of Research and Development 11, 25–33 (1967)
24. Yeager, K.: The MIPS R10000 superscalar microprocessor. IEEE Micro 16(2), 28–40 (1996)

Load-Adaptive Monitor-Driven Hardware for Preventing Embedded Real-Time Systems from Overloads Caused by Excessive Interrupt Rates

Josef Strnadel

Brno University of Technology, IT4Innovations Centre of Excellence
Bozetechova 2, 61266 Brno, Czech Republic
strnadel@fit.vutbr.cz

Abstract. In the paper, principle, analysis and results related to a special embedded hardware/software architecture designed to prevent the real-time software from both timing disturbances and interrupt overloads is presented. It is supposed that the software is driven by a real-time operating system and that the software is critical, so it is expected not to fail. The architecture is composed of an FPGA (MCU) utilized to run the hardware (software) part of a critical application. Novelty of the proposed architecture can be seen in the fact it is able to adapt interrupt service rates to the actual software load, the priority of a task being executed by the MCU and priorities of interrupts occured. The load and priority are monitored by the FPGA on basis of low-overhead signals produced by the MCU for minimizing impacts of the load-monitoring hardware to the software execution because of the monitoring process.

Keywords: task, operating system, load monitoring, interrupt control, scheduling, overload prevention, priority space.

1 Introduction and Problem Formulation

If the load hypothesis is not defined precisely or there are no computational resources available to process the peak load, then a conflict can arise between specified and real behaviors of a system, so the system can fail to operate correctly. Especially, it holds for *embedded systems* (ES) required to be both I/O intensive and *real-time* (RT). Such an ES must be able to react to stimuli both correctly and on-time even though the stimuli are of various rates and (a)periodicity and the ES is equipped with very limited computational resources. Typically, occurence of a stimulus is signalized by an interrupt (INT) mechanism, advantage of which can be seen in its high reactivity. Disadvantage of the mechanism is that each INT occurence and related service routine (ISR) are assigned computational resources prior to the main-loop instructions. As a consequence, the SW part may stop working correctly or collapse suddenly as the INT rate (f_{int}) increases. This is typically denoted as the *interrupt overload* (*IOV*) problem, seriousness of which grows with criticality of the SW.

C. Hochberger et al. (Eds.): ARCS 2013, LNCS 7767, pp. 98–109, 2013.

Thus, a critical ES must be designed so that it may never give up to recover even if the load hypothesis is violated by the reality [3]. Several solutions exist to solve the IOV problem, e.g. [3, 6–8, 10, 12, 14, 16, 17].

The paper is organized as follows. In the section 2, the background related to the research is outlined. In particular, basic terms related to real-time systems are summarized there along with the solved problem definition and typical solutions (2.1). In the section 3, the proposed HW solution to the problem is presented with a special attention paid to monitoring interface and signal generation details w.r.t. proposed HW monitor unit (3.1, 3.2) and its operating principle 3.3. In the section 3.4, experimental results achieved by the proposed solution are presented and compared to results of typical solutions to the problem followed by the sum of crucial implementation overheads w.r.t. proposed monitor and the section 4 concludes the paper.

2   Research Background

The paper is related to systems, perfection of which is based on both the *correctness* and the *timeliness* of the outputs. Such a system – i.e., that is able to produce the right response to given stimuli *on time* – is called an *RT system* [1]. For event-driven RT systems, it is typical that each stimulus (considered as an event) is associated with a computational unit called a *task*, responsible to react correctly to the event. There are two basic types of RT tasks: *hard* and *soft* [2,4]. For hard tasks it holds their timing constraints must be strictly met; violating any of them can lead to a failure of the system. The latter (soft) constraints are not required to be strictly met as their violation typically leads to a temporal degradation of some system services only, but not to a failure of the system as a whole. While hard tasks are typically running at high priority levels, soft tasks are running at lower priorities because they are less time-critical than the hard tasks. To organize task executions in time (i.e., to *schedule* them to meet their timing and other constraints) and to simplify design and analysis of an RT system, *RT operating systems* (RTOS) are often used [2,4]. In the paper, it is supposed the critical SW is driven by an RTOS.

2.1   Interrupt Overload Problem Solutions

In existing works those problems are typically solved w.r.t. INT management: i) the *timing disturbance* problem composed mainly of a *disturbance due to soft real-time* (RT) *tasks* and *priority inversion* sub-problems [6,7,14] and ii) the *predictability* problem originating from the ES inability to predict arrival times and the rate of INTs induced by external events [10, 12]. The timing disturbance problem can be efficiently solved at the kernel level – e.g., it was shown in [6], [7] that ESes can suffer significantly from a *disjoint priority space* where ISRs are serviced by the HW prior to tasks managed by the SW; as the solution, they suggested to implement a *joint priority space* so the ISR and task priorities can be mutually compared to detect the highest-priority ISR/task in the joint set.

They suggested not to service an INT immediately in its ISR but later in an associated (deferred) task – called an *interrupt service task, IST* – running at a predefined task-level priority. At the ISR level, it is supposed only necessary actions are performed such as INT acknowledge or signaling the corresponding IST. It was shown the concept minimizes disturbance effects induced by interrupting high-level tasks by ISRs serviced by low-level ISTs. Similar approaches can be found e.g., in [14, 16, 17]. However, although the solutions minimize the disturbances produced by ISRs, they do not solve the predictability problem. They are still susceptible to INT-overload scenarios in which the CPU can be overloaded when the INT interarrival times ($t_{arrival}$) are very close to or smaller than the ISR context switch time [15].

The latter (predictability) problem solutions – presented e.g. in [6,10,12] – are typically designed to bound the $t_{arrival}$ times (or, maximal interrupt arrival rate f_{int}). In [12], the INT overload prevention solutions – called *interrupt limiters* (*IL*) there – are classified to SW ILs (*SIL*) and HW ILs, (*HIL*). The SILs can be classified to the following sub-types:

i) *Polling SIL.* It is designed to check periodically (with $t_{arrival}$ period) if any event flag is set or not. If it is then an IST corresponding to the event is started. A timer or a well-tuned block of instructions can be utilized to start a new polling period after t_{timer} units of time.

ii) *Strict SIL.* It works as follows: an ISR prologue is modified to disable INTs (except those from timers) and configure a one-shot timer to expire after $t_{arrival}$ units measured from the INT occurence time (t_{req}). After it expires, INTs are re-enabled. Main disadvantage of the approach can be seen in the fact INTs are practically doubled as each external INT request leads to an internal INT utilized to signalize the one-shot timer expiration.

iii) *Bursty SIL.* It is designed to reduce the double-INT overhead w.r.t. strict SIL. Comparing to the strict SIL, the bursty SIL is driven by the two parameters: *maximum arrival rate* ($f_{arrival} = 1/t_{arrival}$) and *maximum burst size* (N). The reduction is based on the following idea: INTs are disabled after a burst of $N_{\geq 2}$ requests rather than disabled after each INT request. An ISR prologue is modified to increment the counter; INTs are disabled as soon as the counter reaches N. INTs are re-enabled and the counter is reset after a timer overflows (after $t_{arrival}$ time units measured from t_{req}).

In the latter (HIL) approach [6], INT requests are processed before they are directed to the device the ES runs on – a HIL guarantees that at most one INT is directed to the device within a time interval long $t_{arrival}$ units (i.e., the HIL is designed to limit f_{int} to a predefined, fixed maximum $f_{arrival}$ rate). Further solution to the HIL – based on the *Real-Time Bridge* (RTB) concept – was presented by Pellizzoni [10]: Each I/O interface is serviced by a separate RTB able to buffer all incoming/outgoing traffic to/from peripherals, and deliver it predictably according to the actual scheduling policy; the PCI(e) bus is utilized to interconnect the RTB-based HIL and the control parts of the ES based on a high-performance (1Ghz Intel Q6700 quad-CPU) platform.

3 Proposed Solution

It can be concluded that actual solutions to the IOV problem are either limited to solving one of the timing disturbance and predictability problems, they are too complex for (limited) embedded realizations, they require significant modifications and/or extensions of common *commercial off-the-shelf (COTS)* components or they inherently worsen the RT-task schedulability as they increase the CPU utilization factor. Motivation and goals of the research w.r.t. this paper can be summarized as follows: *Reachability:* to offer a solution to the IOV problem on basis of instruments accessible at the market, i.e., using COTS components such as MCUs/FPGAs and operating systems (OSes), *Generality:* the solution must result to an architecture that is general enough to abstract from products of particular producers and is able to solve both the timing disturbance and predictability problems, *Simplicity:* the solution must reduce a need to modify existing components to a minimum, *Adaptability:* the solution must be able to adapt the INT service rate to the actual SW load and constraints implying from the system specification.

3.1 Architecture

To achieve the above-mentioned goals, we have decided i) to utilize an FPGA (for realization a HIL function) and an MCU (for executing the safe part of an RTOS-driven ES) as the realization platforms for our monitor-based architecture, ii) to define a monitoring protocol and interface between FPGA and MCU, iii) to describe a monitoring hardware in VHDL for its implementation into the FPGA and iv) to analyze RTOS kernel changes and overheads necessary to realize the monitoring protocol and interface at the MCU side.

In the proposed solution, we have decided to combine the existing RTB concept [10] with the joint task/IST scheduling [6, 7, 14] and novel load-monitoring solution able to adapt the INT management mechanism to the actual SW load. Design and utilization of the monitoring protocol/interface for load-estimation purposes as well as the estimation mechanism itself can be seen as the most important contributions of this paper. Main idea of the proposed solution can be summarized as follows: the FPGA is designed to preprocess all INTs before they are directed to the MCU; each interface (IFC_i) able to generate an INT request is processed by a separate RTB responsible for processing stimuli related to the INT – during the high load of the MCU's CPU any INT is buffered by the FPGA until the CPU is underloaded or the INT priority is higher than the priority of the task running in the RTOS; then the INT is directed to the MCU. Buffers w.r.t. the RTBs must be of a "sufficiently large" capacity to store stalled communication related to delayed INTs.

3.2 Monitoring Signals: Timing and Overheads

Details related to the MON_INT to MON_SLACK signals (see Fig. 1) produced by the MCU for the monitoring purposes are summarized as follows:

i) *Start:* The signal generation begins just after a free-running hardware timer (*TIM*) is started to periodically generate an INT for signalizing new tick of the (logical) operating system time. The start is signalled by producing a short pulse at each of the MON_INT to MON_SLACK lines (Fig. 1, A). The overheads w.r.t. the short pulse generation can be summarized as follows. Number of FPGA/MCU pins needed to realize the monitoring interface is

$$N_{pins} = 4 + n \qquad (1)$$

where n is the joint priority bit-width. Moreover, for the SW part it holds that few instructions must be added to the end of the TIM-start routine in order to produce a short pulse at each of the lines; this increases the ES-startup time by about few CPU cycles ($t_{STARTovr}$), number of which depends on pins and instructions selected to control the lines.

ii) *ISR-Presense Monitor:* Each INT prologue (epilogue) is modified to set the MON_INT signal to HIGH (LOW) just at the beginning (end) of an ISR body to ease the monitoring of ISR execution times. This extends the ISR execution a bit (e.g., one instruction for setting and one for clearing the line), but in a deterministic and the same way across all ISRs except of the TIM-ISR (let the execution delay implying from the extension be denoted as t_{ISRovr}). Moreover, execution of the (special) TIM-ISR is signalled by generating a short pulse at the MON_TICK line.

So, the TIM-ISR execution time is increased by about

$$t_{TICKovr} = 2 \times t_{ISRovr} \qquad (2)$$

because of the signal generation. ISR nesting is disallowed. This saves limited embedded resources such as memory and simplifies the ES analysis, but puts greater demands on ISR-coding efficiency – execution of an ISR must be as short as possible not to delay the execution of a consecutive ISR, which could be of higher priority.

iii) *Context-Switch Monitor:* The MON_CTX signal is set to HIGH each time the task-level context switch (*CTXSW*) is being (re)stored; otherwise, it is set to LOW. Pulse between A, B parts in Fig. 1 represent a (half) CTXSW to the very first task to run while pulses between B, C (C, D and D, E)

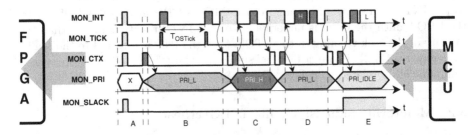

Fig. 1. An illustration to the monitoring signals/interface introduced in [15]

represent (full) CTXSWs between the tasks – i.e., the CTXSWs formed of context store (the light filled area) and context restore (the dark filled area) parts. In Fig. 1, it is supposed the full CTXSW is performed in the ISR body of a special (Exception/Trap/Software Interrupt) instruction, so MON_INT is HIGH too. Each CTXSW is processed in the critical section (INT disable) mode, so an extra response delay is added to INTs arisen during a CTXSW execution. The SW overhead related to generating the signal is similar to those presented above – one instruct. to set, one to clear the line per half CTXSW ($t_{HCTXovr}$), i.e., twice as much for the full CTXSW:

$$t_{CTXovr} = 2 \times t_{HCTXovr}. \tag{3}$$

iv) *Priority Monitor:* The MON_PRI signal is utilized to monitor the running-task priority. The signal is set in the context restore phase of the CTXSW (as soon as the priority is known). Let the execution overhead needed to adjust the MON_PRI line be denoted as t_{PRIovr}. So, the total CTXSW overhead is

$$t_{CTXovr} = 2 \times t_{HCTXovr} + t_{PRIovr} \tag{4}$$

In Fig. 1, it is illustrated how the value of MON_PRI changes if a lower priority task (PRI_L priority, part B) is preempted by a higher priority task (PRI_H priority, part C) and then back to PRI_L (part D) after the higher priority task becomes unready. If there is no ready task in the system (part E) then the *idle task* is started (i.e., MON_PRI is set to PRI_IDLE).

v) *Slack Monitor:* The MON_SLACK signal is utilized to detect slack time in the schedule. The value of the signal is given by the formula (where PRI_{Hmin} is the least significant hard-level priority):

$$\text{MON\_SLACK} = \begin{cases} HIGH & if((\text{MON\_PRI} = PRI\_IDLE) or (\text{MON\_PRI} \le PRI_{Hmin})), \\ LOW & \text{otherwise.} \end{cases} \tag{5}$$

3.3 Proposed HIL: Operation Principle

In this paragraph, the operation principle of the FPGA-based HIL proposed in the paper is described. A special attention is paid there to principles utilized to process the monitoring signals by the FPGA. For the description, let the $PRI : S_{INT} \cup S_\tau \to N$ be a function assigning a joint-priority value to an INT ($INT_i \in S_{INT}$ where S_{INT} is the set of all INT sources) or a task ($\tau_i \in S_\tau$ where S_τ is the set of all non-IST tasks). Let A be a preemptive, fixed-priority assignment policy, let $S_\tau = \{\tau_1, \ldots, \tau_m, \tau_{m+1}, \ldots, \tau_n\}$ be the set of all tasks to be scheduled by A and let the following subsets be distinguished in the S_τ set: the set ($S_{\tau H} = \{\tau_1, \ldots, \tau_m\}$) of *hard* tasks, the set ($S_{\tau S} = \{\tau_{m+1}, \ldots, \tau_n\}$) of *soft* tasks, the set ($S_{\tau P}$) of *periodic* tasks forming a repetitive part of the ES behavior and the set ($S_{\tau A}$) of *aperiodic* event-driven tasks being released/executed once iff an event (INT) occurs.

It is supposed these parameters are known for a $\tau_i \in S_\tau$: r_i (release time), C_i (worst-case exec. t.), D_i (relative deadline), T_i (period; for an aperiodic task it is set to D_i or – if it is known – to the min. interarrival t. of a corresponding INT). Alike, it is supposed these parameters are known for a $INT_i \in S_{INT}$: C_{INT_i} (worst-case INT_i service t.), W_{INT_i} (worst-case data bandwidth w.r.t. INT_i).

The proposed architecture was designed to meet the following requirements: i) the CPU will not get overloaded by an excessive stream of INTs, ii) timing constraints of hard tasks will be always met, iii) soft tasks will be executed if a slack time is detected on the MON_SLACK line or if the CPU is not fully loaded by the hard tasks, iv) the worst-case blocking-time boundary w.r.t. INTs is known. In [15] it is shown that the requirements can be met if a new INT (INT_i) is signaled to the CPU after at least one of the conditions (7) – (9) is satisfied along with (6). To avoid a non-deterministic behavior, the conditions are evaluated in the following, left-to-right order: (7), (8), (9).

i) *NoISR Condition:*
$$MON\_INT = LOW \tag{6}$$

ii) *Priority Condition:*
$$PRI(INT_i) > MON\_PRI. \tag{7}$$

INT nesting is not allowed, so a new highest-priority INT is i) blocked at most by one (recently executed) lower-priority ISR and ii) directed to the CPU just after the actual ISR ends.

iii) *Underload Condition:* the total CPU load (ρ) at hard-PRI levels plus the C_{INT_i}-induced load is smaller than 100% where $\rho = max_{i=1,...,m}(\rho_i(t))$ and

$$\rho_i(t) = \frac{\sum_{d_k \leq d_i} rem_k(t)}{(d_i - t)} \times 100 \tag{8}$$

is the CPU load of a hard-task $\tau_i \in S_{\tau H}$ in the $< t, d_i >$ interval, t is actual time, $d_i = r_i + D_i$ ($d_k = r_k + D_k$) is the absolute deadline of a task τ_i (τ_k) and $rem_k(t) = C_k - run_k(t)$ is the remaining execution time of a hard-task $\tau_k \in S_{\tau H}$ in time t where $run_k(t)$ is the consumed exe-time of the task τ_k in time t measured on a basis of monitoring the MON_PRI=$PRI(\tau_k)$ width.

iv) *Slack Condition:*
$$MON\_SLACK = HIGH. \tag{9}$$

The maximum number of INTs allowed between consecutive hard-level executions (an implicit update interval) is

$$N_{INT}^{max}(t) = \lfloor \frac{(100 - \rho(t)) \times (d_{max} - t)}{100 \times C_{INT}} \rfloor \tag{10}$$

where $C_{INT} = max_{\forall i}(C_{INT_i})$ is the worst-case execution overhead related to servicing an INT and $d_{max} = max_{i=1,...,m}(d_i)$. If time $t' \leq d_{max}$ exists for which it holds that $w_{int}(t', t'')$ – i.e. the accumulated MON_INT'HIGH observed from the last N_{INT}^{max} update done in t" – exceeds the $\lfloor \frac{t'-t''}{C_{INT}} \rfloor \times C_{INT}$ value then no INT is forwarded to the MCU until the exceeding is over, excluding INTs satisfying the (7) condition.

Actually, MON_TICK and MON_CTX are not involved in the formulas; they are utilized to measure the actual OSTime value/jitter and gather CTXSW statistics only. Crucial lemmas (theorems) w.r.t. impact of the architecture to the parameters of an RT system can be found in [15] along with outlines of the corresponding proofs. Because of the limited space, they are not included in this paper. Instead, more details related to experimental results and implementation overheads are presented in the next. Details related to inner structure of the proposed monitoring-driven limiter can be seen in Fig. 3 – each INT is recognized by a separate INT Detect Unit and prospective INT stimulus and related data are stored in the Stall-INT Buffer until the MCU is ready to service the INT.

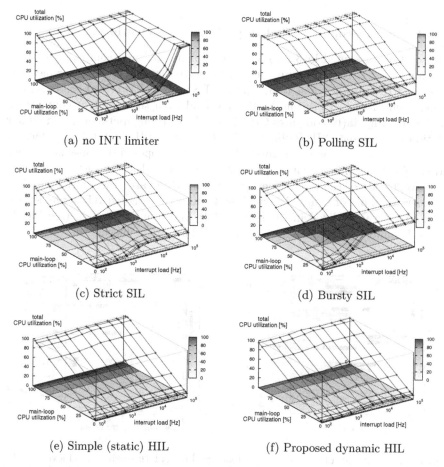

Fig. 2. Comparison of CPU utilization factors of the limiter techniques for $f_{arrival} = 4kHz$. It can be seen that our approach (f) offers "small" CPU utilization comparable to (e) while the other approaches need a higher (c, d) or constant (b) utilization to offer the same level of the IOV protection.

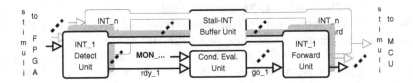

Fig. 3. Block schema of the proposed load-adaptive limiter

The MCU readiness is analyzed by the Condition Evaluation Unit – designed to evaluate the (6) to (10) formulas – and signalled to the INT Forward Unit responsible to forward the INT stimulus to the MCU along with its data. All the mentioned units work in parallel.

3.4   Solution Properties and Implementation Overheads

The solution presented in 3.1 to 3.3 was implemented and compared to those presented in 2.1. In the figures, it can be seen that for high f_{int} values our *dynamic HIL* solution is able to prevent the ES from INT overload and to service higher number of INTs during CPU underload than the others at comparable CPU loads. Fig. 4a(b) compares CPU loads (INT throughputs) achieved by our solution and common SIL (polling, strict, bursty) and HIL (static) approaches.

In order to analyze practical applicability of the proposed IOV mechanism, we have decided to summarize its implementation overheads. Because the overheads w.r.t. MCU side of the mechanism are minimal (they are practically limited to inserting a couple of simple instructions to into the original RT kernel source code, which was outlined in the section 3.2), the summary herein (see Fig. 5, Fig. 6) is limited to overheads w.r.t. the HW part of the mechanism.

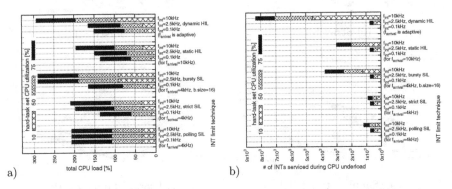

Fig. 4. Comparing accumulated a) CPU loads and b) INT throughputs achieved by the proposed solution (the topmost 3 columns denoted as "dynamic HIL") and by common SIL (polling, strict, bursty) and static HIL approaches. For each of them (vert. axis) results are plotted for 3 various f_{int} values: $0.1kHz$, $2.5kHz$ and $10kHz$, determined by $f_{arrival}$ and by *burst size* values (where applicable).

The HW was targeted to Xilinx Spartan6 family and synthesized using Xilinx ISE 13.1. Device utilization data (such as No. Slice Reg., No. Slice LUTs, No. fully used LUT-FF pairs, No. bonded IOBs and No. BUFG/CTRLs) were collected from Device Utilization Summary report produced by ISE after the synthesis process was over (terminology was taken from the ISE reports).

The remaining data present in the ISE reports were processed to estimate the number of slices needed to implement our limiter into particular Spartan6 devices (Fig. 6). It was estimated that the maximum number of INTs limited by an on-chip Spartan6 realization of the adaptive INT limiter proposed in this paper is about 250. Higher number leads to exhaustion of bonded IOB resources and cannot be implemented on a Spartan6 device. It can be seen that some of the resources are more critical as their utilization is constantly high or grows significantly with decreasing complexity of Spartan6 device while some of them are less critical as their utilization is near to low-constant value across the devices. No. slices needed for implementations are summarized in the Fig. 6c and detailed (for the low-end devices) in Fig. 6b. As common real-time kernels support not more than 256 priority levels, it can be concluded that the presented Spartan6-realization of the limiter is able to limit up to 32–250 INT stimuli.

Limits of memory needed to store data related to interrupts delayed by the FPGA both to prevent the monitored CPU from excessive interrupt stimuli and to guarantee timeliness of responses related to critical interrupts are as follows. The maximum memory size available on-chip of a Spartan6 device along with the limiter mechanism is 6164 kbit (xc6slx150). In the Fig. 6a, details to low-end devices are presented. It can be seen that for XC6SLX9/XC6SLX16 (XC6SLX25) devices, about 600 (1100) kbits can be stored on-chip of an FPGA if the number of limited interrupt sources is not much greater than 32. Otherwise, the maximum of available on-chip memory decreases significantly, so an external memory must be utilized for the purpose. However, in that case, an extra on-chip FPGA resources are needed to implement the controller of such a memory.

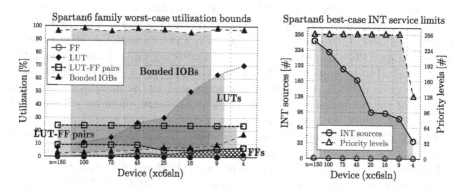

Fig. 5. Summary of utilization bounds (the left sub-figure) and service limits (the right sub-figure) w.r.t. Spartan6 realizations of the proposed IOV mechanism

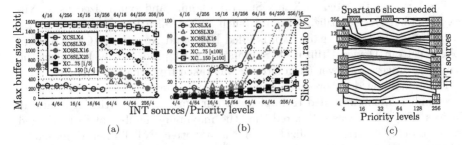

Fig. 6. Requirements and limits w.r.t. on-chip Spartan6 realizations of the adaptive limiter solution proposed in the paper depicted as functions of i) number of limited interrupts and ii) number of supported priority levels. As a Spartan6-slice is composed of 4 LUTs and 8 FFs, ISE outputs were transformed into the number of slices (N_{Slices}) value using the formula $N_{Slices} = (N_{pairs} + N_{LUTs})/4 + N_{FFs}/8$ where i) N_{pairs} is the number of fully used LUT-FF pairs (each of them composed of 1 LUT and 2 FFs – i.e., a slice it is composed of 4 LUT-FF pairs), ii) N_{LUTs} is the number of LUTs not paired with a FF and iii) N_{FFs} is the number of FFs not paired with a LUT.

4   Conclusion

In the paper, a novel hardware solution to the INT overload problem was presented. Novelty of the solution can be seen in the fact it shows that although an RTOS is equipped with a very simple, but properly designed interface then it is possible to precisely monitor its dynamic load by a simple external device and utilize this dynamic information to adapt the INT service rate to the actual load, so the CPU running the safe part of an RT application is not threatened by low-priority INT sources. For the implementation of the proposed approach, common COST components (μC/OS-II RTOS running on ARM Cortex-A9 and Spartan6 FPGA) were utilized to show the applicability and implementation overheads w.r.t. the proposed approach, but it should be emphasized there that the proposed approach is general enough to be realized using another RTOS, MCU/CPU or FPGA. Moreover, an RTOS is not required to run on an MCU/CPU (it can be run e.g. on an FPGA to produce the same monitoring signals) and the monitor is not required to be implemented by an FPGA (instead, a different device such as CPU can be utilized supposing it is able to analyze the monitoring signals). Because of the adaptability, the presented architecture offers an efficient and low-cost load-driven solution to the timing disturbance and predictability problems w.r.t. INT management, which was shown in the paper. Future research activities w.r.t. the paper are going to be focused on real-world applications and real-traffic measurements based on the proposed load-adaptive architecture.

This work has been partially supported by the RECOMP MSMT project (National Support for Project Reduced Certification Costs Using Trusted Multi-core Platforms), the Research Plan No. MSM 0021630528 (Security-Oriented Research in Information Technology), the BUT FIT-S-11-1 and the IT4Innovations Centre of Excellence CZ.1.05/1.1.00/02.0070.

References

1. Cheng, A.M.K.: Real-Time Systems, Scheduling, Analysis, and Verification. John Wiley & Sons, Hoboken (2002)
2. Cottet, F., Delacroix, J., Kaiser, C., Mammeri, Z.: Scheduling in Real-Time Systems. John Wiley & Sons, Hoboken (2002)
3. Kopetz, H.: On the Fault Hypothesis for a Safety-Critical Real-Time System. In: Broy, M., Krüger, I.H., Meisinger, M. (eds.) ASWSD 2004. LNCS, vol. 4147, pp. 31–42. Springer, Heidelberg (2006)
4. Laplante, P.A.: Real-Time Systems Design and Analysis. Wiley-IEEE Press, Hoboken (2004)
5. Lee, M., Lee, J., Shyshkalov, A., Seo, J., Hong, I., Shin, I.: On Interrupt Scheduling Based On Process Priority For Predictable Real-Time Behavior. SIGBED Rev. 7(1), 6:1–6:4 (2010)
6. Leyva-del-Foyo, L.E., Mejia-Alvarez, P.: Custom interrupt management for realtime and embedded system kernels. In: Proceedings of the Embedded Real-Time Systems Implementation Workshop at the 25th IEEE International Real-Time Systems Symposium, p. 8. IEEE Computer Society, United States (2004)
7. Leyva-del-Foyo, L.E., Mejia-Alvarez, P., Niz, D.: Predictable interrupt management for real time kernels over conventional pc hardware. In: Proceedings of the IEEE Real-Time and Embedded Technology and Applications Symposium, pp. 14–23. IEEE Computer Society, Washington, DC (2006)
8. Lee, M., Lee, J., Shyskalov, A., Seo, J., Hong, I., Shin, I.: On interrupt scheduling based on process priority for predictable real-time behavior. In: ACM SIGBED Review - Special Issue on the RTSS 2009 WiP Session, 6th article, p. 4 (2010)
9. Parmer, G., West, R.: Predictable interrupt management and scheduling in the composite component-based system. In: Proc. of the Real-Time Systems Symposium, pp. 232–243. IEEE Computer Society, Washington, DC (2008)
10. Pellizzoni, R.: Predictable and monitored execution for cots-based real-time embedded systems. Ph.D. thesis, University of Illinois at Urbana-Champaign (2010)
11. Regehr, J.: Safe And Structured Use Of Interrupts In Real-Time And Embedded Software. In: Lee, I., Leung, J.Y.-T., Son, S.H. (eds.) Handbook of Real-Time and Embedded Systems, pp. 16-1–16-12. Chapman & Hall/CRC, US (2007)
12. Regehr, J., Duongsaa, U.: Preventing interrupt overload. In: Proceedings of the ACM SIGPLAN/SIGBED Conference on Languages, Compilers, and Tools For Embedded Systems, pp. 50–58. ACM, New York (2005)
13. Regnier, P., Lima, G., Barreto, L.: Evaluation Of Interrupt Handling Timeliness in Real-Time Linux. SIGOPS Oper. Syst. Rev. 42(6), 52–63 (2008)
14. Scheler, F., Hofer, W., Oechslein, B., Pfister, R., Schroder-Preikschat, W., Lohmann, D.: Parallel, hardware-supported interrupt handling in an event-trigered real-time operating system. In: Proc. of the Int. Conf. on Computers, Architectures and Synthesis of Embedded Systems, pp. 167–174. ACM (2009)
15. Strnadel, J.: Monitoring-Driven HW/SW Interrupt Overload Prevention for Embedded Real-Time Systems. In: Proc. of the 15th IEEE Int. Symposium on Design and Diagnostics of Electronic Circuits and Systems, IEEE CS, pp. 121–126 (2012)
16. Zhang, Y.: Prediction-based interrupt scheduling. In: WiP Proc. of the 30th IEEE Real-Time Systems Symposium, pp. 81–84. University of Texas, San Antonio (2009)
17. Zhang, Y., West, R.: Process-aware interrupt scheduling and accounting. In: Proceedings of the 27th IEEE International Real-Time Systems Symposium, pp. 191–201. IEEE Computer Society, Los Alamitos (2006)

Producer-Consumer: The Programming Model for Future Many-Core Processors

Arnau Prat-Pérez[1], David Dominguez-Sal[1,3], Josep-Lluis Larriba-Pey[1], and Pedro Trancoso[2]

[1] DAMA-UPC, Universitat Politècnica de Catalunya
Barcelona, Spain
{aprat,ddomings,larri}@ac.upc.edu
[2] Department of Computer Science, University of Cyprus
Nicosia, Cyprus
pedro@cs.ucy.ac.cy
[3] Sparsity Technologies
Barcelona, Spain

Abstract. The massive addition of cores on a chip is adding more pressure to the accesses to main memory. In order to avoid this bottleneck, we propose the use of a simple producer-consumer model, which allows for the temporary results to be transferred directly from one task to another. These data transfer operations are performed within the chip, using on-chip memory, thus avoiding costly off-chip memory accesses. We implement this model on a real many-core processor, the 48-core Intel Single-chip Cloud Computer processor using its on-chip memory facilities. We find that the Producer-Consumer model adapts to such architectures and allow to achieve good task and data parallelism. For the evaluation of the proposed platform we implement a graph-based application using the Producer-Consumer model. Our tests show that the model scales very well as it takes advantage of the on-chip memory. The execution times of our implementation are up to 9 times faster than the baseline implementation, which relies on storing the temporary results to main memory.

1 Introduction

The recent efforts in new processor development are geared towards the integration of more cores in a single chip. Currently, we find processors in the market with more than ten cores and the designs aim at including more. However, as the trend in adding more cores to the processor proceeds, we are facing with new challenges. More cores in the same chip lead to an increased pressure in the interconnection network and integrated memory controllers, higher synchronization costs and fewer shared resources. In such processors, the traditional shared memory programs (e.g: openMP like) face severe hurdles such as limited cache coherence mechanisms and private memory spaces for each core that difficult the deployment of efficient shared memory code.

The new prototype of many core processor developed at Intel is the Single-chip Cloud Computer (SCC) [1]. This processor is built with 48 cores, and has

C. Hochberger et al. (Eds.): ARCS 2013, LNCS 7767, pp. 110–121, 2013.

a new architecture that intends to integrate hundreds of cores once it gets into production stage. The SCC has a single memory space for all the cores, but the two levels of cache between the main memory and the processor are not coherent among cores. The synchronization of data among cores using shared memory requires the flush of the caches [1]. Flushing the caches impose synchronization barriers and disables the cache hierarchy benefits, which makes flushing not advisable for high performance computing. As a solution, the SCC offers a small memory space inside the chip oriented to send messages between cores and facilitate the implementation of message passing parallel programs (e.g. MPI-like).

In this paper, we take the Intel SCC as a reference of the upcoming many-core processors and study the usage of the Producer-Consumer model as a scalable programming model for future many-core architectures. We propose an implementation of the model for the Intel SCC, where the memory in the chip is divided in as many sections as cores are available, and is used as buffers to implement a Producer-Consumer framework. Our proposal, *Task&DataParallel*, makes use of a double buffer solution that allows simultaneous production and consumption on the same buffer.

We test our Production-Consumer implementation on graph algorithms because they are good representatives of memory intensive applications with heterogeneous data access patterns. We select the triangle counting [2], which consists on computing the number of triangles where a node of a graph participates. This computation is the core of spam detection [2] or social network analysis algorithms [3]. The experimental results show that the Producer-Consumer model scales well for a large number of cores, sometimes super-linearly thanks to the exploitation of the on-chip memory of the Intel SCC. We prove that the *Task&DataParallel* implementation of the Producer-Consumer model is able to exploit both data and task parallelism, achieving high scalability and performance (running up to 9 times faster than a baseline working on main memory).

This paper is organized as follows: in Section 2, we present the many-core architecture and in particular we describe the Intel SCC architecture and review the parallel programming paradigms; in Section 3 we review the Producer-Consumer programming model and its applications; in Section 4, we describe the different implementations of the Producer-Consumer programming model for the Intel SCC; in Section 5, we present the experimental setup; in Section 6, we discuss the experimental results; in Section 7, we overview the related work and finally in Section 8 we present the conclusions of the work.

2   Many-Core Architecture

In this section, we first describe the main characteristics of many-core architectures, and we present details of the Intel SCC platform. Second, we revisit the two main parallel programming paradigms.

2.1 Hardware

Many-core architectures, are characterized by having tens or even hundreds of cores. This allows to perform calculations and to process large amounts of data in parallel. However, the presence of such amount of cores leads to simpler cores, for example, without hardware support for cache-coherency, since these mechanisms would result in a bottleneck and make the exploitation of parallelism harder. This is the main reason why, until nowadays, the usage of many-core architectures has been restricted to specific domains, where the applications are inherently parallel, such as GPUs for graphic processing. Hence, there is a need of more complex and flexible architectures, aimed at satisfying the processing demands of general purpose applications. One proposed architecture that attempts to solve this problem is the Single-chip Cloud Computer (SCC) proposed by Intel [1].

The Intel SCC experimental processor is a 48-core vehicle created by Intel Labs as a platform for many-core software research. This is a clustered architecture composed of P54C cores, grouped in tiles containing two cores each. Each tile (pair of two cores) has a router, forming a communication mesh within all the chip to access the four DDR3 memory controllers.

The Intel SCC has an aggregated address space of 64 GB of memory. However, each P54C core is able to address 4 GB. In our experiments, each core has assigned a private region of memory of total size divided by 48. What makes the Intel SCC special is its non-coherent memory hierarchy. Each core has a non coherent L1 and L2 caches, of 16KB and 256KB respectively, with a cache line size of 32 bytes. Since the caches are non-coherent, is the programmer the responsible of maintaining the coherency of the caches manually. For this reason, the Intel SCC provides a fast core-to-core communication, consisting on 384KB of on-chip memory (also called the Message Passing Buffer(MPB)). Each tile is assigned 16KB of the buffer (8KB for each core), which is is addressable by any core. We will call each 8KB section assigned to each core, as an MPB section. Finally, in order to synchronize the access to the MPB and the memory by all the cores, the system provides 48 globally accessible test-and-set registers.

2.2 Parallel Programming Paradigms For Many-Core Processors

We review the two principal paradigms for exploiting the parallelism of many-core architectures: data parallel paradigm, and task parallel paradigm [4].

In **data parallel** paradigm, the data is split into subsets, each of one is then processed independently by a processing unit in parallel. Applications that map to this paradigm achieve a large degree of parallelism, sometimes achieving super-linear speedups because of cache line re-usage. However, due to the nature of the existing applications, data dependencies are common and splitting the data is not always possible.

In **task parallel** paradigm, each processing unit is devoted to execute a specific task. These tasks can be either subtasks inside an application or different instances of the same application. However, similarly to the data parallel paradigm, sometimes is difficult to identify such tasks, or even executing different instances of the same application is not possible due to a lack of data.

3   Scalable Programming Model: Producer-Consumer

The goal of this work is to analyze the scalability of the Producer-Consumer (P/C) model as a general purpose programming model for future many-core processors. In the P/C model, the program is divided into tasks which adopt the role of a Producer, a Consumer or both. The Producers are tasks that operate on the input data and produce the results, which are then sent to the Consumers. The Consumers are the tasks that receive the data from the Producers, operate on the data and then produce the results, which can be either stored in main memory or forwarded to the next Consumer in the P/C chain (and hence performing the Producer's role too).

The Producers and the Consumers are independent tasks that can be executed in concurrently as long as they have available data to consume and available resources to store the results they produce. Hence, the task parallelism parallelism is exploited. Furthermore, the input data of the tasks, can be split and distributed among multiple instances of both Producers and Consumers, allowing the partitioning of the data and the execution of multiple tasks in parallel. This way, we are also exploiting the data parallelism.

Finally, from a programming point of view, the P/C model allows the programmer to abstract and focus only on each individual task, which is isolated and self contained, and let a hypothetic task scheduler to execute the tasks efficiently in order to optimize the usage of the available resources.

The P/C model is used in many and varied applications. In a GUI system, the Producer is in charge of gathering all the input events while the Consumer use this events to perform the corresponding actions. In an MPEG-4 video encoder [5], the Producer distributes the frames among a set of Consumers, that encode them. The P/C model can also be applied to more complex systems, where the computations are divided into subsystems of different nature. Each of this subsystem can be either be a Producer, a Consumer or both. For example, in computer games, game engines are composed by different subsystems like the physics subsystem, the AI subsystem, the input subsystem and the renderer, which are executed asynchronously following a P/C model [6].

In this paper, we will focus on the triangle counting problem [2]. The problem consists of computing, for each node in a graph, the number of triangles the node belongs to. The counting of triangles in graphs has several applications, such as detecting web spam [2] or content quality in networks [7]. Also, several studies [3] show that social networks are characterized by having lots of triangles, and the computation of local triangle count is of high importance to study the characteristics and topology of these networks.

Given a graph $G(V, E)$ (where V is the set of nodes and E is the set of edges), the Producers compute, for each edge e in E, the number of triangles the edge e belongs to. Given an edge e connecting two nodes a and b, the number of triangles of this edges corresponds to the size of the intersection between the adjacency lists of nodes a and b. In order to exploit data parallelism, different Producer instances are created, and each of them is assigned a subset of the edges to process. Then, the Consumers read the results produced by the Producers and accumulate, for each node, the number of triangles where the edges incident to the node participate in. Several instances of Consumers are created, and each of them accumulates the result of a subset of the nodes of the graph. All the Producers and the Consumers are executed concurrently, as long as the data is produced and consumed.

4   Efficient SCC Implementation

In this section, we present three different implementations for the P/C model on the Intel SCC: the *DataParallelMsg* (which serves as the baseline implementation), the *DataParallelMsgBlk* and the *Task&DataParallel* implementations. Even though the implementations are described for the target architecture, the model and the concepts are general enough to be applied to any other architecture that includes an MPB like structure. As long as the encapsulation processes evolve, more transistors can be added into a chip, which are used to include more devices, bigger caches and resources. On chip memory buffers have been already used in many-core architectures such as GPUs [8], and we expect to be a common feature in future many-core designs due to the possibilities they offer.

In all the implementations, the input data is loaded and replicated into the main memory assigned to each core. This data is read only, so no synchronization between the different cores is needed to maintain the coherency of this data. Consider P cores being used by these implementations.

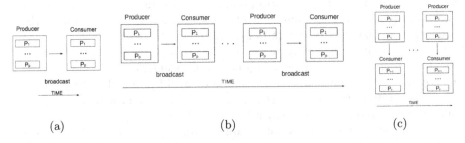

(a)   (b)   (c)

Fig. 1. (a)The *DataParallelMsg* implementation scheme. (b)The *DataParallelMsgBlk* implementation scheme. (c)The *Task&DataParallel* implementation scheme.

DataParallelMsg: This implementation follows the data parallel paradigm and uses main memory to exchange the data between the tasks. This means that only one step (either the Producer or the Consumer step) is executed at a given time. Figure 1-(a) shows the execution flow and how the P processors are distributed among the Producer and the Consumer step. In this approach, all the cores execute the Producer step first, and when it is completed, all the cores execute the Consumer step. All the cores P are assigned to the step being under execution, so each core is responsible for $1/P$ of the computations. The results computed by each core, are stored into main memory. Once all the cores have finished executing the Producer step, the results are broadcast to the other cores, by storing their results into their MPB sections. The other cores read the results and store it again into their addressable main memory. Once all the cores have all the data, the Consumer step starts. Note that, since the MPB sections are smaller than the amount of data to be transfered by each core, this is transfered iteratively in multiple chunks of size of the MPB section.

DataParallelMsgBlk: This implementation, as depicted in Figure 1-(b), follows the data parallel programming model like the previous implementation presented. However, in this implementation, the results in the Producer step are iteratively produced in blocks of the size of the MPB section, instead of producing all the results and then broadcast them. The Producers produce a chunk of results and store them directly into their own MPB section, instead of storing them into main memory. Once all the Producers have finished to produce their chunk of data, the cores consume the data produced by the rest directly from the MPBs of the others, and execute the Consumers step. The process iterates until all the computations from the Producer step have been performed. The goal of this approach is to benefit from keeping all the data produced in the Producers' step inside the chip, instead of copying it into the main memory and hence achieving better performance.

Task&DataParallel: The goal of this implementation, is to fully benefit from the presence of the MPB present in the SCC, by implementing a version based on the task and data parallel paradigm. In this approach we have k cores as Producers, and $P - k$ cores as Consumers and all cores execute their task the same time. The Producers produce the data and store it directly into their MPB section, while the Consumers consume this data to perform their computations. Figure 1-(c) shows the scheme of the application with the different cores assigned to the tasks. Note that one step can have more cores than others, depending on the complexity of the computation performed by the step.

A Producer computes and produces data as long as there is space in its MPB section. Once the buffer is filled, it waits until the data is consumed by all the consumers and the buffer is freed. Once the Producer has performed all the computations, it finishes. On the other hand, a Consumer waits for the data to be in the buffer. Once the data is available, it consumes it and tells the corresponding Producer that the data has been consumed. In order to reduce the contention on the buffer between Producers and Consumers, a double buffering scheme is used in every MPB section. Figure 2 shows how each of the 8KB MPB section is divided and used.

The first 8128 bytes of each MPB section are used to implement the double buffering scheme. The last 4 bytes of each on-chip memory buffer are used for the synchronization mechanism. We store a 32bit (4 bytes) at the end of the section which we call the "communication flag", in order to implement the synchronization protocol. The flags store information about which consumers have read the data in the buffer and which is the region of the double buffer from which they have to read. In order to guarantee the atomic access to each communication

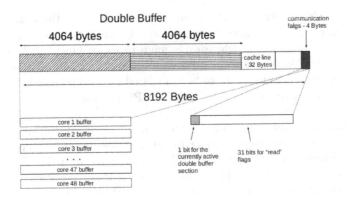

Fig. 2. The division of every 8KB section of the MPB assigned to each core

flag, we use one of the 48 test-and-set registers (one for each Producer) available on the Intel SCC chip.

The goal of this approach is two fold. From the one hand, we achieve and overlap between computations and data distribution, reducing the communication cost and improving the scalability. On the other hand, we keep the data flowing inside the chip by using the MPB, and hence we reduce the number of accesses the main memory.

5   Experimental Setup

For this work, we have used a real many-core system, the Intel Single Chip Cloud Computing (Intel SCC) experimental processor, RockyLake version configured with 32GB of main memory. The frequencies of the tiles, mesh and memory are 533, 800 and 800 Mhz respectively. The operating system used for the Intel SCC cores is the Linux kernel provided by the RCCE SCC Kit 1.3.0.

To test the performance of the different implementations proposed, for the P/C model, we have implemented the local triangle count problem described in Section 3. The input graphs, are built with a graph generator [9], which creates graphs with social network statistics. We generate two graphs: one with 100K nodes and 1M edge (*small*), and another one with 1M nodes and 10M edges (*big*). Each measure is obtained by averaging five executions.

Note that it is not the objective of this work to focus on the improvement of this particular application. Our aim is to test the usage of the Intel SCC in real complex applications such as graph processing, and to prove the scalability of the P/C model for such architectures with an on chip memory buffer. We show the results in terms of speedup since what we want to analyze is the scalability of the proposed model, using a case-study application, on a sample architecture.

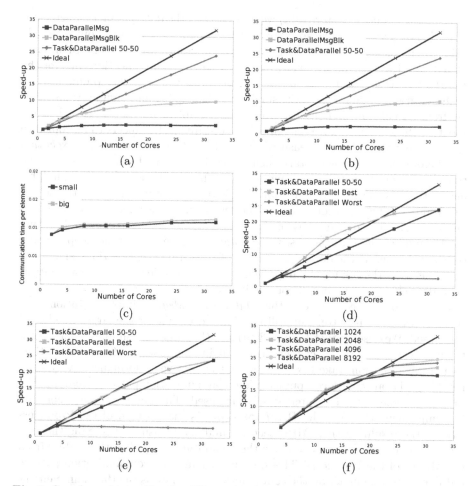

Fig. 3. Speed-up obtained by the different implementations proposed for the: (a) small graph and (b) big graph. (c) Normalized communication time for the *DataParallelMsg* for the small and big graphs. Speedup for the *Task&DataParallel* implementation with different configurations for a variable number of cores for the (d) small and (e) big graph. (f) Speedup for the *Task&DataParallel* implementation with different buffer sizes.

6   Experimental Results

In Figure 3, we depict the speedup for the different implementations described in Section 4 with an increasing number of cores. We present the results for both the *small* and *big* graphs in Figure 3-(a) and 3-(b), respectively. The *50-50* indicates that there is an equal number of Producers and Consumers running in parallel and the *Ideal* line represents the ideal speedup. The speedup is computed taking the *DataParallelMsg* execution with one core only as reference.

From the results in Figure 3-(a) we observe that the data parallel implementations do not scale well. The speedup for the baseline is limited to approximately 2.6x, independently of the number of cores used to solve the problem. In order to understand the speedup behavior, we measured the communication time for the *DataParallelMsg* implementation. In Figure 3-(c), we show the communication time per graph node for both the small and big graphs, for configurations ranging from 2 to 32 cores for the *DataParallelMsg* implementation. This is the time spent by the system to have the data produced by the Producers to be copied to all the Consumers. This is measured after all Producers have finished execution and before the Consumers start their execution. First of all, we see that the time spent per element is the same for both the small and the big graph. This means that the total communication cost is directly proportional to the size of the results produced. Second, we see that the communication cost per element is almost constant, independently of the number of cores. This means that as long as the number of cores increases, the total communication time keeps almost constant, becoming the dominant portion of the total execution time, and hence acting as a bottleneck for the improvement. This justifies why the scalability is degraded when the number of cores is increased.

For the optimized version, the *DataParallelMsgBlk* implementation, the speedup scales a bit better but still it is limited to 10x for the larger number of cores used. We observe that Figures 3-(a) and (b) show very similar results. Even though the input data size changes, resulting in an impact on the execution time (big graph executions take 10x more time), the relative performance is very similar. This is because both computation and communication patterns maintain the same even when different input graphs are used. The main difference between this implementation and the *DataParallelMsg* is that instead of the Producers writing the results in their MPB sections and the Consumers copying them to main memory, the Consumers make the computations by directly reading from the MPB's of the Producers. This does not change the communication pattern but does have an impact on the communication latency as the the main memory accesses are avoided. Consequently, we can observe that the speedup for this optimized version follows a similar trend to the *DataParallelMsg* implementation but the speedup achieved is higher once the communication fixed cost is lower.

Finally, while both data parallel implementations showed a limit in their speedup, the *Task&DataParallel* implementation shows a near linear speedup even for large number of cores (about 24x of speedup for 32 cores). The P/C model has a major benefit compared with the other models studied, which is the characteristics that Producers and Consumers are executing at the same time in a pipelining way. Thus, we are able to hide the communication cost with the Producer and Consumer computation. Consequently we do not observe a limit in the speedup. The reason for the speedup to be slightly below the ideal has to do with another fact which is related to load balancing and contention on the double buffer space used to exchange the results between Producers and Consumers.

6.1   Task Assignment

As mentioned previously, in our proposal there are multiple Producers and Consumers. One difficulty is to determine, for a given number of cores, the optimal distribution of Producers and Consumers. Without any proper runtime analysis, a naive bet is to assign one half of the cores to the Producer role and one half of the cores to the Consumer role. We will call this the *50-50* strategy, which is the strategy used in the results presented in the last section. In order to study the performance impact of the task assignment, we have executed the application on different configurations ranging from 2 up to 30 Producers and 2 up to 30 Consumers, with a maximum of 32 cores in total. In Figure 3-(d) and (b) we show, for each fixed number of cores, the speedup for the worst, the best, the ideal, and the *50-50* configurations.

From the results in Figure 3-(d) and (e) we observe that the *50-50* strategy performs well, close to the *Best* and *Ideal*. It is also relevant to notice that the gap between the *Best* and *Worst* is quite large. This is an indication that smarter dynamic schemes for task assignment may be required to achieve good performance.

6.2   Internal Memory Size

In this section we analyze the impact of the size of the MPB on the performance of the application. We have tested our P/C model with different sizes for the MPB sections. Figure 3-(f) shows the speedup of the *Task&DataParallel* implementation for different buffer sizes: 1024, 2048, 4096, 8192 bytes per core. We observe that, the larger the buffer size, the better the scalability. This is because the cores can spend more time computing than being stalled waiting for writing or reading from the MPBs. However, it seems that after a certain number of cores, there is an upper bound on the performance gain which is independent of the size of the buffer (the difference in the performance between using 4096 bytes or 8192 bytes of MPB sections' size is minimal). This means that, after a certain point, there are other factors which affect the more the scalability such as load balancing, and hence, the MPB does not need to be very large, keeping the architecture simpler.

7   Related Work

Parallel systems have been around for a very long time. One of the major issues with these systems has been programmability. Several parallel programming models have emerged from research projects and standards. Most parallelism has been exploited using the fork-join model implemented using either shared-memory or message-passing. The most common library for shared-memory is OpenMP while the most common for message-passing is MPI. The programmability issue has recently become more serious as processors with multiple cores are becoming widespread. Thus, parallelism is now reaching all, resulting in a need for more simpler ways to exploit that available parallelism. A considerable effort has been put into organizing existing models into what is called parallel programming patterns [4]. This allows programmers to express their algorithms into one or more of the proposed patterns which then can be easily mapped to an efficient implementation for the target architecture. NVIDIA has developed CUDA [10] for programming their GPUs but many believe that a similar paradigm can be also used for many-core processors [11]. Intel is putting some effort into Cilk [12] as a programming language for parallel systems as well as a streaming language Ct which inherits some concepts from RapidMine [13]. IBM is developing X10 [14] a language for parallel programming using the partitioned address space model. Another large effort has been put by Google with their MapReduce model [15]. In this model the authors try to simplify the parallel program as to be able to split them into two phases the Map and the Reduce. Even though MapReduce has been originally developed for large scale multiprocessor systems, it is currently also exploited for multi-core architectures [16] and GPUs [17]. Many researchers believe that the models offered so far require a large effort from the programmer and thus have proposed Transactional Memory [18], a model that exploits parallelism in a speculative way. Others, in order to reduce the large synchronization overheads, have started to look at models that are based on the more efficient data-flow model of execution such as Data-Driven Multithreading [19].

8   Conclusions and Future Work

In this work, we have analyzed the usage of the P/C parallel model in a modern many-core architecture such as the Intel SCC. The Intel SCC, serves as a reference of how future many-core architectures for general purpose computing will look like. The results suggests that the P/C model adapts well to that architecture thanks to the presence of the MPB, which reduces the latency in the communication and the number of main memory accesses. We observed that, with a relatively small MPB, this model scales for a large number of cores (achieving about 24x of speedup for 32 cores, and about 9 times faster than the baseline implementation). Furthermore, we also showed that even though the static task assignment seems to perform well, dynamic task assignment strategies are able to deliver better performance.

As future work, we intend to develop a library to implement applications mapping the P/C model or to exploit the characteristics of these architectures for other models such as MapReduce and Data-Driven Multithreading.

Acknowledgments. The members of DAMA-UPC thank the Ministry of Science and Innovation of Spain and Generalitat de Catalunya, for grant numbers TIN2009-14560-C03-03 and GRC-1187 respectively, and IBM CAS Canada Research for their strategic research grant. David Dominguez-Sal thanks the Ministry of Science and Innovation of Spain for the grant Torres Quevedo PTQ-11-04970. The authors would like to thank Intel Labs for their support with the supply of the Intel SCC machine used in this paper. Arnau Prat-Pérez would like to thank the HiPEAC network for their collaboration grant. Finally, the authors would like to thank Andreas Diavastos, Panayiotis Petrides and the rest of the members of the CASPER research group (www.cs.ucy.ac.cy/carch/casper) for their key support in the realization of this work.

References

1. Mattson, T., Riepen, M., Lehnig, T., Brett, P., Haas, W., Kennedy, P., Howard, J., Vangal, S., Borkar, N., Ruhl, G., Dighe, S.: he 48-core SCC processor: the Programmer's view. In: SC, pp. 1–11. IEEE Computer Society (2010)
2. Becchetti, L., Boldi, P., Castillo, C., Gionis, A.: Efficient Semi-streaming Algorithms for Local Triangle Counting in Massive Graphs. In: KDD, pp. 16–24 (2008)
3. Leskovec, J., Backstrom, L., Kumar, R., Tomkins, A.: Microscopic evolution of social networks. In: KDD, pp. 462–470. ACM (2008)
4. Mattson, T., Sanders, B., Massingill, B.: Patterns for Parallel Programming. Addison-Wesley Professional (2004)
5. Hamosfakidis, A., Paker, Y., Cosmas, J.: A Study of Concurrency in MPEG-4 Video Encoder. In: ICMCS, pp. 204–207. IEEE (1998)
6. Tulip, J., Bekkema, J., Nesbitt, K.: Multi-threaded Game Engine Design. In: CGIE, pp. 9–14. Murdoch University (2006)
7. Welser, H., Gleave, E., Fisher, D., Smith, M.: Visualizing the Signatures of Social Roles in Online Discussion Groups. JoSS 8(2), 1–31 (2007)
8. Andrews, J., Baker, N.: Xbox 360 System Architecture. IEEE Micro 26(2), 25–37 (2006)
9. Lancichinetti, A., Fortunato, S., Radicchi, F.: Benchmark graphs for testing community detection algorithms. Physical Review E 78(4), 046110 (2008)
10. Nvidia, C.: Nvidia CUDA Programming Guide (2012), http://docs.nvidia.com/cuda/index.html
11. Stratton, J.A., Stone, S.S., Hwu, W.-M.W.: MCUDA: An Efficient Implementation of CUDA Kernels for Multi-core CPUs. In: Amaral, J.N. (ed.) LCPC 2008. LNCS, vol. 5335, pp. 16–30. Springer, Heidelberg (2008)
12. Kim, W., Voss, M.: Multicore Desktop Programming with Intel Threading Building Blocks. IEEE Software 28(1), 23–31 (2011)
13. McCool, M., D'Amora, B.: Programming Using RapidMind on the Cell BE. In: SC, p. 222. ACM (2006)
14. Saraswat, V., Sarkar, V., von Praun, C.: X10: Concurrent Programming for Modern Architectures. In: PPoPP, p. 271. ACM (2007)
15. Dean, J., Ghemawat, S.: MapReduce: Simplified Data Processing on Large Clusters. CACM 51(1), 107–113 (2008)
16. Yoo, R., Romano, A., Kozyrakis, C.: Phoenix rebirth: Scalable MapReduce on a Large-scale Shared-memory System. In: IISWC, pp. 198–207 (October 2009)
17. He, B., Fang, W., Luo, Q., Govindaraju, N.K., Wang, T.: Mars: a MapReduce Framework on Graphics Processors. In: PACT, pp. 260–269 (2008)
18. Herlihy, M., Moss, J.: Transactional memory: Architectural Support for Lock-free Data Structures. SIGARCH 21(2), 289–300 (1993)
19. Kyriacou, C., Evripidou, P., Trancoso, P.: Data-Driven Multithreading Using Conventional Microprocessors. TPDS 17, 1176–1188 (2006)

A Highly Dependable Self-adaptive Mixed-Signal Multi-core System-on-Chip

Benjamin Betting, Julius von Rosen, Lars Hedrich, and Uwe Brinkschulte

Institute for Computer Science
Johann Wolfgang Goethe-University,
Frankfurt am Main, Germany
{betting,brinkschulte}@es.cs.uni-frankfurt.de,
{jrosen,hedrich}@em.cs.uni-frankfurt.de

Abstract. In this article we propose a design of a dependable self-organizing and adaptive mixed-signal SoC. With respect to organic computing, we introduce an artificial hormone system (AHS) as general control mechanism. The AHS is an implementation of a completely decentralized, self-organizing task allocation mechanism using self-X properties. To minimize the increase in complexity especially with respect to the analog parts, several different implementations are introduced. Besides the basics of the hormone controlled architecture, the paper presents the mapping onto a SoC, an evaluation of a completely simulated AHS-controlled SoC implementing the different approaches and validating the functionality, stability and upper timing boundaries and showing the improvements in system reliability.

Keywords: Mixed Signal System-on-Chips, Artificial Hormone System.

1 Introduction

The general idea of a self adaptive mixed-signal multi-core System-on-Chip (SoC) combines several research topics related to mixed-signal processing, multithreaded/ multicore architectures, self-organizing and organic computing. The main goal is the development and evaluation of a high dependable, self-organizing mixed-signal SoC. Therefore, also failure modeling, especially regarding analog components, is in the focus of this project. The most relevant failures considered here are degradation through aging, electromigration and temperature instability.

The basic idea of the project[1] is the usage of a generalized heterogeneous Chip-Multi-Processor (CMP) system for mixed-signal processing. The functionality of the SoC is spread across different types of cores. A generalized core concept is issued, which covers the capability of executing one or more tasks on each core. Cores are e.g., processing cores, interface cores, timer cores, special purpose cores, etc. Although, a slight specialization of cores is done due to the principal difference of analog to digital cores. Generalized task notation represents software-programmed tasks, such as data processing or supporting input, and hardware oriented tasks, as camera readout or engine control.

---

[1] This research program is supported by the German Research Foundation (DFG) as part of the priority program "Dependable Embedded Systems" (SPP 1500 - spp1500.itec.kit.edu - MixedCoreSoC).

C. Hochberger et al. (Eds.): ARCS 2013, LNCS 7767, pp. 122–133, 2013.
© Springer-Verlag Berlin Heidelberg 2013

To ensure the self-organization of the system for task-allocation and reliability, an artificial hormone system (AHS) is used as global middleware realized in hard- and software. The assignment of tasks to cores in the mixed-signal CMP is completely handled by the AHS. It has to deal with task reallocation, mixed signal task migration and different kinds of failures. The cores are interconnected via a crossbar-network and provide redundant interfaces to the environment.

2 General SoC Architecture

Our general system architecture is based on a generalized core and task concept for reliable mixed-signal SoC. Therefore, we turned from nowadays likely standard SoC architecture consisting of active digital processing cores and rather reactive digital and analog components like memories, timers, interfaces, converters or amplifiers into a completely heterogeneous many-core architecture, tracing the assumption of a generalized core and task concept. Within this, the entire functionality of the SoC is spread up into different types of cores (Fig. 1). In fact, each core type represents a specialized SoC function realized by specific circuits in the domain of analog, digital or mixed-signal. Consequently, each activity of the SoC is considered as a task to be executed on a suitable core. This generalized core and task concept offers a wide range of flexibility by dynamically assigning tasks to cores for proactive and reactive failure handling. To cover a large amount of typical mixed-signal SoC applications, we focused on elementary core templates for processing, interfacing, analog as well as special purposes.

In order to keep the correlation between the types of cores and corresponding tasks, the notion of **generalized core** declares the capability of core units, being able to execute one or more generalized tasks. Further the **generalized task** concept covers the classification of all software as well as hardware related tasks. Tasks can be represented as coded programs executable on processing cores or as formal task descriptions defining the activities and timing of interface cores, analog cores, memory cores, etc. To give an example of such a formal task description for other than processing cores, an

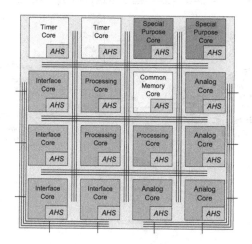

Fig. 1. General MixedCoreSoC architecture

interface task could be described by the message to send, the sending and receiving task ids, and the requested transmission format (e.g. serial link, asynchronous transmission, baud-rate 19200, no parity, ...). Assigning generalized tasks to generalized cores means to execute either the coded program or the formal task description on the selected core. Some cores are able to execute completely different types of task. A timer task can be executed in hardware by a timer core, but as well in software by a processor core. This increases the flexibility and thus the dependability of our approach.

3   Artificial Hormone System for Task Assignment

To realize the dynamic assignment of tasks to cores, a middleware architecture is necessary. Here, we have selected an Artificial Hormone System (AHS), which has been proven to be a highly robust and completely decentralized task assignment mechanism [1]. The aim of the AHS is to assign tasks to cores in a self-organizing way i.e., it uses three main types of hormones:

Eager value. This hormone type determines the suitability of a core to execute a task. The higher the hormonal value the better the ability of the core to execute the task.
Suppressor. This hormone type lowers the suitability of a task execution on a core. Suppressors are subtracted from eager values.
Accelerator. This hormone type favors the execution of a task on a core. Accelerators are added to eager values.

More details on these subtypes of hormones are presented when needed, because they are used for fine tuning of the AHS and do not contribute to its basic understanding.

We have to distinguish between received hormones and hormones to be sent and also between tasks and cores. Therefore, we use Latin letters such as i as task indices and Greek letters such as γ as core indices. A hormone of any type denoted as $H^{i\gamma}$ with

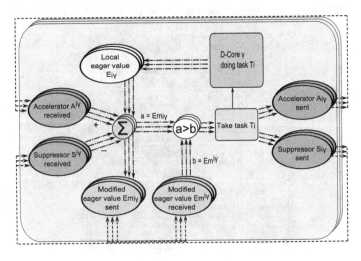

Fig. 2. Basic Hormone Balancing Control Loop

superscripted indices signifies that this hormone is dedicated to and will be received by core γ and task T_i. A hormone of any type denoted as $H_{i\gamma}$ signifies that this hormone is sent by core γ and task T_i to other cores.

The task assignment happens in the following way: Each core periodically executes the hormone based control loop presented in Fig. 2. Core γ receives the modified eager values $Em^{i\gamma}$, suppressors $S^{i\gamma}$ and accelerators $A^{i\gamma}$ for each task T_i from each core in the network. Then, core γ computes the modified eager values $Em_{i\gamma}$ for all of its tasks by adding the received accelerators and subtracting the received suppressors from the local eager value. These modified eager values are now distributed to the other cores. If the modified eager value $Em_{i\gamma}$ on core γ is higher than all received modified eager values for task T_i, core γ decides to take this task, because it is best suited. If a task T_i is taken on core γ, it also distributes a suppressor $S_{i\gamma}$ dedicated to the same task on all other cores. This limits the number of allocations of the tasks. Depending on the strength of this suppressor, the task is taken only once or several times. Furthermore, the core distributes an accelerator $A_{i\gamma}$ to its neighbored cores to attract tasks cooperating with task T_i to neighbored cores thus forming clusters of tasks. Furthermore, local suppressors S_{loc} to indicate the load of a core and local accelerators A_{loc} to keep tasks from migrating too easily thus avoiding task oscillation exists.

· Our approach is completely decentralized and offers self-X properties:
Self-configuration in terms of finding an initial task allocation by exchanging hormones, *self-optimization* by task reallocation when hormone levels change, and *self-healing* by automatic task reassignment. In terms of self-healing, our approach offers the opportunity of both, reactive and proactive system behavior [2]. Since reactive self-healing covers the system's capability in automatic task reassignment in case of core and task crashes, proactive self-healing adapts an task assignment with respect to general failures (not only crashes) and failure sources on cores in order to prevent crashing. The main idea is to emit local suppressor hormones reflecting the current level of failures and failure risk on a core. These failure suppressors rebalance the hormone levels in a way that tasks are assigned more likely to cores with low failure rates or risks. Based on that, we implemented further suppressors for single event errors, temperature and aging. The error suppressor is based on the error history of a task and is used for any type of task error. The temperature suppressor is linked to the current temperature of a core, because high temperature is considered to increase the failure risk. The aging suppressor represents the degradation of a core which becomes affected by negative bias temperature instability (NBTI), hot carrier instability (HCI) etc. The detection of single event, temperature and aging related errors is performed via core monitoring. Within this, task error detection uses parity check of internal data paths and shadowing of register files. Furthermore, several core execution units (e.g. ALU) use multi-path execution to detect errors during calculation (wrong task results). Degradation is detected through monitor circuits for e.g., output stages which measure the input-output voltage difference of transistors threshold voltage. The temperature level can be monitored via heat sensors for e.g., ring-oscillators spread on the chip.

In addition, the self-configuration is real-time capable. Tight upper time bounds are given for self-configuration, these are presented in detail in [3,1]. The hormone loop is stable as long as for each task the sum of suppressors is bigger than the sum of accelerators. The derived stability rules guide as well the proper selection of initial hormone values.

4 AHS and the Analog Domain

To extend the AHS to the analog domain, the characteristics and properties of the analog cores need to be incorporated into the concept of the hormone system as well. We will present two concepts to transfer the AHS to handle analog cores and to furthermore transfer the hormone signal processing in the analog domain.

4.1 Analog Artificial Hormone System

The Analog Artificial Hormone System (AAHS), is the concept of the AHS using pure analog components. The hormone is not a message anymore, which is broadcasted at the network of the SoC, but a signal put on the wires connecting analog cores on the SoC. The hormone level has to be remodeled as a voltage or a current.

The iteration steps are replaced by continuous time operation. The core γ constantly receives signals and is constantly deciding, whether to take or leave the task T_i. Leaving it results in no change at all. However, as soon as the task T_i is taken, two actions are performed. The global accelerator/suppressor signal is pulled down globally, to prevent other cores from taking the task. In order to reduce the signaling, accelerator and suppressors are modeled on one wire using either positive or negative values. While the global accelerator/suppressor signal is pulled down, the local accelerator/suppressor signal is drawn up to keep the task running. Otherwise the core would drop the already taken task immediately. Different time constants for both loops are needed and can be easily established in the analog design process. This decision process is done continuously for every hormone the core is assigned to. Due to this continuous character of the AAHS, tasks on a core are selected simultaneously in time. Hence the reaction time of the hormone system could be relaxed. The analog circuit implementation has not to be very fast and can therefore be power efficient. The signal can either be voltage- or current-based. Both options have slightly different hardware architecture due to their addition principles of voltages and/or currents. However, the basic principle in decentralized task assignment stays and it implements self-X properties, too.

4.2 Artificial Hormone System with Analog Components

Another approach is the Artificial Hormone System with Analog components (AHS-A). This approach is an adaptation of the digital AHS to control analog cores (AHS-A). The hormone system is implemented in the simple digital way described above. To connect to the analog cores, analog-digital-converters (ADC) and digital-analog-converters (DAC) are needed for communication. In the simplest form, these converters are 1-bit converters to transport the *take task* and *health status* from the digital to the analog domain and vice versa. However, more detailed information about the *health status* can be coded with more bits into the local eager value to improve the task balancing on slightly

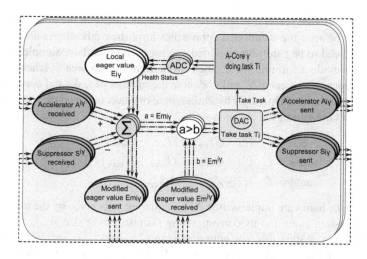

Fig. 3. Hormone based control loop for analog cores (AHS-A)

degraded analog cores. Fig. 3 shows the hormone cycle of this artificial hormone system
with analog components.

The core γ, more precisely the hormone loop *decision stage* of the core is still dealing with digital hormone processing. After the decision is done, the information within
the hormone is translated into a signal for the analog core. Therefore, AHS-A is a
mixed-signal hormone system, using AHS as its base and integrating analog components. According to digital AHS, self-X features, especially the self-optimization and
self-healing criterion, is met. Noise, stability and other analog signal processing issues
are mostly avoided, since the major part of the AHS is still digital.

4.3 Mixed-signal SoC with Digital and Analog Cores

The next question is how to join the hormone systems for digital and analog cores.
Regarding the AHS and the AAHS, the simplest solution is to run both independently.
Self-X properties are still offered on both domains, but with no communication and
hence no coordination of tasks throughout the systems. This leads to a violation of the
self-optimization and self-healing concept with respect to tasks which would be able
to migrate between analog and digital cores (e.g. Filtering Tasks or PWM vs. direct
analog. Limitations in task migration across both domains lowers the system's flexibility towards a real mixed-signal approach. To respond to this violation of the self-
optimization criteria within an implementation of independently working AAHS and
AHS, the hormone system need to be cut down to one again. Therefore the analog cores
need to be connected to the digital hormone system, which is done using the AHS-A.
Within this, the analog and digital cores are connected by a unique digital hormone
system, while hormones are transformed to the analog domain within each analog core.
On the downside, this rises the complexity. Furthermore, to allow task migration between analog and digital cores, a sophisticated data switching methodology is provided
to maintain task communication besides hormones. If a task migrates from a digital to

an analog core or vice versa, it is still able to communicate with the other cooperating tasks. As can be seen the mentioned approaches have their advantages and disadvantages, which need to be carefully weighted against each other. For example, equations 1, 2, and 3 provide a formula for a quick estimation in chip area overhead for each approach. Uppercase letters of T and C denote the number of tasks and cores, while Z represents the amount of OpAmp's to administrate one task on one core and D denotes the amount of OpAmps of the decision-unit.

$$ahs = C \cdot ((T \cdot G_{reg}) + G_{ahs}) \cdot A_{gate} \tag{1}$$

$$ahs\text{-}a = C \cdot ((T \cdot G_{reg}) + G_{ahs} + G_{env}) \cdot A_{gate} \tag{2}$$

$$aahs = C \cdot ((T \cdot Z) + D) \cdot A_{opamp} \tag{3}$$

The chip area of hardware implemented AHS (equation 1) is given by the total amount of required system gates and its corresponding manufacturing size A_{gate} of one gate within the design. Within this, the notion of both G_{reg} and G_{ahs} represents the local gate count for the self-synchronized hormone loop mechanism implemented in hardware on one core. Thereby, G_{ahs} denotes the gate count of the loop logic (adders, subtracters, comparators etc.). The notion G_{reg} represents gate count of the register overhead (cycle and accumulation registers) required for each task on one core. The parameter A_{gate} depends on the chosen processing technology (e.g, 180nm).

Table 1. Comparison of the proposed hormone system implementations

	AHS	AAHS	AHS-A
gates/ OP's	23.360	120 OpAmp's	24.040
needed chip area	$0.284mm^2$	$0.360mm^2$	$0.293mm^2$
percentage of core	12.75%	18.75%	13.1%
min. self-config. time	613.5 ns	$5\mu s$	735.75 ns
min. communication time	20 ns	$1\mu s$	20 ns
min. cycle time	122.3 ns	$5\mu s$	145.75 ns

According to the equations 1, 2, and 3 with $T = 5$, $Z = 2$, $C = 10$, $D = 2$, $G_{reg} = 384$, $G_{ahs} = 416$ and $G_{env} = 68$, estimated by a 180nm CMOS processing technology of Xilinx Inc., considering the total amount of system NAND gates within the design netlist, each given with 2 inputs and at least $12.2\mu m^2$. Percentage of core within AHS, AHS-A considers the use of MB-Lite RISC processing cores.

The chip area needed for AHS-A is calculated by extending equation 1 for hardware based AHS slightly. Thereby, just the overhead in gate count for required hormone translation between both domains of analog and digital is added to already estimated gate count for each core (Fig. 3). Therefore, the notion G_{env} denotes the number of gates required for simple ADC/DAC converters.

A comparison between all approaches is shown in Table 1, considering a SoC example chip with 10 cores and an occurrence of 5 possible tasks for each core. All implementations are feasible. Especially AAHS in combination with AHS, although disabling analog/digital migrations, has a few key points, which makes it still interesting for further consideration.

5 Evaluation

In cause of the nonstandard design, requiring a dynamic virtual environment of mixed-signal cores, regular evaluation tools are very slow. Hence for further analysis, a self implemented hormone simulator application for the AHS has been developed [4] and extended to incorporate analog cores and corresponding hormones. Besides the capability of simulating a dynamic processing grid, containing multiple mixed signal cores, the provision of self-X properties is realized. As a test scenario we used the assignment of 16 different tasks upon a grid arrangement of 4x4 heterogeneous cores. The evaluation focuses on self-healing of dynamic failures during runtime. As a reference, we first run a simulation with deactivated self-healing. After the self-configuration process the hormone cycle was deactivated. Failures caused by single event upsets, aging and temperature effects have been created by a stochastic process according to corresponding failure models described. During simulation, transient and permanent failures leading to task or core crashes are considered. Fig. 4 shows the result.

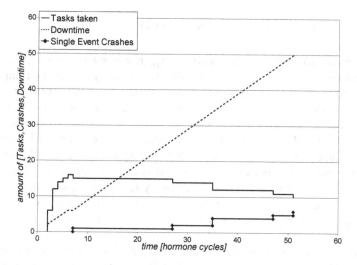

Fig. 4. Behavior of 16 AHS cores with deactivated self-healing

After system startup, all 16 tasks are allocated by self-configuration. This process is finished at hormone cycle 6, so at that time the system is operational. Already at hormone cycle 7 the first failure, a single event upset, crashed one task. More task crashes due to single event upsets followed at hormone cycles 25, 37, 47 and 51 further reducing the number of active tasks. No aging or temperature based failures occurred up to that point in time. So, starting from hormone cycle 7 the system is no longer operational as can be seen by the linearly increasing system downtime (single dotted line) resulting in a downtime ratio of $50/51 = 155/158 = 0.98 = 98\%$ at hormone cycle 51.

Fig. 5 shows the same scenario with self-healing activated by the hormone cycle. To be comparable, the stochastic process creating the failures was initialized with the

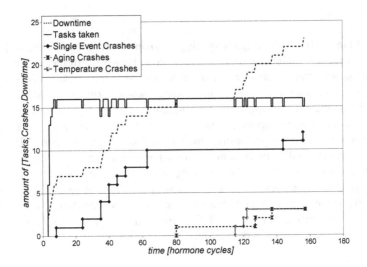

Fig. 5. Behavior of 16 AHS cores with reactive self-healing

same random seed to produce identical events. Again, the system comes operational by allocating all 16 tasks at hormone cycle 6 while at hormone cycle 7 the first single event upset occurred crashing a task. This caused the corresponding task suppressor to vanish. Due to the resulting hormone imbalance, this task is reallocated at cycle 8 bringing the system back online. The same happens for the following failures. Every time a task is crashed by a failure, the hormone system compensates this event by task reallocation or reassignment. Beginning at hormone cycle 81, aging and temperature based crashes occur as well and are compensated. Even so the system downtime still increases due to these crashes, it increase much slower and the system always comes back online, as long as enough cores are available to take all tasks (either by other cores or regeneration of the crashed cores). The downtime ratio is $23/158 = 0.14 = 14\%$ at hormone cycle 158.

The behavior shown is a pure reactive self-healing process. To allow proactive failure handling, additional suppressors can be applied. By monitoring, e.g., failures and temperature, suppressors can be emitted for cores with high temperature or failure count. This favors reliable and cool cores in comparison to unreliable and hot ones. The major effect of this proactive reallocation behavior is shown in Fig. 6, where temperature suppressors are proportional emitted to the raising temperature load. This successively reduces the suitability (eager value) of the core until tasks get migrated to other cores. As a result of the sinking workload, the temperature and the temperature suppressor are declining. The temperature and load are balancing at a reasonable level. The proactive task assignment increases the reliability by preventing cores from total failing, using a rebalance of the workload via task distribution on different cores. The system downtime compared to the reactive simulation is reduced significantly to $14/158 = 0.089 = 8.9\%$ at hormone cycle 158.

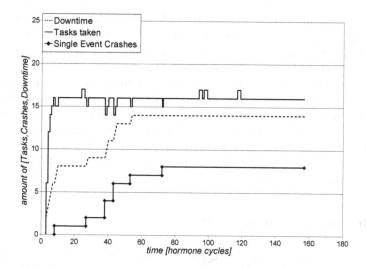

Fig. 6. Behavior of 16 AHS cores with proactive system behavior

Table 2. Comparison between none self-healing, reactive and proactive system behavior towards downtime reduction

Self-healing	Downtime	Failure/Crashes(Fig.)	
None	$155/158 = 0.98 = \mathbf{98\%}$	84/18	(4)
Reactive	$23/158 = 0.146 = \mathbf{14.6\%}$	84/18	(5)
Proactive	$14/158 = 0.089 = \mathbf{8.9\%}$	42/8	(6)

In conclusion, the evaluation shows the major advantage of the hormone cycle for task assignment. Comparing with the results of the first simulation the system achieves an excellent enhancement in downtime optimization thus improving dependability in a significant way, which is shown in Table 2.

6   Related Work

Currently there exist only a few approaches of task assignment in middleware on future CMP based mixed-signal SoC. The approach of [5] traces the assumption of a reliable multi-layered MPSoC architecture against thermal issues due to increasing task processing. This concept internalizes a proactive task migration on cooler cores by a distributed hierarchical agent-based system. It avoids single points of failure, but is restricted to thermal management domain and no mixed-signal is used. Another approach using also the assumption of an distributed agent system is shown in [6]. The author presents an algorithmic schedule for task distribution on a processing grid. In contrast to our approach, it is absolutely different using centralized elements so called Group Manager's (GM), responsible for the internal controlling in a clustered bunch of tasks. Unless a single GM-instance fails, there is no possibility for restoring the corresponding group information, which implies a single point of failure vulnerability.

With this increasing number of mixed-signal SoC, the analog part forms a bottleneck for the design. Failure models are not yet well understood and as predictable as for digital systems. This even gets worse, because of new failure mechanisms like "Hot Carrier Injection" (HCI) [7], "Negative Bias Temperature Instability" (NBTI) [8,9] or Electromigration (EM) [10]. Another aspect is aging and its effects on for example threshold voltage drifts, as shown at [11]. Recent research focuses on this and identifies circuits and its parts, which are sensitive for the reliability ([12,13]) or create tools for partly aided and automated design ([14]). Concepts of redundancy of analog components has been shown for fault-tolerant methodologies (i.e. [15]). Though, a generalized concept, that deals with redundancy, as needed for the hormone system and task allocation, has yet not been taken into account.

7 Conclusion and Future Work

In summary, this paper presented an approach of a highly dependable self-organizing mixed-signal SoC. Besides a reliable general SoC architecture using generalized cores and tasks, an artificial hormone system is used for decentralized task allocation.

In prospection and future work, further investigation upon reliability and superiority aspects especially with a real prototypic SoC hardware implementation have to be conducted to validate the simulation results and to confirm the timing behavior. Therefore, we intend the development of a real demonstrator application in the field of automotive driven assistance control. For this, the SoC is admitted controlling a complex reconnaissance and exploration vehicle used for navigation purposes. The corresponding SoC prototype will be build by distributing the different parts and components within the available SoC approaches of AHS, AAHS, and AHS-A to the corresponding related circuit domain. Then, circuit domain related techniques for rapid prototyping will be used to build up the corresponding parts (e.g. FPGA, FPAA, or breadboards). The first aim is to control the vehicle autonomously by using the SoC prototype as control unit, processing and monitoring different high class mixed-signal tasks in actoric and sensorics. As a major scientific yield, we expect validation and verification results of the functionality in real timing behavior, failure dependability, and collaborating communication as well as the workability in mixed-signal domain of the SoC.

References

1. von Renteln, A., Brinkschulte, U., Pacher, M.: The Artificial Hormone System - An Organic Middleware for Self-organising Real-Time Task Allocation. In: Organic Computing - A Paradigm Shift for Complex Systems. Springer, Basel (2011)
2. Betting, B., Pacher, M., Brinkschulte, U.: Development and Evaluation of a Self-Adaptive Organic Middleware for Highly Dependable System-on-Chips. In: 8th International Conference on Autonomic and Autonomous Systems (ICAS 2012), St. Maarten, Netherlands Antilles (March 2012)
3. Brinkschulte, U., Pacher, M., von Renteln, A.: An Artificial Hormone System for Self-Organizing Real-Time Task Allocation in Organic Middleware. In: Organic Computing. Springer (2008)

4. von Renteln, A., Weiss, M., Brinkschulte, U.: Examining Task Distribution by an Artificial Hormone System Based Middleware. In: 11th IEEE International Symposium on Object/component/service-oriented Real-time Distributed Computing (ISORC 2008), Orlando, Florida, USA, May 5-7 (2008)
5. Ebi, T., Rauchfuss, H., Herkersdorf, A., Henkel, J.: Agent-Based Thermal Management Using Real-Time I/O Communication Relocation for 3D Many-Cores. In: Ayala, J.L., García-Cámara, B., Prieto, M., Ruggiero, M., Sicard, G. (eds.) PATMOS 2011. LNCS, vol. 6951, pp. 112–121. Springer, Heidelberg (2011)
6. Bittencourt, L.F., Madeira, E.R.M., Cicerre, F.R.L., Buzato, L.E.: A path clustering heuristic for scheduling task graphs onto a grid. In: 3rd International Workshop on Middleware for Grid Computing (MGC 2005), Grenoble, France (2005)
7. Li, X., Qin, J., Huang, B., Zhang, X., Bernstein, J.: Sram circuit-failure modeling and reliability simulation with spice. IEEE Transactions on Device and Materials Reliability 6(2), 235–246 (2006)
8. Salfelder, F., Hedrich, L.: An NBTI model for efficient transient simulation of analogue circuits. In: Proc. eda Workshop 2011, pp. 27–32. VDE Verlag (2011)
9. Grasser, T., Entner, R., Triebl, O., Enichlmair, H., Minixhofer, R.: Tcad modeling of negative bias temperature instability. SISPAD, 330–333 (September 2006)
10. Papanikolaou, A., Wang, H., Miranda, M., Catthoor, F.: Reliability issues in deep deep submicron technologies: time-dependent variability and its impact on embedded system design, 121 (2007)
11. Lorenz, D., Georgakos, G., Schlichtmann, U.: Aging analysis of circuit timing considering nbti and hci. In: IOLTS 2009 (2009)
12. Jha, N.K., Reddy, P.S., Sharma, D.K., Rao, V.R.: NBTI Degradation and Its Impact for Analog Circuit Reliability. IEEE Transactions on Electron Devices 52, 2609–2615 (2005)
13. Yan, B., Fan, Q., Bernstein, J., Qin, J., Dai, J.: Reliability simulation and circuit-failure analysis in analog and mixed-signal applications. IEEE Transactions on Device and Materials Reliability 9(3), 339–347 (2009)
14. Gielen, G.: Cad tools for embedded analogue circuits in mixed-signal integrated systems on chip. IEE Proceedings Computers and Digital Techniques 152(3), 317–332 (2005)
15. Askari, S., Nourani, M.: Highly reliable analog filter design using analog voting. In: Saudi International Electronics, Communications and Photonics Conference (SIECPC), pp. 1–6 (April 2011)

Inter-warp Instruction Temporal Locality in Deep-Multithreaded GPUs

Ahmad Lashgar[1], Amirali Baniasadi[2], and Ahmad Khonsari[1,3]

[1] School of Electrical and Computer Engineering, University College of Engineering,
University of Tehran, Tehran, Iran
[2] Electrical and Computer Engineering Department, University of Victoria,
Victoria, British Columbia, Canada
[3] School of Computer Science, Institute for Research in Fundamental Sciences,
Tehran, Iran
a.lashgar@ece.ut.ac.ir, amirali@ece.uvic.ca, ak@ipm.ir

Abstract. GPUs employ thousands of threads per core to achieve high throughput. These threads exhibit localities in control-flow, instruction and data addresses and values. In this study we investigate inter-warp instruction temporal locality and show that during short intervals a significant share of fetched instructions are fetched unnecessarily. This observation provides several opportunities to enhance GPUs. We discuss different possibilities and evaluate filter cache as a case study. Moreover, we investigate how variations in microarchitectural parameters impacts potential filter cache benefits in GPUs.

Keywords: Multi-threaded processors, Energy-efficient design, Pipeline front-end.

1 Introduction

Innovative microarchitectural solutions have used locality to enhance processor performance in several ways (e.g., caches, branch predictors, etc). Many studies have investigated locality in CPUs. Locality in GPUs [3], however, has not received the same level of attention.

In this study we explore Inter-warp Instruction Temporal Locality (or simply ITL). ITL represents our observation that a small number of static instructions account for a significant portion of dynamic instructions fetched and decoded during short intervals and within the same stream multiprocessor. We investigate ITL among threads and show how GPUs come with ample ITL.

An important issue contributing to ITL in GPUs is deep multi-threading. GPUs achieve high throughput by employing and interleaving thousands of threads per core. Threads are grouped into coarser independent schedulable elements (called warps) to achieve both scheduling simplicity and SIMD efficiency. The warp scheduler issues instructions from different warps back-to-back filling the pipeline effectively. This pipeline organization amplifies ITL by fetching the same instruction for all warps during short intervals.

C. Hochberger et al. (Eds.): ARCS 2013, LNCS 7767, pp. 134–146, 2012.
© Springer-Verlag Berlin Heidelberg 2012

Moreover, we have observed that the chances of accessing a recently fetched instruction again are higher in GPUs compared to CPUs. For example, our evaluation shows the likelihood of fetching the same instruction within a 64-cycle period is 67% in CPUs. This grows to 82% in GPUs (see Section 5.1 for methodology).

Each generation of GPUs has superseded the precedent generation by increasing the number of executed warps (also referred to as multi-threading depth) and SIMD width. It is expected that deep multithreading will continue to serve an important role in performance growth in GPUs in upcoming years. Therefore, we expect the current trend in ITL in GPUs to continue in near future.

In this work, we list different opportunities to improve energy efficiency in GPUs by exploiting ITL. In particular and as a case study, we evaluate energy savings achievable under filter caches [12] in GPUs. As we show, employing a filter cache eliminates a significant share of the instruction cache accesses, improving the fetch engine's energy efficiency.

The rest of the paper is organized as follows. In Section 2 we study related works. In Section 3 we present the pipeline front-end of GPU microarchitectures and review ITL. We investigate our case study in Section 4. We present experimental setup and simulation results in Section 5. Finally, in Section 6 we offer concluding remarks.

2 Related Works

Locality studies (data or instruction) in GPUs have received less attention compared to CPUs. Collange et al [5] studied data locality in registers and found that register values often appear uniform across threads of a warp. They introduced dynamic mechanisms detecting up to 19% of the register values as uniform. Their mechanism can be exploited to reduce the number of accesses to the register file or reduce the size of vector register file. Gebhart et al [7] observed that the written registers are often read last within three instructions after the write. They introduce a register file cache to reduce the number of accesses to the conventional power-hungry register file. Moreover, to prevent heavy contention on register file cache, they introduce a two-level warp scheduler. At the first-level they maintain a few active warps. At the second-level other inactive warps are stored. Each warp at the first-level has a few registers in the cache. The scheduler issues instructions from these warps for as long as possible. Once a warp at the first-level stalls on the completion of a long latency instruction (due to operand dependency), the scheduler replaces it with a ready warp from the second-level. The mechanism effectively saves 36% of register file power, which translates to 3.8% of chip dynamic power.

Collagne et al. [4] stressed different NVIDIA GPUs by various workloads to reveal the effect of workload on GPU power. They evaluated power for different number of SIMD processors and reported energy per memory access and energy per ALU instruction. Hong and Kim [10] observed that the optimal performance/watt differs for various types of workloads, depending on the number of active cores. They introduced a performance-power model to predict the optimal number of cores for achieving the best performance/watt dynamically. They also reported the contribution of each architectural module to the dynamic power. They found that GPU's front-end

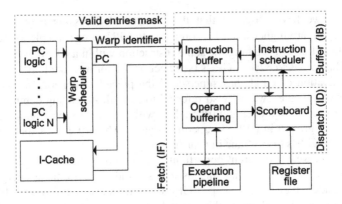

Fig. 1. The microarchitecture of SM's front-end

(fetch, decode, and scheduling) accounts for 18% of GPU's dynamic power. Zhang et al. [21] used a static regression-based model to analyze the performance and power of AMD/ATI GPUs. The analysis shows which units are the most critical to performance and power in GPUs. They found that the fetch engine accounts for 12% of the GPU power and is the 4th among the most important parameters contributing to GPU power. VLIW usage, ALU instructions, and global memory accesses are the other top important parameters. Kasichayanula [11] evaluated two schemes for measuring power in GPUs . In the hardware approach, he used external devices to measure GPU power. In the software approach, NVIDIA NVML library is employed to measure power using GPU performance counters.

3   Observation

3.1   Background

We assume a GPU-like SIMT (Single-Instruction Multiple-Thread) accelerator similar to NVIDIA Tesla. 16 8-wide stream multiprocessors (SM) are connected to six memory controllers through an on-chip crossbar interconnection network. Each SM maintains the context of 1024 concurrent threads. These threads are grouped into coarser independent-schedulable warps. Threads within a warp are executed in an SIMD lock-step manner.

Each SM employs a 24-stage SIMD pipeline for most instructions. In this work, we model the pipeline front-end according to NVIDIA's patents [14, 6, 15]. As shown in Figure 1, SM pipeline front-end consists of three stages: Instruction Fetch (IF), Instruction Buffer (IB), and Instruction Dispatch (ID). IF selects and fetches instructions from concurrent warps. IB buffers the instructions to resolve data dependencies. ID fetches the operands for dependency-free instructions and issues them to the execution pipeline. Below we review each stage in more details.

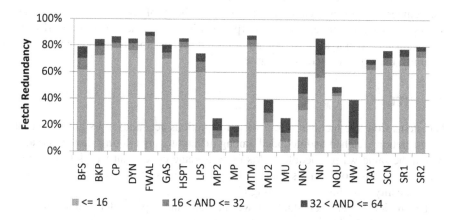

Fig. 2. Fetch redundancy among concurrent warps of SMs during 16, 32, and 64 recent fetches for different benchmarks

Instruction Fetch. IF uses per warp logic to determine the next warp instruction PC, followed by fetching the corresponding instruction through I-Cache. The baseline warp scheduler uses the round-robin policy among warps to select the next instruction from the instruction pool.

IF resolves control dependences among warp instructions using the PC logic module. This module stalls the warp upon a pending branch. PC logic also determines the next active PC of the warp. IF takes one cycle to select the PC and fetch the corresponding instruction from I-Cache to the IB stage if I-Cache hits.

After an instruction is fetched, the warp scheduler sends it to an empty field in the instruction buffer in the next cycle. This empty field is reserved at fetch time and therefore the fetched instruction always finds an empty instruction buffer entry.

Instruction Buffer. Data dependency is resolved through scoreboarding. Instructions communicate only through the register file and operand forwarding is not supported. Once the scoreboard marks the instruction as ready, the scheduler can select the instruction to proceed. The instruction scheduler used at this stage uses round-robin policy.

Instruction Dispatch. ID buffers collect register operands from highly banked register files [15] and issue instructions to the pipeline's back-end as soon as all operands are buffered.

We assume a scoreboard structure similar to [6]. Each scoreboard entry is associated with a different warp and points to the registers having a pending value. This information is maintained at the register region granularity. Each register region is identified using a base (register ID) and an offset (number of register after the base). Each scoreboard entry can keep track of 6 register regions. Scoreboard stalls an instruction due to a RAW/WAR dependency if the input/output operands of the instruction belong to a register region in the warp's scoreboard entry. Note that a warp is stalled if all of its register regions are taken in the scoreboard. Therefore increasing the number of register regions reduces the probability of warp stalls. Our evaluation shows that six register regions per warp are enough to achieve maximum ILP under the evaluated workloads and the employed in-order pipeline. Once an instruction commits, the register region is released.

3.2   ITL

ITL stems from the fact that a few static instructions account for a significant portion of instructions fetched and decoded among different warps during short intervals and within the same warp scheduler. SMs often execute concurrent warps from the same kernel code. Moreover, the scheduler keeps the warps at the same pace to improve cache locality [13], further increasing ITL.

To provide better understanding we measure and report fetch redundancy as an indication of ITL. Fetch redundancy reports the percentage of instructions already fetched by other currently active warps recently. We measure fetch redundancy in different recency windows (16, 32, and 64). We present our findings in Figure 2.

Average fetch redundancy is 53%, 59%, and 67%for recency window sizes of 16, 32, and 64, respectively. Highly parallel benchmarks, which employ a high number of blocks per grid with a few branch divergences (e.g., CP, HSPT, and NN), show higher fetch redundancy. Other benchmarks, which have fewer concurrent warps (e.g., GAS, SR2, and NW), or more diverging branches (e.g., MP2, MP, MU2, MU, NQU), exhibit less fetch redundancy.

3.3   Exploiting ITL

In this section, we briefly go over possible power and performance benefits achievable using ITL in GPUs.

Fetch/Decode Bypassing. Loop buffering stores the decoded word of loop instructions in a dedicated buffer and skips fetch/decode as long as the thread proceeds inside the loop [9]. The challenge in CPUs is to find loop boundaries effectively and fitting the entire loop in the buffer. GPUs can take advantage of bypassing by storing the most recent decoded warp instructions and reusing them later by other warps.

Reducing the Size of Instruction Buffer. We have observed that for ~42% of instruction fetches, the corresponding decoded instruction already exists in the instruction buffer (in the entries dedicated to other warps). The instruction fetch/decode process can be bypassed by reading the decoded word from the instruction buffer. A more efficient alternative is to share similar entries among warps to reduce instruction buffer size.

Reducing Accesses to I-Cache. ITL can be used to filter accesses to I-Cache. This can be done by using a filter cache or row buffer [12]. Filter cache uses temporal locality to reduce cache miss rate by storing the most recent fetched instructions. Row buffer stores the last accessed I-Cache block (row) and serves fetch requests for blocks residing in the buffer. In the next section we evaluate energy saving opportunities provided by filter cache.

4   Using ITL Case Study in GPUs: Filter Cache

Exploiting filter caches (FC) in current GPUs requires minor modifications to the baseline pipeline front-end (described in section 3.1). FC is probed using the next program counter (PC) to fetch. If the instruction look-up hits during FC tag check, the following I-Cache access is prevented, else the instruction is fetched through the conventional path from I-Cache. Missing instructions update FC later.

Table 1. Front-end area, leakage power, read/write energy, and access delay measured by CACTI [16]

	Area (μm²)	Leakage (mW)	Energy per R/W (pJ)	Delay (ps)
I-Cache tag	229	0.03	0.13	115.94
I-Cache data	18204	1.78	4.30	221.20
Instruction Buf.	2600	0.16	1.00	137.59
Scoreboard	6921	0.24	1.57	162.17
Operand Buf.	24173	0.53	4.16	174.05
FC tag (32-entry)	266	0.03	0.14	117.28
FC data (32-entry)	2229	0.11	0.81	161.76
FC tag (16-entry)	155	0.02	0.10	105.47
FC data (16-entry)	1337	0.05	0.57	143.38

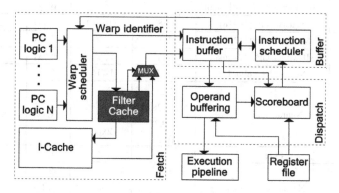

Fig. 3. Modifications made to the instruction fetch stage to implement an FC-enhanced SM

Microarchitecture. Figure 3 shows an FC-enhanced front-end design. The modifications are highlighted over the baseline pipeline microarchitecture. FC is a cache-like structure consisting of two parts, i.e., FC check and FC fetch. FC check is similar to a tag array and compares the incoming PC tags against earlier stored tags. Upon a match, FC forwards the bypass signal to the fetch circuit and prevents instruction fetching. Bypass signal activates FC fetch and sends the instructions associated with the matched PC to the next stage through the multiplexer. Upon a mismatch, the front-end follows the conventional approach.

Timing. Using an FC imposes two delays: FC tag check and multiplexer. Upon FC check hit, fetch stage faces the following delay:

(Warp scheduling) + (FC check) + (FC fetch) + (MUX)

Upon FC mismatch, the delay is:

(Warp scheduling) + (FC check) + (I-Cache) + (MUX)

Table 2. Benchmark characteristics. CTA/SM indicates the maximum number of concurrent blocks per SM which is limited by both parallelism and occupancy.

Abbr.	Name and Suite	Grid Size	Block Size	#Insn	CTA/SM
BFS	BFS Graph [2]	16x(8)	16x(512)	1.4M	1
BKP	Back Propagation [2]	2x(1,64)	2x(16,16)	2.9M	4
CP	Coulumb Poten. [19]	(8,32)	(16,8)	113M	8
DYN	Dyn_Proc [2]	13x(35)	13x(256)	64M	4
FWAL	Fast Wal. Trans. [18]	6x(32) 3x(16) (128)	7x(256) 3x(512)	11M	2, 4
GAS	Gaussian Elimin. [2]	48x(3,3)	48x(16,16)	9M	1
HSPT	Hotspot [2]	(43,43)	(16,16)	76M	2
LPS	Laplace 3D [1]	(4,25)	(32,4)	81M	6
MP2	MUMmer-GPU++ [8] big	(196)	(256)	139M	2
MP	MUMmer-GPU++ [8] small	(1)	(256)	0.3M	1
MTM	Matrix Multiply [18]	(5,8)	(16,16)	2.4M	4
MU2	MUMmer-GPU [2] big	(196)	(256)	75M	4
MU	MUMmer-GPU [2] small	(1)	(100)	0.2M	1
NNC	Nearest Neighbor [2]	4x(938)	4x(16)	5.9M	8
NN	Neural Network [1]	(6,28) (25,28) (100,28) (10,28)	(13,13) (5,5) 2x(1)	68M	5, 8
NQU	N-Queen [1]	(256)	(96)	1.2M	1
NW	Needleman-Wun. [2]	2x(1) ... 2x(31) (32)	63x(16)	12M	2
RAY	Ray Tracing [1]	(16,32)	(16,8)	64M	3
SCN	Scan [18]	(64)	(256)	3.6M	4
SR1	Speckle Reducing [2] big	4x(8,8)	4x(16,16)	9.5M	2, 3
SR2	Speckle Reducing [2] small	4x(4,4)	4x(16,16)	2.4M	1

Our study shows that MUX delay is negligible compared to the rest and can be ignored. Table 1 reports the access latency of FC tag, FC data, I-Cache tag, and I-Cache data. IF delay for FC check hit/miss scenario is 0.28ns/0.45ns plus warp scheduling delay. The evaluated front-end runs under 1.3 GHz (0.77ns clock period). For warp scheduling delays below 0.32 ns (0.77 ns - 0.45 ns), FC-enhanced SM does not impose extra cycles. Under the pessimistic scenario where warp scheduling's delay exceeds 0.32 ns, IF should be pipelined into two stages. Under such circumstances, warp scheduling and FC check are done at the first stage. The second stage decides whether to fetch the instruction from FC or I-Cache. This design

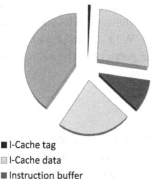

- ■ I-Cache tag
- ▨ I-Cache data
- ■ Instruction buffer
- ☐ Scoreboard
- ▨ Operand Collector and buffering

Fig. 4. SM's front-end energy breakdown

Table 3. Baseline configurations for GPGPU-sim

NoC	
#SMs : #Memory Ctrls	16 : 6
#SM Sharing a Network Interface	2
Clocking	
Core	1300 MHz
Interconnect	650 MHz
DRAM	800 MHz
Memory	
#Banks Per Memory Ctrls	8
DRAM Scheduling Policy	FCFS
SM	
Warp size : SIMD width	32 : 8
Thread/SM	1024
Register file : Shared memory	64KB : 16KB

extends the pipeline depth by a cycle compared to the baseline resulting in a performance loss less than 1%.

Hardware Overhead. FC- enhanced SM requires two auxiliary structures. First, a multiplexer is used to select between two 64-bit instruction words. Second, additional storage is needed for the FC module to temporarily store a small number of instructions. Our simulations show that a 32-entry FC captures a significant share of fetch redundancy. The 32-entry FC imposes 4.7% area overhead compared to a conventional pipeline front-end.

5   Experiments

5.1   Methodology

We used GPGPU-sim v2.1.1b [1] to model the baseline architecture described in Section 3. We configured GPGPU-sim with the parameters shown in Table 3. We have extended GPGPU-sim to model the discussed FC-enhanced pipeline front-end. We extended the simulator to model 4KB 4-way 4-set [20] I-Cache per SM (32 8-byte instructions per line). On a cache miss, the associated warp is stalled for 300 cycles to access the cache block in global memory. Requests from different warps are merged through I-Cache per warp MSHRs. We used benchmarks from Rodinia benchmark suite [2], CUDA SDK 2.3 [18], Parboil [19], and the benchmarks distributed with GPGPU-sim. We also included the MUMmerGPU++ [8] third-party sequence alignment program. Table 3 shows benchmarks' characteristics.

We report both static and dynamic power. We use CACTI 6.5 [16] to estimate the power dissipation, area, and latency of an FC-enhanced SM compared to the baseline under 32nm technology. For small sized modules, like the operand collector, we scaled the number linearly to extrapolate the parameters. We extracted 6 samples of larger caches (keeping I/O bits, associativity, and other parameters the same) from CACTI to find the line's parameters.

5.2   Experimental Results

In this section, we first report the energy breakdown of the baseline architecture. Then we report the percentage of I-Cache accesses filtered by FC and the associated energy savings. Finally, we evaluate filter caches under various microarchitectural changes.

Energy Breakdown. Figure 4 presents the energy breakdown for the SM pipeline front-end for the evaluated workloads. The operand collector and the associated buffering are the most energy consuming parts accounting for 40% of dynamic power. I-Cache, which is the target of this case study, is second, accounting for 27%.

FC Hit Rate. Table 4 reports FC hit rate, which is equal to percentage of the I-Cache accesses filtered. FC check hit rate reaches a maximum of ~100%. Hit rate is above 60% for coherent control-flow compute-intensive workloads like CP, DYN, HSPT, LPS, and MTM. FC shows lower hit rate in control-flow intensive workloads with high branch divergence (e.g., MU2, and MP2). This is due to the fact that these benchmarks exhibit lower ITL as warps often follow different diverging paths. Hit rate is also low for workloads with limited warp-level parallelism (MU, NW, MP, SR2, and NQU). Lower number of concurrent warps reduces the chance of instruction reuse and consequently FC hit rate.

Energy Saving. Table 1 reports die area, leakage power, read/write energy per access, and access latency for modules with significant energy contribution in the pipeline front-end. We assume two ports per I-Cache and FC caches, one read port and one write port. Using a 32-entry FC cache, front-end static power increases by 5.0%. Assuming 16KB register file (7.46 mW leakage), 16KB shared data cache (5.80 mW leakage), 5KB texture cache (1.93 mW leakage), and 2KB L1 constant cache (0.82 mW leakage) per SM, FC imposes less than 0.7% leakage power per SM.

Table 4. FC energy saving compared to the baseline as measured by CACTI [16]

	FC hit rate	Baseline I-Cache energy (nJ)	I-Cache + FC energy (nJ)	Front-end energy-saving using FC
BFS	97%	644.11	270.93	12%
BKP	96%	500.14	216.86	9%
CP	100%	16532.20	6616.15	7%
DYN	93%	9882.86	4435.14	8%
FWAL	96%	1730.16	740.77	8%
GAS	87%	1218.70	592.08	7%
HSPT	89%	12076.70	5676.64	8%
LPS	83%	14955.05	7625.97	8%
MP2	33%	67872.12	57354.82	2%
MP	30%	161.40	139.78	2%
MTM	95%	347.37	153.66	8%
MU2	49%	43099.85	31846.11	5%
MU	39%	100.32	81.10	4%
NNC	76%	1718.39	963.81	10%
NN	99%	132820.86	53780.92	19%
NQU	50%	217.81	159.97	5%
NW	70%	5627.29	3356.63	10%
RAY	76%	10520.69	5945.77	6%
SCN	97%	562.47	240.70	9%
SR1	87%	1430.76	699.11	8%
SR2	84%	368.94	189.63	7%

In Table 4, we report the dynamic energy consumption of the baseline I-Cache compared to the FC-enhanced design (I-Cache + FC). As reported, FC can reduce I-Cache energy from 13% (MP) to 60% (CP). This translates to from 2% (MP benchmark) to 19% (NN benchmark) of the overall pipeline front-end dynamic energy reduction. Assuming an 18% overall energy share for the front-end [10], an FC-enhanced GPU saves up to 3.4% of the dynamic energy.

Sensitivity Analysis. In this section we report FC hit rate and energy reduction under variations in multithreading depth, FC size, and warp scheduler. We evaluate filter caches for 512 threads per SM, 16-entry FC, and a two-level warp scheduler [17] as an alternative to our baseline 32-entry FC, 1024 threads per SM, and round-robin warp scheduler.

Employing the two-level scheduler improves memory latency hiding. Two-level scheduler divides the warps into multiple fetch groups and gives the highest priority to the warps belonging to the fetch group of the last issued warp. This mechanism can hide the memory accesses made in one fetch group using the computations of other fetch groups. We choose 8 warps per fetch group to achieve maximum latency hiding.

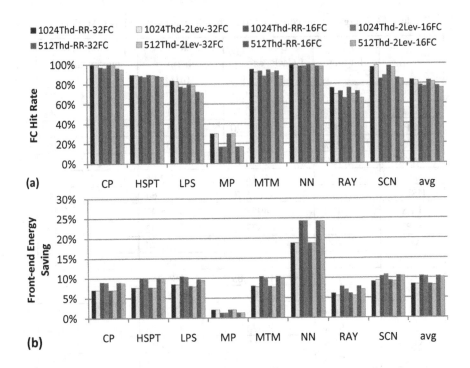

Fig. 5. Sensitivity for a) FC hit rate and b) front-end energy reduction to the multithreading depth (1024 and 512), warp scheduling policy (RR for round-robin and 2Lev for two-level scheduler), and FC size (32 and 16) for different benchmarks.

Figure 5 reports FC hit rate and front-end energy reduction for different combinations: multithreading depth (1024, and 512), FC sizes (32, and 16), and warp schedulers (RR, and 2Lev). In the interest of space we report average and a few representative benchmarks.

Multithreading Depth. Reducing multithreading depth is expected to reduce ITL. CP, LPS, and SCN are among the benchmarks that have enough parallelism to run more than 512 threads per SM. As reported, reducing multithreading depth to 512 threads reduces FC hit rate up to 6% (in LPS) compared to 1024 threads per SM but has minor impact on energy reduction.

Warp Scheduler. We expect to see lower FC hit rate under 2Lev compared to RR under fixed FC size and multithreading depth. This is because 2Lev keeps the warps of different fetch groups at different paces reducing the ITL. As reported, 2Lev often impacts FC hit rate but insignificantly.

FC Size. Among the parameters studied here, FC size has the highest impact. Lower FC size reduces FC hit rate. However, smaller FC comes with lower energy overhead.

As reported, a 16-entry FC has a lower FC hit rate (on average of 9% to 10% percent) compared to a 32-entry. However, since the 16-entry consumes less energy, it still shows higher energy reduction.

6   Conclusion

In this study we showed that there is high temporal instruction locality in GPU microarchitectures for general-purpose computations. Concurrent warps fetch and decode the same instruction frequently providing an opportunity to design a more efficient pipeline front-end. We suggested different possibilities to exploit this locality to improve performance, energy, and area. We investigated filter cache as a case study. We found that a simple direct-map filter cache per SM can eliminate 30% to ~100% of I-Cache requests reducing pipeline front-end energy up to 19%. We have evaluated our results under various microarchitectural changes including multithreading depth, warp scheduling, and filter cache size.

Acknowledgement. The authors like to thank anonymous reviewers. This work was partially supported by School of Computer Science at Institute for Research in Fundamental Sciences (IPM).

References

1. Bakhoda, A., Yuan, G.L., Fung, W.W.L., Wong, H., Aamodt, T.M.: Analyzing CUDA workloads using a detailed GPU simulator. In: Proc. of ISPASS 2009, pp. 163–174 (2009)
2. Che, S., Boyer, M., Meng, J., Tarjan, D., Sheaffer, J.W., Sang-Ha, L., Skadron, K.: Rodinia: A benchmark suite for heterogeneous computing. In: Proc. of IEEE International Symposium on Workload Characterization (IISWC), pp. 44–54 (2009)
3. Collagne, S.: Exploiting all forms of parallel locality in many-thread architectures. ALF Research Group Seminar, IRISA, Rennes (December 21, 2011)
4. Collange, S., Defour, D., Tisserand, A.: Power Consumption of GPUs from a Software Perspective. In: Proc. of the 9th International Conference on Computational Science (ICCS), pp. 914–923 (2009)
5. Collange, S., Defour, D., Zhang, Y.: Dynamic Detection of Uniform and Affine Vectors in GPGPU Computations. In: Lin, H.-X., Alexander, M., Forsell, M., Knüpfer, A., Prodan, R., Sousa, L., Streit, A. (eds.) Euro-Par 2009. LNCS, vol. 6043, pp. 46–55. Springer, Heidelberg (2010)
6. Coon, B.W., Mills, P.C., Oberman, S.F., Siu, M.Y.: Tracking register usage during multithreaded processing using a scoreboard. United States Patent, Patent number: 7434032
7. Gebhart, M., Johnson, D.R., Tarjan, D., Keckler, S.W., Dally, W.J., Lindholm, E., Skadron, K.: Energy-efficient mechanisms for managing thread context in throughput processors. In: Proc. of the 38th Annual International Symposium on Computer Architecture (ISCA), pp. 235–246 (2011)
8. Gharaibeh, A., Ripeanu, M.: Size Matters: Space/Time Tradeoffs to Improve GPGPU Applications Performance. In: Proc. of ACM/IEEE International Conference for High Performance Computing, Networking, Storage and Analysis, pp. 1–12 (2010)

9. Hiraki, M., Bajwa, R.S., Kojima, H., Gorny, D.J., Nitta, K., Shri, A.: Stage-skip pipeline: a low power processor architecture using a decoded instruction buffer. In: International Symposium on Low Power Electronics and Design, pp. 353–358 (1996)

10. Hong, S., Kim, H.: An Integrated GPU Power and Performance Model. In: Proc. of ISCA 2010, pp. 280–289 (2010)

11. Kasichayanula, K.K.: Power Aware Computing on GPUs. Master Thesis Dissertation, University of Tennessee, Knoxville (May 2012)

12. Kin, J., Gupta, M., Mangione-Smith, W.H.: The filter cache: an energy efficient memory structure. In: Proc. of MICRO 1997, pp. 184–193 (1997)

13. Lindholm, J.E., Coon, B.W., Wierzbicki, J., Stoll, R.J., Oberman, S.F.: Credit-Based Streaming Multiprocessor Warp Scheduling. United States Patent, application number: 12/885,299

14. Lindholm, J.E., Coon, B.W., Moy, S.S.: Across-thread out-of-order instruction dispatch in a multithreaded microprocessor. United States Patent, Patent number: 7676657

15. Liu, S., Lindholm, J.E., Siu, M.Y., Coon, B.W., Oberman, S.F.: Operand collector architecture. United States Patent, Patent number: 7834881

16. Muralimanohar, N., Balasubramonian, R., Jouppi, N.: Optimizing NUCA Organizations and Wiring Alternatives for Large Caches with CACTI 6.0. In: Proc. of MICRO 2007, pp. 3–14 (2007)

17. Narasiman, V., Shebanow, M., Lee, C.J., Miftakhutdinov, R., Mutlu, O., Patt, Y.N.: Improving GPU performance via large warps and two-level warp scheduling. In: Proc. of MICRO 2011, pp. 308–317 (2011)

18. NVIDIA Corp. NVIDIA CUDA SDK 2.3

19. Stratton, J.A., Rodrigues, C., Sung, I.J., Obeid, N., Chang, L.W., Anssari, N., Liu, G.D., Hwu, W.M.W.: Parboil: A Revised Benchmark Suite for Scientific and Commercial Throughput Computing. IMPACT Technical Report (2012)

20. Wong, H., Papadopoulou, M.M., Sadooghi-Alvandi, M., Moshovos, A.: Demystifying GPU microarchitecture through microbenchmarking. In: Proc. of ISPASS 2010, pp. 235–246 (2010)

21. Zhang, Y., Hu, Y., Li, B., Peng, L.: Performance and Power Analysis of ATI GPU: A Statistical Approach. In: 6th IEEE International Conference on Networking, Architecture and Storage (NAS), pp. 149–158 (2011)

GALS-CMP: Chip-Multiprocessor for GALS Embedded Systems

Muhammad Nadeem, HeeJong Park, Zhenmin Li,
Morteza Biglari-Abhari, and Zoran Salcic

Department of Electrical & Computer Engineering,
University of Auckland, Private Bag 92019,
Auckland 1142, New Zealand
{m.abhari,z.salcic}@auckland.ac.nz

Abstract. In this paper we present a novel multi-processor architecture for concurrent execution of programs that follow the Globally Asynchronous Locally Synchronous (GALS) formal model of computation. Programs are specified using the SystemJ concurrent programming language, suitable for modeling heterogeneous embedded applications that contain reactive and control driven parts and interact with the external environment. The proposed architecture is based on separating the control-driven and data-driven operations and executing them on distinct cores that support both types of operations, implemented as two modes within the single processor core. Each core can switch between two modes without any overhead. The core as the basic building block of the multiprocessor extends Java Optimized Processor (JOP), suitable for data-driven transformational operations, with control-oriented constructs that implement concurrency, reactivity, and control flow in SystemJ. Experimental evaluation over a range of benchmarks shows significant performance improvements over the existing platforms developed for the execution of the SystemJ program.

Keywords: GALS Processors, Reactive Processors, Chip-multiprocessors, Concurrent embedded systems.

1 Introduction

A wide range of embedded systems consist of multiple concurrent behaviors containing both control-dominated and data-dominated operations. These behaviors also interact with each other and with the environment repeatedly reading inputs, doing computations and generating outputs. They typically have different requirements on response times; hence, they need to run concurrently at different speeds. These systems are often modeled using GALS (Globally Asynchronous Locally Synchronous) model of computation. Although Java can be used to program such systems, it has never been an obvious choice due to the presence of a large piece of software in the form of Java Virtual Machine (JVM), as an additional layer, and garbage collector resulting in increased memory and execution cost. Java is not suitable for the hard real-time systems due to garbage

C. Hochberger et al. (Eds.): ARCS 2013, LNCS 7767, pp. 147–158, 2013.
© Springer-Verlag Berlin Heidelberg 2013

collector which typically causes non-deterministic pauses in the application due to unpredictable invocation times and length of these pauses. In addition, Java threads and concurrency constructs introduce non-determinism in program execution and make it hard to analyze the execution behavior of the program. Also the lack of statements for modeling reactive control structures, support of synchronous reactive model of computation, and frequent occurrence of context switching to support thread-based concurrency reduce its efficiency.

SystemJ [1] is a system-level programming language which extends Java with synchronous and asynchronous concurrency and reactivity, making it suitable for designing complex embedded programs. The language allows use of full Java as usual object oriented sequential programming language, and does not recommend using Java concurrency (threads), but relies on its own concurrency model based on formal GALS model of computation (MoC). It extends Java with Esterel-like [2] constructs for the synchronous concurrency and reactivity, and CSP-like [3] constructs for the asynchronous concurrency. Synchronous parts of SystemJ programs are deterministic and suitable for real-time applications if the continuous blocks of java code embedded into those programs have bounded execution times.

A SystemJ program consists of multiple asynchronous processes, called clock-domains (CD), which are described at the top design level. The clock-domains are composed together with the asynchronous parallel operator ($><$). Each clock-domain consists of a number of synchronous concurrent processes, called reactions, which execute in lock-step, driven by a logical clock, called tick. A synchronous program reacts to its environment in a sequence of ticks, and computations within a tick are assumed to be instantaneous, i.e., as if the processor executing them was infinitely fast (synchrony hypothesis). The reactions communicate within a clock-domain, as well as with the external environment (input/output) through signals, which are broadcast and present within the current tick and comply with synchronous reactive MoC [2]. Communication between reactions in different clock-domains is carried out through the exchange of messages over channels, which are semantically the same as channels used in CSP MoC [3]. Besides operations on signals and channels, SystemJ allows free use of Java data objects and sequential statements in its reactions, and those statements are considered instantaneous in terms of logical time (i.e. they do not consume logical time or ticks).

Control flow of a SystemJ program incorporates scheduling of all reactions and clock-domains, as well as communication between reactions, and communication with the external environment. The data-driven computations and transformations are performed in Java.

This paper presents a homogeneous chip-multiprocessor architecture for executing programs described in SystemJ referred to as GALS-CMP. The multiprocessor is based on the use of multiple JOP-Plus [4] cores, which are particularly suitable for separation of SystemJ reactivity and concurrency control flow on one hand, and sequential Java computations, on the other hand. This is used as the basis of two modes of JOP-Plus operation, particularly efficient for execution of single clock domain and all synchronous reactions in it.

The rest of the paper is organized as follows. Section 2 presents the previous related works. Details of the GALS-CMP architecture including the interconnect fabric, the distribution of clock-domain processing on multiple cores and the inter clock-domain communication are presented in Section 3. Section 4 presents the details of the compilation and the execution flow of the system. The experiment results and evaluation of GALS-CMP performance are given in Section 5. Finally, Section 6 presents the conclusions and future work directions.

2   Related Works

SystemJ programs can be compiled and executed using various approaches. The early approach was using TReK [5] run-time Java library, which required additional memory. Also, the language was introduced informally and without a compiler so SystemJ mechanisms were used through suitable application programming interface. In another approach the SystemJ program is transformed to an intermediate format called AGRC (Asynchronous GRaph Code) and the compiler back-end produces a single threaded Java code [1] that can be executed on processors with JVM or on Java processors, such as JOP [6], resulting in more efficient execution than those that target JVM. These JOP Java programs can also be analyzed and their worst case execution times estimated [6]. An attempt to extend JOP byte code repertoire and support SystemJ reactivity resulted in more efficient execution of SystemJ programs [7], but SystemJ's powerful concurrency model in this case is implemented in Java and inherits the same deficiencies as previous implementations due to the lack of efficient mechanism (unconditional goto) to control the program flow. The compilation approach [8] separates the concurrency and control flow (CRCF) of SystemJ program, presented as special instructions, from Java control flow (JCF), presented in Java, and they are executed on two different processors [8], [9]. Further attempts reported in [9], [4], extend JOP and execute both control-dominated and data-dominated computations on a single processor resulting in efficient execution in terms of both execution times and resources used.

Although, the execution of SystemJ programs on a single processor can be efficient and economical, it may suffer from poor response time due to cyclic scheduling of the asynchronous behaviors called clock domains [1]. These programs respond to the environment events only once at every logical clock cycle (tick) of the clock-domain execution. Hence, for each clock-domain, system will be able to interact with the environment only when it resumes the execution of the same clock-domain after executing all other clock-domains. The SystemJ programs offer high degree of concurrency at clock-domain level which could be exploited to boost the performance of the system if clock domains are executed in parallel. The single processor approach is unable to exploit this parallelism and fails to make efficient use of it. Furthermore, achieving higher performance out of a piece of silicon by increasing the system clock frequency results in higher power consumption.

3   GALS-CMP Architecture

A SystemJ program uses local synchronous concurrency and global asynchronous concurrency. This can be exploited by introducing hardware platforms consisting of multiple cores to provide parallel and faster execution. To achieve efficient execution, we divide programs into concurrent operations at the clock-domain boundaries during compilation and then we distribute these concurrent operations to the cores. In other words, each part of the compiled program to be executed on a core comprises of the CRCF and JCF code for a complete clock-domain. In this section we describe the GALS-CMP system in detail.

3.1   GALS-CMP System

The GALS-CMP follows the methodology adopted by the time predictable multi-processor system JopCMP [10]. It consists of multiple JOP-Plus cores, connected to the shared memory through an arbiter using a SoC bus as shown in Fig. 1. Each core uses a local method cache, stack cache and the CRCF memory, which contains the control code of a SystemJ clock-domain, to reduce the shared memory accesses. Shared memory is used to store Java data computations (JCF) made of a collection of Java methods that are loaded upon call from the control code into local method caches of individual cores before they are executed. Also, shared memory is used to store the JVM run time data areas. Furthermore, the depicted GALS-CMP architecture shows a synchronization unit which has the responsibility to coordinate access to the shared objects by a mutual exclusion mechanism. On-chip IO devices, such as a controller for real-time Ethernet or a real-time field bus, may be mapped to shared memory addresses and are connected via the memory arbiter.

All cores are connected to each other and to the memory via simple SoC interconnect (SimpCon) [11] which provides point-to-point interconnections between components. All cores communicate with each other through the shared memory and an arbiter is used when multiple masters try to access the same slave.

Both control-dominated and data-dominated processing is split at the clock-domain boundaries. This means that an entire clock domain must execute on the same processing core. However, a single processing core may execute any number of clock-domains. The allocation of clock-domains to the processors is done statically at the compile time. The designer is offered with the specific choice of executing the clock-domain on different processors.

3.2   Inter Clock-Domain Communication

The distribution of clock-domains on different cores gives rise to the problem of communication between the clock-domains. In SystemJ, all communication between clock-domains must take place through channels, which are implemented as Java objects shared by the respective clock-domains. The exchange of data using channels on traditional JVM based processors is implemented by passing Java objects between Java methods and classes on the same JVM, which

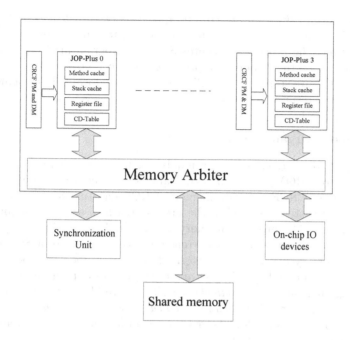

Fig. 1. GALS-CMP system

entails passing references. All the cores of GALS-CMP are connected to the single shared memory and the communication between clock-domains is handled by passing object references of channels in Java. The shared memory also contains channel status signals to implement the rendezvous used in data exchange. The inter clock-domain communication in GALS-CMP is more efficient than the one adopted by the multiprocessor system in [8]. The two clock-domains communicating each to the other and executing on different processors have more expensive communication mechanism in terms of execution time and memory requirements as channel objects need to be transferred physically instead of passing references. In case of GALS-CMP, channel communication takes place by passing object reference to the other clock-domain irrespective of whether they are allocated to the same core or on different cores.

3.3 Base Core

The core used as basis for the GALS-CMP provides a seamless integration of both control and data execution modes in one processor called JOP-Plus [4]. The control execution is capable of invoking the data computations in Java, which then returns to the control directly. The main idea is to provide support for the two separate components of the control flow in SystemJ programs, Concurrency and Reactive Control Flow (CRCF) and Java Control Flow (JCF), by extending the instruction set of the original JOP while using single execution unit and data-path. This allows resultant core to appear as two "logical" processors, or, alternatively, as a processor executing in two different modes of execution. At any given time, the processor executes SystemJ program in either of the two modes and uses all the resources of processor. The code parts corresponding to CRCF and JCF are stored in two different memories, local CRCF memory and shared memory, respectively.

3.4   Memory Organization

Each GALS-CMP core consists of a number of memories; *method* cache, stack cache, microcode ROM, and translation-table. Other memory components such as Register-File, CRCF program memory, CRCF data memory and a number of temporary registers are part of the processor, which are used in the CRCF execution mode. The program memory of the CRCF holds the compiled and assembled code implementing concurrency and control flow of a SystemJ program. The memory depth is parameterized depending upon the code size, but maximum size is limited to 64K. There are two sources of program instructions: CRCF program memory and *method* cache. Therefore, the CRCF memory shares the program counter register with the *method* cache. The *method* cache serves as the instruction cache for JCF. The byte-codes for a complete method are loaded into the cache before execution.

The CRCF data memory (DM) contains the data structure for the concurrency and control flow statements of the SystemJ program (CRCF). The DM is 16-bits wide and the depth is not fixed and maximum size depends on the number of clock-domains. The register file (RF) is used for temporary storage of the operands when executing CRCF and is functionally the same as the register file in [8,9]. The Register-File consists of 16 16-bit registers, which are not visible in the JCF mode. The *method* cache holds a complete Java method prior to its execution. The clock-domain table is created in a very small memory and is used for holding the address of particular methods.

The main memory is situated external to the core and can be divided into two parts: application (program) area and heap. The application area consists of per-class structures such as run-time constant pool, field and method data, and the code for methods and constructors, as well as interned Strings. The heap is a run-time data area from which memory for all class instances and arrays are allocated. The application area also contains the code for JCF methods, loader method and CRCF wrapper for each CPU and the main method. The channels are implemented as the Java object and reside in the heap part of the main memory. These objects are shared among the clock-domains running on the same or different cores. The access to the objects by the multiple concurrent clock-domains on different cores is synchronized by using the lock which guarantees the mutual exclusion.

3.5   CD-Table

The CD-table holds the addresses of the first JCF method structure of each clock-domain which helps in calculating the address of any method being invoked directly from CRCF. In the GALS-CMP architecture, each processor core executes different clock-domain(s); therefore, each processor needs to store the base address of corresponding JCF. All these addresses are stored in a CD-table. The clock-domain number acts as the index of the table and each entry in the table consists of the address of the structure of the first method of that clock-domain. All the JCF methods, each representing a data-computation node, are arranged in ascending order making it possible to calculate the address of structure of any method provided its offset from the base method is given. This offset is provided during the data-call. The CD-table, implemented in a RAM has parameterized number of entries equal to the number of clock-domains. The clock-domain number acts as the address for the RAM and address of the structure of base method for that clock-domain is read which is used to calculate the address of the desired method to be invoked.

3.6   Instruction Fetch

There are two different memories which hold the program code for two different modes: method cache for the JCF mode and CRCF program memory. The program memory source for the next instruction to be fetched is controlled through *mode_control* flag, which defines the mode of operation. If *mode_control* flag is set, the next instruction to be executed is always fetched from the CRCF program memory. On the other hand, resetting of the flag results in fetching of the next instruction to be executed from the method cache. This flag is set and reset while switching from the CRCF mode to JCF or vice versa. Both memories share the program counter (*jpc*); therefore, its value is saved when switching to the JCF mode. The switching from JCF to CRCF mode does not require storing the address as the memory subsystem provides the method start address in the cache every time a JCF method is loaded into it.

4   GALS-CMP Compilation and Execution Flow

The compilation and execution flow for GALS-CMP is shown in Fig. 2. The GALS programs described in SystemJ are compiled by using the approach where CRCF is separated from JCF. The CRCF code is compiled first; the resulting code is wrapped in an array as shown in Fig. 2 and stored in heap. On start up the compiled CRCF code is stored in the program memories of the respective processor cores. The allocation of clock-domains to the processors is done statically at the compile time. The designer is offered with the specific choice of executing the clock-domain(s) separately on different processors. The compiler generates separate CRCF (CRCF.asm) and JCF (JCF.java) code for each processor consisting of the CRCF and JCF codes for the clock-domains assigned

to this particular processor. The assembler assembles the CRCF assembly code
and generates .hex file (CRCF.hex). The CRCF wrapper fragments this code
and wraps them into Java arrays (CRCF.java). The Java code responsible for
downloading the CRCF code, called CRCF loader, is generated and combined
with the JCF.java to produce the code to be executed on each core (*core.java*).
All the signals and variables local to these clock-domains being executed on
the same core are declared here. Finally, all the clock-domains are assigned to
the respective cores physically in the main method of class *GALSCMP.java*.
The shared channel objects, through which the clock domains communicate, are
declared inside the same class. The application class is compiled by *javac* and
produces the class file which is further processed by the JOP specific tool to
produce the GALS-CMP final code. It also generates the code for the CD-table.
The application is downloaded into main memory by the core whose *id* is 0. Once
the start up is completed, all the cores start executing respective clock-domains.
Each core starts in Java mode and downloads the CRCF code from the heap
into CRCF program memory. After the CRCF program memory is initialized,
the core switches the mode and start executing in control mode by fetching the
instructions from the CRCF program memory.

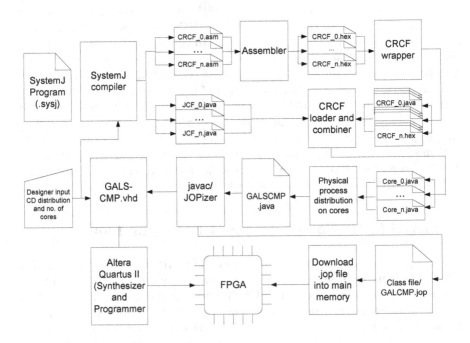

Fig. 2. Compilation and execution flow

4.1 JCF Invocation and Return

When invoking a JCF method to perform data-computation, the address of next (returning) CRCF instruction is stored in a register and the address of the structure of the base method of the clock-domain to be executed is fetched from the CD-table. The address of the structure of the required method is calculated using the address of the structure of base method. The structure record of a method resides in main memory and holds the information such as constant pool address, argument count, variable count, method start address and code length, in the encoded form. The method start address and code length are extracted and the information is passed to the memory subsystem for loading the method code into the cache. At the same time, the *mode_control* flag is reset making the method cache default memory for read/write operations. The next byte-code is fetched from the method cache and JCF method execution starts.

When returning from the JCF to the CRCF mode, the result is available as the top element of stack. The result is written to the CRCF data memory at a location pointed to by data-lock position. The address of next CRCF instruction to be executed is stored in a register; it is loaded into Java program counter and *mode_control* flag is set. The next instruction is fetched from the CRCF program memory, and method cache does not require being loaded with CRCF program code as it permanently resides in the CRCF program memory.

5 Experimental Results

This section presents the results of experiments conducted to evaluate and compare our proposed GALS-CMP multiprocessor architecture with a single processor approach, called base core, to execute the SystemJ programs. All presented data have been collected from the experiments carried out by using the cycle-accurate ModelSim simulator for 2, 3 and 4 core systems all running at 50 MHz clock. The system is capable of running at frequency higher than 50 MHz but the results presented are for 50 MHz clock for fair comparison with earlier published results.

The benchmarks are selected to show the effectiveness of the approach for the SystemJ GALS program execution. The benchmarks include asynchronous examples which are heterogeneous in nature both with and without involving any clock-domain communication. The benchmarks without any inter clock-domain communication include the two and four clock-domain version of demoloop (dl), *dl2* and *dl4*, respectively. They consist of two or four identical clock-domains respectively each comprising of four reactions and these clock-domains run independently without involving any communication between them. This benchmark has minimal data computation without any accesses to shared data structures and synchronization needs. The asynchronous case is represented by an asynchronous protocol stack (*aps* with two clock-domains, and *aps3* with three clock-domains), and *pump controller* examples. In both cases of *aps*, the first clock-domain is used to model the packet generation process, and the second clock-domain implements the stack itself as mentioned previously. The *aps3* implements two protocol stacks pre-senting a case where network generator sends data at a rate higher than what can be handled by a single protocol stack. Therefore, the generator sends to two different stacks alternately. The *pump controller* example consists of two clock-domains and nine reactions in total. It models the control of a pump inside a mine which may have high methane levels. The pump pumps out water whenever the water level exceeds the desired level and is turned on only if methane level is below a certain limit. Whenever methane level goes above that limit, the controller must stop the pump and wait until right methane level is restored. If methane level goes too high, then the pump is stopped immediately and an ALARM is generated.

The execution speed comparisons are given in terms of the average response time of the clock-domain and the application execution time. The response time is defined as the average time taken by the clock-domain to respond to the environment at the end of its logical tick. A logical tick is the time interval between two logical time consuming statements and may have variable time depending on the amount of computation enclosed between these two statements. The application response time is defined as the time between the application input sampled and final output generation and may involve multiple logical ticks. It takes into account the time needed by the cores and in addition the time taken for communication between the processing elements to exchange the information, if needed.

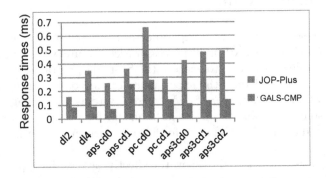

Fig. 3. Comparison of applications' execution

The results in Fig. 3 show that GALS-CMP outperforms the single processor execution in terms of response time. The GALS-CMP with 2 cores has between 2 and almost 4 times reduction in response time when executing the benchmarks which do not involve any clock-domain communication and have minimal data computations. This can be attributed to two factors: firstly, the use of multipro-cessor system and secondly, the local storage of the CRCF program as provided in the base core. The control dominated programs contain minimal data com-putations, so they do not need to access the main memory to fetch the JCF method into the cache. Therefore, the gain is almost proportional to the number of processor cores. Increasing the number of clock-domains increases the response time, which is evident from the results for the benchmarks *aps* and its variant *aps3*. The improvement in response time is achieved through concurrent execution of the clock-domains. The clock-domains run independently and respond to the environment at the end of each of their logical ticks which is in contrast to the single processor approach where clock-domains are executed cyclically one after the other. The clock-domains in the later case are able to respond to the environment signals only after all the clock-domains have finished their execution resulting in increased response time. The GALS-CMP is expected to suffer from degradation in the clock-domain tick time due to the shared memory as the bandwidth is divided equally among all the nodes of the GALS-CMP. In case of control-dominated applications with minimal data-computation, the tick time is not expected to suffer by much as the code implementing the concurrency and control flow is stored in a separate local memory and, therefore, it is not affected by the constraints on memory bandwidth due to shared memory.

Fig. 4 shows the gain in application execution times for benchmark examples against the single processor execution. The results indicate that the application execution times are improved by almost 100% when we migrate from single core to two core system when executing control dominated applications such as *dl2*. But this gain is not linear when going from 2 to 4 core systems as evident from *dl4* benchmark. This is due to the constraints on shared memory bandwidth. The *aps* and *pump controller* examples are 85% and 89% faster, respectively. Both of these examples involve the channel communication; therefore, some of the time is consumed in physical transfer of data over channels. Further addition to this time is the fact that the channel objects reside in heap, which is implemented in shared main memory resulting in delayed access due to memory bandwidth constraints.

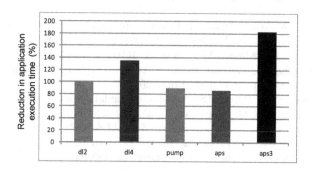

Fig. 4. Comparison of applications' execution

6   Conclusion and Future Work

We have described a new multiprocessor platform, GALS-CMP, for the execution of concurrent programs written in the GALS programming language SystemJ. We demonstrated the effectiveness of the approach by running different benchmark examples and comparing the measurements against the single processor approach. This processor outperforms other execution platforms for SystemJ in terms of clock-domain response-time and the overall application response time.

In the current implementation, the CRCF code is stored in on-chip memory whereas JCF code is stored in the main memory which is shared among all the processing cores. The sharing of memory bandwidth results in the degradation of performance as the processing cores compete for the bandwidth to fetch the JCF code to method cache prior to its execution. So, providing the local storage for JCF code will ease the pressure on the shared memory bandwidth. At present, channel-based communication takes place through the shared memory. We plan to investigate hardware support for point-to-point channel communication among the processing cores.

References

1. Malik, A., Salcic, Z., Roop, P.S., Girault, A.: SystemJ: A GALS language for system level design. Comput. Lang. Syst. Struct. 36(4), 317–344 (2010)
2. Berry, G.: The semantics of pure Esterel (1993)
3. Hoare, C.A.R.: Communicating sequential processes. Prentice-Hall, Inc. (1985)
4. Nadeem, M., Biglari-Abhari, M., Salcic, Z.: JOP-Plus - A processor for efficient execution of Java programs extended with GALS concurrency. In: 17th Asia and South Pacific Design Automation Conference (ASP-DAC), January 30-February 2, pp. 17–22 (2012)
5. Gruian, F., Roop, P., Salcic, Z., Radojevic, I.: The SystemJ approach to system-level design. In: Proceedings of the fourth ACM and IEEE International Conference on Formal Methods and Models for Co-Design, MEMOCODE 2006, pp. 149–158 (2006)
6. Schoeberl, M.: A Java processor architecture for embedded real-time systems. Elsevier Journal of Systems Architecture 42(1-2), 265–286 (2008)
7. Nadeem, M., Biglari-Abhari, M., Salcic, Z.: RJOP - A customized Java processor for reactive embedded systems. In: 48th ACM/EDAC/IEEE Design Automation Conference (DAC), pp. 1038–1043 (June 2011)
8. Malik, A., Salcic, Z., Roop, P.S.: SystemJ compilation using the tandem virtual machine approach. ACM Trans. Des. 14(3), 34:1–34:37 (2009)
9. Nadeem, M., Biglari-Abhari, M., Salcic, Z.: GALS-JOP: A Java embedded processor for GALS reactive programs. In: IEEE Ninth International Conference on Dependable, Autonomic and Secure Computing (DASC), pp. 292–299 (December 2011)
10. Pitter, C., Schoeberl, M.: A real-time Java chip-multiprocessor. ACM Trans. Embed. Comput. Syst. 10(1), 9:1–9:34 (2010)
11. Schoeberl, M.: JOP Reference Handbook: Building Embedded Systems with a Java Processor (2009)

HW/SW Tradeoffs for Dynamic Message Scheduling in Controller Area Network (CAN)

Tobias Ziermann[1], Zoran Salcic[2] and Jürgen Teich[1]

[1] University of Erlangen-Nuremberg, Germany
{tobias.ziermann,teich}@informatik.uni-erlangen.de
[2] The University of Auckland, New Zealand

Abstract. Designers of distributed embedded control systems face many design challenges related to change of system configuration, functionality and number of participating computing nodes, which affect the usage of the communication bus. The concept of self-adaptivity of participating nodes plays an important role in reducing design effort while guaranteeing high system performance. The dynamic offset adaptation algorithm (DynOAA) for adaptive message scheduling reduces average message response times in CAN-based systems with high bus loads. This technique has in previous work proven its benefit in simulation. However, it is still necessary to test the algorithm in a real physical environment. In this paper, we use FPGAs with their capability of performing rapid system prototyping. Our design space exploration shows that both pure software and pure hardware implementations are possible. However, parts of the software implementation require a significant amount of computation. As a result a mixed HW/SW implementation is proposed.

1 Introduction

Distributed control systems use communication buses for communication between their components, which are usually called electronic control units (ECUs) or just nodes. The most common communication bus is the Controller Area Network (CAN) [1] is used in automotive, industrial control, medical and other similar applications [5,12,13]. Industrial communication buses, such as CAN, typically have fairly low nominal transmission speed and bandwidth, but also very short response times. However, when multiple messages are sent from multiple nodes at the same time, the messages with low priorities can have long response times, sometimes leading to starvation. This problem becomes even worse at the high bus loads, for example in modern cars that contain more than 70 ECUs [14]. Because the underlying CAN bus has limited bandwidth, this inevitably results in increased message response times. From this reason the bus has to be run at low bus utilization. A possible solution would be to increase the bandwidth by using another communication bus or by using multiple CAN segments at higher cost. In this paper, we propose to retain the existing CAN infrastructure and add the intelligence to the nodes that result in better scheduling of messages

C. Hochberger et al. (Eds.): ARCS 2013, LNCS 7767, pp. 159–170, 2013.
© Springer-Verlag Berlin Heidelberg 2013

and shortening of the average message response times, while at the same time allowing higher utilization of the bus.

The main idea of this approach is based on the distribution and dispersion of message release times, thus alleviating the problem of simultaneously released messages. Assuming that messages released by different nodes are periodic, offsets are added to the release times using a dynamic offset adaptation algorithm or DynOAA [17]), where each node that releases messages monitors the traffic on the bus and adapts the offsets as the traffic on the bus changes. DynOAA, which has been analyzed using simulation models only, achieves reduction of the average of maximum message response times, avoids the analytical worst case, and enables the use of the same bus at higher bus loads.

In order to apply the algorithm in real distributed setting it is necessary to verify that the actual implementations with limited resources are able to perform similar to the simulation results. In addition, this has to be achieved within acceptable cost. As the acceptable solutions may be combinations of hardware and software, FPGAs prototyping is an almost ideal way to explore different solutions. Moreover, FPGAs allow software-only implementations using a soft-core processor, pure hardware solutions or solutions that combine hardware and software to achieve the same functionality on a single platform. Finally, in foreseeable future it is expected that FPGAs are utilized in the ECUs of the final system [7,8], too. In this paper, we use the developed prototypes and test-bed to analyze performance of DynOAA in the real implementation setting. Tests on the real system are more realistic and require less time than those in simulations.

This paper is organized as follows. In Section 2, we describe DynOAA, which is the basis for the following sections. Section 3 evaluates the HW/SW-tradeoffs and proposes a mixed hardware and software implementation of DynOAA. Section 4 shows the performance of the pure hardware and pure software solution on a prototype with initial measurements. Conclusions are given in Section 5.

2   Dynamic Message Scheduling Using Offset Adaptation

Current analytical techniques for calculating the message response times for priority-based buses are overly pessimistic [6,11], and result in very conservative designs with low bus utilization. On the other end of the spectrum are approaches that use simulation models of the behavior and measure the message response times [9,15,16]. These approaches are based on the assumption of random release times of messages by the system nodes, which may, in the worst case, result in simultaneous release of messages by multiple or all nodes. The DynOAA approach belongs to the later group, but uses adaptation of offsets to control the otherwise random release times.

2.1   Problem Definition

The proposed approach for message scheduling specifically targets soft real-time systems. As soft real-time we consider system where satisfying timing constraints is important for the system functionality, but missing the deadlines once in a while will not result in malfunction of the system. Typical examples of such applications are found in the body network of an automotive embedded system [14]. For example, a rain sensitive wiper needs to react in time on the changing environment, but some delayed messages will not cause a system failure.

The CAN system consists of a set of nodes, i.e. ECUs, each executing one or more tasks, which release messages, typically periodically. In our model, we abstract the tasks by considering only the mechanism used to release messages called a stream. A stream s_i is characterized by a transmission time, by a period (time between any two consecutive messages generated by stream s_i) and an offset. The offset is relative to a global time reference. It can therefore drift over time, because the local time reference differs from the global one. In our approach to calculating offsets, we assume that the individual streams are not bound by any constraints, but rather can freely be set by the designer [10]. The hyperperiod P is the least common multiple of all periods. Assuming a synchronous system, the schedule is finally periodic with the period equal to the hyper-period. A message is a single release or CAN frame of the stream. The time between a message release and the start of its uninterrupted transfer over the bus is the response time of the message. We do not add the constant non-preemptive time to transfer the message to the response time, thus a zero response time is always the best possible case for any message regardless of its length. This simplifies comparisons between different schedules.

To compare our results, we use the rating function called the average weighted worst case response time, or AWW, originally proposed in [17], which enables us to differentiate the quality of different message scheduling schemes:

$$AWW(t) = \frac{\sum_{i=1}^{k} \frac{WCRT_i(t-P,t)}{T_i}}{k} \tag{1}$$

where $WCRT_i(t - P, t)$ is the measured worst case response time of the stream i that has period T_i in the last hyper-period P and k is the total number of streams generating messages. The function $AWW(t)$ takes into account that the streams with large periods are more sensitive to large response times, because each WCRT is weighted with its corresponding period. Finally, the sum is divided by the number of streams to get the average rating per stream. This also allows comparison of different scenarios with different numbers of streams.

2.2 Dynamic Offset Adaptation Algorithm (DynOAA)

In our approach, we use the dynamic offset adaptation algorithm (DynOAA) introduced in [17], which changes offsets over time following the change of the traffic on the CAN bus. DynOAA is run on each node independently and periodically. An illustration of the operation of DynOAA for one stream is shown in Fig. 1. In the upper part of the figure, on the top of the time line, the periodically released messages of the stream are indicated by small arrows. The larger arrows on the bottom of the time line indicate the instances when the

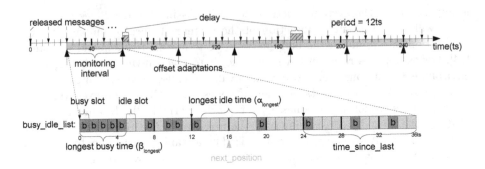

Fig. 1. DynOAA illustration - timing diagram and busy_idle_list on a single node

adaptations start or when DynOAA is executed. Each algorithm run consists of a traffic monitoring phase and a delay phase. During the monitoring phase, a list called busy_idle_list is created. It is a circular list, meaning the last element is adjacent to the first element. An example of it is shown in the lower part of Fig. 1. It contains, for each time slot during the monitoring phase, an idle element if the bus is idle and a busy element if the bus is busy. If not mentioned otherwise a time slot has the length of the transmission time of one CAN bit. From the busy_idle_list, we can find the longest idle time $\alpha_{longest}$ and longest busy time $\beta_{longest}$, which are the maximum continuous intervals when the bus was idle or busy, respectively. During the delay phase, the next message of the stream is then delayed, i.e., the offset is adjusted, so that a message in the next monitoring phase is released in the middle of $\alpha_{longest}$ (next_position).

In distributed systems, all streams are considered independent of each other. If more than one stream starts to execute the adaptation simultaneously, there is a high probability that the value of the next_position will be identical at more than one stream. Instead of spreading, the message release times would in that case be clustered around the same time instant. Therefore, we need to ensure that only one stream is adapting its offsets at the same time. This is accomplished by introducing a unique criterion for all streams, which ensures that the stream that is the first in the longest busy time $\beta_{longest}$ will adapt its offset. The probability that a message will be delayed depends on the number of preceding messages. If the message is not preceded by any other message, the message cannot be delayed. Therefore, it makes sense to choose the first message from the $\beta_{longest}$ to adapt. All communication controllers have to adhere to this unique protocol individually.

3   HW/SW Exploration

The proposed algorithm from the previous section is not directly applicable to an embedded platform (ECU). In this section, we introduce and analyze purely software-based and hardware-based implementations of DynOAA. Then, based on these observations a mixed HW/SW solution is proposed.

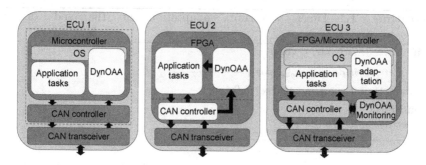

Fig. 2. Different ECU architectures and how DynOAA could be integrated. The dashed boxes indicate a possible integration on a single IC.

In our model, we assume it is possible to control the offsets of message streams. In a real application, the messages are triggered by tasks running periodically on the ECUs. Therefore, in order to control the message release and also the offset, we suggest doing it via controlling the task release.

3.1 Design Alternatives for DynOAA

Figure 2 shows examples of three different implementation alternatives of ECUs with DynOAA. ECU 1 represents the currently most often used architecture, where one or several microcontrollers are responsible for the execution of the application tasks. Because of the limited computation power, the the communication protocol needs dedicated hardware support. This hardware unit is integrated into the microcontroller as indicated by the dashed box or is a separate integrated circuit (IC). Finally, a CAN transceiver is needed to establish the physical communication with the bus. In this setup type, typically an operating system is responsible for scheduling the application tasks. To include DynOAA, the releases of the tasks need to be controlled either by integrating DynOAA to the operating system (as additional component of a scheduler) or by running DynOAA as an application task reporting the desired release times to the operating system.

ECU 2 uses an FPGA for computation and communication [2]. Here, the application tasks are implemented as hardware modules running in parallel to each other. Typically the application tasks are triggered periodically. In this type of ECU, DynOAA could be integrated by implementing it as a hardware component which triggers the application tasks with the adapted schedule. In this setup, the CAN controller could be implemented as dedicated hardware module similar to the implemented application tasks.

ECU 3 represents a solution where DynOAA is implemented as a HW/SW solution. A general purpose DynOAA monitoring unit unloads the CPU of monitoring the traffic on the bus, while the adaptation is implemented as software integrated into the operating system (see Section 3.4).

Algorithm 1. Timer interrupt: adaptation at the end of the *monitoring interval*

1: **if** $(\beta_{longest}.isSender)$ **then**
2:     $next\_position = \alpha_{longest}.pos + \frac{\alpha_{longest}.length}{2}$
3:     $\text{adapt}(next\_position \bmod period)$
4: **end if**
5: $\text{reset}(\alpha/\beta_{current/longest})$

In the following sections, we describe in more details two implementation alternatives: (1) an interrupt-based implementation, which is better suited as software implementation on existing processors, and (2) a polling-based implementation, which is better suited as a hardware implementation that works in parallel with existing processors.

3.2   Software Implementation

Typical microcontrollers have processors ranging from simple 8-bit microprocessors to powerful 32-bit processors. In order to estimate the class of controllers DynOAA can be run on, we provide an interrupt-based alternative of DynOAA to measure the computational requirements. Interrupts are generated by the CAN controller and by a timer of the microcontroller. The CAN controller raises interrupts when the reception of a message starts and when it finishes. For example, the CAN controller inside the AT90CAN32/64/128 microcontroller series [3] offers these interrupts. A timer with the period equal to the length of the monitoring interval is used to trigger the adaptation and to provide the current position when a CAN controller interrupt is raised. Therefore, the timer needs to be set to increment by one whenever one time slot passes, i.e. after transmission time of one CAN bit. The implementation of DynOAA requires storing the longest and the current busy and idle time. Each time is characterized by a position (*.pos*), by a length (*.length*) and a Boolean whether the stream that is running the algorithm is sender of the first message of that busy time (*.isSender*). The id of the first message of the busy time has to be stored, if the ECU runs more than one stream.

The principle of operation of the interrupt service routines is as follows. The timer interrupt (Alg. 1) delays the task if it is the first of the longest busy time and resets all variables for the next monitoring phase. The start of reception interrupt (Alg. 2) updates the longest idle time $\alpha_{longest}$ if necessary. In addition, the position and whether it is sender or not of the current busy time is updated, if the received message starts a new busy time. This is the case if the distance between the last two messages, i.e. $\alpha_{current}$, is greater than a threshold (δ). In the ideal case, when transmission of delayed messages starts immediately $\delta = 0$. But depending on the accuracy of the involved microcontrollers the threshold needs to be increased. The end of reception interrupt (Alg. 3) updates the longest busy time if necessary and stores the current timer position for the next interrupt.

Algorithm 2. CAN controller interrupt: start of reception

1: $\alpha_{current}.length = currentCount - \alpha_{current}.pos$

2: **if** $\alpha_{longest}.length < \alpha_{current}.length$ **then**

3:    $\alpha_{longest} = \alpha_{current}$

4: **end if**

5: **if** $(\alpha_{current}.length > \delta)$ **then**

6:    $\beta_{current}.pos = currentCount$

7:    $\beta_{current}.isSender = isCurrentSender()$

8: **end if**

Algorithm 3. CAN controller interrupt: end of reception

1: $\beta_{current}.length = currentCount - \beta_{current}.pos$

2: **if** $\beta_{longest}.length < \beta_{current}.length$ **then**

3:    $\beta_{longest} = \beta_{current}$

4: **end if**

5: $\alpha_{current}.pos = currentCount$

In summary, the interrupt-based implementation requires seven unsigned integers and two Boolean values (or two 16-bit values, if several streams are adapted). In our example scenarios, when using the time of the transmission of one CAN bit per time slot on a 500kbit CAN with a monitoring interval of 2 sec, the integer needs to have the maximum value

$$integer_{max} = \frac{2\,sec}{2\,\mu s} = 10^6 < 2^{20}. \tag{2}$$

The total amount of computation depends on the frequency of the interrupts. The CAN controller interrupts can be predicted by assuming the worst case of sending the shortest message all the time, in our example around 80 bits * $(1/500kbit/s) = 160us$. During each interrupt only a few comparisons and subtractions need to be calculated. The timer interrupt is only raised every 2 seconds, so its computation requirements can be neglected.

In order to verify the amount of computation, we implemented the algorithm on a Nios 2 32-bit processor instantiated on an Altera Cyclone II 2C70 FPGA running at 100 MHz. The used CAN controller is a VHDL module that is implemented on the FPGA as hardware. The memory requirement is minimal using seven 32-bit and two 16-bit integer that makes a total of 32 bytes. The number of cycles required to calculate the CAN controller interrupts is always below 2500 cycles (25us). However, the overhead for entering and leaving the interrupt is in the order of 100us that it dominates the calculation overhead.

3.3   Hardware Implementation

A polling-based hardware implementation does not use any processor resources and can be done in parallel with processor operation. We prototyped this implementation in an FPGA and as such it can be used on ECUs that use FPGAs. However, the design could be easily ported on an ASIC, too. Alg. 4 shows the pseudo code of this approach.

In order to perform the algorithm, only the longest and the current busy and idle time ($\beta/\alpha_{current/longest}$) need to be stored similar to the software implementation in the previous section. During the monitoring phase, each time slot, $\alpha_{current}$ and $\beta_{current}$ are updated by simply counting up the length of $\alpha_{current}$ and reset $\beta_{current}$ when the current slot is idle. When the current slot is busy $\alpha_{current}$ is reset and the length of $\beta_{current}$ is incremented by one. In addition, $\alpha_{current}$ needs to update the position when a new idle time starts and $\beta_{current}$ needs to update isSender when a new busy time starts. After updating, the length of the current idle time $\alpha_{current}.length$ is compared with the length of the longest idle time $\alpha_{longest}.length$ and, if necessary, updated. The same is done for the busy times. During the adaptation, if the node is the sender of the first busy slot of the longest busy time, next_position is calculated and the node adapts by delaying its next release time.

Algorithm 4. Polling-based DynOAA implementation

1: // monitoring:
2: init($\alpha/\beta_{current/longest}$)
3: **for** (each time slot) **do**
4:      update($\alpha/\beta_{current}$)
5:      **if** $\alpha_{longest}.length < \alpha_{current}.length$ **then**
6:          $\alpha_{longest} = \alpha_{current}$
7:      **end if**
8:      **if** $\beta_{longest}.length < \beta_{current}.length$ **then**
9:          $\beta_{longest} = \beta_{current}$
10:     **end if**
11: **end for**
12: // adaptation/delay:
13: **if** ($\beta_{longest}.isSender$) **then**
14:     $next\_position = \alpha_{longest}.pos + \frac{\alpha_{longest}.length}{2}$
15:     adapt($next\_position \bmod period$)
16: **end if**

In summary, this implementation of DynOAA requires six 20-bit unsigned integers according to 2 and two Boolean values to be stored in registers. Similar to the software implementation, DynOAA can be used for several streams by storing the id of the first message of the busy time instead of only a Boolean.

The amount of computation is very low, because in every time slot the FPGA carries out a few simple comparisons and increments, and at the end of every monitoring carries out interval two integer additions, a division by two and a modulo operation.

We designed the polling-based approach as hardware module in VHDL and implemented it on FPGA to verify the overhead. The algorithm is designed as a finite state machine using a counter, three flag bits and 16 registers resulting in a memory requirement of 38 bytes. Considering today's size and computation power of FPGAs the requirements for DynOAA in hardware can be neglected.

3.4   HW/SW-Solution

Running DynOAA as a purely software-based solution allows its straightforward integration to a typical ECUs. However, the analysis of the computation overhead shows that the monitoring requires the most processing time as it is in the worst case triggered every 160 us. It is necessary to interrupts to trigger monitoring, because otherwise the acquired information would be corrupted. The interrupt can, depending on the used microcontroller, cause a significant overhead. In addition, the use of interrupts can have negative effects on the timing behavior of the applications running on the microcontroller. Therefore, this approach is suitable only for ECUs with powerful processors. The duration of the delay phase is mainly affected by the adaptation of the schedule. It is not necessary to trigger the adaptation by an interrupt, as it is not timing critical. Instead, we suggest integrating the delay phase into the scheduler of the operating system.

A pure hardware implementation of DynOAA is the most efficient one, as the required resources are negligible and performance is highest. However, DynOAA needs to control the release of the applications, and therefore, hardware/software communication is necessary.

Due to these facts, we propose to implement the monitoring phase in a hardware unit and the delay phase in software as a part of the operating system. With the growing popularity and use of FPGAs in the control domain, this design could be implemented on an FPGA using a softcore processor for software part of the algorithm and dedicated hardware unit for monitoring phase. Alternatively, the hardware unit could be integrated within standard microcontrollers. The hardware unit implements the polling-based approach in Alg. 4, and generates $\alpha_{longest}$ and the id of the first message of $\beta_{longest}$. A reset signal on the hardware unit resets $\alpha_{longest}$ and $\beta_{longest}$, and starts the next monitoring interval. The adaptation is triggered periodically by the operating system. It reads the values from the hardware unit, delays the appropriate stream and resets the hardware unit. This way the computation burden by DynOAA is reduced to almost zero by moving the computational intensive part to hardware. The area requirement of the hardware unit is also very small. In order to make the hardware unit general purpose, it needs to be able to adjust the length of one time slot, i.e., length of the transmission of one CAN bit. Microcontrollers that include a CAN controller already have a register to set the speed of the CAN, which could be then read by the hardware unit.

4   Results

In this section, results for a hardware-based and software-based DynOAA using a prototype setup implementation on two FPGAs are shown. The hardware-based implementation uses two Xilinx XC5VLX100T FPGAs that communicate each to the other over a real CAN bus to explore the effects of a distributed embedded system. The software-based implementation is run on a Nios 2 processor instantiated on two Altera Cyclone II 2C70 FPGAs. Using two FPGAs, we can emulate close to real world examples from the automotive domain [4] which typically consist of 10 to 20 ECUs with up to 300 streams. Figure 3 shows the setup of the prototype, where each ECU is implemented according to ECU 1 or 2 template in Fig. 2. The streams are equally distributed on both ECUs. Each ECU module has three basic components: (1) the CAN controller is responsible for the communication protocol, (2) the DynOAA module implements the scheduler for the application tasks that can run either purely periodically (fixed random offsets) or use DynOAA. In the software-based implementation the operating system is reduced to the periodic or DynOAA scheduler. (3) the application tasks collect the response times and include them in the data field of the CAN messages. These response times are collected by the evaluation module, which calculates the AWW and transmits it to a PC for evaluation.

Using this setup, measurements were taken to compare the performance of DynOAA to fixed offsets using a hardware-based or software-based implementation as shown in Fig. 4. The initial or fixed offsets are chosen uniformly distributed and are equal for all shown runs. The measurements show that using DynOAA improves the AWW in average almost by a factor of two. In addition, the behavior of using the hardware-based or software-based implementation is similar when using DynOAA. The difference between the hardware-based and software-based implementation when using fixed offsets exists, because the AWW is mainly influenced by the offset between both FPGAs. This offset is initially random depending on the sequence of turning on the FPGAs and then changes over time depending on the clock drift between the FPGAs.

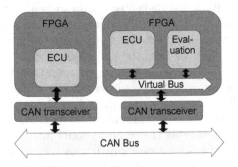

Fig. 3. Schematic of the prototype setup

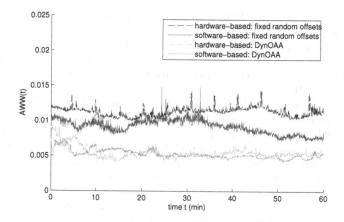

Fig. 4. Value of the AWW over time for a scenario with 85% bus load using DynOAA or fixed random offsets run as the hardware-based or software-based implementation

5   Conclusion

FPGAs are used to prototype alternatives for integrating the dynamic offset adaptation of message scheduling into current ECUs. A software only solution, which can easily be run on any ECU, was developed first. The solution has been implemented and tested on a softcore processor. Furthermore, a design of DynOAA especially suited for hardware implemented ECUs is proposed and developed. Based on hardware and software solutions an FPGA test-bed of the CAN bus system emulating a complete typical automotive bus has been established. The analysis shows that the monitoring part of the algorithm requires a considerable amount of computation that suggests the use of a general purpose hardware accelerator. This accelerator could be included as a hardware module into future specialized microcontrollers. In case using an FPGA in the ECU, it is possible to use a softcore processor with reconfigurable hardware accelerators. The experiments on the test-bed show the same performance in terms of average weighted maximum response times independent of the implementation. In summary, we have shown that self-adaptive methods are realistically applicable in embedded distributed control systems.

Acknowledgment. This work was supported in part by the German Research Foundation (DFG) under contract TE 163/15-1.

References

1. CAN specification 2.0 b. Robert Bosch GmbH, Stuttgart, Germany (1991)
2. Anthony, R., Rettberg, A., Chen, D., Jahnich, I., de Boer, G., Ekelin, C.: Towards a dynamically reconfigurable automotive control system architecture. In: Embedded System Design: Topics, Techniques and Trends, pp. 71–84 (2007)

3. Atmel Corporation. 8-bit AVR Microcontroller with 32K/64K/128K Bytes of ISP Flash and CAN Controller (2008)
4. Braun, C., Havet, L., Navet, N.: NETCARBENCH: A benchmark for techniques and tools used in the design of automotive communication systems. In: 7th IFAC International Conference on Fieldbuses and Networks in Industrial and Embedded Systems, pp. 321–328 (2007)
5. Bueno, E.J., Hernandez, A., Rodriguez, F.J., Giron, C., Mateos, R., Cobreces, S.: A dsp- and fpga-based industrial control with high-speed communication interfaces for grid converters applied to distributed power generation systems. IEEE Transactions on Industrial Electronics 56(3), 654–669 (2009)
6. Davis, R.I., Burns, A., Bril, R.J., Lukkien, J.J.: Controller Area Network (CAN) schedulability analysis: Refuted, revisited and revised. Real-Time Systems 35(3), 239–272 (2007)
7. Gabrick, M., Nicholson, R., Winters, F., Young, B., Patton, J.: Fpga considerations for automotive applications. In: Proc. SAE Conf. (2006)
8. Galea, F., Gatt, E., Casha, O., Grech, I.: Control unit for a continuous variable transmission for use in an electric car. In: 17th IEEE International Conference on Electronics, Circuits, and Systems (ICECS), pp. 247–250 (December 2010)
9. Gamiz, J., Samitier, J., Fuertes, J.M., Rubies, O.: Practical evaluation of messages latencies in CAN. In: Proceedings of the IEEE Conference on Emerging Technologies and Factory Automation, ETFA 2003, pp. 185–192 (2003)
10. Goossens, J.: Scheduling of offset free systems. Real-Time Systems 24(2), 239–258 (2003)
11. Grenier, M., Havet, L., Navet, N.: Pushing the limits of CAN-scheduling frames with offsets provides a major performance boost. In: Proc. of the 4th European Congress Embedded Real Time Software (ERTS 2008), Toulouse, France (2008)
12. CAN in Automation. Canopen, http://www.canopen.org/
13. Marino, P., Poza, F., Dominguez, M.A., Otero, S.: Electronics in automotive engineering: A top-down approach for implementing industrial fieldbus technologies in city buses and coaches. IEEE Transactions on Industrial Electronics 56(2), 589–600 (2009)
14. Navet, N., Simonot-Lion, F.: Automotive embedded systems handbook. CRC (2009)
15. Samii, S., Rafiliu, S., Eles, P., Peng, Z.: A simulation methodology for worst-case response time estimation of distributed real-time systems. In: Proceedings of the Conference on Design, Automation and Test in Europe, DATE, pp. 556–561. ACM (2008)
16. Zhou, F., Li, S., Hou, X.: Development method of simulation and test system for vehicle body CAN bus based on CANoe. In: 7th World Congress on Intelligent Control and Automation, WCICA, pp. 7515–7519. IEEE (2008)
17. Ziermann, T., Salcic, Z., Teich, J.: DynOAA - dynamic offset adaptation algorithm for improving response times of CAN systems. In: Proc. of Design, Automation, and Test in Europe (DATE), pp. 269–272 (2011)

A Data-Driven Approach for Executing the CG Method on Reconfigurable High-Performance Systems

Fabian Nowak[1], Ingo Besenfelder[1], Wolfgang Karl[1], Mareike Schmidtobreick[2], and Vincent Heuveline[2]

[1] Chair for Computer Architecture, Karlsruhe Institute of Technology
[2] Engineering Mathematics and Computing Lab, Karlsruhe Institute of Technology
ingo@besenfelder.de, firstname.lastname@kit.edu

Abstract. Employing reconfigurable computing systems for numerical applications poses an interesting and promising approach toward increased performance. We study the applicability of the Convey HC-1 for numerical applications by decomposing a preconditioned conjugate gradient (CG) method into several independent kernels that can operate concurrently. To allow overlapped execution and to minimize data transfers, we stream the data between the kernel units using a central buffer set. A microprogrammable control unit orchestrates memory accesses, buffer writes/reads and kernel execution, and allows for further algorithms to be executed on the available kernel units. Solving the Poisson problem can thereby be accelerated up to 10 times compared to a single-threaded software version on the HC-1 and up to 1.2 times compared to a 2-socket hex-core Intel Xeon Westmere system with 24 hardware threads for large problem sizes with only a single application engine.

1 Introduction

Numerical simulations provide great benefit in, for example, engineering and weather forecasting. These simulations need to be carried out as fast as possible to trigger appropriate actions early or to yield more accurate results. There the huge amount of data and the low compute-to-memory-access ratios pose significant problems. Thus, accelerators such as GPUs and FPGAs need to be employed and programmed thoughtfully. Although memory frequently isn't large enough to allow the efficient use of these accelerators, the Convey HC-1 is a promising system architecture that combines large amounts of accelerator-side memory with easy programming models and fast, large FPGAs.

We aim at creating a reusable framework on the HC-1 that solves the data transport problem. Moreover, given the large FPGAs and the small size of arithmetic units in contrast, we aim at exploiting task parallelism to fully leverage the FPGAs and the available memory bandwidth. To efficiently support an overlapping of data transport and the execution of multiple kernels while internally streaming data between the computational units, we additionally implement a microprogrammed control unit. Users may reprogram the unit in order to also employ our implementation for other algorithms. We evaluate our framework by accelerating a preconditioned CG method for the Poisson problem [1]. In this context, the HC-1 is also evaluated for its general ability to accelerate numerical applications by using our approach.

C. Hochberger et al. (Eds.): ARCS 2013, LNCS 7767, pp. 171–182, 2013.

Our results show that with our data-driven, task-parallel approach, HC-1 users can profit from up to 1.2 times the speed of a 2-socket hex-core HyperThreading Intel Xeon Westmere system and up to 10 times the performance of the Intel Xeon 5138 by using only a single application engine (AE). Performance projections indicate that with even larger FPGAs such as on the Convey HC-1^{ex}, much more speedup can be gained when more kernel units run in parallel.

This paper is structured as follows: we first give an overview over related work in Sect. 2, then analyze the CG method toward decomposition for FPGA implementation in Sect. 3. Our design is presented in Sect. 4 and its implementation is given in Sect. 5. The evaluation of our approach is discussed in Sect. 6 before drawing the final conclusions and giving an outlook in Sect. 7.

2 Related Work

For the Convey HC-1, Convey delivers so-called personalities providing general but also application-specific kernel implementations for the four user-programmable FPGAs. The performance of the floating-point vector personality is comparable to 4-5 Intel Westmere cores for stencil computations [2]. Although sparse matrix-vector multiplications conducted by the vector personality suffer from performance issues [3], Nagar et al. investigated in a sophisticated, powerful and fast sparse matrix personality [4] and achieved better results than a single Tesla S1070 GPU in most cases.

Porting numerical applications or selected kernels onto accelerators such as FPGAs and GPUs has already been published extensively. The Conjugate Gradient Method that we consider in this work could be accelerated via double-precision sparse matrix-vector multiplies on reconfigurable computing systems (RCSs), yielding a speedup of 1.3 [5]. With FPGAs being perfectly suited for arithmetics other than floating-point, the CG method can be accelerated on FPGAs via rational fraction implementations that only need few hardware resources and few pipeline stages, but run at high frequencies [6]. DuBois et al. implemented a sparse, non-preconditioned CG method on the SRC MAPStation. They overlapped several parts of the main loop so that the 30 times slower clocked RCS performed comparatively to single-core CPUs [7]. As they used high-level tools only, performance gain can be expected from hand-coded designs.

With the advent of multicores and heterogeneous systems, more research on the kernel's data access patterns was required. Cache-aware formulations of algorithms proved better performance than cache-oblivious ones on different architectures [8]. In addition, programmer-managed memory and data transfers, as necessary on the Cell B.E., showed best absolute and best relative performance in terms of bandwidth usage. For multicores, pinning data and computation to fixed nodes has become important in addition to in-place calculations that minimize cache accesses [9]. With the proposed in-place calculation scheme, the authors were able to frequently obtain performance near the optimum.

Another important aspect of this work poses data-driven, task-parallel program execution. This subject has gained much attraction recently by industry. AMD Heterogeneous Parallel Primitives (HPP) [10] targets at bringing task parallelism, which is not available with OpenCL, to the GPU. StarPU establishes a model to concurrently and asynchronously execute different tasks of an application on different computational units [11]. Their focus is mostly on the necessary task queues and scheduling. When parallelizing the Visualization ToolKit, Vo et al. considered data parallelism, task parallelism, i.e. concurrent execution of independent kernels, and pipeline parallelism, where data are streamed from one unit to another [12]. As a result, Gaussian smoothing can be 5 times faster on an 8-core system. For distributed computing, Active Pebbles [13] with its data-driven nature of performing computations showed to perform similarly to MPI implementations while at the same time being conveniently programmable.

Controlling concurrent execution of kernels or tasks on FPGAs can be achieved via microprogrammed controls [14]. While the pipelined version achieved higher frequency than the non-pipelined version, delayed branches are necessary.

3   A Preconditioned CG Method for FPGA Acceleration

A well-known problem in numerics is to solve the Poisson equation that occurs in electrostatics and mechanical engineering. Let $\Omega \subset \mathbb{R}^2$ be an open and bounded domain and let $f : \Omega \to \mathbb{R}, f \in C(\Omega)$ be a given function. A function $u : \bar{\Omega} \to \mathbb{R}, u \in C^2(\Omega) \cap C(\bar{\Omega})$ is to be found that satisfies $-\Delta u = f$ in Ω, where $\Delta := \frac{\partial^2}{\partial x^2} + \frac{\partial^2}{\partial y^2}$. We further demand homogeneous Dirichlet boundary conditions $u = 0$ on $\partial \Omega$ and set $\Omega = (0,1)^2$ for simplicity. We discretize our domain Ω by an equidistant grid with parameter h to $\Omega_h = \{(x,y) \in \Omega \mid x = k \cdot h, y = l \cdot h, (k,l) \in \mathbb{Z}^2\}$ and approximate $-\Delta$ by means of finite differences

$$-\Delta u = \frac{-u_{j+e_1} - u_{j-e_1} + 4u_j - u_{j+e_2} - u_{j-e_2}}{h^2} + O(h^2), \tag{1}$$

where $u_{j+e_i} := u(x_j + he_i)$ and e_i denotes the ith unit vector. We first apply a lexicographical ordering to the grid points, i.e. starting at one corner of the grid and numbering the nodes consecutively. Then we multiply Equation (1) with h^2 and obtain a matrix A_h with block structure

$$A_h = \begin{pmatrix} T & -I & & \\ -I & T & \ddots & \\ & \ddots & \ddots & -I \\ & & -I & T \end{pmatrix}, \quad T = \begin{pmatrix} 4 & -1 & & \\ -1 & 4 & \ddots & \\ & \ddots & \ddots & -1 \\ & & -1 & 4 \end{pmatrix}, \quad I = \begin{pmatrix} 1 & & \\ & \ddots & \\ & & 1 \end{pmatrix}, \tag{2}$$

and a corresponding right-hand side $b_h(x_j) = h^2 \cdot f(x_j)$. As a result of the sparsity pattern in Equation (2) we can express A_h as the well-known five-point stencil expressing Equation (1), illustrated in Figure 1(a).

Additionally, A_h has the advantage that it is symmetric and positive definite. For solving this kind of linear system, the CG method is the best known iterative technique [15]. The number of necessary iterations for reaching a good approximation to the solution depends on the condition number $\kappa(A)$ through the relation

$$\frac{\|e^{(k)}\|_A}{\|e^{(0)}\|_A} \leq 2 \left(\frac{\sqrt{\kappa(A)} - 1}{\sqrt{\kappa(A)} + 1} \right)^k, \tag{3}$$

(a) Five-point stencil of the Poisson problem (3) discretized by finite differences on an equidistant grid.

(b) Example of a red-black ordering. The rectangles denote the border values given by the boundary condition.

Fig. 1. Applying a 2-dimensional stencil operation onto a red-black reordered grid

where $e^{(k)} = x^{(k)} - x$ is the error in the kth iteration and $\|\cdot\|_A$ the energy norm. This inequality justifies the application of a preconditioner M where $\kappa(M^{-1}A) \ll \kappa(A)$. Conclusively, fewer iterations are necessary to solve the equivalent system $M^{-1}Ax = M^{-1}b$. In our case, M needs to be symmetric and positive definite in order to sustain these properties for the CG method.

An often applied preconditioner for the CG method is a descendant of the Successive-Over-Relaxation (SOR) method. SOR relies on the matrix splitting $\omega A = (D + \omega L) - ((1 - \omega)D - \omega U)$, where D is the diagonal of A, L its strict lower part, U its strict upper part and $\omega \in (0, 2)$ a relaxation parameter. An iteration scheme is then given by

$$(D + \omega L)x^{(k+1)} = \left((1 - \omega)D - \omega L^T\right)x^{(k)} + \omega b, \tag{4}$$

that solves the given equation system under the same premises as the CG method with the fulfilled additional requirement that all diagonal entries are positive. Given the sparsity pattern of our matrix (4), this can be easily translated to a stencil formulation. The drawback of the scheme is that the left-hand side of Equation (4) enforces the calculation of $x^{(k+1)}$ by a serial forward substitution. Using a red-black ordering of the unknowns remedies this drawback so that unknowns with the same color are decoupled from each other as illustrated in Figure 1(b).

An SOR preconditioner is then simply defined as one SOR iteration with the starting vector $x^{(0)}$ chosen to be the null vector and the right-hand side $b = r$. The preconditioner is applied in line 8 of Algorithm 1. To achieve the necessary symmetry, which is violated by the left-hand side in Equation (4), we update consecutively two times with reversed ordering of the unknowns the second time to get a symmetric SOR (SSOR) preconditioner, formally

$$M^{-1} = \omega(2 - \omega)(D + \omega L^T)^{-1}D(D + \omega L)^{-1}. \tag{5}$$

In the case of a red-black ordering, the best relaxation parameter ω is known to be 1, which renders the SSOR a symmetric Gauss-Seidel method. Equation (5) can then be simplified to gain Algorithm 2.

Decomposing the CG method into basic computational units reveals that many tasks can execute in parallel, given enough hardware resources. Furthermore, with the red-black ordering and the SGS preconditioner, the matrix multiplications or calculations

Algorithm 1. Preconditioned Conjugate Gradient method.

1: $r_0 = b - Ax_0$
2: $z_0 = M^{-1}r_0$
3: $p_0 = z_0$
4: **for** $k = 0, 1, \ldots, k_{max}$ **do**
5:     $\alpha_k = \frac{r_k^T z_k}{p_k^T A p_k}$
6:     $x_{k+1} = x_k + \alpha_k p_k$
7:     $r_{k+1} = r_k - \alpha_k A p_k$
8:     $z_{k+1} = M^{-1} r_{k+1}$
9:     **if** $r_{k+1}^T z_{k+1} < TOL$ **then**
10:       exit loop
11:    **end if**
12:     $\beta_k = \frac{r_{k+1}^T z_{k+1}}{r_k^T z_k}$
13:     $p_{k+1} = z_{k+1} + \beta_k p_k$
14: **end for**

Algorithm 2. Red-black symmetric Gauss-Seidel preconditioner (SSOR with $\omega = 1$) as applied in line 8 of Algorithm 1.

1: **for all** z_i in red points **do**
2:     $z_i = (r_i + (r_{j+e_1} + r_{j-e_1} + r_{j+e_2} + r_{j-e_2})/4)/4$
3: **end for**
4: **for all** z_i in black points **do**
5:     $z_i = r_i + (z_{j+e_1} + z_{j-e_1} + z_{j+e_2} + z_{j-e_2})/4$
6: **end for**

of the inverse for the preconditioner can be replaced by stencil operations. This allows streaming the data to the stencil units because for a successive stencil operation, only one more datum is required in the best case. The same applies to all vector operations when a second input stream is connected. This motivates a streaming-oriented implementation where pipeline parallelism can be exploited. We also consider task parallelism where functional units process independent data from several memory locations concurrently in order to fully exploit memory bandwidth.

4   Designing a Data-Driven Architecture

Key to supporting numerical problems are efficient stencil units and descendants, such as the red-black symmetric Gauss-Seidel preconditioner. These units must be provided with enough data, which can be achieved by exploiting memory data width such that two data are delivered within one cycle, thereby exploiting data parallelism. For the HC-1's data width of 64 bits, this means that we implement single-precision floating-point units only.

4.1   Data Buffer Set for Intermediate Storage and Streaming between Units

With only small memories on the FPGAs and comparatively high latencies to outside memory, streaming must be employed. Thereby, many function units can be executed overlappingly, obtaining pipeline parallelism. We therefore designed the buffer set based on FIFOs shown in Fig. 2: a buffer within the set is read only by one distinct function unit. In contrast, any unit can write to any other unit by writing to its buffer. For vector units, the buffers can carry up to 8K elements (around 90×90 resolution of the vector x); scalar buffers are only 64 elements deep. Dependencies in the dataflow (Fig. 4(a)) might lead to livelocks in case data aren't consumed fast enough or the

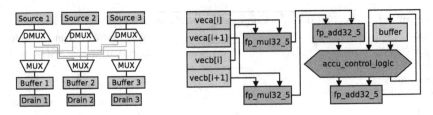

Fig. 2. Buffer set   **Fig. 3.** Scalar product unit

buffers are too small for the problem size. Figure 4(b) illustrates how to bypass them: data on the critical paths are written back to memory and reloaded via memory access units.

4.2 Memory Access

For the input data to be loaded, output data to be written and for overly large intermediate data to be stored temporarily in memories outside the FPGAs, direct memory access (DMA) engines are required. Writing DMA engines consume their assigned buffer, and reading DMA engines feed an arbitrary unit's input buffer so that the corresponding unit can work in a streaming fashion as long as input data are available. The HC-1 has 8 memory controllers (MCs), each for a different column of the memory space. The MCs operates on both clock edges, labelled "odd" and "even" ports, so that there is a total of 16 MC ports available. Instantiating the optional memory crossbar enables any MC to read or write from/to arbitrary addresses. From the analysis phase (cmp. Fig. 4(b)), we know that there is potential for livelocks when all buffers are filled so that data need to be written back to memory at some points within the algorithm implementation. Overall, this amounts to 7 read operations and 3 write operations, so we attach 10 DMA units to the buffer set and to the 16 MCs.

4.3 Vector Operation Units

As can be seen from Algorithm 1, most of the required operations are vector operations. Apart from vector addition and subtraction, the scalar product is required to calculate the A-norm and vectors need to be scaled by α and β, respectively.

The scalar (inner) product of two vectors is a classical reduction operation. With the two-datum buffer width, an implementation can be data-parallel internally by multiplying two vector components in parallel (cmp. Fig. 3 left). Their products then need to be added and then summed up in an accumulation unit (cmp. Fig. 3 bottom right). When the 5-stage pipeline of the product adder is filled, this adder produces one datum per cycle. The accumulating adder will have two valid operands only every second cycle in the beginning, which is handled and buffered by the control logic. This adder produces only partial results in the beginning, which need to be summed up. To achieve this goal, the output is fed back to the control logic. In case three operands are available, one of them is stored temporarily in a buffer and will be added later on automatically. The resulting pipeline has a length of $k = 21$ stages. Additional 26 cycles are required

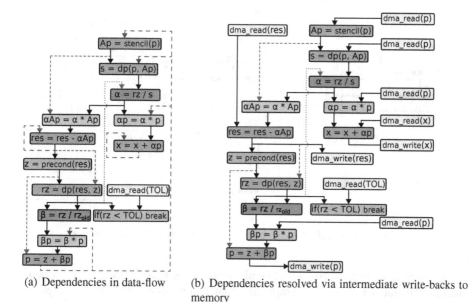

(a) Dependencies in data-flow

(b) Dependencies resolved via intermediate write-backs to memory

Fig. 4. Data-flow graph of the CG method. There are loop-carried dependencies that need to be resolved statically and offline before formulating a data-driven implementation.

for accumulating the buffer's content, resulting in $n + k - 1 + 26 = n + 46$ cycles for a vector of length n. Both adders are custom designs, extended with tags to check when the last two partial sums are added and the final result becomes valid.

Similar to the scalar product unit, the vector adder is given two pairs of elements from vectors a and b and uses two adders to produce two sums, which are finally merged into a 64-bit output register and written to the assigned buffer.

Many numerical implementations make heavy use of the operation $ax + y$, which is also highly applicable to the CG Algorithm 1. However, in this design we stick to two operands only and therefore need to split this operation into a regular vector addition as above and a separate multiplication with a scalar value. Again, the implementation is internally twofold data-parallel. The 32-bit scalar value is read from a 64-element scalar buffer and right-aligned inside the 64 bit.

4.4 Stencil Computation Unit and RBSGS Preconditioner

Nearly random access when fetching all matrix values for a stencil implementation requires four memory accesses on the HC-1 (one for the top, two for the middle, and one for the bottom). This can be avoided by saving the recently read value to internal line buffers of sufficient length. Limited by hardware resources, we use 2048-element line buffers of width 64 bit, which suffice for matrices with up to 4096 columns. As Figure 5 shows, it is sufficient to implement two line buffers because the single new value of the southern element can overwrite the old northern element that is no longer needed.

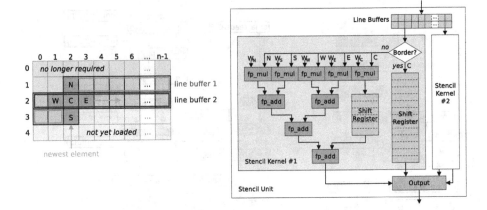

Fig. 5. Streaming southern stencil element only   **Fig. 6.** Pipelined stencil unit

Again, to consume two floating-point numbers per cycle, two kernel units are instantiated as illustrated in Figure 6. Employing four floating-point adders, the weighted stencil elements are added and registered appropriately. Special care is taken of the matrix border values for which no stencil can be calculated: they must also be written to the results streams, but the correct order must be guaranteed. For this purpose, border values are stored temporarily in shift registers.

For the RBSGS implementation, the individual weights for each stencil element from Algorithm 2 are 0.0625 for the neighbors of the black stencils and 0.25 for the neighbors of the red stencils and also for all center values. Thereby, we can avoid multiple scalar multiplications and the divisions as well. The above stencil implementation is slightly modified with different parameters for the red and black part and only computes every second stencil. However, at this stage the full advantage of custom hardware comes out as data locality can be exploited: having just computed the black stencil value, it can already be used as the new southern value in the red kernel unit (and vice versa, depending on the current row). Figure 7 shows the final, fully pipelined design with the necessary shift registers to take care of the correct ordering of all values.

4.5   Scalar Units

Besides vector operations, calculation with scalar values is required. For the scalar division unit (lines 5 and 12 in Algorithm 1), an off-the-shelf floating-point core is connected to a 64-entry scalar input buffer. Upon achieving a distinct threshold, the CG method can terminate. The comparator unit requires a scalar value and a constant, in our case, and is hence connected to a scalar input buffer as well. It is the only unit writing to the control unit that stalls until the result has been written to the register set.

4.6   Microprogrammable Control Unit

The central control unit contains a micro-instruction memory (MIM), a register set, an ALU, a sequencer and connects the functional units such as DMA units, stencil unit,

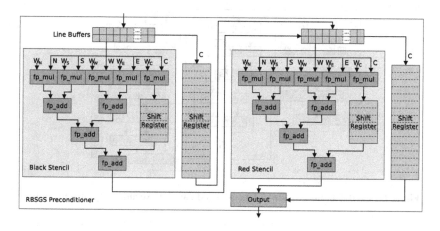

Fig. 7. Pipelined red-black symmetric Gauss-Seidel preconditioner

preconditioner and vector operation units. The MIM can be written by the DMA units. The control unit has a default program that waits for a program-load command from the host, then loads the microprogram to memory and finally executes the given program. The register set consists of 32 64-bit registers directly attached to the Convey coprocessor interface and can also be read and written by micro instructions. The ALU is required to perform adding, subtracting and shifting to implement counters and modify addresses. The sequencer is in charge of modifying the instruction pointer. Instructions are first fetched from the MIM, then they are decoded, and finally executed. Pipelining of the control unit is not required as most operations of the asynchronously running functional units will take many cycles, while the next instruction can already be fetched, decoded, and executed concurrently, so that in the end virtually all functional units can work in parallel despite the non-pipelined control unit.

5   Implementing, Synthesizing, Placing and Routing the Design

Synthesis of the entire Convey HC-1 FPGA project revealed that this design would not fit the device due to too much logic having to be packed too densely and therefore leading to badly routed paths. To overcome this limitation, we split the microprogram for executing the CG method into 4 distinct parts such that within each part, each functional unit is used only once as is depicted in Fig. 8 and accordingly needs to be instantiated only once. This block-wise decomposition achieved timing closure and produced a valid and fully functional bitstream. Its resource consumptions as well as the implementation results of the larger design variant are given for both the HC-1 and the HC-1^{ex} in Tab. 1.

6   Evaluation

We measured the execution times for both our hardware-supported and purely software versions of the single-precision CG method. They were compiled with -O0 for

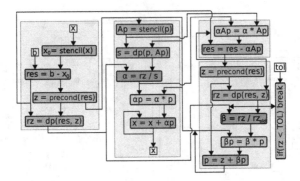

Fig. 8. Blocked data flow of the CG method and parallel execution of few units only

the Open64-based Convey compiler to be comparative with GCC, which is used for the multithreaded versions, unless otherwise noted. Also, no additional optimizations have been applied to our hardware design, yet. For all implementations, stencil calculations have been used instead of matrix multiplications, thereby avoiding the overhead of sparse matrix formats for the sparsely populated finite-differences matrix. As can be seen from Fig. 9, the performance of a single instance (one FPGA) of the modified, blocked coprocessor version is for small problem sizes inferior to a 24-thread version compiled with -O2 executing on a 2-socket hex-core Intel Xeon Westmere, but its advantage comes for large data sizes when generic, portable stencil implementations suffer from cache benefits. Furthermore, based on simulation results we prognosed the to be expected performance of the full design. It suffers not only from not achieving timing closure on the HC-1, but also from lack of block memory on the Virtex-5 such that the buffers only suffice for problems of dimension 90 – for larger problem sizes, intermediate stores and loads to and from memory are needed. For this reason, we also synthesized the full version for the HC-1^{ex}. On the large Virtex-6, there are many more block RAMs available to further increase the size of the buffer set.

In addition to comparing the execution times of the coprocessor design, we are also interested in achievable performance. Figure 10 shows the maximum achievable

Table 1. Resource consumption and achievable timing

Resource	Blocked Variant HC-1	Full Variant HC-1	HC-1^{ex}
Slices	34,311 (66%)	45,210 (87%)	58,039 (48%)
Slice Registers	86,379 (41%)	112,603 (54%)	110,593 (11%)
Slice LUTs	89,445 (43%)	134,381 (64%)	172,114 (36%)
Slice LUT Flip-Flop Pairs	115,181 (55%)	159,820 (77%)	190,879 (40%)
RAMB36	255 (89%)	264 (92%)	274 (38%)
DSP48	110 (57%)	138 (72%)	138 (15%)
Clock	6.643 ns	14.164 ns	14.889 ns
(targeting 6.667 ns timing closure)	(99.6%)	(212%)	(223%)

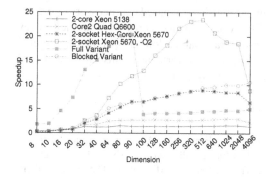

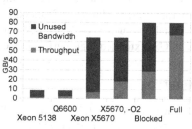

Fig. 9. Speedup of one AE over sequential software version on Intel Xeon 5138 on the Convey HC-1

Fig. 10. Usage of available bandwidth (scaled to 4 Application Engines for the HC-1)

memory bandwidth and the computed or measured throughput for the evaluated architectures. Note that caches and especially the data-driven, buffer-supported AE design would allow for more throughput than available bandwidth. The figure also illustrates that it is possible to exploit the large memory bandwidth on the HC-1 for accelerating computations when all four FPGAs are used on a partitioned problem, i.e., the input data split into a 2×2 grid, or for four different problems in parallel being solved via a single coprocessor call to the four different application engines with distinct parameters each.

7   Conclusions and Outlook

We designed a data-driven, micro-programmable framework for the Convey HC-1 to accelerate entire numerical applications. Reading input data, storing and loading intermediate data, passing data between computational units, and starting them is handled via the microprogram. As an example, we evaluated a preconditioned conjugate gradient solver for the Poisson equation whose sparsely populated matrix can be reordered by means of the red-black scheme. The matrix multiplication could then be replaced by a simple stencil computation. Similarly, the symmetric Gauss-Seidel preconditioner could also be formulated based on stencils. Due to hardware constraints of the chosen HC-1, only few units fit on the FPGA, yielding only a speedup of 1.2 compared to 24 OpenMP threads with optimization level 2, and of 10 compared to a sequential implementation on the HC-1's CPU for 4096×4096 data sets and no optimizations. This could be achieved by exploiting data parallelism within vector units, pipeline parallelism via streaming between successive operations, and task parallelism by concurrent execution of independent functional units.

For the HC-1[ex], our initial design with more functional units will become synthesizable after minor adaptations. The size of the intermediate buffers and buffer sets can be increased there so that larger problems can be solved, potentially doubling the currently achievable performance. Apart from that, a large design space has been opened with regard to the number of DMA and vector units.

Much work is currently being done integrating FPGA-based coprocessors into commodity systems while at the same time FPGA performance increases. With the Convey programming model and advanced, user-programmable, domain-specifically targeted personalities such as our proposed one, many more performance gains can be expected by FPGA-extended high-performance computing systems in future.

References

1. Chen, R.S., Yung, E.K.N., Chan, C., Wang, D.X., Fang, D.G.: Application of the SSOR preconditioned CG algorithm to the vector FEM for 3D full-wave analysis of electromagnetic-field boundary-value problems. IEEE Transactions on Microwave Theory and Techniques 50(4), 1165–1172 (2002)
2. Kunkel, J.M., Nerge, P.: System Performance Comparison of Stencil Operations with the Convey HC-1. Technical report, Research Group: Scientific Computing, University of Hamburg (November 2010)
3. Augustin, W., Weiss, J.P., Heuveline, V.: Convey HC-1 Hybrid Core Computer – The Potential of FPGAs in Numerical Simulation. In: HipHac 2011, pp. 1–8. KIT Scientific Publishing (2011)
4. Nagar, K., Bakos, J.: A Sparse Matrix Personality for the Convey HC-1. In: FCCM 2011, pp. 1–8. IEEE Computer Society (2011)
5. Morris, G.R., Prasanna, V.K., Anderson, R.D.: A Hybrid Approach for Mapping Conjugate Gradient onto an FPGA-Augmented Reconfigurable Supercomputer. In: FCCM 2006, pp. 3–12. IEEE Computer Society (2006)
6. Maslennikow, O., Lepekha, V., Sergyienko, A.: FPGA Implementation of the Conjugate Gradient Method. In: Wyrzykowski, R., Dongarra, J., Meyer, N., Waśniewski, J. (eds.) PPAM 2005. LNCS, vol. 3911, pp. 526–533. Springer, Heidelberg (2006)
7. DuBois, D., DuBois, A., Boorman, T., Connor, C., Poole, S.: An Implementation of the Conjugate Gradient Algorithm on FPGAs. In: FCCM 2008, pp. 296–297. IEEE Computer Society (2008)
8. Kamil, S., Datta, K., Williams, S., Oliker, L., Shalf, J., Yelick, K.: Implicit and explicit optimizations for stencil computations. In: Proc. of the 2006 Workshop on Memory System Performance and Correctness, pp. 51–60. ACM (2006)
9. Augustin, W., Heuveline, V., Weiss, J.-P.: Optimized Stencil Computation Using In-Place Calculation on Modern Multicore Systems. In: Sips, H., Epema, D., Lin, H.-X. (eds.) Euro-Par 2009. LNCS, vol. 5704, pp. 772–784. Springer, Heidelberg (2009)
10. Gaster, B.R., Howes, L.: Can GPGPU Programming Be Liberated from the Data-Parallel Bottleneck? IEEE Computer 45, 42–52 (2012)
11. Augonnet, C., Thibault, S., Namyst, R., Wacrenier, P.-A.: STARPU: A Unified Platform for Task Scheduling on Heterogeneous Multicore Architectures. In: Sips, H., Epema, D., Lin, H.-X. (eds.) Euro-Par 2009. LNCS, vol. 5704, pp. 863–874. Springer, Heidelberg (2009)
12. Vo, H.T., Comba, J.L., Geveci, B., Silva, C.T.: Streaming-Enabled Parallel Data Flow Framework in the Visualization ToolKit. IEEE Computing in Science Engineering 13(5), 72–83 (2011)
13. Willcock, J.J., Hoefler, T., Edmonds, N.G., Lumsdaine, A.: Active Pebbles: Parallel Programming for Data-Driven Applications. In: ICS 2011, pp. 235–244. ACM (2011)
14. Bomar, B.W.: Implementation of Microprogrammed Control in FPGAs. IEEE Transactions on Industrial Electronics 49(2), 415–422 (2002)
15. Saad, Y.: Iterative methods for sparse linear systems, 2nd edn. Society for Industrial and Applied Mathematics (SIAM) (2003)

Custom Reconfigurable Architecture Based on Virtex 5 Lookup Tables

Rico Backasch[1] and Christian Hochberger[2]

[1] Chair for Embedded Systems
Dresden University of Technology
Department of Computer Science
Institute for Computer Engineering
`rico.backasch@tu-dresden.de`
[2] Computer Systems Group
Department of Electrical Engineering and Information Technology
Technical University of Darmstadt
`hochberger@rs.tu-darmstadt.de`

Abstract. Reconfigurable architectures combine the high flexibility of general purpose processors with the high performance of specialized hardware architectures. They can be implemented on field programmable gate arrays or on custom coarse grain reconfigurable arrays (CGRA). Often the CGRAs are designed in a domain specific way. In this contribution, we present a mixture of both: a domain specific custom reconfigurable architecture implemented with the help of a particular feature of modern Virtex FPGAs (Virtex 5 and up). We show that our custom architecture joins the qualities of both alternatives: a full hardware implementation and a reconfigurable solution based on vendor tools. Our custom tool for the programming of the architecture performs considerably faster than using partial reconfiguration and the standard vendor tools and is smaller than a full hardware solution.

Keywords: Custom Architecture, Dynamic Partial Reconfiguration, Trace Analyzing.

1 Introduction

For the past 20 years, reconfigurable architectures have been promoted for many different application areas. They offer better performance than general purpose processors, but can be adapted to the needs of individual applications within their applications domain. Also, reconfigurable architectures allow to apply a particular chip design to more than one application, thereby leading to a better amortization of the non recurring costs. Eventually, reconfigurable architectures may even provide virtualization of hardware, as different parts of the application can be mapped to the reconfigurable resources at different times.

Field programmable gate arrays (FPGAs) based on lookup tables (LUTs) are reconfigurable by design, as the content of the table can be exchanged for different applications (as well as the routing configuration). In case that individual

C. Hochberger et al. (Eds.): ARCS 2013, LNCS 7767, pp. 183–194, 2013.

tables can be exchanged at runtime, such a system is typically considered a dynamically partial reconfigurable system. The advantage of this approach is that some part of the FPGA can execute the application while other parts of the FPGA are being reconfigured for later use.

Unfortunately, the usage of the partial reconfiguration feature is rather complicated. The designer has to apply a special tool flow and the design itself needs to be tailored to this approach. For a long period, the required tool support was available only upon request to the FPGA manufacturer. In fact, some FPGA vendors considered partial reconfiguration so critical, that neither their tools included support for this, nor did they publish the required information to implement the required tools on your own.

Nevertheless, partial reconfiguration allows the designer to adapt a circuit to the specific requirements of an application much quicker. Only the exchanged part of the circuit needs to be synthesized. Especially the physical synthesis (place and route) is completed faster as if the whole chip had to be treated.

Although partial reconfiguration offers advantages over the traditional development approach, it is still not often used since the handling of the tools is rather complicated. Alternatively, the designer can implement a domain specific reconfigurable architecture on the FPGA. In this case the designer also needs to supply the tools which are required to program this architecture. Even if this may be a lot of additional work, it might improve the applicability of the system, since the requirements of the end user can be regarded in the specific synthesis tool.

The focus of this paper is to show the rewards for building your own custom reconfigurable architecture. Compared with two alternatives (1) a full hardware implementation that can be switched into different modes or 2) using dynamic partial reconfiguration), a domain specific reconfigurable architecture and an accompanying tool can provide the best of both alternatives. It can be reconfigured much faster than using partial reconfiguration, but consumes much fewer resources than the full hardware implementation.

The remainder of this paper is organized as follows. The following section gives an overview of the application domain that is considered for this work. Following, in section 3 we discuss the different implementation alternatives and our own reconfigurable architecture. Section 4 gives a short evaluation of the three alternative approaches to customize the hardware for the application. Eventually, section 5 gives a conclusion and sketches some future activities.

2   Application Domain

Modern embedded systems contain thousands of lines of software code, often even for several processor cores working in parallel. Debugging this code has become a very time consuming part of the overall software development process.

Runtime verification [1] has successfully been used in complex software scenarios to assess the software quality and to identify and eliminate bugs. A runtime verification system tests defined properties of the running software by analyzing software traces. Properties are defined in form of linear temporal logic formulas (LTL[2]).

Our aim is to analyze the trace data of embedded processors on the fly. The analysis should be able to check for arbitrary properties of the executed code. To this end, we use an FPGA to process trace data in real-time which are generated from trace systems like ARM ETM[3], NEXUS[4], MCDS[5] or hidICE[6]. Our verification system consists of a module which processes the trace data and another module, which analyzes this processed data. Customizing the trace processing seems to involve to much design effort, so that we decided to build a rather generic trace processing module. It generates 150 boolean signals (so called propositions), which are derived from many different sources: reaching a particular source line, reading or writing variables, counting instructions in particular address ranges, aggregations of all these conditions and even comparisons of these aggregations with predefined constants. Checking these propositions is usually done by a finite state machine (FSM). We implement this FSM in a microprogrammed way to simplify the exchange of the transition function.

Eventually, trace processing generates much more propositions than we can handle as input signals for the microprogrammed FSM. Fortunately, studies have shown, that the number of required propositions within one rule is below six[7]. Hence, we build the microprogrammed FSM with six inputs. In turn, we need a third component that selects the right properties for the FSM. This selection must be newly defined every time the FSM is exchanged.

In our system, we added a very small soft core called SpartanMC[8] as reconfiguration manager to exchange the FSM memory and to handle the reconfiguration of the selection module. Figure 1 shows the described system with the incomming trace data which is processed and has to be routed the the FSM.

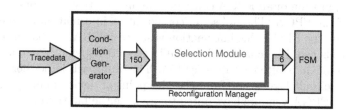

Fig. 1. System Overview with producer and consumer

3   Implementation

The selection module can be implemented in three different ways: A full hardware implementation, dynamic partial reconfiguration and a domain specific reconfigurable architecture, which we will now discuss in detail.

3.1   Full Hardware Implementation (Multiplexer)

The first realization idea is building six 150 to 1 multiplexer, each with a 8bit select signal. It is shown in figure 2. This is the simplest solution, but also the biggest. In terms of reconfiguration time, it is the fastest routing module.

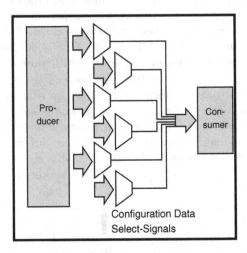

Fig. 2. Multiplexer Solution

3.2   Partial Reconfiguration

The main function of the module is to create a direct connection from one input to one output, which is a very simple line of code in a hardware description language. Partial Reconfiguration can be used to implement and download this connection into the device.

The configuration of an FPGA consists of many bits that control the internal operation of the FPGA. The full set of configuration information is called a bitstream. Inside the FPGA this information is stored in SRAM cells. In principle, all SRAM cells could be connected as one large shift register. Then, a full configuration could be shifted into the FPGA. This approach is neither from the viewpoint of circuit layout nor from the viewpoint of device management very useful. Thus, FPGA vendors have opted to organize the bitstream into so called frames. Each frame that is shifted into the device, carries an address information. Typically, the frame is shifted into a central shift register and then loaded in parallel into the appropriate SRAM cells.

This approach allows the bitstream to selectively reconfigure individual frames within the FPGA. Early FPGAs used full columns of the FPGA as frames. Modern FPGAs use segments of one column as frames and thus can address the configuration information more fine grained.

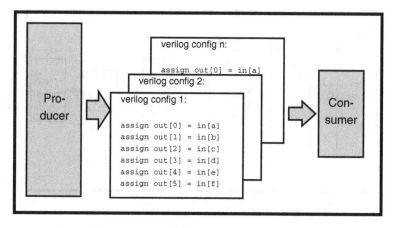

Fig. 3. System with partial reconfiguration

If a bitstream that is loaded into the device does not contain all configuration frames it is called a partial bitstream. Engineering such a partial bitstream is non trivial. Therefore, the FPGA vendors did not supply the tool support for a long time, but now it is available.

One of the problems that have to be solved for partial reconfiguration is the connection between the static part of the design and the reconfigured region. Care must be taken, such that no illegal situation arises during reconfiguration (i.e. two outputs actively driving a single wire segment). For this purpose, so called bus macros must be inserted into the design (nowadays built with LUTs). In order to do this automatically, the designer has to identify a geometrical region which is the target of the reconfiguration and he has to define an interface to the reconfigurable region (typically done by inserting a black box model into the verilog code).

The tools now allow the designer to specify the functionality of the reconfigurable area in the usual manner (HDL or schematic). The tool flow then produces a mapped circuit which is in turn placed and routed (obeying the region restrictions of the reconfigurable area). Eventually, a bitstream is created that only contains the frames which are affected by the reconfigurable region.

Figure 3 shows how partial reconfiguration can be used in our application domain. The main part that needs to be configured individually for each specification is the selection of conditions. Condition selection is thus delegated to a partial reconfigurable region and a new configuration is computed for each new specification.

3.3   Custom Architecture

Working with the partial reconfiguration is not very easy for a person that has no knowledge about FPGAs. But our application should be used by such people. Thus we developed our own reconfigurable routing architecture which is powerful

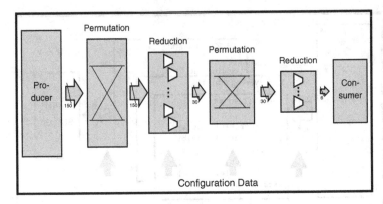

Fig. 4. System with reconfigurable architecture

enough to realize the required function and can be easily and fast configured. Figure 4 shows the system with our architecture.

Basic Elements. The basic idea of our architecture is to build a static network of basic elements and change the behavior of this network without a new synthesis. These basic elements are called *configurable lookup tables (CFGLUT)* and are a version of the *shift register lookup tables*, which are primitives of Virtex 5 and newer Xilinx FPGAs. These lookup tables have 5 inputs and two outputs. One output deals with all 5 inputs and the other one only with the lower 4 inputs. Our approach uses only the first output. Figure 5 shows such a basic element. These lookup tables work like normal lookup tables, but have additional connections to exchange the behavior. The behavior of a 5-input lookup table is defined by a 32 bit wide memory inside the table. Every combination of the inputs addresses one bit of this memory. Normally, the value of this memory is calculated by the synthesis-tool. Configurable lookup tables provide access to this memory through four extra connections. The connections are *serial data in*, *configure enable*, *configuration clock* and *serial data out*. With these signals, the memory can be used like a shift register and the behavior of the table can be exchanged manually. Because the memory content is shifted serially, 32 clock cycles are required to reconfigure one lookup table.

Reduction Stages. As described in section 2, we have to provide six output signals. Thus, we use six parallel *CFGLUT* to reduces 30 input signals to 6 output signals. The possible combinations are limited because only a block of 5 signals can be combined into one output signal as the affected table has five inputs (see figure 5). This structure of tables can realize a reduction of signals and is called reduction stage with a width of 6 (*red[width]*)[1]. It is shown in figure 6. Unfortunately, only using this structure would prevent us from routing adjacent input signals to the consumer.

---

[1] red[width] means a reduction stage that reduces $5 \cdot width$ signals to *width* signals. A red[1] is one basic element and a red[6] reduces 30 signals to 6 signals.

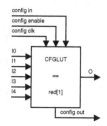

Fig. 5. A configurable lookup table

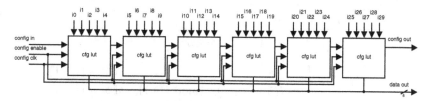

Fig. 6. Reduction stage: red[6]

Permutation Stages. There are 30! possibilities to combine the 30 input signals and one combination of these signals is called a permutation. It is infeasible and not necessary to use all possible permutations. Instead, five different permutations are used in the implemented architecture. An important step is to choose only permutations which are not equal. Two permutations are equal when the input signals of a lookup table of the first permutation are only a shuffled version of the input signals of the same lookup table in the second permutation. For example, table 1 shows 3 different input signal permutations of a reduction stage with width two and the equation 1 shows the realized functions of the two basic elements. Permutation *P1* is equal to permutation *P2* because the two *CFGLUT*s realize the same function in both permutations. They are redundant. If this property is valid for each pair of tables in two permutations, both are equal. Permutation *P3* is not equal to *P1* or *P2* because each *CFGLUT* has a different set of input signals.

The architecture tries to select permutations which are not equal. The mapping of an input signal to an output signal of one permutation is done by equation 2 where x is the number of the input signal in the input vector, i size of the input vector, j the number of the permutation and $f(x, j)$ the position of the signal in the output vector. The number of input signals (i) has to be a multiply of 5 because a basic element has five inputs and one output. The verilog implementation of a permutation is a for-loop which assigns every input signal to the output signal calculated with the given equation. Every permutation is followed by a reduction stage and five parallel instances are called permutation stage.

Table 1. Example permutations at red[2]

Signal	P1	P2	P3
CFGLUT 0 0	0	4	0
1	1	3	5
2	2	2	1
3	3	1	6
4	4	0	2
CFGLUT 1 5	5	9	7
6	6	8	3
7	7	7	8
8	8	6	4
9	9	5	9

$$P1 \begin{cases} out[0] & = f(i0, i1, i2, i3, i4) \\ out[1] & = f(i5, i6, i7, i8, i9) \end{cases}$$

$$P2 \begin{cases} out[0] & = f(i0, i1, i2, i3, i4) \\ out[1] & = f(i5, i6, i7, i8, i9) \end{cases}$$

$$P3 \begin{cases} out[0] & = f(i0, i1, i2, i5, i6) \\ out[1] & = f(i3, i4, i7, i8, i9) \end{cases}$$

$$(1)$$

$$f(x, j) = \begin{cases} x, & \text{if } x = (i - 1) \\ x * ((5 * j) + 1) \pmod{i - 1}, & \text{if } x \neq (i - 1) \end{cases}$$

$$i = \text{size of inputvector(constant)}$$

$$\text{x = input signal } (0 \ldots \text{i-1}), \text{j = number of permutation } (0 \ldots 4)$$

$$(2)$$

Altogether, with one permutation stage and one reduction stage we provide an architecture which combines 30 input signals to six output signals. In our application we want to select six signals out of 150, so we put a second reduction and permutation stage in front of the first one with a width of 30 which has 150 input signals and 30 output signals.

Resource Estimation. A reduction stage has as many CFGLUTs as output signals. This means that a small reduction stage consists of 6 CFGLUTs and a large reduction stage consists of 30 CFGLUTs. A permutation stage consists of 5 reduction stages. Table 2 gives an overview of the used lookup tables in the implemented architecture.

As one can see, there are 216 LUTs in the design which are connected serially. Each lookup table comprises 32 bit of memory. In other words, the whole configuration data for this structure contains 6912 bit ($32 \, bit * 216$) and needs the same amount of clock cycles to be shifted into the CFGLUTs. Given a configuration clock of 50Mhz, 13,824 μs are required to configure the architecture.

Configuring this architecture is as simple as the architecture itself. Only 3 Pins are required to shift the data in. In our case we put a small microcontroller[8] into the design. This controller does not only configure the LUT structure but also configures and controls other parts of the hardware e.g. the FSM memory. The controller receives the configuration data through a USB connection and shifts it into the chain of lookup tables. However, a simple JTAG-Controller can also do the configuration.

Configuration- & Download-Tool. The behavior of the presented architecture is defined by a configuration which consists of the memory of the configurable

Table 2. Resource Consumption

Stage	Number of CFGLUT	Note
small reduction stage	6	reduces 30 signals to six signals
small permutation stage	30	shuffles 30 signals
large reduction stage	30	reduces 150 signals zu 30 signals
large permutation stage	150	shuffles 150 signals
total	216	+ Overhead for programming logic

lookup tables. Computing a configuration for this network of tables is done on a hosts PC with a special tool, similar to the partial reconfiguration tool flow.

The tool has to know the architecture of the network. For this reason, the architecture is modeled in the tool as a set of connected objects. In future versions, the architecture can be described as an XML-structure and from this structure the model can be generated. The model includes all connections of the tables which allows using a simple search algorithm. Up to now, the network is used as a simple routing network. So the function in the tables realize the mapping of one of the inputs to the output. Unused inputs are not interesting and are set to *don't care*.

The implemented algorithm is a depth-first-search starting at the outputs of the architecture. It searches a path through the tables and always tries the first input of the table. If there is another table connected to this input, the first input of this table is used to find the path. If there is no other table, the algorithm checks if the reached input port is the expected port. If it is the wrong port, it goes back to the last found table and tries the next input as long as there are untried inputs. If all five input-paths fail, the algorithm goes one table back and so on. If the expected port is reached, the path will be marked as used and the configuration values are stored in the model. The five configuration values are shown in table 3. If the algorithm comes back to the starting point without a positive search result, the algorithm is stopped and the tool exits with an error. Future versions will try to delete existing connections, find different paths for the deleted connections and then find a path for the failing connection (essentially leading to a full backtracking algorithm).

The values of the lookup tables are stored in the model of the architecture. As mentioned above, the model is an exact copy of the real hardware. The bitstream generation is as easy as the search algorithm. In other words the algorithm walks along the configuration signals, fetches the configuration value of each table and writes it into the bitstream. The generated bitstream can be shifted into the real tables.

Summary. The reconfigurable architecture is a network of configurable LUTs as basic elements. As shown in figure 7 the architecture is structured into 4 stages, 2 permutation stages and 2 reduction stages. Permutation stages are parallel reductions stages with shuffled input connections. The first permutation stage shuffles 150 signals. The following reduction stage reduces the number of

Table 3. Routing Information

active input	value of lut memory
0	0xAAAAAAAA
1	0xCCCCCCCC
2	0xF0F0F0F0
3	0xFF00FF00
4	0xFFFF0000

signals to 30. These 30 signals are shuffled in the third stage which is the second permutation stage. The last stage is the second reduction stage and reduces the number of signals to six. All lookup tables are connected serially with its configuration signals which allows to change their behavior through a bitstream.

4   Evaluation

All three presented solutions have been implemented, tested and compared with each other. The results are shown in table 4.

The custom architecture requires 28% fewer lookup tables than the full featured multiplexer. Also generating and downloading a new configuration is more than two orders of magnitude faster as the partial reconfiguration approach because the algorithm is much simpler as the algorithms of the partial reconfiguration tool flow.

To avoid the compute time of partial reconfiguration and to prevent the user from the high complexity of this tool chain, one might think to precompute all possible configurations This is not possible, because on a single core computer this takes $156 \cdot 10^6$ years. Also if one partial reconfiguration bitfile requires $50KB$ storage, you have to spent $468PB$ for all configurations. The custom architecture does not require additional storage space because the configuration data is held in the LUT.

An important question to the network is: can this network route all possible combination of six chosen inputs through the LUTs to the output pins. To answer

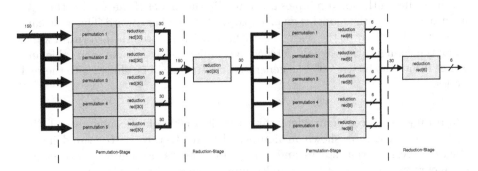

Fig. 7. Stages of reconfigurable architecture

Table 4. Solution comparison

	multiplexer	partial reconfiguration	custom architecture
tool runtime (s)	0	502	2
download (s)	0	1	10
resources (LUT)	300	0	216

this question we checked all expedient possibilities. Expedient possibilities are all combinations were never input is routed to two different outputs. The number of this combinations are calculated in equation 3. This check showed that 98.6% of this combinations can be mapped to our architecture.

$$x = \binom{150}{6} = 10,293 \cdot 10^{12} \tag{3}$$

Another important issue is the delay of the implemented module. The delay of the partial reconfiguration realization depends on the functions implemented in the module while the delay is fixed in our approach because every signal has to pass 4 stages. Also the delay of the multiplexer is constant. The minimal delay of the partial reconfiguration realization is the delay of two LUTs, because the inserted bus macros are built with LUTs.

An advantage of our approach is the usability. The user does not have to know anything about writing Verilog or VHDL, synthesis tools or FPGA development. The user has to define the function and the developed tool does everything else, which is in contrast to using complicated synthesis tools.

5   Conclusion

We have analyzed three different implementations of a signal selection box: A full hardware multiplexer, a dynamic partial reconfiguration of the FPGA and a custum reconfigurable architecture.

The last one is a network of configurable lookup tables which are primitives of the Virtex 5 and newer Xilinx FPGAs. We implemented reduction stages with these basic elements to reduce the number of input signals. We also built permutation stages to increase the number of mappable combinations of the input signals. The architecture is a composition of 216 lookup tables and all tables form one long shift register through their configuration ports.

A tool on the host PC computes a configuration for this network. This config-uration is send to a microcontroller which configures the tables. Our approach is ~ 200 times faster than the partial reconfiguration approach and consumes $\sim 2/3$ of the resources of the full hardware multiplexer.

Compared with the reconfigurable approach, our architecture has the advan-tage of a fixed delay and fixed resource consumption. Furthermore the user doesn't have to install a synthesis tool or have to know how a hardware description language.

Compared with the full hardware multiplexer, our architecture has the huge advantage that it is possible to compute combined condition signals in the network, which is impossible in the multiplexer.

In the future, we will improve the tool in order to support this combinatorial usage of the network. Also, we will extend the algorithm to support a better backtracking, in order to find an optimal solution. Additionally, we think that other permutation schemes might provide better routeability with less resource consumption, so we want to explore different permutation schemes as well.

References

1. Leucker, M., Schallhart, C.: A brief account of runtime verification. Journal of Logic and Algebraic Programming 78(5), 293–303 (2009)
2. Bauer, A., Leucker, M., Schallhart, C.: Runtime verification for LTL and TLTL. ACM Transactions on Software Engineering and Methodology (TOSEM) (2009) (in press)
3. ARM: Coresight (2011), http://www.arm.com/products/system-ip/coresight/index.php
4. NEXUS-Forum: The Nexus 5001 forum (2011), http://nexus5001.org
5. Infineon: MCDS - multi-core debug solution (2011), http://www.infineon.com
6. Hochberger, C., Weiss, A.: Acquiring an exhaustive, continuous and real-time trace from socs. In: IEEE International Conference on Computer Design, ICCD 2008, pp. 356–362 (October 2008)
7. Dwyer, M.B., Avrunin, G.S., Corbett, J.C.: Patterns in property specifications for finite-state verification. In: International Conference on Software Engineering (ICSE), pp. 411–420. IEEE (1999)
8. Hempel, G., Hochberger, C.: A resource optimized SoC kit for FPGAs. In: Bertels, K., Najjar, W.A., van Genderen, A.J., Vassiliadis, S. (eds.) International Conference on Field Programmable Logic and Applications (FPL 2007), pp. 761–764. IEEE (2007)

Profiling Energy Consumption of I/O Functions in Embedded Applications

Shiao-Li Tsao, Cheng-Kun Yu, and Yi-Hsin Chang

Department of Computer Science, National Chiao Tung University, Hsinchu, Taiwan
sltsao@cs.nctu.edu.tw, {louis.ckyu,changyihsin}@gmail.com

Abstract. I/O operations consume a significant portion of energy of an embedded system. To profile the energy consumption of I/O requests issued by a specific application helps developers to understand the energy consumption of the software and to further optimize the energy efficiency of the designs. However, most of the existing energy profiling tools concentrate on the energy consumption analyses of processors and memory, and provide limited supports to associate the energy consumption of an I/O device with high-level I/O function calls. In this paper, we propose and implement a generic framework, called energy **pro**filing **m**odule (**EPROM**), which can estimate the energy consumption of I/O requests in application processes. The experimental results based on two typical I/O devices, i.e. WLAN and TFT-LCD, demonstrate that our proposed framework can provide accurate estimates on the energy consumption of I/O function calls and the errors between the estimation and measurement results are below 4%.

Keywords: Energy Efficiency, Energy Profiling and Estimation, Embedded System, I/Os.

1 Introduction

The energy efficiency becomes one of the most important design considerations for embedded devices such as mobile phones and tablets [1]. Considering more and more embedded devices offer Internet-based and cloud-based services, the energy consumption of I/O devices such as display and wireless communication becomes a critical design issue [4].

To understand the energy consumption of an embedded application and the energy consumption of each function in the application helps developers to diagnose energy consumption problems. Moreover, many power saving and power management strategies rely on accurate energy estimation of an embedded system [2-3]. Therefore, technologies that estimate and monitor the energy consumption of embedded applications become very important. To estimate the energy consumption of an I/O device and to associate the energy consumption of the I/O device with its I/O requests (e.g. I/O function calls) is even more challenging since application processes generate I/O requests simultaneously and the I/O requests are scheduled by operating system (OS) in an asynchronous manner. In this paper, we propose a generic I/O energy profiling

C. Hochberger et al. (Eds.): ARCS 2013, LNCS 7767, pp. 195–206, 2013.

framework, called energy **pro**filing **m**odule (EPROM), to associate the energy consumption of an I/O device with I/O requests issued by embedded applications. The
proposed framework is implemented in the Linux kernel 2.6.15 running on an embedded system. The experimental results based on two typical I/O devices, i.e. WLAN and
TFT-LCD, demonstrate that the energy estimation error is less than 4%. With the proposed tool, developers can obtain accurate energy estimation of I/O events and optimize the energy efficiency of the software designs and power management policies.

The rest of the paper is organized as follows. Section 2 summarizes the related
work. Section 3 presents design concept and implementation of the proposed framework. Section 4 analyzes the experimental results. Finally, we conclude this study in
Section 5.

2   Related Work

With increasing attention to energy consumption issues of embedded devices, a number of energy estimation tools have been proposed. The existing solutions for estimating the energy consumption of an embedded system can be categorized into
measurement-based and model-based approaches. For measurement-based approaches, the energy consumption is measured by an external equipment such as a
multi-meter, data acquisition card (DAQ), or an oscilloscope [5-6]. For example,
PowerScope [5] is a measurement-based energy profiling tool which can associate the
energy consumption of an processor with software activities. However, they did not
consider I/O events and the synchronization between the measurement equipment and
the target system may introduce estimation error.

Model-based approaches estimate the power consumption of an embedded system
according to power models at different granularities such as transistor-level, architec-
ture-level and instruction-level [7-8]. Depending on the granularity that the power
model considers, the estimation process may spend a period of time to get an energy
report of the software. Since developers may want to modify applications and see its
energy efficiency, they prefer fast energy estimation of the applications. Therefore,
running embedded applications on a target embedded system and estimating the energy
consumption of embedded applications based on performance counters and high-level
power models have been considered. For example, processors with hardware performance counters can monitor the performance events, such as cache misses, TLB hits,
and these parameters reflect the system activities which are strongly correlated with the
energy consumption of the system [9-11]. [12-15] gather high-level software activities
such as execution time, processor utilization, memory utilization, and power states of
components to evaluate the energy consumption of software. In [12], the tool provides
application-level energy analyses, and [13] further supports on-line energy profiling.
[14] and [15] estimate the energy consumption of applications running on virtual machine such as Java virtual machine on mobile devices and notebooks. Most of the previous work focused on the energy consumption estimation of processors and systems,
but did not elaborate the energy consumption issues of I/O devices. Some studies proposed power models for I/O devices. For example, wireless communication interface is

one of the most power-consuming devices. Factors such as packet sizes, the transmission rates, the radio frequency (RF) power level influence the power consumption of a wireless communication interface. In [16], a linear formulation of the energy consumption of a wireless communication interface was presented. In [17], the detailed energy model based on the energy per bit goodput for a WLAN interface was proposed. Although above tools and models can help the energy consumption estimation of an I/O device, a generic framework in operating system which can dynamically and flexibly monitor the energy consumption of I/O activities and estimate the energy consumption of an I/O function call in a application process has not been explored. This study proposes a generic energy profiling framework to associate energy consumption of I/O devices with high-level software I/O requests so that the process-level and function-level energy consumption estimation of I/O events can be obtained.

3   Profiling Energy Consumption of I/O Events

3.1   Methodology

The application processes first generate I/O requests to operating system (OS). OS then schedules resources such as CPU, memory, wireless communication interface, display, etc. to serve these high-level requests. However, following characteristics cause problems to correlate the energy consumption of I/O devices with I/O requests.

1. Operating system usually performs a scatter-gather technique on I/O requests to improve I/O efficiency. Therefore, we cannot associate the energy consumed by an I/O device for handling one I/O request with only one process or one function call.
2. I/O are usually asynchronous. The asynchronous occurs in two scenarios. The first scenario is that an application process may invoke an I/O function but the request is not scheduled and performed at an I/O device immediately. The other scenario is that when an I/O event occurs, the event does not always correlate with the application process that is currently running on the processor. Therefore, we may not charge the energy consumption of an I/O device purely based on the time that the I/O event occurs.
3. OS usually removes the process identifier (ID) when the process passes an I/O request to OS and device drivers. The link between an I/O operation at the I/O device and an I/O function call at the software is missing.

The relationship between I/O function calls and I/O operations performed by the I/O device could be one-to-one, many-to-one, one-to-many mapping. For example, transmitting a large packet by using the socket application program interface (API) are usually fragmented into a number of small packet data units (PDUs), and then PDUs are transmitted by a network interface. Therefore, we propose a framework in the OS kernel to associate necessary information with I/O requests so that the application process and/or function call that issues the I/O requests and introduces the energy consumption can be easily identified.

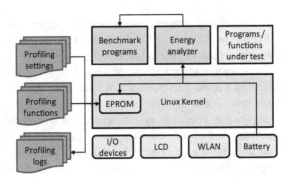

Fig. 1. Architecture of the proposed EPROM

Before the EPROM starts to profile the I/O energy consumption of an application process or a function call in an application process, a calibration process has to be conducted first. Fig. 1 shows the architecture of the EPROM. The calibration process is done by an energy analyzer and benchmark programs. The energy analyzer implements the energy consumption model of a specific I/O device, runs the benchmark programs, and collects the energy consumption measurements. A benchmark program is to test all operations and/or states of an I/O device. For example, the benchmark program for WLAN is to set the WLAN interface to the doze mode, i.e. deep sleep mode, idle mode and to collect the information while the interface receives and transmits packets at different speeds. The benchmark program for TFT-LCD is to set TFT-LCD to different brightness levels and different colors at various sizes of areas. The energy models and benchmark programs can be easily extended in order to support more I/O devices in the proposed framework. While the benchmark programs are running, the energy analyzer collects the system activities from the EPROM and the energy consumption of the system from measurement devices such as an external meter or an internal battery controller. After a period of tests, the energy analyzer can derive the parameters of energy consumption model of an I/O device based regression analyses. We use WLAN to describe the detailed calibration procedures.

To perform I/O requests, processor and memory also involve and consume energy. In the below model, we only consider the energy consumption of a WLAN interface and ignore the energy consumption of processor and memory for processing the I/O operations. Several existing processor and memory energy profiling tools such as [12-15] have been integrated with the proposed framework to support full system profiling. Before the benchmark program starts, the energy analyzer first stops all unnecessary processes, measures the system base energy consumption, and notifies the EPROM to track the I/O activities of the WLAN interface. We use below model to estimate WLAN energy consumption:

$$E_{WLAN} = P_{doze} \cdot T_{doze} + P_{idle} \cdot T_{idle} + \sum_{i=1}^{n_{TX}^{PK}}(P_{TX}^{MTX(PK_{TX}^i)} \cdot T_{TX}(PK_{TX}^i)) + \sum_{i=1}^{n_{RX}^{PK}}(P_{RX}^{MRX(PK_{RX}^i)} \cdot T_{RX}(PK_{RX}^i)).$$

E_{WLAN} is the extra energy consumption during the benchmark period and it can be measured by an external meter or a battery controller. We assume the extra energy consumption is introduced by WLAN only. T_{doze} and T_{idle} are the time periods that a

WLAN interface stays in the doze (deep sleep) and idle mode. The benchmark program first stops transmitting packets, sets the WLAN interface to the doze mode and idle mode for a period. Then, P_{doze} and P_{idle} can be derived. To derive other parameters of the WLAN energy consumption model, the benchmark program randomly generates a number of packets to access public websites, and the EPROM traces the I/O activities in the OS and device drive. The ERPOM also adjusts the modulation and coding schemes for transmitting packets so that packets can be delivered at different speeds. Assume that the EPROM detects total n_{TX}^{PK} packets transmitted by the benchmark program and reports $T_{TX}(i)$ as the time for transmitting packet i using the $M_{TX}(i)^{th}$ modulation and coding scheme. Similar, the EPROM detects n_{RX}^{PK} packets received by the benchmark program and reports $T_{RX}(i)$ as the time for receiving packet i using the $M_{RX}(i)^{th}$ modulation and coding scheme. After running the benchmark tests, the EPROM collects the time for transmitting and receiving each packet and its corresponding modulation and coding scheme, i.e. $T_{TX}(i)$, $T_{RX}(i)$, $M_{TX}(i)$, and $M_{RX}(i)$. With a number of iterations, the energy analyzer is able to derive the average power consumption per bit for transmitting and receiving a packet at different modulation and coding schemes, i.e. different transmission/reception speeds, by using regression analysis technique. We define the average power consumption per bit for transmitting and receiving a packet as P_{TX}^i ,P_{RX}^i , $i = 1,...,m$, respectively, and m is the number of modulation and coding schemes that an WLAN interface can support. The calibration process is to calibrate the parameters such as P_{doze}, P_{idle}, P_{TX}^i ,P_{RX}^i , $i = 1,...,m$ for the energy consumption model of a WLAN interface. With these parameters, the EPROM can collect the WLAN activities such as T_{doze}, T_{idle}, $T_{TX}(i)$, $T_{RX}(i)$, $M_{TX}(i)$, and $M_{RX}(i)$, and estimate the energy consumption of WLAN I/O requests.

The proposed EPROM is a kernel module and uses /proc file system to communicate with the energy analyzer. A developer can turn on/off the energy profiling of a specific I/O device by enabling or disabling the flag in /proc. The EPROM monitors the kernel activities related to the I/O devices that the developer specifies and saves the I/O logs to a kernel buffer. Before the EPROM starts to monitor the activities of the I/O devices, it reads a setting file and loads another profiling module which contains profiling functions for the I/O devices into the kernel memory. Based on the setting file, the EPROM knows the probe points in the kernel and drivers that the EPROM has to insert the related profiling functions. The probe points that the EPROM should instrument are kernel addresses or kernel function names which can be further translated into kernel addresses based on the kernel symbol table. The probe points are the functions which handle the I/O requests and perform scatter-gather operations of the I/O requests. The profiling functions are to gather I/O activities so that the EPROM can refer the activity information to estimate the energy consumption of I/O requests. These profiling functions and probe points are I/O specific. Each I/O device may have its own probe points and profiling functions. The EPROM uses a generic design to read the settings, probe points, and profiling functions information from the user space so that developers can further add probe points and profiling functions for newly added I/O devices. Therefore, energy profiling on the new I/O devices can be supported.

An example to register profiling functions to the WLAN probe points such as transport layer send/recv functions and WLAN driver send/recv functions in the kernel space is illustrated in Fig. 2. We apply the dynamic kernel instrumentation technology which is similar to Kprobes [19] to implement the above procedures. First (step ❶), when a developer enables the profiling flag, the probe points and profiling functions are loaded and the profiling functions are further registered as un-defined instruction handlers. Second (step ❷), the EPROM finds the probe points in the kernel memory, replaces the entry instructions of the functions with un-defined or break instructions (depending on the architecture). Once the processor executes the un-defined instructions, it traps an un-defined exception. The profiling functions are called in the un-defined instruction handler (Step ❸). The profiling functions can be identified, run, and return (step ❹). With the dynamic kernel instrumentation, we do not have to recompile the kernel and can dynamically determine the I/O devices to profile during the run-time. Also, no additional overhead is introduced for these I/O devices which are not monitored.

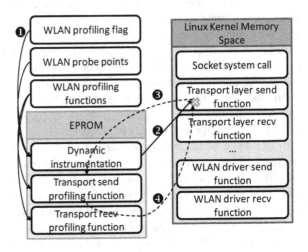

Fig. 2. An example of dynamic instrumentation in the EPROM

3.2   Energy Profiling of a WLAN Interface

In order to evaluate software-level energy consumption, we construct process-level and function-level energy model based on below models. The energy consumption of a WLAN interface can be rewritten as: $E_{WLAN} = E_{WLAN}^{SYS} + \sum_{i \in all\ PIDs} E_{TX}^i + \sum_{i \in all\ PIDs} E_{RX}^i$, where E_{WLAN}^{SYS} is the WLAN power consumption that the WLAN interface stays in the doze and idle mode, and E_{TX}^i and E_{RX}^i are the energy consumption of packet transmission and reception for process i. Since the WLAN power consumption during the doze and idle mode depends on user configuration and the WLAN enable and disable policy, we therefore consider the base energy consumption of WLAN, i.e. $E_{WLAN}^{SYS} = P_{doze} \times T_{doze} + P_{idle} \times T_{idle}$ as a system operation cost and does not charge it to any process or function. For a specific process, say process pid, it may transmit or receive certain amount of packets.

Therefore, the energy consumption of WLAN introduced by process pid is defined as $E_{TX}^{pid} + E_{RX}^{pid}$. Assume, process pid calls I/O transmission functions, e.g. `send()`, for $n_{TX}^{pid,IO}$ times to send packets and calls I/O reception functions, e.g. `recv()`, for $n_{RX}^{pid,IO}$ times to receive packets. We thus can calculate the process-level WLAN energy consumption of process pid as: $E_{TX}^{pid} = \sum_{i=1}^{n_{TX}^{pid,IO}} E_{TX}^{pid,i}$ and $E_{RX}^{pid} = \sum_{i=1}^{n_{RX}^{pid,IO}} E_{RX}^{pid,i}$, where $E_{TX}^{pid,i}$ and $E_{RX}^{pid,i}$ are the energy consumption of the ith I/O transmission and reception function call for process pid, respectively. As we mentioned before, an I/O transmission function invokes the kernel and copies the data to the kernel to send the data may be further fragmented into packet data units (PDUs), and the PDUs are transmitted by the device. Therefore, we define: $IO_{TX}^{pid,p} = \{PK_{TX}^{pid,p_1}, PK_{TX}^{pid,p_2}, ..., PK_{TX}^{pid,p_q}\}$, where the data for the pth I/O transmission function call is divided into p_q PDUs which are transmitted by the device. We can then estimate the energy consumption of the pth I/O transmission function call for process pid as: $E_{TX}^{pid,p} = \sum_{i=1}^{q} P_{TX}^{M(PK_{TX}^{pid,p_i})} \times T_{TX}(PK_{TX}^{pid,p_i})$. The transmission time for packet PK_{TX}^{pid,p_i} can be estimated by: $T_{TX}(PK_{TX}^{pid,p_i}) = (S(PK_{TX}^{pid,p_i}) + S_h)/(R_{TX}^{M(PK_{TX}^{pid,p_i})})$, where $M(PK_{TX}^{pid,p_i})$ is the modulation and coding scheme for transmitting packet PK_{TX}^{pid,p_i}, $R_{TX}^{M(PK_{TX}^{pid,p_i})}$ is the transmission rate under the $M(PK_{TX}^{pid,p_i})^{th}$ modulation and coding scheme, $S(PK_{TX}^{pid,p_i})$ is the size of packet PK_{TX}^{pid,p_i} and S_h is the header size of the PDU. We can also estimate the energy consumption of the pth I/O reception function call for process pid as: $E_{RX}^{pid,p} = \sum_{i=1}^{q} P_{RX}^{M(PK_{RX}^{pid,p_i})} \times T_{RX}(PK_{RX}^{pid,p_i})$ and the reception time for packet PK_{RX}^{pid,p_i} can be estimated by: $T_{RX}(PK_{RX}^{pid,p_i}) = (S(PK_{RX}^{pid,p_i}) + S_h)/(R_{RX}^{M(PK_{RX}^{pid,p_i})})$. According to above calculations, we can estimate the energy consumption of I/O requests for a specific application process and the energy consumption of a specific I/O function call in an application process. Fig. 3 and Fig. 4 illustrate the implementation details of the EPROM for tracking an I/O transmission and reception function call and estimating their energy consumption.

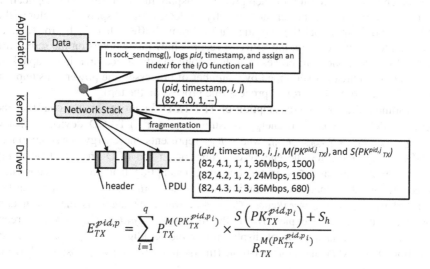

Fig. 3. Tracking I/O transmitting function calls for WLAN

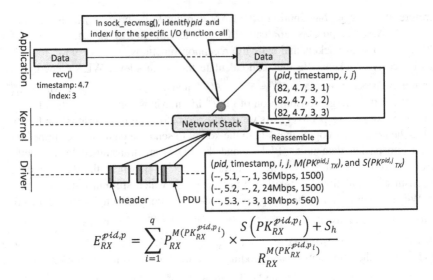

$$E_{RX}^{pid,p} = \sum_{i=1}^{q} P_{RX}^{M(PK_{RX}^{pid,p_i})} \times \frac{S\left(PK_{RX}^{pid,p_i}\right) + S_h}{R_{RX}^{M(PK_{RX}^{pid,p_i})}}$$

Fig. 4. Tracking I/O reception function calls for WLAN

3.3   Energy Profiling of a TFT-LCD

Display is also one of the major energy-consuming devices for embedded systems. For a TFT-LCD, the power consumption is determined by the brightness levels of the backlight of the LCD screen. For an OLED, the power consumption is related to the displayed objects and their colors [20]. In this study, we use a TFT-LCD as an example, the design can be applied to the OLED system. The EPROM monitors the area of the screen which each process occupies and the backlight levels of the LCD to estimate the energy consumption of each process. Display function calls from application processes to the frame buffer are directly reflected the display. Therefore, the EPROM module monitors the activities at the frame buffer when each process may write data to it. Furthermore, the EPROM records how many pixels on the screen are occupied by an application process and how long the displayed area is occupied on the screen. If an area is overlapped by a number of processes, the power consumption is only charged to the foreground process (the process on the top).

To estimate the energy consumption of TFT-LCD for processes, we construct the energy model for LCD. The energy consumption of a TFT-LCD device is: $E_{LCD} = E_{LCD}^{SYS} + \sum_{i \in all\ PIDs} E_{LCD}^{i} + \sum_{i \in all\ PIDs} E_{LCD}^{i}$, where E_{LCD} represents the energy consumption of TFT-LCD, E_{LCD}^{SYS} indicates the energy consumption of the LCD areas that operating system manipulates, and E_{LCD}^{i} is the energy consumption that process i consumes. Moreover, the LCD energy consumption that process pid introduces can be further estimated by: $E_{LCD}^{pid} = \sum_{i \in pid} AreaRatio_i \times T_{LCD}^{i} \times P_{LCD}^{i}$, where $AreaRatio_i$ is the screen area ratios that process pid occupies, T_{LCD}^{i} is the time process pid displays on the screen, P_{LCD}^{j} is the power consumption of display under the backlight level j. For the implementation, the EPROM monitors a 4-tuple (timestamp, PID, drawing position, drawing area) information from the frame buffer. The EPROM also tracks the display I/O function calls so that the energy consumption of each process can be derived.

4 Experimental Results

4.1 Experimental Environment

The measurement equipment includes a current probe and a data acquisition (DAQ). The current clamp uses Hall effect to measure the current flow of the I/O devices, and the data acquisition collects the measurements from the current clamp. The experimental platform is an embedded system evaluation board with an Intel XScale PXA270 processor. A TFT-LCD and a WLAN USB adaptor are connected to the experimental platform as the I/O devices. The TFT-LCD is 3.5" display with a 320×240 resolution, supporting 16-bit color depth. The WLAN USB adaptor supports 802.11b/g. The benchmarking programs execute on the experimental platform which runs the Linux kernel 2.6.15 with the proposed EPROM.

4.2 Experimental Results

The experiments are separated into three parts. The first part shows the overhead of our proposed framework. The second and third parts are WLAN and TFT-LCD experiments, respectively. The WLAN and TFT-LCD experiments verify the accuracy of the energy estimation.

We use ping utility to ping the local host and default gateway for 30 times to evaluate the profiling overhead introduced by the EPROM. The one way delay which indicates the overhead introduced by the EPROM increase only 3.5%-7%. For these I/O devices which are not monitored, the EPROM introduces zero overhead.

The second experiment uses different link speeds to send 1MB data. Table 1 shows that using lower link speeds to send packets consumes much more energy than that using higher link speeds. We compare the estimated energy with the measured results, and find that the errors are below 4%.

In the third experiment, TX represents a process to send 1MB data using UDP, and RX represents a process to receive 1MB data using UDP. The symbol "+" indicates the processes execute in order, and the symbol "&" indicates the processes execute simultaneously. We compare the total estimated energy with total measured energy, and calculate the estimation error. Table 2 illustrates that the error is less than 3% in each testing. In different cases such as running in order or concurrently, the results show each TX or RX process consumes the similar energy. The results match our expectations. The link rates for receiving packets are decided by the access point (AP). Since the AP changes the link rate according to the manufacture's rate algorithm, the AP does not use the highest link rate to transmit each packet. Therefore, the energy consumption of packet reception process is larger than energy consumption of packet transmission process in the experiment.

Table 1. Energy consumption for transmitting 1MB data under different link speeds

Link Rate	Tx Time (ms)	Idle Time (s)	Tx Energy (mJ)	Idle Energy (J)	Estimated Energy (J)	Measured Energy (J)	Error
54Mbps	154.55	1.91	275.10	2.491	2.766	2.839	2.58%
48Mbps	173.87	1.89	309.48	2.467	2.777	2.851	2.60%
36Mbps	231.82	1.83	412.64	2.391	2.803	2.903	3.43%
24Mbps	347.73	1.72	618.97	2.240	2.858	2.882	0.82%
18Mbps	463.64	1.60	825.29	2.089	2.915	2.977	2.09%
12Mbps	695.47	1.37	1237.93	1.785	3.023	3.095	2.33%
9Mbps	927.29	1.14	1650.57	1.484	3.135	3.190	1.73%

Table 2. Energy consumption of combined tests

Exec.	Test Set	Tx Time (ms)	Rx Time (ms)	Idle Time (s)	Tx Energy (mJ)	Rx Energy (mJ)	Idle Energy (J)	Total Estimated Energy (J)	Total Measured Energy (J)	Error(%)
one	TX	155	0	2	275	0.0	2.49	2.77	2.79	0.7
+	TX	155	0	4	275	0.00	4.93	5.48	5.54	1.0
	TX	155	0		275	0.00				
&	TX	154	0	3	275	0.00	4.29	4.82	4.91	1.8
	TX	154	0		275	0.00				
one	RX	0	323	2	0	514	2.27	2.79	2.84	1.8
+	RX	0	326	4	0	518	5.00	6.02	6.20	3.0
	RX	0	313		0	498				
&	RX	0	315	6	0	501	7.28	8.311	8.435	1.5
	RX	0	331		0	526				
+	TX	155	0	3	275	0	4.52	5.297	5.429	2.4
	RX	0	316		0	502				
&	TX	155	0	3	275	0	4.25	5.070	5.129	1.2
	RX	0	343		0	546				

4.2.1   TFT-LCD Experiment

In TFT-LCD experiments, we prepare a script that four processes draw the screen in a pre-defined order. Process 1 uses the full screen from time 0 to 4. Process 2 pops up at time 4, and occupies 25% screen (process 1 now uses 75%). Process 2 ends at time 6, and process 3 and process 1 share the screen from time 6 to 9. Finally, process 1 and process 3 both end. Process 4 uses the full screen from time 9 to 14. According to the profiling on the frame buffer, we obtain when, where, and the area each process writes to the frame buffer. Hence, we apply the LCD power model and the profiling information to estimate energy consumption of each process. Experimental results demonstrate the error between measurement and estimated energy consumption of TFT-LCD is merely 1.93%.

5   Conclusions

In this paper, we proposed a generic framework to profile the energy consumption of functions and application processes. The framework assists developers to dynamically decide the I/O devices to monitor and obtain accurate energy estimation of I/O events so that they can optimize the energy efficiency of the software designs and power management policies. We implemented the proposed idea in the Linux and PXA270 platform. Experimental results based on WLAN and TFT-LCD demonstrate that our proposed framework can provide accurate estimations on the energy consumption of I/O events and the errors between the estimation and measurement results are below 4% for WLAN and 2% for TFT-LCD.

Acknowledgment. The authors would like to thank MediaTek Inc. and National Science Council of the Republic of China for financially supporting this research under Contract No. 101-2219-E-009-010-, 101-2220-E-009-036-, 101-2918-I-009-004-, 101-2915-I-009-022, 101-3113-P-006-020-, 101-2219-E-009-001-, and Institute for Information Industry under the "Advanced Sensing Platform and Green Energy Application Technology Project" which is subsidized by the Ministry of Economy Affairs of the Republic of China.

References

1. Starner, T.E.: Powerful Change Part 1: Batteries and Possible Alternatives for the Mobile Market. IEEE Pervasive Computing 2, 86–88 (2003)
2. Cho, Y., Chang, N.: Energy-Aware Clock-Frequency Assignment in Microprocessors and Memory Devices for Dynamic Voltage Scaling. IEEE Transactions on Computer-Aided Design of Integrated Circuits and Systems 26, 1030–1040 (2006)
3. Anand, M., Nightingale, E.B., Flinn, J.: Self-tuning Wireless Network Power Management. Wireless Networks 11, 451–469 (2005)
4. Palit, R., Singh, A., Naik, K.: Modeling the Energy Cost of Application on Portable Wireless Devices. In: Proceedings of the 11th International Symposium on Modeling, Analysis and Simulation of Wireless and Mobile Systems (2008)
5. Flinn, J., Satyanarayanan, M.: PowerScope: a Tool for Profiling the Energy Usage of Mobile Applications. In: Proceedings of the 2nd IEEE Workshop on Mobile Computing Systems and Applications (1999)
6. Xian, C., Cai, L., Lu, Y.-H.: Power Measurement of Software Programs on Computers With Multiple I/O Components. IEEE Transactions on Instrumentation and Measurement 56, 2079–2086 (2007)
7. Tiwari, V., Malik, S., Wolfe, A.: Power Analysis of Embedded Software: a First Step Towards Software Power Minimization. In: Proceedings of the 1994 IEEE/ACM International Conference on Computer-Aided Design (1994)
8. Tan, T.K., Raghunathan, A., Jha, N.K.: EMSIM: an Energy Simulation Framework for an Embedded Operating System. In: Proceedings of the IEEE International Symposium on Circuits and Systems (2002)
9. Kadayif, I., Chinoda, T., Kandemir, M., Vijaykirsnan, N., Irwin, M.J., Sivasubramaniam, A.: vEC: Virtual Energy Counters. In: Proceedings of the 2001 ACM SIGPLAN-SIGSOFT Workshop on Program Analysis for Software Tools and Engineering (2001)
10. Choi, W., Kim, H., Song, W., Song, J., Kim, J.: ePRO-MP: Energy PRofiler and Optimizer for MultiProcessors. In: Proceedings of Design, Automation and Test in Europe Conference, France (2009)

11. Contreras, G., Martonosi, M.: Power Prediction for Intel XScale Processors Using Performance Monitoring Unit Events. In: Proceedings of the 2005 International Symposium on Low Power Electronics and Design (2005)
12. Kansal, A., Zhao, F.: Fine-grained Energy Profiling for Power-aware Application Design. In: Proceedings of the Workshop on Measurement and Modeling of Computer Systems (2008)
13. Do, T., Rawshdeh, S., Shi, W.: pTop: A Process-level Power Profiling Tool. In: Proceedings of the Workshop on Power Aware Computing and Systems (2009)
14. Dong, M., Zhong, L.: Self-constructive, High-rate Energy Modeling for Battery-powered Mobile Systems. In: Proc. ACM/USENIX Int. Conf. Mobile Systems, Applications, and Services, MobiSys (2011)
15. Kansal, A., Zhao, F., Liu, J., Kothari, N., Bhattacharya, A.: Virtual Machine Power Metering and Provisioning. In: ACM Symposium on Cloud Computing, SOCC (2010)
16. Feeney, L.: Investigating the Energy Consumption of an IEEE 802.11 Network Interface. SICS Technical Report (1999)
17. Ebert, J., Aier, S., Kofahl, G., Becker, A., Burns, B., Wolisz, A.: Measurement and Simulation of the Energy Consumption of an WLAN Interface. TKN Technical Report (2002)
18. Dugam, J.: Iperf (2010), http://sourceforge.net/projects/iperf/
19. Moore, R.: A Universal Dynamic Trace for Linux and other Operating Systems. In: 2001 USENIX Annual Technical Conference (2001)
20. Dong, M., Zhong, L.: Power Modeling and Optimization for OLED Displays. IEEE Transactions on Mobile Computing (2012)

An Application-Aware Cache Replacement Policy for Last-Level Caches

Tripti S. Warrier, B. Anupama, and Madhu Mutyam

PACE Laboratory, Computer Science and Engineering Department,
Indian Institute of Technology Madras, Chennai, India-600036
{tripti,anupama,madhu}@cse.iitm.ac.in

Abstract. Current day multicore processors employ multi-level cache hierarchy with one or two levels of private caches and a shared last-level cache (LLC). Efficient cache replacement policies at LLC are essential for reducing the off-chip memory traffic as well as contention for memory bandwidth. Cache replacement techniques for unicore LLCs may not be efficient for multicore LLCs as multicore LLCs can be shared by applications with varying access behavior, running simultaneously. One application may dominate another by flooding of cache requests and evicting the useful data of the other application.

This paper proposes a new cache replacement policy for shared LLC called *Application-aware Cache Replacement* (ACR). ACR policy prevents victimizing low-access rate application by a high-access rate application. It dynamically keeps track of maximum life-time of cache lines in shared LLC for each concurrent application and helps in efficient utilization of the cache space. Experimental evaluation of ACR technique for 2-core and 4-core systems using SPEC CPU 2000 and 2006 benchmark suites shows significant speed-up improvement over the *least recently used* and *thread-aware dynamic re-reference interval prediction* techniques.

1 Introduction

Modern multi-core processors support multiple levels of cache to improve performance. Most often the LLC in such systems is shared among concurrent applications. Implementing an efficient LLC management policy is essential for reduction in off-chip memory traffic and bandwidth since it has a direct impact on power consumption of the system. One of the key features involved in cache management is the replacement policy. An ideal replacement policy will victimize cache lines that are accessed farthest in future and retain the data with high temporal locality [1]. But all practical cache replacement policies take victim selection decision by *predicting* the cache line that is going to be re-referenced farthest in future. The effectiveness of such replacement policies depends on the prediction accuracy.

Least recently used (LRU) policy is one of the most commonly used cache replacement techniques. LRU policy predicts near re-reference for a cache line accessed recently and distant re-reference for one without reference. There are

C. Hochberger et al. (Eds.): ARCS 2013, LNCS 7767, pp. 207–219, 2013.

several drawbacks with the LRU technique: 1) it looses the access history if it encounters a burst of references of length more than the associativity; 2) it can victimize a frequently accessed cache line over a less-frequently but recently accessed cache line; 3) it performs badly for working sets larger than the cache size; and 4) it may not be effective for multicore LLC as applications with varying access patterns share the LLC. Since the performance gap between the theoretical optimal [1] and LRU technique is large, several cache replacement techniques have been proposed for unicore LLCs [2, 3] to improve the cache efficiency.

In multicore processors, concurrent execution of applications demands significant memory bandwidth. This is provided by multi-level cache hierarchy with one or two levels of private caches and a shared LLC. As LLC can be shared by parallelly running applications with varying access behavior, the replacement techniques proposed for unicore LLC may not be effective for multicore LLC. If such applications conflict with each other, system-wide performance can be significantly degraded. One application may dominate another by flooding cache requests and evicting the useful data of the other application. Performance of most of the cache replacement techniques proposed for multicore LLCs [4, 5, 6, 7, 8] depends on the data access patterns of specific workloads.

This work takes a different approach for replacement of a cache line from LLC by exploiting the non-uniform access rates and access behaviors of applications. It proposes an *Application-aware Cache Replacement* (ACR) policy. Apart from being access rate aware, ACR technique dynamically adapts the eviction process to the varying access patterns of applications. ACR technique is compared with LRU policy and state-of-the-art *thread-aware dynamic RRIP* (TA-DRRIP) [5] policy using SPEC CPU 2000 and 2006 benchmarks. ACR policy achieves (geometric mean) speed-up of 8.62% and 5.08% over LRU and TA-DRRIP policies, respectively, for 4-core workloads. The major contribution of the work is that the proposed replacement technique works well for workloads with both LRU friendly and scan access patterns as opposed to TA-DRRIP, which is not the best replacement technique for LRU friendly workloads.

2   Related Work

Several cache eviction policies have been proposed in the literature for both unicore and multicore systems. Discussion in this section is restricted to techniques that are relevant to proposed techniques.

Counter-based replacement technique [3] for unicore LLC predicts access interval using a counter for each cache line. All counters in a set are incremented on an access and a cache line whose counter value exceeds a given threshold is selected as victim.

The use of reuse information during victim selection for unicore LLC has been exploited in [2]. PC-based prediction method [2] predicts the reuse distance and uses the predicted values for cache eviction. On a cache miss, if the predicted reuse distance of the memory reference is higher than the reuse distance seen by all cache lines in the set, the requested data is directly sent to the processor without storing it in the cache. Otherwise, a cache line with highest reuse distance is replaced with the requested data.

To avoid keeping one time accessed cache lines for longer time, Bimodal Insertion Policy (BIP) [6] inserts most of the cache lines at the LRU position and place the others at MRU. But some applications are benefited if the cache lines are inserted at LRU position. In order to work with this varying behavior, dynamic insertion policy (DIP) [6] chooses either LRU or BIP policies at run-time. When it comes to multicore LLC, DIP technique is extended with thread-awareness [4], wherein each thread selects between LRU or BIP policies at run-time.

Static and dynamic cache replacement techniques based on re-reference interval prediction (RRIP) are proposed in [5]. Static RRIP (SRRIP) is scan-resistant, but not thrash-resistant. Thrashing is avoided by adopting an approach similar to BIP in bimodal RRIP (BRRIP). Both thrashing and non-thrashing access patterns are handled in dynamic RRIP (DRRIP), which selects between BRRIP or SRRIP for a given application using set-dueling monitors (SDMs)[6]. DRRIP policy does not have recency information. It inserts cache lines with low priority and changes it priority to highest only on a hit. During victim selection, it always searches from left and selects any cache line with lowest priority. If there are no suitable candidates, it keeps on changing the priority of all the cache lines till it finds a cache line with lowest priority. In case there are multiple cache lines with lowest priority, the search from left might not give the best victim candidate as the low priority of the chosen victim could be either due to its insertion or insertions of other cache lines. Hence, DRRIP policy does not always work well with LRU friendly applications. The work is extended to handle multi-programmed workloads in thread-aware dynamic RRIP (TA-DRRIP). With the help of two SDMs per application, TA-DRRIP dynamically selects either SRRIP or BRRIP in the presence of other application.

The promotion/insertion pseudo partitioning (PIPP) technique [8] has different priority positions for insertion of cache lines that belong to different applications. On a hit, accessed cache line is promoted by one position up in the priority chain. During promotion of cache lines, the applications with low priority position for insertion face stiff competition from those with high priority position for insertion. Hence, identifying suitable application-specific priority positions is critical for achieving good performance in PIPP technique.

Adaptive timekeeping replacement [7] uses the cache decay concept in cache line level for managing shared LLC. Operating system assigns three levels of priorities to the application and hardware assigns decay intervals accordingly. When a cache line is not accessed within the decay interval, it becomes a potential victim block. The main drawback with the technique is that it cannot distinguish between two or more applications having the same priority values.

Thrasher caging [9] identifies thrashing application that degrades the performance of multicore processor. The thrasher detection is based on the absolute number of misses from the cores. Once an application is detected as a thrasher application, reduced number of cache ways will be allocated.

Table 1. LLC statistics for SPEC CPU 2000 and 2006 benchmarks[1]

SPEC	LLC statistics		SPEC	LLC statistics	
benchmark	APKI	Miss Rate (%)	benchmark	APKI	Miss Rate (%)
164.gzip	1.22	17.08	429.mcf	64.47	90.91
168.wupwise	3.01	99.13	435.gromacs	1.72	19.59
171.swim	22.89	99.98	437.leslie3d	9.15	82.64
172.mgrid	12.32	64.95	444.namd	0.68	98.68
173.applu	20.16	99.92	450.soplex	2.94	35.67
175.vpr	11.78	27.48	454.calculix	0.91	62.92
177.mesa	0.72	91.53	456.hmmer	2.14	71.36
178.galgel	14.09	43.91	458.sjeng	0.37	79.98
179.art	129.64	78.81	459.GemsFDTD	0.006	70.98
186.crafty	0.58	9.65	462.libquantum	6.72	99.64
193.fma3d	0.00051	100	464.h264ref	0.88	10.41
300.twolf	15.24	32.37	470.lbm	32.07	99.99
401.bzip2	5.18	43.57			

3   Motivation

In a multi-core scenario, multiple applications compete with each other for space in LLC. The access rates and behavior of these applications are different from one another and their accesses to LLC are filtered by caches closer to the processors.

Access Rates of Applications: Table 1 shows the *accesses per kilo instructions* ($APKI$) at LLC of different SPEC CPU 2000 and 2006 benchmark suites [10] with 3-level cache hierarchy in a single core environment. In a shared LLC with LRU replacement policy, high access rate application can dominate low access rate application. Figure 1 shows the cache line occupancy of a particular cache set for an application (*hmmer*) when it is concurrently executing with a lower access rate application (*calculix*) and a higher access rate application (*libquantum*). The average number of cache lines in the cache for *hmmer* reduces from 8.5 to 5.7 when the co-executing application is *libquantum* instead of *calculix*. This corresponds to a performance loss of 11.2% in IPC for *hmmer* due to *libquantum*.

Figure 2 gives a typical access in a 2-core system at time T1 (=3848587115 simulation cycle) with *hmmer-libquantum* during which *libquantum* flushes the application cache lines of *hmmer*. It shows that the number of cache lines in a particular set from *hmmer* (*libquantum*) is changed from 7 (8) to 2 (14) during an interval of 16 accesses to the set. This is because the LRU replacement policy is unaware of the difference in accesses across the applications. It selects the LRU candidate from an eviction chain that is common to both the applications. Due to the variation in access rate, the cache lines of low access rate application are pushed to the LRU position of priority chain and will be flushed out by the cache lines that belong to high access rate application. In such case, it is better to prevent an application from evicting a cache line of another application [11].

---

[1] Refer Section 5 for simulation setup.

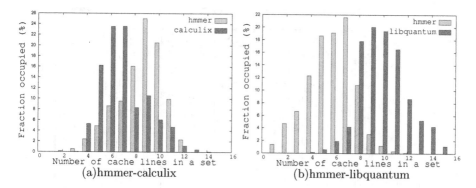

Fig. 1. The distribution of cache lines for set 56 in LLC when *hmmer* is executing with lower (*calculix*) and higher (*libquantum*) APKI applications

Hence, access rate aware eviction policy can improve the overall performance of the system.

Access Pattern of Applications: Access rate of an application does not give any insight on the temporal locality of the application. Relying just on application-wise access rates for cache replacement may sometimes degrade the performance of the system. As can be seen from Table 1, benchmarks such as *mesa* and *namd* have low APKI and very high miss rates. When such an application is co-scheduled with high access rate application, the access count based strategies can penalize the latter. This is of disadvantage because high access rate application is penalized without considering the temporal locality of individual applications. Hence, the replacement policy should also be aware of the access recency behavior of the overall system along with access rate.

Each application has different reuse patterns, which can change during various stages of the execution. Figure 3 shows the hit-behavior of SPEC CPU 2000 and 2006 benchmark suites in a single core environment with 1MB 16-way set associative LLC. The hit behavior is measured in terms of *hit-gap* of the cache lines. The *hit-hap* of a cache line is defined as the number of accesses to the corresponding set between consecutive accesses to the cache line. The graph provides percentage of hits covered for different *hit-gap* values. Most of the applications

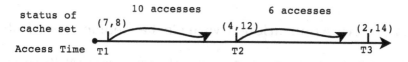

Fig. 2. Access sequence for *hmmer-libquantum* for set-56. The cache occupancy status is denoted by (a,b), where a is number of cache lines that belong to *hmmer* and b is number of cache lines that belong to *libquantum*.

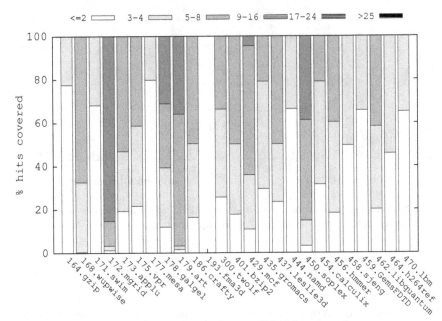

Fig. 3. *hit-gap* for single core SPEC benchmarks

cover their hits by a *hit-gap* of 16 and *fma3d* does not have hits at all. Even
when an application gets the entire share of LLC, the *hit-gap* is not increasing
beyond a particular value. For example, applications such as *gzip, swim, mesa,
namd, sjeng, GemsFDTD, h264ref* and *lbm* cover most of their hits by a *hit-gap*
of 4. If a cache line of one of these applications is present in the cache for more
than 4 accesses to the set, it is highly likely that the cache line will not be ref-
erenced again. This maximum value of *hit-gap* will give the maximum life-time
required by any cache line of the application in the cache. The maximum *hit-gap*
when tracked dynamically can be used during cache line eviction. The use of
maximum *hit-gap* will ensure that all cache lines of an application are present in
the cache for only allotted time. Hence, the use of maximum *hit-gap* information
can facilitate better utilization of available cache space.

In conclusion, variation in access counts, access recency, and *hit-gaps* across
different applications motivates an alternate cache replacement policy. The next
section proposes such policy.

4   ACR: An Application-Aware Cache Replacement Policy

The paper proposes an application aware cache replacement (ACR) policy for
shared LLCs. To make the policy access rate aware, separate local eviction priority chains are maintained for different cores. The length of each chain is dynamically changed at run-time to make *ACR* policy access pattern aware.

ACR technique updates the eviction priority of only those cache lines that belong to the referencing application and maintains separate eviction priority chains for each application. It is seen in Section 3 that for low-access and low-hit rate applications, separate replacement chains that are aware of the access rates of applications is not sufficent and can sometime degrade the performance. Keeping a tab on the order of access recency among concurrent applications for individual sets along with access counts is of use here. Further in case of victim selection if multiple applications have victims with same eviction priority, the access recency information can be used to guarantee performance similar to LRU policy.

The study of *hit-gaps* of cache lines for different applications in Section 3 also shows that each application has different maximum residency period for its cache lines. This maximum residency period for each application can be used to limit the length of individual eviction priority chain as the cache lines are unlikely to be reference after this period. ACR policy changes the length of the individual eviction priority chain based on the application-wise maximum *hit-gap*. ACR policy dynamically tracks the maximum *hit-gaps* of an application for each interval and uses it as the predicted life-time or *predicted-hit-gap* (*PHG*) for the next interval. We consider the maximum hit-gap observed for the prediction to avoid any additional miss penalties due to insufficient prediction of cache life-time. Special care is taken in the absence of hit for an application in an interval, as the reason for no hits could be an error in the *predicted hit-gap*.

Implementation: ACR technique uses the following registers/counters for implementation:

- n-bit saturating counter called *hit-gap* counter (*HG*) for each cache line to keep track of individual access counts.
- $N*logN$ bits per cache set to maintain application-wise access recency order (LRU chain), where N is the number of cores in the system.
- Two n-bit application-wise counters, *predicted-hit-gap* (*PHG*) and *shadow predicted-hit-gap* (*sPHG*). *PHG* value is the predicted life time for current interval and *sPHG* value is the learned maximum *hit-gap* during the current interval (to be used as the predicted life-time for the next interval).
- 1-bit *hitFlag* per application, which is set on a hit for the application.

Access Rate Awareness: On every access to a set, *HG* counters of all cache lines in the set that belong to the accessed application are incremented. The counter value of a cache line at any given time is an estimate of its life-time in the cache after its last access. This time is measured in terms of the number of accesses to the cache set. A cache line with the highest counter value is the oldest cache line without access in the set. If an access is a hit, the counter of the corresponding cache line is reset. The value of the counter at the time of hit is the *hit-gap* of the cache line and so is called the *hit-gap* (*HG*) counter. Whenever a new cache line is inserted, its *HG* value is set to 0. Each access to the cache also updates the application wise LRU chain corresponding to that set.

Access Pattern Awareness: For dynamically tracking the application life-time (maximum *hit-gap*) the total number of cache sets s is divided into p *monitor*

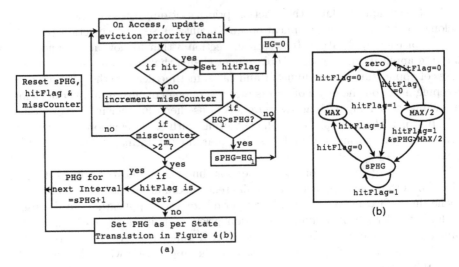

Fig. 4. Illustration of ACR policy (a) Flowchart illustrating dynamic update of PHG. (b) Computation of PHG at the end of an interval.

sets and $(s - p)$ *normal sets*. The predicted life-time for all monitor sets is fixed at $MAX = 2^n - 1$ to ensure the maximum possibility of *hit-gap* for cache lines in monitor sets. The hit gaps of the monitor and normal sets are tracked and stored as $sPHG$ for each interval of 2^m misses (implemented using an m-bit *missCounter*) for LLC and the PHG value is updated at the end of each interval (Figure 4(a)). At the start of each interval $sPHG$ and $hitFlag$ are reset. During each hit to a cache line l of an application i, if $HG_l > sPHG_i$, then $sPHG_i$ is set to HG_l. At the end of the interval, $sPHG_i$ stores the maximum *hit-gap* of the application. If $hitFlag_i$ is set, PHG_i for the next interval is set to $sPHG_i + 1$. If the $hitFlag_i$ is reset, the application had no hits during the interval. This could be because of insufficient PHG, which is tackled using the FSM shown in Figure 4(b). In case of no hit, the FSM gives the application maximum time in cache for the next interval, i.e., $PHG = MAX$. If the status of the $hitFlag$ continuous to remain reset, it means the application has thrashing behavior, and so $sPHG$ is reset. To make sure such application is given opportunity to remain in the cache if its behavior changes, PHG alternates between 0 and $\frac{MAX}{2}$. Note that if at any point the application encounters a hit, the value of $sPHG$ is used for PHG for the next interval.

Victim Selection: As maximum time in the cache for a cache line l of an application i is when $HG_l = PHG_i$, the cache line with minimum predicted life-time will be one with $\min(PHG_i - HG_l)$. Hence on a miss, the victim in the absence of invalid cache line is the cache line with $\min(PHG_i - HG_l)$. The search for victim cache line starts from LRU core so that the cache line that has minimum life in the cache from a core that is least recently used is evicted.

Note that in the absence of *monitor sets* in the PHG computation, the chances of the value of $sPHG$ being larger than PHG would be very less as all cache

Table 2. Architectural parameters of the simulated system

IL1 caches	32KB, 64B, 4-way, 1 cycles, 1W and 2R ports, LRU
DL1 caches	32KB, 64B, 4-way, 1 cycles, 1W and 2R ports, LRU
L2 cache	256KB, 64B, 8-way, 10 cycles, private, LRU
LLC	1MB per-core, 64B, 16-way, 35 cycle, shared, non-inclusive
Main memory	200 cycles

lines with $HG = PHG$ are evicted. Any hit in the monitor or normal cache set can change the value of $sPHG$ as long as the *hit-gap* of the current hit is greater than the present value of $sPHG$. Also, the victim selection procedure is not in the critical path and hence the search involved in the algorithm does not affect the system performance.

Whenever a cache encounters scan access pattern, the corresponding cache lines become victim candidates faster by virtue of application based HG modification. Such scan patterns will not have hits due to which cache lines of such applications will be predicted to have smaller life-time in the cache. Hence, ACR policy is scan resistant irrespective of the length of the scan chain unlike SRRIP. ACR policy is aware of access recency and so can perform well for LRU friendly applications. Hence in contrast to TA-DRRIP, ACR policy can perform well for applications that have access patterns that can be LRU friendly or scan.

5   Evaluation

Our technique is evaluated with 3-level cache hierarchy having private L1 and L2 caches with shared LLC. Table 2 gives other details of the system configuration used in experimentation. Workloads using set of 26 SPEC CPU 2000 and 2006 benchmark suites [10] (refer to Table 1), compiled for ALPHA ISA, are executed on GEM5 simulator [12]. All the benchmarks are executed using reference inputs. Applications are fast-forwarded for 900 million instructions and then warmed up for next 100 million instructions. The statistics are recorded for the next 1 billion instructions for each application. As ACR technique is access rate aware, we consider workloads with mix of low (L) and high (H) APKI values. Applications with $APKI > 6$ are categorized as H and others are categorized as L. The workload mixes are categorized based on the number of low and high APKI applications. For 2- and 4-core systems, we have 3 $((\#L, \#H) = \{(2,0),(1,1),(0,2)\})$ and 5 $((\#L, \#H) = \{(4,0),(3,1),(2,2),(1,3),(0,4)\})$ categories of workloads, respectively. About 20 mixes are considered for each class of workloads in both 2- and 4-core systems.

Results and Analysis: ACR policy is compared with LRU and TA-DRRIP [5] techniques. We consider 4-bit HG counter, 12-bit *missCounter* and 128 monitor sets for ACR policy. TA-DRRIP [5] is implemented with $2N$ SDMs, where N is the number of cores, with 32 sets each to learn the insertion decision of each

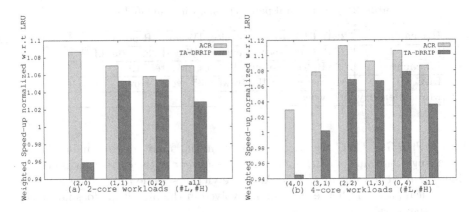

Fig. 5. Performance comparison of ACR policy with LRU and TA-DRRIP policies

application. A 10-bit dedicated PSEL counter is used to decide the core-wise insertion policy.

Effect on System Performance: Performance of multiple applications that execute concurrently is evaluated using weighted speedup. Weighted speedup gives the improvement in execution time compared to the baseline configuration. Figure 5(a) shows the performance improvement of ACR policy for 2-core system compared to LRU and TA-DRRIP policies in various categories of workloads. ACR policy achieves speed-up of 7.02% and 4.16% (geometric mean) with respect to LRU and TA-DRRIP policies, respectively.

Similar behavior for 4-core systems can be observed in Figure 5(b). The geometric mean of performance improvement of ACR policy as compared to LRU and TA-DRRIP techniques are 8.6% and 5.03%, respectively. ACR policy outperforms LRU and TA-DRRIP policies in all categories of workloads for both 2- and 4-core systems. The difference in performance improvement between ACR and TA-DRRIP policies is largest for (2,0) and (4,0) workload categories in 2- and 4-core systems, respectively. This difference reduces as the number of H category applications increases in the workloads. Most of the applications in L category have low miss rate or good temporal locality (refer to Table 1) with LRU policy and hence are LRU friendly. ACR policy improves the performance of workloads with LRU friendly patterns as the modification of eviction priority chain for each application is similar to LRU chain update. On the other hand, TA-DRRIP policy does not have recency information and hence degrades the performance of workloads with similar access patterns. Further, due to the dynamic update of length of the eviction priority chain based on *hit-gap* in ACR policy, applications with scan patterns will have shorter life-time in the cache. Hence ACR policy is able to improve performance of workloads with both scan and LRU friendly patterns. With increase in high access rate applications in the workloads, both ACR and TA-DRRIP policies have improved performance but the performance of ACR policy is still higher than that of TA-DRRIP technique as it is access rate aware along with being access pattern aware.

Figure 6 shows the speedup improvement of ACR and TA-DRRIP policies in a 4-core system with respect to LRU technique for all the workloads. It can be observed that unlike TA-DRRIP, the performance of ACR is always better than LRU policy.

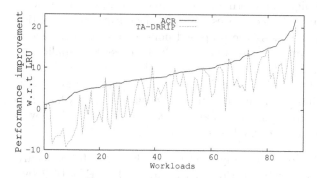

Fig. 6. Effectiveness of ACR and TA-DRRIP policies for all workloads in 4-core system.

Table 3. Overhead of replacement policies for 4-core system with 4-MB LLC

Replacement Policy	Overhead
LRU	$32KB$
TA - DRRIP	$\approx 16KB$
ACR	$\approx 36KB$

Victim selection procedure for our technique involves comparing the counter values to identify the victim candidate. This procedure is similar to that of LRU. Since the victim selection is in parallel to memory access, it does not increase the critical path to the processor. For a 'k-way' set associative cache, LRU and TA-DRRIP replacement policies have an overhead of $k * logk$ and $2 * k$ bits per cache set, respectively. In addition, TA-DRRIP has 10-bit PSEL counter per core to support SDMs. ACR policy has an overhead of $k * logk$ (for HG counters) + $NlogN$ (to implement core-wise LRU), where N is the number of cores in the system. In addition to this, ACR policy has two 4-bit register for PHG and $sPHG$, and one 1-bit register for $hitFloag$ per application and a single 12-bit $misCounter$. Table 3 shows the overhead involved in implementation of LRU, TA-DRRIP, and ACR replacement policies for 4-core system with 4MB LLC. Even though ACR policy incurs slightly larger area overhead than TA-DRRIP, ACR achieves significant performance improvement in both 2- and 4-core systems. Hence it can be used in environments where performance is critical and hardware overhead is not a constraint.

Effect of the size of HG counter: Performance of 2- and 4-core systems is evaluated for different sizes of the HG counter. Performance of ACR policy improves with the increase in the number of bits in the HG counter from 3 bits to 5 bits for both 2- and 4-core systems. Increase in the number of bits for HG counter provides better control on the length of eviction priority chains. This gain is almost constant on increasing the size of HG counter beyond 5 bits. Thus, we consider 4-bit HG counter as it provides significant performance improvement without incurring much hardware overhead.

6 Conclusion

A cache eviction policy for multicore shared LLC is proposed to exploit application wise access rate and pattern. Evaluation of ACR technique using SPEC CPU 2000 and 2006 benchmark suites has shown to improve the performance with respect to LRU and TA-RRIP techniques. Experiments on 2- and 4-core systems indicate that incorporating awareness of access-rates and *hit-gaps* during cache eviction will improve the LLC utilization. As the proposed policy is aware of the access rates of the applications, it prevents domination of high access rate application over low access rate application. It also performs well in the presence of both LRU friendly and scan access patterns. As part of future work, we plan to i) look at the challenges of using this technique in a multi-threaded scenario; ii) apply fine grain control on the life of individual cache lines of applications at run-time along with the coarse grain maximum life constraints exerted by ACR policy.

Acknowledgement. This work was supported in part by grant from Department of Science and Technology, India, Project No. SR/S3/EECE/0018/2009.

References

[1] Belady, L.: A study of replacement algorithms for a virtual-storage computer. IBM Systems Journal 5(2), 78–101 (1966)

[2] Keramidas, G., Petoumenos, P., Kaxiras, S.: Cache replacement based on reuse distance prediction. In: International Conference on Computer Design (2007)

[3] Kharbutli, M., Solihin, Y.: Counter-based cache replacement and bypassing algorithms. IEEE Transactions on Computers 57 (2008)

[4] Jaleel, A., Hasenplaugh, W., Qureshi, M., Sebot, J., Steely Jr., S.C., Emer, J.: Adaptive insertion policies for managing shared caches. In: ACM International Conference on Parallel Architectures and Compilation Techniques, pp. 208–219 (2008)

[5] Jaleel, A., Theobald, K.B., Steely Jr., S.C., Emer, J.: High performance cache replacement using re-reference interval prediction (RRIP). In: ACM International Symposium on Computer Architecture, pp. 60–71 (2010)

[6] Qureshi, M.K., Jaleel, A., Patt, Y.N., Steely Jr., S.C., Emer, J.: Adaptive insertion policies for high-performance caching. In: ACM International Symposium on Computer Architecture, pp. 381–391 (2007)

[7] Wu, C.J., Martonosi, M.: Adaptive timekeeping replacement: Fine-grained capacity management for shared cmp caches. ACM Transactions on Architecture and Code Optimization 11, 27 (2011)

[8] Xie, Y., Loh, G.H.: PIPP: Promotion/insertion pseudo-partitioning of multi-core shared caches. In: ACM International Symposium on Computer Architecture, pp. 174–183 (2009)

[9] Xie, Y., Loh, G.H.: Scalable Shared-Cache Management by Containing Thrashing Workloads. In: Patt, Y.N., Foglia, P., Duesterwald, E., Faraboschi, P., Martorell, X. (eds.) HiPEAC 2010. LNCS, vol. 5952, pp. 262–276. Springer, Heidelberg (2010)

[10] SPEC CPU benchmark suite, http://www.spec.org

[11] Srikantaiah, S., Kandemir, M.: Irwin: Adaptive set pinning: Managing shared caches in chip multiprocessors. In: International Conference on Architectural Support for Programming Languages and Operating Systems, pp. 135–144 (2008)

[12] Binkert, N., Beckmann, B., Black, G., Reinhardt, S.K., Saidi, A., Basu, A., Hestness, J., Hower, D.R., Krishna, T., Sardashti, S., Sen, R., Sewell, K., Shoaib, M., Vaish, N., Hill, M.D., Wood, D.A.: The GEM5 simulator. ACM SIGARCH Computer Architecture News 39, 1–7 (2011)

Deploying Hardware Locks to Improve Performance and Energy Efficiency of Hardware Transactional Memory

Epifanio Gaona[1], José L. Abellán[1], Manuel E. Acacio[1], and Juan Fernández[2]

[1] Universidad de Murcia, Spain
{fanios.gr,jl.abellan,meacacio}@ditec.um.es
[2] Intel Barcelona Research Center, Spain
juan.fernandez@intel.com

Abstract. In the search for new paradigms to simplify multithreaded programming, Transactional Memory (TM) is currently being advocated as a promising alternative to lock-based synchronization. Among the two most important alternatives proposed for conflict detection and data versioning in today's Hardware Transactional Memory systems (HTMs), the *Lazy-Lazy* one allows increased concurrency, potentially bringing higher performance levels in most cases. Unfortunately, the implementation of the commit protocol in *Lazy-Lazy* systems results in increased complexity and has severe impact on performance and energy consumption. In this work, we propose GCommit, an efficient and low cost hardware implementation of the SEQ commit protocol based on the use of hardware locks. Specifically, GCommit deploys hardware locks to ensure exclusive access to shared data at commit time. Implementing this functionality using dedicated hardware brings important benefits in terms of execution time as well as energy consumption with respect to traditional commit protocols that use the general-purpose interconnection network. Additionally, our proposal has negligible requirements in terms of area. Results for a 16-core CMP show that the GCommit protocol obtains average reductions of 15.7% and 13.7% in terms of execution time and energy consumption, respectively, compared with a traditional implementation of Scalable TCC with SEQ, a high-performance commit protocol proposed in the literature.

1 Introduction and Motivation

In recent years the emphasis in microprocessor design has shifted from high performance to high efficiency, measured as cycles per watt. Therefore energy consumption constitutes a fundamental aspect in processor design that has made major processor vendors to evolve towards multicore architectures. On the other hand, whereas it is expected that the number of cores in multicore architectures will grow, reaching even hundreds of them in the next years, multithreaded programming remains a challenging task, even for experienced programmers.

In this context, Transactional Memory (TM) has arisen as a promising alternative to lock-based synchronization, and industry is moving to incorporating

C. Hochberger et al. (Eds.): ARCS 2013, LNCS 7767, pp. 220–231, 2013.
© Springer-Verlag Berlin Heidelberg 2013

TM support at the hardware level (e.g. Intel's Haswell microarchitecture [1]). TM borrows the concept of transaction from the database world and brings it into the shared-memory programming model [2]. Transactions are no more than blocks of code whose execution must satisfy the serializability and atomicity properties. Programmers simply declare the transaction boundaries leaving the burden of how to guarantee such properties to the underlying TM system thereafter.

In Hardware Transactional Memory (HTM) systems, the hardware provides the illusion that each transaction is executed atomically and in isolation while threads are executing in parallel (transactions are speculatively executed). HTM systems usually work at cache line level. Conceptually, each transaction is associated two initially-empty read and write sets that are populated every time a transactional access is issued. A transaction can commit only after the HTM system can assure that there are no other running transactions whose write sets collide with its read or write sets. The commit process makes the read and write sets visible to the whole system. HTM systems are usually classified attending to how they tackle with data version management (VM) and conflict detection (CD). In this work we focus our attention on the extensively used *Lazy-Lazy* systems.

Lazy-Lazy systems are called optimistic since they perform data accesses as if there were no data dependencies. Nevertheless, at commit time, it must be verified that there are no conflicts with other transactions. This step represents in some cases a significant fraction of the total transactional execution time [3]. We can distinguish two different tasks during the *commit*: (1) acquiring privileges and (2) making changes visible. The former, also known as *precommit* subphase, ensures compliance with the serializability and atomicity properties by enforcing commit ordering between transactions with clashing read and write sets. The latter propagates transactionally modified data to the memory hierarchy.

In this work, we present GCommit, an efficient and low cost hardware implementation of the SEQ commit protocol [4] used in Scalable TCC system [5] (STCC-SEQ). The main particularity of GCommit is that it deploys hardware locks to reduce the duration of the *commit* phase (more precisely the *precommit* component), and consequently, to improve performance and reduce energy consumption. More specifically, GCommit is implemented assuming *GLocks* hardware locks [6], which are slightly modified. Glocks present really short acquirement and release latencies even in the case of high contention. Taking advantage of these characteristics, a GLock can be employed to ensure exclusive access to a rank of addresses at *precommit* time, as L2 cache banks do in STCC-SEQ. Implementing this functionality using dedicated hardware brings important benefits in terms of execution time as well as energy consumption with respect to traditional implementations of commit protocols that use the general-purpose interconnection network to coordinate commit ordering. Additionally, our proposal entails negligible overhead in terms of area. Results for a 16-core CMP show that GCommit accelerates the *precommit* subphase about 68.5% on average, which results in average reductions of 15.7% and 13.7% in terms of execution time and energy consumption when compared with STCC-SEQ.

2   GCommit: Efficient Commits in HTM Systems

In this section we start with a description of the original scheme of Sequential Commit (SEQ) and its most advanced algorithm up to date: SEQ-PRO. Afterwards, we continue with a brief explanation of GLocks [6], the main hardware component of GCommit, and how they have to be adapted to our proposal. Finally, we detail the design and implementation of GCommit.

2.1   STCC with Sequential Commit (STCC-SEQ)

In *Lazy-Lazy* systems, transactions are allowed to run as if they were alone in the system. Only when a transaction reaches its end and before it is allowed to propagate their results, conflicts are checked. This stage is known as the commit phase. Sequential Commit (SEQ) is nowadays the most popular commit algorithm for *Lazy-Lazy* HTM systems. Instead of employing a centralized arbiter to enforce commit ordering, SEQ makes use of the L2 directory banks to manage an implicit order between transactions with clashing read and write sets. To do so it tries to book every directory (L2 cache bank) in its read and write sets. A directory belongs to that sets if at least one transactional address belongs to the corresponding L2 cache bank. The process is explained below:

1) A committing transaction sends a request message to each directory in its read and write sets in ascending order. This prevents deadlock conditions. In the case of two different transactions competing to commit, only the first that achieves to book the first conflicting directory will continue with the process. The other transaction will have to wait till the completion of the first one.
2) Once a transaction has booked a particular directory, an "Occupied" bit is set and an ACK message is sent back. Other requests will be buffered.
3) The precommit phase finishes once a transaction has collected all the ACKs from every directory bank in its read and write sets.
4) The transaction's write set is sent to the reserved directory banks. Involved memory lines will be marked as Owned and invalidations will be sent to the other sharers of theses lines to signal a conflict with this transaction. When all the ACKs for these invalidations has been received, the directory bank clears its "Occupied" bit. If another transaction is waiting to book the directory bank, then an ACK message is sent to it.
5) The transaction ends with a release message to the directories in its read set. The scheme above represents the basic approach where Read-After-Read (RAR) situations are managed as a possible source of conflict. This happens when two transactions share the same directory bank in their read sets. Although in this case there is no conflict between the transactions (the directory is only used for reads), SEQ only allows one of the transactions to book the directory, delaying the commit of the other. An advanced algorithm called SEQ with Parallel Reader Optimization (SEQ-PRO) distinguishes between directories booked by read and write access, allowing several transactions to occupy the same directory bank for

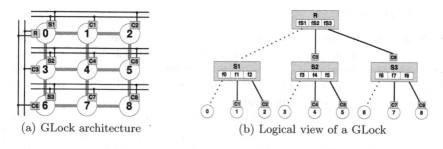

(a) GLock architecture   (b) Logical view of a GLock

Fig. 1. Implementation of a GLock in a 9-core CMP

read accesses. To do so, several Read "Occupied" bits (and one Write "Occupied" bit) are required in every directory bank.

2.2 GLocks

The design of a GLock for a 9-core CMP is shown in Figure 1(a). Every GLock is made up of two kind of components: *G-lines* (finer black lines) and controllers (R, Sx, and Cx). Each G-line is able to transmit one bit signal across one dimension of the chip in one cycle. Thanks to that property and its distributed tree design (figure 1(b)), a GLock can guarantee access to the critical section in two or four cycles in absent of contention. Figure 1(b) represents the logical tree view of a GLock. The lock request travels till the root controller (R) with one cycle in each step and the ACK/token signal performs the same in the opposite direction (4 cycles). In case the intermediate controller (Sx) already had the token, then this node has enough privileges to ensure access to the GLock without asking the root (2 cycles). In addition, an implementation of GLocks using regular wires (not G-lines) has also been studied. This implementation relies on a mainstream industrial synthesis toolflow and on an STMicroelectronics 45 nm standard cell technology library. The placement-aware logic synthesis is performed through Synopsys Physical Compiler. Assuming an area equal to $550{\times}550\mu m^2$ (each core) it is obtained that the size of a GLock is $3.62\mu m^2$, which represents 0.07% of the total area employed (this is true also for 32 cores). This marginal overhead also will lead to a negligible impact on power dissipation as is specified in [6]. Details about the operation, implementation and scalability of GLocks can be found in [6].

In order to be used in GCommit, GLocks had to be minimally customized. In particular, we extend the behavior of GLocks to manage release petitions (unlock) even if the ACK signal that grants access to the lock has not been sent yet. In particular, this behavior is found when a transaction is aborted just after requesting access to a GLock, and the corresponding ACK has not been received. In this case, and as part of the abort, the transaction desists from its request to commit by explicitly sending the release signal to the lock manager.

2.3   GCommit

GCommit is a hardware implementation of the SEQ commit algorithm used in STCC. Instead of using the directory banks as a distributed arbiter, GCommit employs one or several GLocks [6] to enable transactions to commit. According to our experiments, a GLock is at least ten times faster than the usual network where cache coherence messages flow.

For SEQ, the decision of employing as much directories as L2 cache banks is natural since the directory itself is usually split in that way. Nevertheless GCommit needs a separate hardware mechanism that does not scale naturally with system size. Each GLock is not implemented as a central arbiter. Its design is spread along the whole system and $C - 1$ G-lines are needed for one GLock, where C represents the number of cores. To keep GCommit simple, we assume that each GLock logically protects a rank of addresses. The assignment is done statically by means of the next formula: $D \ mod \ G$. Where D is the directory ID and G represents the number of GLocks used by GCommit. This additional mapping does not entails any overhead.

When a transaction wants to commit, it tries to acquire all the GLocks (with a lock request) in its read and write sets (instead of the L2 cache banks) in ascending order to avoid deadlock conditions. To do so, a transaction requests the first GLock. If no other transaction has already acquired that GLock, it will receive an ACK signal giving it exclusive access over the addresses protected by the lock. On the contrary, the GLock will delay the ACK till the other transaction keeping the lock at that moment, releases (unlock) the GLock. After collecting all ACKs from the GLocks involved in the read and write sets, the precommit subphase finishes. After that the transaction has the certainty that no other transaction will abort it, and hence, it proceeds making its write set visible to the L2 cache as in the SEQ protocol (second phase of the commit). Finally, after collecting all the acknowledgments to the invalidations sent by the cache coherence protocol as part of the propagation of its writes, the transaction must unlock all the previously granted GLocks (just one cycle). This is another difference between the original SEQ implementation and GCommit, since SEQ only needs to send a release message to the read directories. Nevertheless GLocks' acquisitions and releases do not travel along the main interconnection network, but are sent using the specialized hardware deployed by GLocks. This results in very significant savings in terms of network traffic (Section 4).

3   Evaluation Environment

3.1   System Settings

We use a full-system execution-driven simulation based on the Wisconsin GEMS toolset [7], in conjunction with Wind River Simics [8]. We rely on the detailed timing model for the memory subsystem provided by GEMS's Ruby module, with the Simics in-order processor model. Simics provides functional correctness for the SPARC ISA and boots an unmodified Solaris 10. We simulate a tiled

Table 1. Parameters of Orion

Parameter	Value
in_port	6
tech_point	45
Vdd	1.0
transistor type	NVT
flit_width	128 (bits)

Table 2. Workloads and inputs

Benchmark	Input
Genome	-g512 -s32 -n32768
Intruder	-a10 -l16 -n4096 -s1
Kmeans-high	-m15 -n15 -t0.05 -i random-n2048-d16-c16
Kmeans-low	-m40 -n40 -t0.05 -i random-n2048-d16-c16
Labyrinth	-i random-x32-y32-z3-n96
Ssca2	-s14 -i1.0 -u1.0 -l9 -p9
Vacation-high	-n4 -q60 -u90 -r1048576 -t4096
Vacation-low	-n2 -q90 -u98 -r1048576 -t4096
Yada	-a10 -i ttimeu10000.2

CMP system configured as described next. We assume a 16-core configuration with private L1 I&D caches and a shared, multibanked L2 cache consisting of 16 banks of 512KB each. The L1 caches maintain inclusion with the shared L2 cache. The private L1 data caches are kept coherent through an on-chip directory (at L2 cache banks), which maintains bit-vectors of sharers and implements the MESI protocol. All tiles are connected through a router-based 2D-mesh network. In this 4×4 2D-network, each router has between 5 and 7 ports.

To compute energy consumption in the on-chip memory hierarchy we consider both the caches and the interconnection network. Energy consumed by the interconnection network has been measured based on Orion 2.0 [9]. In particular, we have extended the network simulator provided by GEMS with the consumption model included in Orion. Table 1 shows the values of some of the parameters assumed for the interconnection network. On the other hand, the amount of energy spent in the memory structures (L1, L2, Write Buffer) has been measured based on the consumption model of CACTI 5.3 rev 174 [10]. In the case of the L2 cache, we distinguish the accesses that return cache blocks from those that only involve the tags' part of the L2 cache. To account for the energy consumed by the GLocks we assume the implementation presented in [6].

The Ruby module provides support for a naive implementation of a *Lazy-Lazy* system. We have extended it in order to achieve an implementation that mimics the behavior of Scalable-TCC with the sequential commit algorithm (STCC-SEQ) described in [4]. We have implemented GCommit on top of STCC-SEQ. For that, all we had to change was the commit protocol. In GCommit, all commits are performed in hardware using the mechanism described in Section 2. The remaining aspects are identical in both GCommit and STCC-SEQ. Finally, we have also evaluated the parallel reader optimization for STCC-SEQ (STCC-SEQPRO [4]). This optimization allows multiple transactions to simultaneously occupy a directory as long as none of these transactions write to this directory.

3.2   Workloads

For the evaluation, we use nine transactional benchmarks extracted from the STAMP suite [11]. We evaluate STAMP applications using the recommended input size in each case. The application *Bayes* was excluded since it exhibits unpredictable behavior and high variability in its execution times [12]. Results presented have been averaged over twenty runs for each application, each with very minor randomization of some system parameters just sufficient to excite different interleavings. Table 2 describes the benchmarks and the values of the input parameters used in this work.

4   Results

In this section, we present the results obtained for the *Lazy-Lazy* systems previously described (STCC-SEQ, GCommit and STCC-SEQPRO) in terms of execution time, energy consumption and network traffic. For GCommit we assume different number of GLocks. *Gx* in the next figures represents an implementation of GCommit with x GLocks. Results for *G16* have been omitted in the energy and traffic graphs since they coincide with those obtained with less GLocks.

4.1   Execution Time Results

Figure 2 shows the relative breakdown of the execution times obtained for STCC-SEQ, STCC-GCommit and STCC-SEQPRO (SEQ, GCommit and SEQPRO from here on respectively). In all cases, execution times have been normalized with respect to those obtained with SEQ. Moreover, to have clear understanding of the results Figure 2 divides the execution times into the following categories: *Abort* (time spent during aborts), *Back-off* (delay time between an abort and the next re-execution), *Barrier* (time spent in barriers), *Commit* (time needed to propagate the write sets to the memory hierarchy), *Non_xact* (time spent in non-transactional execution), *Precommitting* –or *precommit* phase– (time taken to acquire privileges to commit–book the corresponding directory modules/GLock), *Xact_useful* (useful transactional time) and *Xact_wasted* (transactional time wasted because of aborts).

As it can be derived from Figure 2, GCommit shows noticeable improvements in overall performance with respect to both SEQ and SEQPRO (average reduction of 15.7% and 11.3% respectively). It is important to note that these improvements come as a result of a significant reduction in the amount of time needed to complete the *precommit* phase (*Precommitting* category in the bars). Observe also that GCommit consistently reduces the duration of the *precommit* phase in all applications (68.5% on average compared with SEQ). On the other hand, the distinction between reads and writes carried out in SEQPRO results in small improvements over SEQ (average reduction of only 5.1%), which are mainly a consequence of the reductions in the *precommit* phase in just two of the nine applications (*Kmeans-high* and *Ssca2*). The other important conclusion that can be extracted from Figure 2 is that the number of GLocks needed to obtain full potential of GCommit is just one. All bars labeled with *Gx* obtain almost the same result and hence, G1 is presented as the best tradeoff between complexity and performance. On the one hand, with only one GLock, GCommit precludes the possibility of parallel commits since all the transactions willing to commit will have to compete for the same GLock during the *precommit* phase. On the other hand, the more GLocks GCommit uses, the more GLocks must be

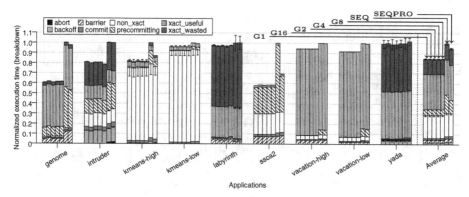

Fig. 2. Breakdown of the execution times

booked, thus enlarging the duration of the *precommit* phase. In this way, the benefits of having several GLocks are offset by the increased number of steps in the booking process. Moreover, the fact that our proposal reduces drastically the duration of the *precommit* phase also minimizes the possibility of transactions competing for the same resources.

The discussion below highlights important observations and presents insights gained from a detailed analysis of the interaction between the three commit algorithms and the behavior of individual workloads.

Genome. This workload exhibits moderate to high degree of contention. The average number of directory banks that must be booked is considerably high (10-16). This supposes a considerable number of steps that enlarge the duration of the *precommit* phase. Additionally, the distinction between read and write accesses enabled by SEQPRO barely improves execution time.

Intruder. This workload shows high contention with three transactions. Nevertheless, only transaction with TID0 accumulates the most important part of the aborts. Reducing the time needed in the arbitration process (booking directories/GLocks) benefits the global execution by 20%.

Kmeans (high/low). Despite the fact that this benchmark is mainly non transactional, there are some differences in *Kmeans-high*. In this case, there are three transactions but only TID0 and TID1 represent important fractions of transactional execution time. Parallel commits are allowed only between threads running transactions with different TIDs. Nevertheless, *Kmeans* is highly concurrent, so the efficiency of GCommit exceeds its lack of parallel commits.

Labyrinth. Results for this workload depend significantly on the interleaving of threads. Its most important transaction (TID1) presents large write sets and a long execution time. An abort is extremely costly and when a transaction commits, it is frequent that other transactions must abort. Tansactional execution phases dominate overall time, and the commit algorithm is not relevant.

Ssca2. It has a large number of tiny transactions that favors parallel reader optimization of SEQPRO allowing multiple parallel commits. On the other hand

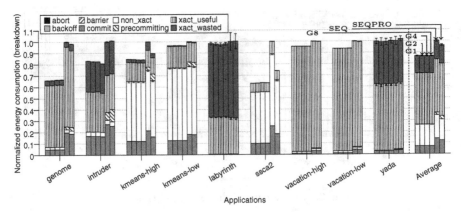

Fig. 3. Energy consumed (breakdown)

SEQ obtains the worst results due to the serialization that introduces in RAR situations. GCommit beats SEQ because of its minimum delay to book every directory/GLock. Parallel Reader Optimization (PRO) applied to GCommit can improve its performance even more.

Vacation (high/low). This benchmark does not exhibit real conflicts. The number of directory banks booked for writing and the low level of contention eliminate any possibility of parallel commits. Only the fast commits enabled by GCommit can make *precommitting* time disappear.

Yada. It has a large working set and exhibits high contention. The dominant transaction (TID2) spreads its large write set (69.3 addresses) among all L2 banks, hindering parallel commits. The frequency of the aborts makes *xact_wasted* time the most important fraction in the total execution.

4.2 Energy and Network Traffic Results

Figure 3 shows the dynamic energy consumption for the three systems considered in this work. As before, results have been normalized with respect to SEQ. Additionally, we split the energy consumed in each case into the same categories than in Section 4.1. To do so, we track the amount of energy consumed during each one of the categories. For messages sent through the general-purpose interconnection, we track data accesses in any cache structure and Write Buffer as well as other possible messages generated because of the first one, and accumulate all this energy consumption into the corresponding execution phase of the transaction that issued the original message.

As with execution time, our proposal significantly improves overall energy consumption compared to SEQ and, as shown in Figure 3, average reductions of 13.7% are obtained. The energy due to the *precommit* phase is virtually eliminated in GCommit. Our proposal does not issue any messages on the general-purpose interconnect, and the energy consumed during the *precommit* phase comes just from

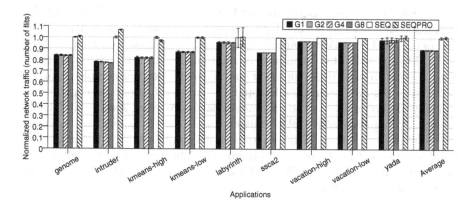

Fig. 4. Normalized network traffic

the much more efficient dedicated links and controllers of the GLocks. Additionally, in both SEQ and SEQPRO, several directory banks must be reserved and therefore much more steps have to be done (except with G16). Network traffic (measured as number of flits) generated by SEQ, SEQPRO and GCommit is shown in Figure 4. As in Figure 3, results have been normalized with respect to those obtained with SEQ. As it can be seen, GCommit entails smaller traffic levels than the other approaches (reductions of 10.6% on average). On the other hand, the amount of energy spent during *precommitting* is small in the case of SEQ and SEQPRO. The number of control messages across the network during this arbitration period is moderate in both protocols, so part of the improvements in energy consumption come from the reduction in the number of aborts that GCommit entails. This is why the amount of energy due to *backoff* is also reduced in GCommit.

5   Related Work

Research in Hardware Transactional Memory (HTM) has been very active since the introduction of multicores in mainstream computing. The initial proposal by Herlihy *et al.* [13] was revived in the previous decade with more sophisticated designs like TCC [14] or LogTM-SE [15]. HTM systems have been traditionally classified into two categories according to the approaches to version management (VM) and conflict detection (CD) that they implement: *Eager-Eager* and *Lazy-Lazy* (VM and CD respectively). Although *Lazy-Lazy* HTMs have been identified as being more efficient than eager designs [16], the necessity of en-masse publication of updates at commit time raises issues of scalability and several hybrid approaches (FlexTM [16], ZEBRA [17]) have been recently proposed.

TCC [14] has probably been the most seminal *Lazy-Lazy* system. The original design which was based on a bus was later adapted to a more scalable architecture that uses directory-based coherence, giving rise to Scalable-TCC [5]. Subsequently, Pugsley *et al.* proposed STCC-SEQ and STCC-SEQPRO to significantly reduce commit time in Scalable-TCC [4]. Both STCC-SEQ and STCC-SEQPRO are free of deadlocks/livelocks, do not employ a centralized agent and allow for parallel commits. In this work we study a hardware implementation of an algorithm similar to STCC-SEQ and show that to improve commit bandwidth it is more important to reduce *commit transfer time* (time that goes since a transaction completes commit until another one gets permission to commit) than enabling parallel commits.

Finally, GCommit is based on the use of hardware locks, specifically GLocks, presented by Abellán *et al.* [6]. A GLock makes use of G-lines [18] to deploy a distributed design that let transactions fast commit during their arbitration period at commit time (*precommit* phase). This efficient hardware imitates the behaviour of directories in STCC-SEQ but it completes each step of the *precommit* phase much more faster.

6   Conclusions

In this work we have presented GCommit, a new hardware approach to commit algorithms in *Lazy-Lazy* HTM systems. GCommit implements a hardware approximation to the STCC-SEQ commit algorithm that dramatically accelerates the *precommit* subphase of a commit. GCommit is implemented using hardware locks, more specifically GLocks. A GLock allows access to its critical section in 2 or 4 cycles in absent of contention. GCommit exploits that quality to replace the reservation of directory banks during the *precommit* phase in STCC-SEQ with the acquisition of one or several GLocks. Now each GLock protects access to the same rank of addresses (its critical section) than the previous directory bank. GCommit can use several GLocks in its implementation. Nevertheless we find that with a single GLock, GCommit achieves the maximum performance and energy savings with the minimal hardware complexity.

We evaluate our proposal using full-system simulations of a 16-core CMP running several STAMP applications, and compare it against a traditional implementation of STCC-SEQ and STCC-SEQPRO. We find that GCommit accelerates the *precommit* subphase about 68.5% on average, which results in average reductions of 15.7% and 13.7% in terms of execution time and energy consumption, respectively, compared with STCC-SEQ. Additionally, our proposal has negligible requirements in terms of area. Finally, although GCommit does not enable parallel commits–with only one GLock–(contrary to STCC-SEQ), because of the particularities of transactional applications it is more important to ensure short *precommitting* time than enabling parallel commits at the cost of increasing the duration of the process (for example, by increasing the time to acquire every GLock).

Acknowledgment. This work was supported by the Spanish MINECO under grant TIN2012-38341-C04. Epifanio Gaona Ramírez is supported by fellowship 09503/FPI/08 from Fundación Séneca, Agencia Regional de Ciencia y Tecnología de la Región de Murcia (II PCTRM).

References

1. Kanter, D.: Analysis of Haswell's transactional memory. In: Real World Technologies (Febuary 15, 2012)
2. Herlihy, M., Eliot, J., Moss, B.: Transactional memory: Architectural support for lock-free data structures. In: ISCA 20 (May 1993)
3. Gaona-Ramírez, E., Titos-Gil, R., Fernández, J., Acacio, M.E.: Characterizing energy consumption in hardware transactional memory systems. In: SBAC-PAD-22 (October 2010)
4. Pugsley, S.H., Awasthi, M., Madan, N., Muralimanohar, N., Balasubramonian, R.: Scalable and reliable communication for hardware transactional memory. In: PACT-17 (October 2008)
5. Chafi, H., Casper, J., Carlstrom, B.D., McDonald, A., Minh, C.C., Baek, W., Kozyrakis, C., Olukotun, K.: A scalable, non-blocking approach to transactional memory. In: HPCA-13 (February 2007)
6. Abellán, J.L., Fernández, J., Acacio, M.E.: Design of an efficient communication infrastructure for highly-contended locks in many-core cmps. Journal of Parallel and Distributed Computing (July 2012)
7. Martin, M.M.K., Sorin, D.J., Beckmann, B.M., Marty, M.R., Xu, M., Alameldeen, A.R., Moore, K.E., Hill, M.D., Wood, D.A.: Multifacet's general execution-driven multiprocessor simulator (GEMS) toolset. SIGARCH CAN 33(4), 92–99 (2005)
8. Magnusson, P.S., Christensson, M., Eskilson, J., Forsgren, D., Hallberg, G., Hogberg, J., Larsson, F., Moestedt, A., Werner, B.: Simics: A full system simulation platform. IEEE Computer 35, 50–58 (2002)
9. Kahng, A.B., Li, B., Peh, L.S., Samadi, K.: ORION 2.0: A fast and accurate NoC power and area model for early-stage design space exploration. In: DATE-13 (March 2009)
10. HP Labs, http://quid.hpl.hp.com:9081/cacti
11. Minh, C.C., Chung, J., Kozyrakis, C., Olukotun, K.: STAMP: Stanford transactional applications for multi-processing. In: IISWC-4 (September 2008)
12. Dragojevic, A., Guerraoui, R.: Predicting the scalability of an STM. In: Transact-05 (April 2010)
13. Herlihy, M., Moss, J.E.B.: Transactional memory: Architectural support for lock-free data structures. SIGARCH CAN 21(2), 289–300 (1993)
14. Hammond, L., Wong, V., Chen, M.K., Carlstrom, B.D., Davis, J.D., Hertzberg, B., Prabhu, M.K., Wijaya, H., Kozyrakis, C., Olukotun, K.: Transactional memory coherence and consistency. In: ISCA-31 (June 2004)
15. Yen, L., Bobba, J., Marty, M.R., Moore, K.E., Volos, H., Hill, M.D., Swift, M.M., Wood, D.A.: LogTM-SE: Decoupling hardware transactional memory from caches. In: HPCA-13 (February 2007)
16. Shriraman, A., Dwarkadas, S., Scott, M.L.: Flexible decoupled transactional memory support. In: ISCA-35 (June 2008)
17. Titos, J.R., Negi, A., Acacio, M.E., García, J.M., Stenström, P.: ZEBRA: A data-centric, hybrid-policy hardware transactional memory design. In: ICS-25 (June 2011)
18. Krishna, T., Kumar, A., Peh, L.S., Postman, J., Chiang, P., Erez, M.: Express virtual channels with capacitively driven global links. IEEE Micro 29(4), 48–61 (2009)

Self-adaptation for Mobile Robot Algorithms Using Organic Computing Principles

Jan Hartmann[1], Walter Stechele[2], and Erik Maehle[1]

[1] Institute for Computer Engineering, Universität zu Lübeck
[2] Institute for Integrated Systems, Technische Universität München

Abstract. Many mobile robot algorithms require tedious tuning of parameters and are, then, often suitable to only a limited number of situations. Yet, as mobile robots are to be employed in various fields from industrial settings to our private homes, changes in the environment will occur frequently. Organic computing principles such as self-organization, self-adaptation, or self-healing can provide solutions to react to new situations, e.g. provide fault tolerance. We therefore propose a biologically inspired self-adaptation scheme to enable complex algorithms to adapt to different environments. The proposed scheme is implemented using the Organic Robot Control Architecture (ORCA) and Learning Classifier Tables (LCT). Preliminary experiments are performed using a graph-based Visual Simultaneous Localization and Mapping (SLAM) algorithm and a publicly available benchmark set, showing improvements in terms of runtime and accuracy.

1 Introduction

The Organic Robot Control Architecture (ORCA, [1]) is a software architecture that enables the development of self-x properties for mobile robots. While ORCA was only applied to simple problem sets, e.g. servo control or walking gate generation, previously, in this work, ORCA is extended by utilizing Learning Classifier Systems (LCS, [2]) as the main method for self-adaptation, so that it can be applied to a broad range of algorithms. Now, in ORCA algorithms are organized in a modular and hierarchical fashion. The LCS analyze the output of a module and apply changes to algorithm parameters or exchange parts of the algorithm. In operation, the LCS further employ unsupervised machine learning to determine, which actions have most improved the algorithm performance, e.g. runtime or accuracy, and adjust itself accordingly.

A Visual Simultaneous Localization and Mapping (SLAM) algorithm has been chosen as a test scenario for its popularity, the ability to modularize the algorithm, and the large impact of changes in the environment to the algorithm's performance. ORCA and LCS are implemented in the Robot Operating System (ROS) framework[1], which supports the modular approach of ORCA. We extend existing interfaces for manual reconfiguration of parameters to allow for an easy incorporation of self-adaptation capabilities into other projects.

---

[1] http://www.ros.org/wiki

C. Hochberger et al. (Eds.): ARCS 2013, LNCS 7767, pp. 232–243, 2013.
© Springer-Verlag Berlin Heidelberg 2013

As software systems become larger and the underlying hardware is often distributed and heterogeneous, self-adaptive software has been extensively studied. Self-adaptive software systems vary widely in the degree of adaptation, scale, and view-point of the approach. A comparison of different formal descriptions of self-adaptation architectures can be found in [3]. Self-adaptive software in terms of self-managed system architectures is introduced in [4]. A survey from an engineering point of view is given in [5], posing open questions for future research. Some of these questions are addressed in this work, e.g. the transparent integration into existing projects through ROS.

Our approach, given the various definitions in the previously mentioned surveys, must be seen as an architecture-based self-adaptation approach, governed by the Organic Robot Control Architecture ORCA. It further exhibits the properties of a control loop-based self-adaptation scheme. A similar biology-inspired approach was introduced with the generic Observer/Controller architecture [6]. Another approach to self-adaptation architectures was proposed by the IBM Autonomic Computing Initiative[2], specifically the Monitor-Analyze-Plan-Execute (MAPE) Model, which was e.g. implemented in the Rainbow framework [7]. Similarly to organic computing, ORCA, and other Observer/Controller architectures, autonomic computing and Rainbow utilize a biologically inspired approach. Yet, the main application lies in large-scale server infrastructures.

In the field of mobile robots, self-adaptation has been studied on the level of physically reconfigurable robots [8] and cooperating robot teams [9]. While the main goal of robots that seamlessly adapt to the environment remains similar, the problem set discussed in this paper requires a higher degree of software-centered self-adaptation. Generally, in comparison to other self-adaptation schemes, the approach presented in this paper mainly contributes in three areas. Firstly, the approach is tailored to complex mobile robot algorithms. To reduce the engineering time and raise the degrees of freedom for such complex algorithms, secondly, unsupervised machine learning was introduced to the self-adaptation process. Lastly, a simple means of applying self-adaptation to existing projects is proposed by the integration into the ROS framework.

The remainder of this paper is structured as follows. First, the different methods used in this work are introduced in Sec. 2. Then, details on the implementation of the proposed self-adaptation framework are presented in Sec. 3. Finally, preliminary results are shown in Sec. 4 and discussed in Sec. 5.

2   Methods

In this section, the main building blocks of the self-adaptation approach, which is presented in this work, will be introduced in more detail.

2.1   The Organic Robot Control Architecture

The Organic Robot Control Architecture (ORCA, [1]) was developed in the German Research Foundation (DFG) priority program "Organic Computing" at the

---

[2] http://www.research.ibm.com/autonomic/

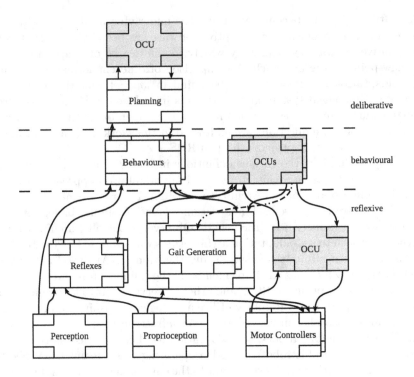

Fig. 1. Using the Organic Robot Control Architecture (ORCA) for the six-legged walking robot OSCAR. Basic Control Units (BCU, white) guarantee the functionality of the system under normal condition. In case of anomalies, Organic Control Units (OCU, gray) may change parameters of the gait generation and motor control BCUs to ensure that the robot reaches its goal in the best still possible way.

Institute for Computer Engineering at the University of Lübeck in cooperation with the University of Osnabrück and the Fraunhofer IAIS. ORCA is a modular and hierarchically structured software architecture, which is aimed to aid the development of self-x properties in mobile robots.

In ORCA, the functionality of a system in a fault-free state is guaranteed by the Basic Control Units (BCU). Organic Control Units (OCU) supervise the BCUs as well as other OCUs and may change parameters of the supervised modules in case of anomalies, i.e. disturbances that stem from the environment or the inner state of the robot. Further, with the means of Health Signals, the state of any unit may be described in a hierarchical fashion.

The capabilities of ORCA have been demonstrated on the six-legged walking machine OSCAR (Fig. 1). OSCAR is able to adapt to its environment, e.g. different kinds of terrain [10], or hardware failures, e.g. the amputation of a leg [11]. Re-planning of paths through difficult terrain based on the general health status of the robot has been investigated in [12]. A number of BCUs execute the basic functionality: planning, reactive behaviors, and walking. OCUs can adjust the walking gait generation as well as the parameters of the servo motor controller to ensure the best possible walking in any situation.

In this paper, the ORCA architecture is utilized to bring organic computing principles to a more general and a more complex set of mobile robot algorithms.

2.2   Visual SLAM as Demonstration Algorithm

The estimation of the position of a robot in an unknown environment - Simultaneous Localization and Mapping (SLAM) - is one of the most important problems of mobile robotics. Solutions using cameras to construct a map of the environment especially pose several challenges. Realtime capability in large environments, due to the complexity of the image processing algorithms that are typically used, remains an open issue. The impact of changes in the environment is largely ignored.

Such unsolved problems make Visual SLAM a good algorithm to demonstrate the capabilities of our self-adaptation approach. Using the ORCA OCU/ BCU scheme, Learning Classifier Tables (LCT), as described in the next section, are used to adjust parameters of the different parts of the Visual SLAM algorithm to ensure high efficiency in terms of runtime and accuracy, depending on the environment and state of the algorithm and robot. Further, parts of the algorithm may be exchanged, e.g. the means by which the robot movement is estimated.

2.3   Learning Classifier Tables

In this work, OCUs are implemented using Learning Classifier Tables (LCT, [13]). LCT are based on Learning Classifier Systems (LCS, [14]), but allow for an efficient hardware implementation, which will be an important goal for future improvements to this work. A LCT rule table consists of a set of rules with specific conditions, actions, and a fitness value. The fitness value governs which rule that matches the current conditions is selected. It is updated based on a reward, which reflects the general performance of the algorithm, e.g. runtime or accuracy. While an extension to learning via genetic algorithms is provided by LCT, this work solely relies on the fitness update for learning, due to the limited scope of the presented preliminary results.

Fig. 2 shows an example LCT for the proposed demonstration algorithm. A total of 10 conditions are evaluated. The conditions reflect information about the environment, e.g. the amount of information that can be obtained from the current image, as well as the inner state of the robot, e.g. the current robot speed. Thirteen different actions are applied, which change the supervised module by either reconfiguring part of the module or changing a specific parameter. Matching rules are selected based on the conditions, where for each rule a condition must apply, if the rule value at the corresponding position is 1, must not apply for a value of 0, and is ignored otherwise. Similarly, for a selected rule, a specific action is performed, if the rule value at the corresponding position is 1.

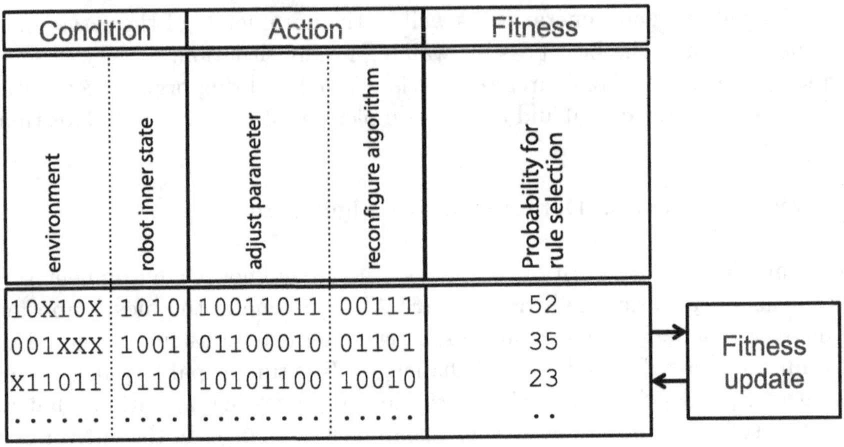

Condition		Action		Fitness
environment	robot inner state	adjust parameter	reconfigure algorithm	Probability for rule selection
10X10X	1010	10011011	00111	52
001XXX	1001	01100010	01101	35
X11011	0110	10101100	10010	23
. . . . . .	. . . .	. . . .	. . . . .	. .

Fitness update

Fig. 2. Example of a Learning Classifier Table (LCT) for the proposed demonstration algorithm

3   Implementation

This section will explain the Visual SLAM implementation and show the LCT ruleset that is used to adapt the Visual SLAM algorithm.

3.1   Visual SLAM Implementation

The proposed Visual SLAM algorithm largely follows the popular graph-based solution, which is e.g. utilized in [15] and [16]. Fig. 3 shows the general dataflow of a graph-based SLAM solution. Features are extracted from the camera image to estimate the robot movement. If the robot has traveled a distance larger than T, a new node is added to the SLAM graph. The extracted features are used to link existing nodes in the vicinity of the new node by estimating the linear transformation between the two nodes. Finally, the graph is optimized based on the robot movement as well as the links between nodes, which were estimated based on the features.

In this work, the RGBD camera Microsoft Kinect[3] is used. The Kinect provides a RGB image as well as depth information for each pixel through a structured light approach. The Features from Accelerated Segment Test (FAST, [17]) feature detector and Binary Robust Independent Elementary Features (BRIEF, [18]) feature descriptor are used for feature extraction. The graph is optimized using g2o [19], an efficient framework for least squares graph optimization. The means of estimating the movement of the robot and the transformation between nodes as well as the threshold distance T is governed by the LCT self-adaptation. The robot movement as well as the transformation between nodes is estimated

---

[3] http://www.xbox.com/de-DE/Kinect

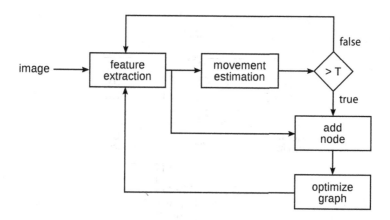

Fig. 3. Simplified dataflow for a graph-based Visual SLAM system

in a Random Sample Consensus (RANSAC) scheme. Two different algorithms may be used to estimate a transformation from feature correspondences. A robust and fast approach, as similarly applied in [15], uses three correspondences and the Singular Value Decomposition (SVD). The more sophisticated EPnP algorithm [20] is less efficient, but generally more accurate.

The proposed Visual SLAM algorithm has been designed for the popular Robot Operating System (ROS) framework. Each BCU and OCU is implemented as a ROS node, i.e. distinct processes that communicate via pre-defined messages. ROS messages are also used as a means of generalized communication between BCUs and OCUs. This will, in future experiments, provide a simple way to introduce the capabilities of self-adaptation to other algorithms. Initial steps in this direction have already been taken by using the *dynamic_reconfigure*[4] message types, which is a generic means for manual reconfiguration of algorithm parameters in ROS.

3.2   Proposed Ruleset

For these experiments, the Visual SLAM algorithm is structured as shown in Fig. 4. The general SLAM algorithm is subdivided into four modules. The graph optimizer, feature extraction, movement estimation, and graph manager (which handles adding new nodes and finding links between different nodes) are each represented by a BCU. Two OCUs perform the self-adaptation for the latter three BCUs. The first OCU supervises the movement and feature extraction BCUs. It adjusts the number of features that are to be extracted. The second OCU adjusts the distance after which to add a new node and the algorithm used to estimate the transformation between nodes.

---

[4] http://www.ros.org/wiki/dynamic_reconfigure

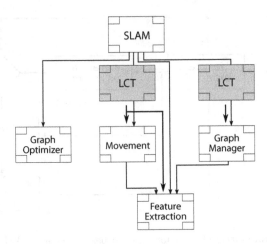

Fig. 4. The proposed graph-based Visual SLAM as structured in ORCA

Table 1. Conditions, actions and rewards that were used in the experiments

conditions	
mean feature score (μ_S)	represents the amount of information that may be gathered from the environment, i.e. high for highly textured environments, low otherwise
robot speed (ν)	influences the rate at which images need to be processed in order to maintain a high accuracy
actions	
number of features (F)	sets the number of features to be extracted to a specific value
new node distance (T)	sets the distance after which a new node is to be added
transformation estimation	sets the algorithm to estimate the transformation between nodes
rewards	
runtime	reward for low runtime
matches	reward for high number of matching features in movement estimation
neighbors	reward for large number of node neighbors

Generally, as shown in Tab. 1, two conditions, two actions that change parameters, one action that reconfigures part of the algorithm, and three rewards were selected in the experiments. Rules may then, for example, look as depicted in Fig. 5.

```
if μ_S < 60 and ν ≥ 0.5 m/s then
|   F = 200
end
if μ_S ≥ 60 then
|   F = 100
end
.
.
.

if μ_S ≥ 60 and ν < 0.5 m/s then
|   T = 0.1m, use EPnP
end
if ν ≥ 0.5 m/s then
|   T = 0.2m, use SVD
end
.
.
.
```

Condition		Action		
$\mu S < 60$	$\nu < 0.5$	$F = 100$	$F = 200$	$F = 300$
1	0	0	1	0
0	X	1	0	0
...		...		

Condition		Action		
$\mu S < 60$	$\nu < 0.5$	use EPnP	$T = 0.1$	$T = 0.2$
0	1	1	1	0
X	0	0	0	1
...		...		

Fig. 5. Example of a ruleset for the Visual SLAM algorithm with four rules. Left: rules in pseudo-code formulation. Right: resulting learning classifier table.

4   Preliminary Results

The self-adaptation for the Visual SLAM algorithm was evaluated using the Freiburg University RGBD SLAM dataset[5]. The dataset provides different test sequences using a handheld Microsoft Kinect as well as ground truth position and orientation of the camera using a highly accurate tracking system. While all test sequences are set in an office environment, they exhibit different kinds of motion (e.g. rotational in *FR1 rpy* or translational in *FR1 xyz*) and different degrees of texture in the image (e.g. low amount of texture in *FR1 floor* or high amount of texture in *FR1 desk*). Therefore, a Visual SLAM algorithm should benefit from self-adaptation in the test sequences.

The proposed Visual SLAM algorithm was tested on all test sequences that were available at the time of writing, with and without self-adaptation. In the latter case, a new node distance of $T = 0.1$, the SVD transformation estimation, and feature numbers of $F = 100$ and $F = 300$ were used, representing the two extremal cases in terms of runtime and accuracy. A full set of rules was used for the learning classifier tables with the conditions, actions, and rewards that were proposed in Sec. 3.2. All rules were initialized with equal fitness. The self-adaption should, now, produce similarly accurate results as when using the highest number of features while significantly improving the runtime.

Tab. 2 shows the runtime, i.e. mean time for a Visual SLAM update, and Root Mean Squared Error (RMSE) in position, averaged over ten runs. Comparing the

---

[5] http://vision.in.tum.de/data/datasets/rgbd-dataset

Table 2. Mean runtime (excluding graph optimization) and Root Mean Squared Error (RMSE) in position of the Visual SLAM algorithm with and without self-adaptation. Length and duration indicate the path length and actual duration of each test sequence. Experiments without self-adaptation were run with $T = 0.1$ and the two extremal number of features, $F = 100$ and $F = 300$. Values are averaged over 10 runs. The best accuracy is highlighted for each sequence. Please refer to [15] for a more detailed description of the dataset and results of the original authors.

Sequence Name	Length (m)	Duration (s)	with Time (s)	with RMSE (m)	without (100) Time (s)	without (100) RMSE (m)	without (300) Time (s)	without (300) RMSE (m)
FR1 360	5.82	28.69	0.114	0.119	0.064	0.129	0.174	**0.105**
FR1 desk2	10.16	24.86	0.142	0.087	0.070	0.118	0.201	**0.066**
FR1 desk	9.26	23.40	0.116	**0.061**	0.068	0.081	0.193	**0.061**
FR1 floor	12.57	49.87	0.160	**0.217**	0.066	0.227	0.190	0.224
FR1 room	15.99	48.90	0.147	**0.139**	0.067	0.186	0.190	0.153
FR1 rpy	1.66	27.67	0.163	**0.042**	0.071	0.049	0.217	0.045
FR1 xyz	7.11	30.09	0.166	**0.023**	0.069	0.032	0.188	0.026
mean			0.144	0.098	0.068	0.118	0.193	**0.097**

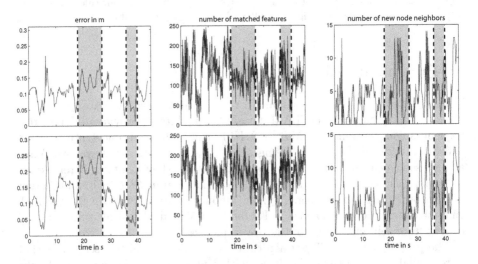

Fig. 6. Illustration of the self-adaptation process for the *FR1 room* test sequence using self adaptation (top) and fixed 300 features (bottom)

two test cases without self-adaptation, as expected, the error decreases significantly with the number of features (-18%), while the update time almost triples. Results with self-adaptation show that by adjusting parameters dynamically, as opposed to the 300 feature case, the runtime can be significantly decreased (-25%) while accuracy is improved in most test sequences.

A more in-depth analysis is shown in Fig. 6, comparing a single test run for the *FR1 room* test sequence with self-adaptation (top) and without self-adaptation

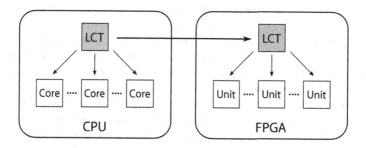

Fig. 7. The proposed hardware platform for self-adaptation and reconfiguration in software and hardware

using 300 features (bottom), with a RMSE of $0.113m$ and $0.145m$ and mean runtime of $0.152s$ and $0.190s$ respectively. The figure shows, from left to right, the error, number of matched features, and number of node neighbors for a new node over time. Two characteristic regions are highlighted.

Generally, both, the number of matched features and the number of node neighbors, directly relate to the accuracy of the algorithm. In the first region (time 18 to 27), the self-adaptation chooses a lower number of features. As this is a part of the test sequence, where a lot of node neighbors can be found, the accuracy will not decrease with a lower number of features, while the runtime improves. Similarly, in the second region (time 36 to 40), the number of node neighbors is low. Here, the self-adaptation chooses to increase the number of features to maintain a high accuracy.

5 Conclusion and Outlook

In this paper, a new method for the self-adaption of mobile robot algorithms has been proposed. The self-adaption is performed within the Organic Robot Control Architecture (ORCA) framework and uses Learning Classifier Tables (LCT) as a means of adapting the parameters of an algorithm or exchanging parts of an algorithm.

The method for self-adaptation was demonstrated using a graph-based Visual SLAM algorithm. Self-adaptation was used to dynamically adjust important parameters and exchange parts of the algorithm. The performance of the Visual SLAM algorithm was evaluated using a publicly available benchmark, showing that, in our setup, self-adaptation may improve runtime significantly while maintaining similar or better accuracy as compared to parameters, which have proven to provide good results in previous experiments.

Of course, the presented experiments only superficially evaluate the full potential of the proposed self-adaptation scheme. Therefore, in future efforts, more thorough experiments will be conducted with larger LCT tables. The performance will be evaluated using the ground truth data for rewards as well as using several consecutive runs to better train the classifier tables. Further, genetic algorithms will be used to alter the LCT rules and find better solutions in larger rulesets, while rewards will be modified based on the current task and state of the robot. For more sophisticated experiments, new datasets will be used, which are tailored to the self-adaptation problem, e.g. with vastly different environments and robot speeds or supplemental information, e.g. the battery charge.

The approaches that were presented in this paper may be applied to any kind of mobile robot algorithm, given appropriate conditions and rewards. Therefore, besides more thorough experiments using the Visual SLAM algorithm, the self-adaptation will be generalized in a way that it can be easily applied to a wide variety of algorithms. This will include the transparent inclusion into the Robot Operating System (ROS) through the *dynamic_reconfigure* interfaces, which is already used by many projects. The automatic generation of a ruleset will be a key part in this effort.

In terms of system architecture, future research will focus on extending our approach to dynamically reconfigurable Field Programmable Gate Arrays (FPGA). Since many advanced mobile robot algorithms are computationally very intensive, CPUs alone are often too slow to assure realtime behavior. A partially reconfigurable FPGA in form of a Multiprocessor System-on-Chip (MPSoC), as shown in Fig. 7, will be used as a co-processor to accelerate parts of the Visual SLAM algorithm, e.g. the feature extraction. Which parts of the software will be executed on the CPU or FPGA is decided based on the current situation, similarly to the self-adaptation methods presented in this paper. Hardware Learning Classifier Tables will govern the dynamic reconfiguration of the FPGA.

Acknowledgement. This work was funded in part by the German Research Foundation (DFG) within priority programme 1183 under grant reference MA 1412/8-2.

References

[1] Brockmann, W., Maehle, E., Grosspietsch, K.E., Rosemann, N., Jakimovski, B.: ORCA: An organic robot control architecture. In: Müller-Schloer, C., Schmeck, H., Ungerer, T. (eds.) Organic Computing - A Paradigm Shilft for Complex Systems. Birkhäuser-Springer (2011)

[2] Wilson, S.W.: Classifier fitness based on accuracy. Evolutionary Computation 3(2), 149–175 (1995)

[3] Bradbury, J.S., Cordy, J.R., Dingel, J., Wermelinger, M.: A survey of self-management in dynamic software architecture specifications. In: ACM SIGSOFT Workshop on Self-Managed Systems (WOSS), pp. 28–33 (2004)

[4] Kramer, J., Magee, J.: Self-managed systems: an architectural challenge. In: Future of Software Engineering (FOSE), pp. 259–268 (2007)

[5] Cheng, B.H., Lemos, R., Giese, H., Inverardi, P., Magee, J., Andersson, J., Becker, B., Bencomo, N., Brun, Y., Cukic, B., Marzo Serugendo, G., Dustdar, S., Finkelstein, A., Gacek, C., Geihs, K., Grassi, V., Karsai, G., Kienle, H.M., Kramer, J., Litoiu, M., Malek, S., Mirandola, R., Müller, H.A., Park, S., Shaw, M., Tichy, M., Tivoli, M., Weyns, D., Whittle, J.: Software engineering for self-adaptive systems, pp. 1–26. Springer, Heidelberg (2009)

[6] Richter, U., Mnif, M., Branke, J., Müller-Schloer, C., Schmeck, H.: Towards a generic observer/controller architecture for organic computing. In: Hochberger, C., Liskowsky, R. (eds.) INFORMATIK 2006 - Informatik für Menschen!, pp. 112–119. Bonner Köllen Verlag (2006)

[7] Garlan, D., Schmerl, B., Cheng, S.W.: Software Architecture-Based Self-Adaptation, pp. 31–55. Springer (2009)

[8] Yu, C.H., Nagpal, R.: Self-adapting modular robotics: A generalized distributed consensus framework. In: IEEE International Conference on Robotics and Automation (ICRA), pp. 1881–1888 (2009)

[9] Edwards, G., Garcia, J., Tajalli, H., Popescu, D., Medvidovic, N., Sukhatme, G., Petrus, B.: Architecture-driven self-adaptation and self-management in robotics systems. In: ICSE Workshop on Software Engineering for Adaptive and Self-Managing Systems (SEAMS), pp. 142–151 (2009)

[10] Al-Homsy, A., Hartmann, J., Maehle, E.: Inclination detection and adaptive walking for low-cost six-legged walking robots using organic computing principles. In: Climbing and Walking Robots (CLAWAR), pp. 173–182 (2012)

[11] Maehle, E., Brockmann, W., Grosspietsch, K.E., El Sayed Auf, A., Jakimovski, B., Krannich, S., Litza, M., Maas, R., Al-Homsy, A.: Application of the organic robot control architecture ORCA to the six-legged walking robot OSCAR. In: Müller-Schloer, C., Schmeck, H., Ungerer, T. (eds.) Organic Computing - A Paradigm Shilft for Complex Systems, Birkhäuser-Springer (2011)

[12] Maas, R., Maehle, E.: Fault tolerant and adaptive path planning for mobile robots based on health signals. In: International Conference on Architecture of Computing Systems (ARCS), Workshop on Dependability and Fault-Tolerance, pp. 58–63 (2011)

[13] Zeppenfeld, J., Bouajila, A., Stechele, W., Herkersdorf, A.: Learning classifier tables for autonomic systems on chip. Lecture Notes in Informatics, vol. 134, pp. 771–778. Springer, GI, Jahrestagung (2008)

[14] Wilson, S.W.: Classifier fitness based on accuracy. Evolutionary Computation 3(2), 149–175 (1995)

[15] Endres, F., Hess, J., Engelhard, N., Sturm, J., Cremers, D., Burgard, W.: An evaluation of the RGB-D SLAM system. In: IEEE International Conference on Robotics and Automation, ICRA (2012)

[16] Strasdat, H., Davison, A.J., Montiel, J., Konolige, K.: Double window optimisation for constant time visual SLAM. In: IEEE International Conference on Computer Vision, ICCV (2011)

[17] Rosten, E., Drummond, T.W.: Machine Learning for High-Speed Corner Detection. In: Leonardis, A., Bischof, H., Pinz, A. (eds.) ECCV 2006. LNCS, vol. 3951, pp. 430–443. Springer, Heidelberg (2006)

[18] Calonder, M., Lepetit, V., Strecha, C., Fua, P.: BRIEF: Binary robust independent elementary features, 778–792 (2010)

[19] Kümmerle, R., Grisetti, G., Strasdat, H., Konolige, K., Burgard, W.: g2o: A general framework for graph optimization. In: IEEE International Conference on Robotics and Automation, ICRA (2011)

[20] Lepetit, V., Moreno-Noguer, F., Fua, P.: EPnP: An accurate O(n) solution to the PnP problem. International Journal of Computer Vision 81(2), 155–166 (2008)

Self-virtualized CAN Controller for Multi-core Processors in Real-Time Applications

Christian Herber, Andre Richter, Holm Rauchfuss, and Andreas Herkersdorf

Technische Universität München, Institute for Integrated Systems,
Arcisstr. 21, 80290 Munich, Germany
{christian.herber,andre.richter,holm.rauchfuss,herkersdorf}@tum.de

Abstract. The long-rising number of electronic control units (ECUs) in cars is a major problem for OEMs, because of high costs and installation space requirements. The complexity could be reduced by the use of multi-core processors, where several ECUs can be repartitioned into virtual machines (VMs) running on one multi-core processor. Such a consolidation of ECUs is challenging, because I/O devices for real-time capable interconnects have to be shared by multiple VMs. In this paper we present a concept for offloading the functionality for CAN controller virtualization into a self-virtualized controller. By means of a thorough real-time analysis, it is shown that proposed solution is capable of real-time message transmission with additional latencies, that are multiple orders smaller than the common deadlines.

Keywords: Embedded Multi-Core Systems, Controller Area Network, Automotive Electronics, Self-Virtualized I/O Devices, Real-Time.

1 Introduction

Electronic functions have been a major driver of innovation in cars for many years. Since the beginning of the 1990s, embedded electronics and software have been increasing by 10% per year [1]. The fast development of electronic functions is responsible for many innovations in cars. The underlying Car-IT architecture is composed of a large number of electronic control units (ECUs) with relative low-performance single-core microcontrollers. They are connected by a set of automotive communication buses, e.g. Controller Area Network (CAN). Common practice for the introduction of a new electronic function has been the implementation of an additional ECU. This approach, however, has reached its limits regarding installation space, complexity and costs, with premium cars employing more than 70 ECUs [2].

An employment of multi-core processors in automotive electronic architectures could help to reduce this complexity, by consolidating the functionality of multiple ECUs into a multi-core powered ECU. To allow running mixed criticality functions side-by-side without one interfering with the other, a virtualization layer must be employed. Putting each function into a separate virtual machine (VM) will guarantee a logical separation in processing resources and memory

C. Hochberger et al. (Eds.): ARCS 2013, LNCS 7767, pp. 244–255, 2013.

space that prevents interference. However, each VM still needs access to the shared I/O devices of the hosting ECU. This is particularly challenging, because real-time requirements are a key factor in the design of automotive embedded systems and virtualizing I/O devices often poses a bottleneck in a virtualized system.

In order to minimize the latency between a VM and a shared I/O device, an efficient way of I/O virtualization is needed. In this paper, we propose a self-virtualized CAN controller as an extension to a conventional CAN controller that allows the transmission of messages from multiple VMs to a CAN bus under real-time constraints.

The remainder of this paper is structured as follows: Section 2 presents related work regarding I/O virtualization. Section 3 introduces basic principles of the CAN protocol. Our proposed concept is discussed in Section 4 and a the corresponding architectural realization is presented in Section 5. Section 6 introduces a real-time analysis method for such a controller. Based on this, Section 7 analyzes a consolidation scenario, and finally, Section 8 concludes this paper.

2   Related Work

Several approaches towards I/O virtualization, i.e. multiplexing and partitioning of the I/O device access for several VMs, have already been researched. Traditional solutions include emulating a device [3] or using paravirtualized front-end/back-end drivers [4].

Both solutions are purely software-based, either via extended functionality in the Virtual Machine Monitor (VMM) or by a dedicated driver VM. While these solutions are capable of circumventing the problem that conventional I/O devices are designed to be accessed from only a single instance, the additional latencies are too high for embedded applications [5]. Furthermore, extension of the trusted computing base of the software leads to side-effects on security, footprint and verification.

Self-virtualized I/O devices [6] [7] can resolve this problem. They offload virtualization routines into the I/O device itself to remove the VMM or driver domain from the I/O data path. In contrast to the aforementioned solutions this leads to reduced additional latencies for I/O virtualization. However, those devices also struggle to provide real-time capability, because they still implement software routines on dedicated RISC processors inside the device for the data processing.

This limitation is overcome in [8] for Ethernet by removing any software from the data path, implementing all virtualization functionality in hardware. Still, certain properties of automotive communication controllers like their unique arbitration schemes have not been addressed in any research. This motivates the development of a self-virtualized CAN controller that enables real-time access for VMs by offloading I/O virtualization functionality into hardware and removing any additional software from the data path.

3   Controller Area Network

Controller Area Network (CAN) is the most widely used bus in automotive embedded systems and supports data rates of up to 1 Mbit/s. Communication on the CAN bus is message based and the nodes do not have a distinct address. It has to be clear from the ID of a message what the associated content is. The ID is transmitted at the beginning of a frame (cf. Fig. 1) and specifies the fixed priority of a message, with low IDs having the highest priority. Because communication is non-preemptive, low priority messages can block the transmission of higher priority messages.

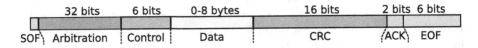

Fig. 1. Format of a CAN data frame with extended ID

The arbitration is performed by each node in a bitwise way. At any point in time when the bus is idle, any CAN node can start transmitting a message. The arbitration uses certain electrical characteristics of the physical bus on which dominant (0) and recessive (1) logic levels can exist. At the beginning of the frame a node will send the identifier and monitor the level present on the bus. If a node monitors a dominant state after transmitting a recessive bit, the arbitration is lost and the message has to be backed off. This scheme is called carrier sense multiple access/bitwise arbitration (CSMA/BA).

4   Concept for a Self-virtualized CAN Controller

In order to enable access to the CAN bus for multiple VMs through a single protocol engine, we propose a concept for a self-virtualized CAN controller as depicted in Fig. 2. It will offer virtual interfaces to the host system that enable real-time capable medium access. The concept is derived from several constraints originating from the nature of the CAN bus itself and considerations regarding flexibility, scalability and efficient use of resources.

When a message gets issued for transmission by the host system to the self-virtualized CAN controller, immediate access to the CAN bus cannot be guaranteed, because it might temporarily be occupied by messages from other nodes. Therefore, messages have to be buffered. Because certain actions from the host system (e.g. disabling one virtual controller) affect only the set of buffered messages associated with a distinct VM, a logical buffer has to be provided for each VM. The total memory demand is application dependent and scales with the number of VMs and messages objects (usually one per message).

To enable a flexible architecture, which can be used in many different application scenarios, the number of messages associated with one virtual interface

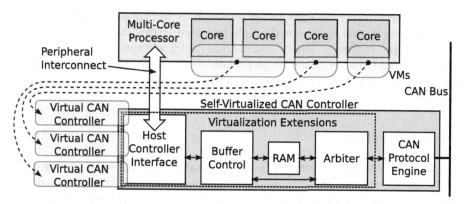

Fig. 2. System-level view at a virtualized multi-core system communicating through a self-virtualized CAN controller

should not be fixed. A common memory shall be shared by all virtual controllers, in which pointer-based data structures are contained for each virtual domain.

More requirements arise from the nature of the CAN bus, which is non-preemptive and uses a fixed priority arbitration scheme. The behavior of each virtual CAN controller should be as close as possible to the behavior of an ideal CAN controller to guarantee optimal performance. Therefore, the highest priority message queued should enter arbitration when the bus goes idle. Selecting this message at the right time is done by the virtualized CAN controller.

The length of a CAN frame is not fixed due to variable payloads and bit stuffing, which makes it hard to determine its actual length and therefore the point in time, when the bus will be idle. The only point, where this information is easily obtained is after the successful transmission. From there on, the internal arbitration has 3 µs of interframe spacing to determine the highest priority message, which will subsequently enter the CAN bus arbitration.

Because an arbitration of all messages requires a number of RAM accesses that scales linearly with the number of buffered messages, it is not feasible for the internal message selection by the virtualized CAN controller. Alternatively, priority queues can be used as buffers, which provide a sorted set (based on CAN ID) of messages for each virtual controller. The priority queue was realized as a binary search tree. This way, only a small subset of messages (one for each virtual domain) has to be compared, allowing a fast arbitration that is independent of the number of buffered messages. On the other hand, the insertion of messages into a priority queue might take longer. How this affects the overall performance of the system evaluated in Sections 6 and 7.

Frames received from the CAN bus are compared to a predefined set of filters for each VM, saved in a random access data structure and fetched by the host application. Back-to-back messages can arrive with a minimum inter-arrival time of 56 µs (standard ID, no payload), resulting in relaxed timing constraints in the receive part. Because the reception of messages is not critical with respect to real-time capability, the remainder of this paper will focus on the transmission.

The concept presented here allows several VMs to access the buffers within the respective virtual controller through dedicated virtual interfaces. The organization of the buffers as binary search trees, which are connected by pointers, enables a flexible use of resources and a fast selection of messages for transmission. The concept should allow real-time applications to communicate within their respective deadline requirements.

5   Architecture

We used the concepts presented above to create a timing accurate SystemC model of the virtualized CAN controller. The structure of the model and the contained components will be explained. A top-level schematic of the modules is shown in the lower half of Fig. 2.

The component presented here receives frames for transmission from a host system. These frames have to be buffered and selected for transmission on the CAN bus, which is connected to the other end of the controller.

The **Host Controller Interface** is used as a test bench in order to achieve an abstraction from actual host systems or peripheral interconnects. Transmission requests can arrive at arbitrary rates and are issued to the buffer control module using a first-come, first-served policy.

The **Buffer Control** module manages the priority queues within the RAM. It is the only component aware of which data structure is actually used (here: binary search tree). Upon an insertion request, the issued message has to be stored at the right position within the RAM. If the inserted message has the highest priority within a virtual controller, a notification will be issued to the arbiter module. In addition to the data structures, general information regarding the buffers is stored in the memory. This includes a pointer to the object of maximum priority for each buffer, which will be used by the arbiter module.

The **Arbiter** has to select the highest priority message from the RAM and issue it for transmission. The selected message should be ready for transmission when the CAN bus goes idle and another arbitration on the CAN bus is possible. The highest priority message within each virtual controller is found by referencing the provided pointer. The overall highest priority message will be issued to the protocol engine in order to enter the CAN bus arbitration.

The implementation of the CAN specification is done within the **Protocol Engine**. Its implementation is similar for all CAN controllers and does not need to be modified here. Within a self-virtualized CAN controller, multiple virtual CAN controllers can be served by one protocol engine.

6   Real-Time Analysis

CAN buses in an automotive context are often used under real-time conditions. This means that messages transmitted via the CAN bus are expected to meet deadline requirements. To determine whether a message will meet its deadline, an analysis for the worst-case message response time is needed. Such a method exists for ideal CAN controllers. For the case of virtualized CAN controllers, this theory has to be extended and is presented in Section 6.2.

6.1 Ideal CAN Nodes

A method for calculating message response times for ideal CAN nodes was published by Davis et al. in 2007 [9]. We will introduce the central ideas here, while the complete theory can be reviewed in the original publication.

The worst-case scenario assumed for message m is the following. At the time the message is queued for transmission, all higher priority messages are also queued. Additionally, a lower priority message has just started transmission on the bus, blocking it for a time B_m. Therefore, after transmission of the blocking lower priority message, all higher priority messages will be transmitted. It is possible that while waiting for transmission further instances of the higher priority messages will be queued. After all these messages are successfully transmitted, message m will start transmission.

The time that has to be considered in a worst-case scenario is called level-m busy period. It starts when a message of priority m or higher is queued ready for transmission and no messages of the same or higher priority waiting for transmission were queued before. It ends when there is no message of priority m or higher queued at the beginning of arbitration. According to [9], it can be iteratively calculated as

$$t_m^{n+1} = B_m + \sum_{\forall k \in hp(m) \cup m} \left\lceil \frac{t_m^n + J_k}{T_k} \right\rceil C_k. \tag{1}$$

Here, $hp(m)$ describes the set of higher priority messages, J_k, T_k and C_k are the queuing jitter, the cycle time and the transmission time of a message k.

It is possible that the level-m busy period is extended beyond the transmission of message m and also the cycle time T_m. This implies that multiple instances might be issued during the worst-case scenario. Instances are represented by the index variable $q \in (0, Q_m - 1)$ with the number of instances being

$$Q_m = \left\lceil \frac{t_m + J_m}{T_m} \right\rceil. \tag{2}$$

The response time for all instances q has to be calculated. The time from the start of the level-m busy period until the transmission of each instance is called the queuing delay and can be determined as

$$w_m^{n+1}(q) = B_m + qC_m + \sum_{\forall k \in hp(m)} \left\lceil \frac{w_m^n(q) + J_k + \tau_{bit}}{T_k} \right\rceil C_k. \tag{3}$$

Finally, the worst-case response time for each message can be computed. It is equal to the sum of the queuing jitter, the time from the queuing of the instance till its transmission and the transmission time of the message itself.

$$R_m(q) = J_m + w_m(q) - qT_m + C_m \tag{4}$$

The worst case response time of a message can then be obtained as the maximum response time of all instances. In most cases, the level-m busy period does not stretch beyond the cycle time T_m and only one instance has to be considered. Even if multiple instances have to be checked, the first instance usually suffers from the longest response time. Nevertheless, it is important not to disregard these cases in order to have a sufficient real-time analysis.

6.2 Self-virtualized CAN Controller

The analysis presented for ideal CAN nodes delivers optimistic results when dealing with non-ideal virtualized CAN nodes, because the shared interface and finite insertion times can result in head-of-line blocking by low priority messages.

We therefore propose a new worst-case scenario for non-ideal virtualized CAN controllers. Because all messages can delay the transmission of message m, they are all ready to be queued up at the same time. Lower priority messages contribute maximum blocking if they are inserted to the RAM before message m.

They are assumed to be inserted in order of increasing priority. This way, the pointer to the object of maximum priority has to be updated after each insertion resulting in maximum insertion times.

Such a blocking is contributed from each virtual CAN controller $v \in \{0, ..., V-1\}$. Because the virtual CAN controllers share a physical interface, they can still induce blocking to each other. This is of course in contrast to the ideal case, where only higher priority messages cause such blocking. The number of messages in one virtual CAN controller v that additionally contribute to the blocking is given as

$$M_{lp(m),v} = |\{k|k \in lp(m) \wedge k \in m_v\}|, \tag{5}$$

where $|\cdot|$ is the cardinality of the set. m_v describes the set of messages in a virtual CAN controller. From the model we determine the time needed for an insertion into a buffer at the n-th level as

$$t_{insrt}(n) = (6+n)/f_{clk}. \tag{6}$$

The insertion times of all messages add up for each virtual CAN controller, leading to an additional blocking by lower priority messages described by

$$B_{virt,m} = \sum_{v=0}^{V-1} \sum_{k=0}^{M_{lp(m),v}-1} t_{insrt}(k). \tag{7}$$

After this time, only higher priority messages or message m itself can be inserted and no further head-of-line blocking is experienced. Although higher priority messages can also block the insertion of message m, they do not contribute additional waiting time, because message m is assumed to enter bus arbitration only when all higher priority messages have been transmitted.

The proposed worst-case scenario assumes that just before a higher priority message is ready for transmission, a low priority message wins the CAN bus arbitration. For simplicity it is assumed that this message has maximum length. This assumption is true for most messages in a CAN configuration, especially for high priority messages. The blocking is therefore determined to be

$$B_m = \max_{k \in lp(m)} (C_k), \tag{8}$$

which is equal to the blocking assumed in [9] for an ideal CAN controller. When computing the overall waiting time only the influence of the blocking of lower priority messages has to be considered additionally.

Such blocking by lower priority messages can occur at multiple points throughout the level-m busy period, effectively extending its duration. This case can occur, when a high priority message gets issued to the controller near the end of the transmission of message m. If the insertion of this high priority message is delayed by head-of-line blocking within the controller, it can miss the CAN bus arbitration and a lower priority message gets transmitted.

While this case seems to be unlikely, it must still be considered in a sufficient real-time analysis. Because it is hard to determine whether this case occurs, we assume it to happen after each transmission of an instance of message m. This is a conservative assumption, however, it will very rarely lead to an increased message response time. Under these considerations the length of the level-m busy period can be determined as

$$t_{virt,m}^{n+1} = Q_m^n B_m + B_{virt,m} + \sum_{\forall k \in hp(m) \cup m} \left\lceil \frac{t_{virt,m}^n + J_k}{T_k} \right\rceil C_k. \tag{9}$$

The length of the level-m busy period is influenced by the number of instances Q_m of message m that have to be considered.

$$Q_m^{n+1} = \left\lceil \frac{t_{virt,m}^n + J_m}{T_m} \right\rceil. \tag{10}$$

Equations (9) and (10) have to be updated in an alternating way until convergence. The bigger Q_m is, the more low priority messages are assumed to extend the level-m busy. If $Q_m = 1$ no additional blocking is considered. Finally, the maximum time from the start of the level-m busy period until an instance q of a message m wins the arbitration and starts transmission is determined as

$$w_m^{virt,n+1}(q) = B_{virt,m} + (q+1)B_m + qC_m + \sum_{\forall k \in hp(m)} \left\lceil \frac{w_{virtm,m}^n(q) + J_k + \tau_{bit}}{T_k} \right\rceil C_k. \tag{11}$$

A couple of observations can be made regarding previously introduced equations. Equation (7) describes the additional blocking experienced with a non-ideal, virtualized CAN controller. The blocking is the greatest for high priority messages, whereas the lowest priority message does not experience any additional blocking.

This blocking increases the overall waiting time at least by its value. It is possible that additional interference occurs from later instances of higher priority messages.

Equation (11) is simplified to (3) if the insertion time t_{insrt} is assumed to be zero. Also, by choosing the number of virtual devices $V = 1$, the equation can be used to characterize non-ideal, non-virtualized controllers that implement similar mechanisms regarding message buffering.

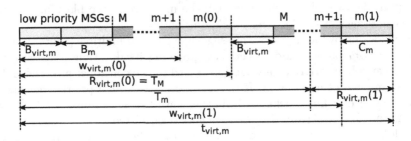

Fig. 3. Bus occupation in a worst-case scenario for message m

Figure 3 summarizes the blocking and waiting experienced by multiple instances of message m. All important measures used are depicted. Here, the head-of-line blocking and finite insertion times cause the insertion of messages to be delayed ($B_{virt,m}$). After all low priority messages are inserted, a transmission of a low priority message is started on the bus (B_m). After the transmission of all higher priority messages, the first instance $m(0)$ of the message wins arbitration. Due to the increased blocking, the level-m busy period is stretched beyond the cycle time of message m and a second instance $m(1)$ has to be considered. Still, instance $m(0)$ experiences the highest overall response time.

7   Results

In the previous sections we presented an architecture as well as a real-time analysis for a self-virtualized CAN controller. Because major parts of the evaluation are based on the analytic approach, its validity and accuracy is discussed first.

For one-on-one comparison, the following case studies were conducted using the same generic traffic pattern. The cycle times are chosen randomly for each message and can take values between 10 ms and 100 ms. 251 messages distributed among 16 (virtual) controllers are generated to achieve a bus load of 75%.

The left graph in Fig. 4 compares the response times of a set of messages obtained from simulation and from the real-time analysis. It is assumed that all messages are transmitted through the same self-virtualized CAN controller.

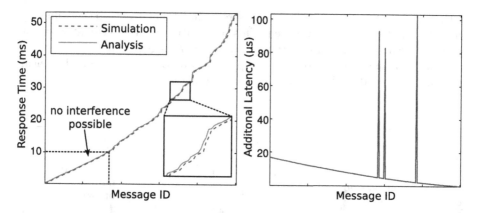

Fig. 4. Left: Comparison of the message response times determined by simulation/analysis. Right: Additional latency compared to an ideal CAN node.

While the curves are nearly overlapping, the response times calculated analytically are strictly bigger. This is to be expected, because the simulation cannot cover the worst-case for each message. These results suggest that the analytic method is capable of providing accurate timing information.

The right graph in Fig. 4 shows the additional latency suffered in this scenario, compared to the case of ideal CAN controllers. For most messages the latency increase is smaller for higher IDs (lower priorities). While this is unfortunate, the absolute values are still orders smaller than the smallest common deadlines in automotive CAN applications (around 10 ms).

For some medium priority messages a strong increase in their response time can be witnessed. This increase is due to additional interference from higher priority messages, caused by the additional delay inside the self-virtualized CAN controller. It is important to note that interference from higher priority messages is generally not possible if the response time of a message is smaller than the smallest cycle time within the network (as indicated in the left half of Fig. 4).

For medium priority messages the latency increase due to the virtualization can peak to values around 100 μs. Deadlines of medium priority messages are usually in the range of 100 ms, so the latency increase seems to be tolerable.

In a similar scenario we evaluated how the latencies are increased if other controllers are repartitioned into a common self-virtualized CAN controller. Out of the 16 controllers, the messages of 8 controllers are subsequently moved to one self-virtualized CAN controller. The rest of the messages are assumed to be transmitted through ideal CAN controllers.

This scenario is relevant, when considering the consolidation of stand-alone ECUs in the VMs of a multi-core processor. It allows us to draw conclusions, how the additional latency scales with respect to the number of VMs/virtual CAN controllers and how messages of different priorities are affected.

The results of this case study are summarized in Fig. 5. All of the results focus on the additional latency that is inflicted to the 17 messages that are first moved to the virtualized CAN controller. The increase in latency seems to scale linearly with the number of VMs employed. This observation is in agreement with the theoretical considerations in Section 6. Equation (7) suggests that the overhead introduced by each virtual device is superimposed. Deviations from the linear trend are grounded in the varying message characteristics.

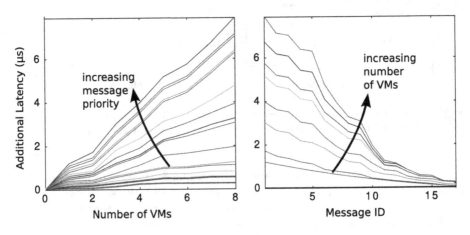

Fig. 5. Additional latency dependent on the number of VMs accessing the CAN bus through a self-virtualized CAN controller. In the left graph, each curve corresponds to one message. In the right graph, the number of VMs is rising with each curve.

For this small set of messages, no additional interference is suffered by any message. Therefore, the overhead is the greatest for high priority messages. This is not generally guaranteed, as Fig. 4 showed. To evaluate, how the response times are actually increased in a concrete scenario, a message response time analysis has to be conducted for the respective configuration.

In this section, the feasibility of the analytic real-time analysis was demonstrated. If no additional interferences occur, high priority messages suffer from the highest additional overheads, which are small compared to common automotive deadlines. Additional interference cannot occur for high priority messages. It was also shown that the additional latency scales roughly linearly with the number of VMs used (e.g. when repartitioning ECUs in a consolidation scenario).

8   Conclusion

In this paper, we proposed a self-virtualized CAN controller architecture that allows multiple VMs to transmit real-time messages onto a CAN bus. It overcomes the limitations imposed by the additional latencies that go along with software based virtualization solutions for I/O devices, and enables applications with real-time requirements. We presented a flexible and scalable concept that enables real-time processing by buffering messages in distinct priority queues associated with each virtual domain. These queues are dynamically managed and implemented as binary search trees. This way, the CAN bus arbitration principles can efficiently be applied to the buffered messages. The architecture we presented differs from ideal CAN nodes, because it has finite insertion times and can induce head-of-line blocking. Based on these limitations we proposed a modified analytical method for calculating worst-case message response times. Using this method, the additional latency suffered by messages in different scenarios was evaluated. It was shown that the additional latency is small compared to common deadlines and that the self-virtualized CAN controller introduced is therefore capable of serving real-time transmissions.

Acknowledgments. This work was funded within the project ARAMiS by the German Federal Ministry for Education and Research with the funding IDs 01|S11035. The responsibility for the content remains with the authors.

References

1. Navet, N., Simonot-Lion, F.: Automotive Embedded Systems Handbook. Industrial Information Technology Series. Taylor & Francis (2008)
2. Fürst, S.: Challenges in the design of automotive software. In: Proceedings of the Conference on Design, Automation and Test in Europe, pp. 256–258 (2010)
3. Barham, P., Dragovic, B., Fraser, K., Hand, S., Harris, T., Ho, A., Neugebauer, A., Pratt, I., Warfield, A.: Xen and the art of virtualization. ACM 37(5), 164 (2003)
4. Pratt, I., Fraser, K., Hand, S., Limpach, C., Warfield, A., Magenheimer, D., Nakajima, J., Mallick, A.: Xen 3.0 and the Art of Virtualization. In: Proceedings of the 2005 Ottawa Linux Symposium, pp. 65–77 (2005)
5. Menon, A., Santos, J., Turner, Y., Janakiraman, G., Zwaenepoel, W.: Diagnosing performance overheads in the xen virtual machine environment. In: Proceedings of the 1st ACM/USENIX International Conference on Virtual Execution Environments, VEE 2005, pp. 13–23. ACM (2005)
6. Raj, H., Schwan, K.: High performance and scalable I/O virtualization via self-virtualized devices. In: Proceedings of the 16th International Symposium on High Performance Distributed Computing, HPDC 2007, pp. 179–188 (2007)
7. Willmann, P., Shafer, J., Carr, D., Menon, A., Rixner, S., Cox, A.L., Zwaenepoel, W.: Concurrent direct network access for virtual machine monitors. In: High Performance Computer Architecture, pp. 306–317 (2007)
8. Rauchfuss, H., Wild, T., Herkersdorf, A.: A network interface card architecture for I/O virtualization in embedded systems. In: Proceedings of the 2nd Conference on I/O Virtualization (2010)
9. Davis, I., Burns, A., Bril, R., Lukkien, J.: Controller Area Network (CAN) schedulability analysis: Refuted, revisited and revised. Real-Time Systems 35(3), 239–272 (2007)

Shrinking L1 Instruction Caches to Improve Energy–Delay in SMT Embedded Processors

Alexandra Ferrerón-Labari, Marta Ortín-Obón, Darío Suárez-Gracia,
Jesús Alastruey-Benedé, and Víctor Viñals-Yúfera

gaZ—DIIS—I3A, Universidad de Zaragoza, Spain
{ferreron,ortin.marta,dario,jalastru,victor}@unizar.es

Abstract. Instruction caches are responsible for a high percentage of the chip energy consumption, becoming a critical issue for battery-powered embedded devices. We can potentially reduce the energy consumption of the first level instruction cache (L1-I) by decreasing its size and associativity. However, demanding applications may suffer a dramatic performance degradation, specially in superscalar multi-threaded processors, where, in each cycle, multiple threads access the L1-I to fetch instructions.

We introduce iLP-NUCA (*Instruction Light Power NUCA*), a new instruction cache that substitutes the conventional L2, improving the Energy-Delay of the system. iLP-NUCA adds a new tree-based transport network topology that reduces latency and energy consumption, regarding former LP-NUCA implementations.

With iLP-NUCA we reduce the size of the L1-I outperforming conventional cache hierarchies, and reducing the overall consumption, independently of the number of threads.

1 Introduction

Superscalar execution cores demand a continuous instruction supply to feed their functional units. Delays due to instruction cache misses affect the instruction flow speed and instruction issue, and hence, performance. Simultaneous Multi-Threading (SMT) is a technique to hide long latency operations, such as cache misses, by the execution of several threads [1]. SMT aims to have all the functional units highly utilized by using a more powerful front-end (fetch unit) that supplies instructions from several threads. Consequently, the aggregated demand of instructions added by SMT makes on-chip instruction caches even more critical.

Instruction caches are responsible for a high amount of the energy consumption of the system. For example, StrongARM SA-100 and ARM 920TTM dissipate the 27% and 25% of the total power in the instruction cache, respectively [2],[3].

Ideally, we would like to have an instruction cache big enough to fit the footprint of the most demanding applications in order to increase their hit rate. However, bigger caches come at the expense of higher access latencies and higher energy consumption per access. Thus, there is a complex trade-off between size, on the one hand, and latency and energy consumption, on the other hand.

C. Hochberger et al. (Eds.): ARCS 2013, LNCS 7767, pp. 256–267, 2013.

Reducing the size of the first level instruction cache (L1-I)—as Qualcomm MSM8960 does [4]—will potentially benefit the system from the energy perspective, but it could affect the cache hit rate, harming performance, and the energy consumption of the second level cache could increase, counteracting other savings.

Recent works propose to dynamically reconfigure the L1 size and associativity, so only part of the ways or part of the sets are active in a given moment [5],[6]. With such an approach, the cache adapts to the behavior of the applications and operates within the optimal size. Other works add a small structure close to the L1-I that captures part of its accesses, increasing the fetch speed, reducing the energy consumption, or both [7],[8].

All of these techniques need to either modify the interface between the first-level cache and the processor, or add additional hardware/software support. We propose a different approach not requiring to modify the interface between the L1-I and the processor. We reduce the L1-I size and associativity, and replace the L2 cache with an iLP-NUCA (*instruction Light Power NUCA*), which minimizes performance degradation and reduces energy consumption.

Our experiments running SPEC CPU2006 show that, for the same L1-I size, iLP-NUCA performs better and consumes less energy than a conventional instruction-only L2. Alternatively, by using iLP-NUCA we can shrink the L1-I from 16KB to 8KB and keep performance, regardless of the number of threads. Specifically, we reduce the energy consumption by 21%, 18%, and 11%, reaching 90%, 95%, and 99% of the ideal performance for 1, 2, and 4 threads, respectively.

This work makes the following contributions:

- We apply a new NUCA organization to the instruction hierarchy. To the best of our knowledge, this is the first work proposing a specific NUCA cache for the instruction hierarchy in both single thread and SMT environments.
- We adapt LP-NUCA for instruction hierarchies (iLP-NUCA). We propose a new instruction-driven transport network-in-cache for iLP-NUCA, based on a tree topology, which improves previous designs. This new topology simultaneously reduces the effective service latency of cache blocks, the number of links, and the energy consumed by the network.
- We propose to shrink L1-I size and associativity to save energy, and maintain an acceptable performance by replacing a conventional L2 with iLP-NUCA. By reducing the size of LI-I, iLP-NUCA provides additional area for the implementation of other components such as accelerators.

The rest of the paper is organized as follows. Section 2 explores iLP-NUCA. In Section 3 the methodology we followed is explained. Section 4 collects the main results. Section 5 presents the related work, and Section 6 concludes.

2   Instruction Light Power NUCA

2.1   LP-NUCA Overview

LP-NUCA [9] extends the conventional L1 capacity by surrounding it with one or more levels of small cache tiles interconnected by specialized networks, as shown in Fig. 1.

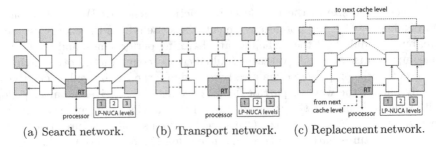

(a) Search network.   (b) Transport network.   (c) Replacement network.

Fig. 1. 3-level LP-NUCA with its three networks-in-cache

The first level of LP-NUCA (root-tile, RT) corresponds to a conventional L1 cache with added network logic. The second level of the conventional hierarchy is replaced by a tiled structure whose effective access time increases gradually. The LP-NUCA design relies on three specialized networks-in-cache: search, transport, and replacement, allowing for a simple implementation, low latency, and high bandwidth. The search network (Fig. 1a) uses a broadcast-tree to propagate miss requests from the RT to the rest of the LP-NUCA levels. The transport network (Fig. 1b) employs a 2-D mesh to deliver hit cache blocks from the tiles to the RT. The replacement network (Fig. 1c) connects tiles by means of an irregular topology to place recently evicted blocks close to the RT, and exploit their temporal locality. Please refer to [9] for further details about the design and implementation of LP-NUCA.

LP-NUCA has never been tested for instruction hierarchies; however, it is a good candidate because it could exploit the temporal code locality, reduce the average memory access time, and be more energy-efficient. Besides, it does not modify the interface between the L1 and the processor. We call the structure adapted to instruction hierarchies iLP-NUCA (*instruction Light Power NUCA*). The following section describes the improvements we propose to successfully adapt LP-NUCA to instruction hierarchies.

2.2 Instruction-Driven Tree-Based Transport Network

Instruction and data hierarchies differentiate in two key aspects. First, the miss instruction bandwidth demand from L1/RT is lower than the corresponding miss data bandwidth demand. In SMT environments (without taking into account the prefetches), the maximum number of requests in iLP-NUCA equals the number of threads being executed. Second, an instruction fetch missing in the first cache level stalls the corresponding thread, preventing the front-end to supply instructions to the pipeline. The L1-I miss resolution time becomes critical forcing the re-evaluation of the search and transport networks.

Previous designs of LP-NUCA utilized a bufferless search network with no flow control, having little margin for latency improvement, and a 2-D mesh for the transport network, because it provides high bandwidth with its path diversity. Figure 2a shows the 2-D mesh topology (solid lines). The numbers in the upper left corner of the tiles represent the round-trip latencies (time since injecting a request into LP-NUCA until the block returns to the processor), assuming a one-cycle tile access time. The main components of the transport network (Fig. 2b) are a switch and two transport buffers (Tbf) that contain hit blocks on their way to the RT. The replacement buffers (Rbf) contain victim blocks waiting for replacement. Hits can occur also in the replacement buffers and, therefore, they must be accessed during a search operation. The transport network relies on buffered flow control, and uses store-and-forward flow control with on/off back-pressure (dashed lines in Figs. 2b and 2c) and two-entry buffers per link.

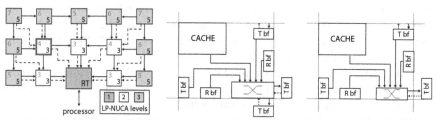

(a) 2-D Mesh (solid lines) and tree-based (dashed lines) transport networks.

(b) 2-D mesh transport components.

(c) Tree-based transport components.

Fig. 2. Transport networks (a)—2-D mesh (solid lines, latencies in upper left corner) and tree-based (dashed lines, latencies in bottom right corner)—and their respective components, (b) and (c), for the example tile (thick box)

A preferable transport network for instructions would offer lower latency, even if that comes at the expense of lower bandwidth. Figure 2a shows in dashed lines an instruction-driven transport network topology based on a minimum degree tree. With this topology the benefit is twofold. On the one hand, we decrease the number of links between tiles to just one transport output link, decreasing the crossbar delay and area (Fig. 2c). On the other hand, latency becomes uniform within each level and most of the tiles decrease their hit latency (numbers on bottom right corner in Fig. 2a), as we need less hops to reach the RT. The latter also reduces the energy consumed by the network when delivering blocks to the RT. Thus, we expect to reduce the average hit latency of blocks in comparison with previous LP-NUCA designs, and the energy consumption of the transport network. This latency reduction could allow us to dramatically shrink the RT (L1-I) because misses can be served faster from the next cache level.

The novel topology increases the number of inputs of the RT multiplexer from 3 to 5 without harming performance. Cycle time remains unchanged because the multiplexer is not in the critical path (it works in parallel with the instruction cache banks).

Finally, the original replacement network offers a good block replacement distribution and, therefore, iLP-NUCA will use the same network topology.

3 Methodology

3.1 Processor Model and Simulation Environment

We model the system summarized in Table 1. Our model is based on state-of-the-art high performance embedded systems such as IBM/LSI PowerPC 476FP [10], NetLogic XLP864 [11], and Freescale QorIQ AMP T2080 [12]. Our system has a more powerful memory hierarchy, and supports 4 hardware threads.

We compare two alternative instruction cache hierarchies. The first one is a conventional setup, named CV, made up of two dedicated instruction/data cache levels, L1-I/D and L2-I/D, and a third level shared by instructions and data, L3. The second one, named iLP, replaces L1-I and L2-I by a three-level iLP-NUCA, that is, L1-I is replaced by the root-tile, and L2-I by two levels of tiles (Le2 and Le3) interconnected as explained in Sect. 2. iLP also replaces L1-D and L2-D by the original data LP-NUCA. We model a perfect data path with L1-D/LP-NUCA caches that always hit, so that result variations only come from instruction activity. Section 4.3 removes this constraint to examine the interaction of iLP-NUCA with the data hierarchy.

We have developed *SMTScalar*, a cycle-accurate execution-based simulator based on SimpleScalar 3.0d for Alpha ISA [13]. SMTScalar heavily extends SimpleScalar to support detailed microarchitectural models, highly configurable memory hierarchies, simultaneous multi-threading execution, and iLP-NUCAs.

Table 1. Simulator micro-architectural parameters. BS, AM, lat, and init stand for block size, access mode, latency, and initiation latency, respectively.

Clock Frequency	1 GHz	Fetch/Decode/Commit	4
ROB/LSQ	64/32 entries	Int/FP/Mem IW	24/16/16 entries
Functional units	3 int ALUs, 2 mem ports, 3 FP units	STB/L2–iLP-NUCA WB/L3 WB	32/16/16 entries
Issue width	4(Int+Mem) + 2FP	TLB miss latency	30 cycles
Branch Predictor	bimodal + gshare	Miss. branch penalty	6 cycles
L1/L2/L3 MSHR	8/8/4 entries	MSHR second. misses	4
Baseline L1/RT [a]	32KB, 4Way, 32B BS, parallel AM, 2-cycle lat, 1-cycle init		
L2-I/L2-D	512KB, 8Way, 32B BS, serial AM, 4-cycle lat, 2-cycle init		
iLP-NUCA rest tiles	32KB, 2Way, 32B BS, parallel AM, levels: 3 (448KB)		
L3	4MB, eDRAM, 16Way, 128B BS, 14-cycle lat, 7-cycle init		
Main Memory	100 cycles/4 cycle inter chunk, 16 Byte bus		

[a] L1: write-through; RT: copy-back; L1/RT: write-around and 2 ports.

We estimate cache access latencies and energy consumption assuming 32nm LSTP (Low STandby Power) technology with Cacti 6.5 [14]. For iLP-NUCA networks-in-cache we derive latency and consumption figures by scaling the data obtained from a real 90nm layout [9].

3.2 Workloads

We use the full SPEC CPU2006 benchmark suite [15], but 483.xalancbmk (which could not be executed in our environment). For each program we simulate 100M representative instructions that were selected following the SimPoints methodology [16]. Caches and branch predictor are warmed up during 200M instructions for one thread experiments. Multi-thread experiments (2 and 4 threads) are multiprogrammed. We utilize *last* as simulation ending policy and collect statistics for the first 100M instructions of each thread. For two thread experiments we run all the benchmarks combinations. For four thread experiments, we assure results are representative by using statistical sampling and taking enough samples to reach 97% of confidence level and less than 3% error [17],[18].

3.3 Metrics

We use two system oriented performance metrics for multiprogrammed workloads: IPC throughput (i.e., committed user instructions summed over all threads divided by total elapsed cycles[1]) and fairness [19], according to the formulas:

$$IPC\ throughput = \sum_{i=1}^{n} IPC_i \qquad fairness = \frac{\min_i \left(\frac{CPI_i^{MT}}{CPI_i^{ST}} \right)}{\max_i \left(\frac{CPI_i^{MT}}{CPI_i^{ST}} \right)}$$

where IPC, CPI, ST and MT refer to instructions per cycle, cycles per instruction, single thread, and multi-threaded execution, respectively.

Regarding energy consumption, we report the total energy consumed by the cache hierarchy. We compute the Energy-Delay and Energy-Delay^2 products taking into account the energy consumption of the memory hierarchy[2] and the execution time (delay). We follow the Li *et al.* approach for SMT environments [20], and account for all the energy consumed until the last thread commits 100M instructions.

4 Evaluation

4.1 Impact of the Tree-Based Transport Network

The new tree-based network-in-cache reduces the tiles degree regarding the former 2-D mesh. The transport components (see Fig. 2c) are the two input transport buffers and the switch. From the hardware implementation of LP-NUCA [9], we know that each buffer accounts for one third of the energy consumption, and so does the switch. Our new network simplifies the switch removing one output link. From the original layout we estimate that these changes reduce the components energy consumption by 20%.

---

[1] The use of IPC throughput is safe because there are no synchronization instructions.
[2] In general, we have observed that the processor activity implementing iLP-NUCA decreases slightly, due to a reduction in the speculation depth.

We compare the former 2-D mesh with the tree-based transport network in a system with a 3–level iLP-NUCA (4-way, 32KB root-tile).

Our results show that the tree-based transport network reduces the average service latency by 8%, with bigger gains in tiles located on more distant levels. Thus, the effectiveness of the new network strongly depends on the amount of reused blocks that those levels capture, which tends to be low except in some benchmarks, such as 447.dealII. Finally, the tree-based network does not experience contention because the number of simultaneous requests is low.

Energy savings are more noticeable when executing several threads. With 2 threads the new transport network consumes 4.7% less energy than the former 2-D mesh; with 4 threads energy savings reach 6%.

4.2   Instruction Cache Energy/Performance Trade-Offs

We compare two alternative instruction cache hierarchies (CV and iLP), as explained in Sect. 3.1. In this section we assume a perfect L1 data cache, so that result variations will only come from instruction activity. We are also interested in analyzing the sensitivity of CV and iLP to a possible L1-I/RT downsizing. Hence, we reduce the L1-I/RT size and associativity from 4-way, 32KB (baseline) to 2-way 16KB, 8KB, and 4KB. Next, we show results of energy, performance, and fairness for all the above configurations, considering the system loaded by one, two, or four threads.

Energy Consumption. Figure 3 shows the total energy consumption for 1, 2, and 4 threads. Each bar corresponds to one configuration, and represents the added energy consumption of all the executed workloads. We plot the dynamic energy of the different caches accessed by instructions (L1-I, L2-I, and L3), and group the total static energy on top. In order to analyze the results in Fig. 3 we first highlight some obvious facts; namely, i) the dynamic energy of L1-I and RT matches, as both caches have a very similar complexity; ii) the static energy is almost constant for a given number of threads, except for the smallest L1-I cache in the CV system loaded with 4 threads, due to its significant slowdown; and iii) the L3 cache spends a negligible amount of dynamic energy, because hitting in L2-I is the norm. Bearing this in mind, to gain an insight into the best choice we should concentrate on the energy transfer between the L1-I and the L2-I as we change L1-I size and number of threads.

In configurations with 32KB 4-way L1-I/RT, the dynamic energy consumed by the L2-I or by the levels 2 and 3 of iLP-NUCA (Le2+Le3 in Fig. 3) is similar and very small, though it increases as the number of threads grow. We can conclude that the instruction footprints of most applications fit in the L1-I cache.

As we shrink the L1-I/RT size, the energy per access decreases and so does the total energy of L1-I/RT. However, smaller L1-I/RT caches fail to capture the required footprint and the number of misses increase. In turn, the growing number of first-level misses increases the dynamic energy consumption in L2-I or Le2+Le3, and, eventually, the total energy consumption increases. Underloaded systems, executing one or two threads, present a similar behavior: overall energy

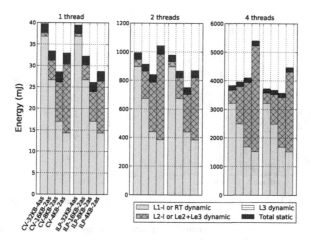

Fig. 3. Energy consumption of several CV and iLP cache configurations—labeled with type (CV vs. iLP) and L1-I/RT size and associativity—for 1, 2, and 4 threads

reduction for 16KB and 8KB L1-I/RT caches, and overall increase for 4KB. However, in the fully loaded system, when executing four threads, as the first level shrinks and the working set moves to the second level, the behavior of CV and iLP clearly departs. CV hierarchies do not allow L1-I reduction, because the energy transfer between levels is always detrimental for the overall spending. In contrast, iLP hierarchies benefit from RT reduction up to 8KB. All in all, for any configuration and number of threads, iLP-NUCA always consumes less energy than the conventional hierarchy, and the preferable configuration is an iLP-NUCA with a 2-way 8KB RT.

Performance and Fairness. Figure 4a shows the IPC throughputs harmonic mean and Fig. 4b the fairness distributions for the considered configurations.

When reducing the first-level size the miss ratio increases, and performance lowers in both CV and iLP systems. With iLP-NUCA the performance degradation is lower: for the same size of L1-I/RT, iLP-NUCA performs better, regardless of the number of threads. In the conventional system loaded with a single thread, as L1-I reduces to 16KB, 8KB, and 4KB, the IPC throughput decreases 5.8%, 12.5%, and 20%, respectively. In the iLP-NUCA system, performance also decreases, yet the gradient is less and the 32KB IPC throughput is slightly better.

When considering two threads, the former observations hold, but now the sensitivity to the first-level cache size is softened by the ability of SMT to hide long latency operations by interleaving useful work from other threads. In the conventional system loaded with two threads, as L1-I reduces to 16KB, 8KB, and 4KB, the IPC throughput reduces 3%, 6.3%, and 10.5%, respectively, while in the iLP system the reductions are 1.1%, 3.2%, and 6%, respectively.

With four threads differences are smaller. The occupancy of the functional units is higher and there are more threads to hide the processor stalls due to

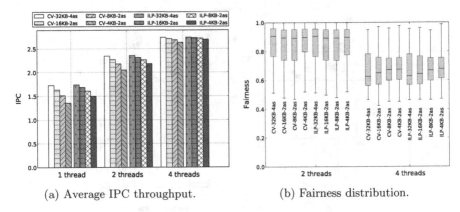

(a) Average IPC throughput.   (b) Fairness distribution.

Fig. 4. Harmonic mean of IPC throughputs and fairness distribution—labeled with type (CV vs. iLP) and L1-I/RT size and associativity

instruction misses. As the first level shrinks, iLP-NUCA keeps performance degradation below 1.5%, while conventional caches lose up to 3.5%, on average.

As expected, since we keep the first-level cache latency constant, from a performance standpoint it is always better to select the largest size. However, if we can afford some losses when the system is underloaded (one or two threads), an iLP system with 16KB or 8KB will keep an acceptable performance and use less energy. For example, an iLP system implementing a 8KB RT would reach the performance of a CV system with a 16KB L1-I, but saving 21%, 18%, and 11% of energy, for 1, 2, and 4 threads, respectively.

Regarding the fairness among threads, let us consider Fig. 4b where each candlestick represents the minimum, the quartile 25, the median, the quartile 75, and the maximum of the fairness distribution. A fairness figure close to 1.0 means an even resource distribution. Lower figures mean unfair execution, where some threads are slowed down much more than others. As we can see in Fig. 4b, the fairness distribution for two and four threads is quite similar in CV and iLP systems. We can conclude that implementing an iLP system is not detrimental at all from a fairness standpoint.

Energy-Delay and Energy-Delay^2. Figure 5 shows the Energy-Delay and Energy-Delay^2 products normalized to the baseline (CV-32KB-4ass). Configurations with iLP-NUCA present better (lower) ED and ED^2 results, independent of the number of threads. We find bigger differences when the L1-I cache is smaller and the pressure on the next levels higher. Again, the optimal configuration would be an iLP-NUCA with a 2-way, 8KB RT, whose normalized ED values are 0.70, 0.8, and 0.94, for 1, 2, and 4 threads respectively. ED^2 values are 0.73, 0.82, and 0.95, respectively.

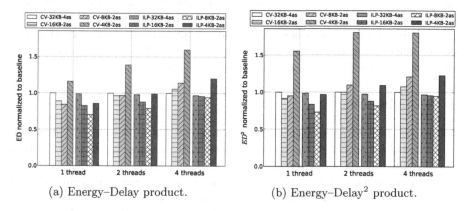

(a) Energy–Delay product.   (b) Energy–Delay^2 product.

Fig. 5. ED (Fig. 5a) and ED^2 (Fig. 5b) products for 1, 2, and 4 threads. Values are normalized to baseline (CV-32KB-4ass).

4.3   Evaluating iLP-NUCA with a Non-ideal Data Cache Hierarchy

We evaluated our proposal with a non-ideal data path, using a conventional L1-D/L2-D pair, and the original data LP-NUCA. We just summarize some results due to the lack of space. The benefit now is twofold: we reduce the fetch latency on the instruction side (iLP-NUCA), and we reduce the load latency as well as increasing the store bandwidth on the data side (LP-NUCA). This allows for energy reductions up to 28%, 28%, and 27% for 1, 2, and 4 threads, respectively, while achieving greater IPC throughput, on average, regardless of the number of threads. Thus, former conclusions hold, encouraging the use of iLP-NUCA. A 2-way, 8KB RT is reinforced as the best candidate for our workloads.

5   Related Work

Several works have addressed the instruction cache energy consumption problem by adding hardware structures between the processor and the first-level instruction cache (L1-I) to capture instruction fetches [7],[8],[21]. These proposals add extra hardware structures between the processor and the instruction cache. They reduce the amount of access to the L1-I, but at the expense of introducing extra fetch latency when a miss to these structures occurs. On the contrary, we keep the interface between the processor and the L1-I, and these designs could be implemented in front of our system.

Reconfigurable caches try to adapt dynamically to applications requirements obtaining great energy reductions, but they modify the cache structures [22],[5],[6]. A variable size or associativity allows the hosting of applications or program phases with big working set requirements and reduces the energy consumption when the requirements are small. Apart from complexity, a reconfiguration drawback appears when predictions are wrong and the cache becomes under- or over-sized. Nonetheless, merging reconfiguration with iLP-NUCA would be an interesting future work, for example switching on/off iLP-NUCA levels.

These works do not consider multi-threaded applications, where several threads that run together and share a small structure (such as a filter or victim cache) could interfere each other by evicting useful blocks of other threads.

6 Conclusions

Current high-performance embedded processors require a powerful instruction cache hierarchy with low energy consumption. Most designs rely on large first level instruction (L1-I) caches that, for many applications and a low number of executing threads, spends an undue amount of energy. However, shrinking L1-I caches naively harms the performance of many applications, specially when the processor becomes loaded up to its maximum number of threads. In order to simultaneously improve the performance and energy consumption of the instruction cache hierarchy, we propose iLP-NUCA, a structure that replaces a conventional L1-I/L2-I cache pair by several levels of richly interconnected cache tiles. We provide iLP-NUCA with a new transport network-in-cache, reducing blocks average service latency by 8%, and the energy consumption of the network.

We compare our proposal with a state-of-the-art conventional three level cache hierarchy, where L1-I and L2-I are dedicated to instructions, and L3 is shared. From our experiments we can conclude that iLP-NUCA performs better and consumes less energy for the same L1-I/RT size, independently of the number of threads. Furthermore, iLP-NUCA achieves the performance of a conventional hierarchy with a double sized L1-I, saving a great amount of energy. For instance, if we compare a conventional 2-way, 16KB L1-I against an iLP-NUCA with a 2-way, 8KB RT, we found equal performance and energy savings of 21%, 18%, and 11% for 1, 2, and 4 threads, respectively.

Acknowledgments. This work was supported in part by grants TIN2010-21291-C02-01 (Spanish Government, European ERDF), gaZ: T48 research group (Aragón Government, European ESF), Consolider CSD2007-00050 (Spanish Government), and HiPEAC-3 NoE. The authors would like to thank Manolis Katevenis for his suggestions about the transport network.

References

1. Tullsen, D.M., Eggers, S.J., Levy, H.M.: Simultaneous multithreading: maximizing on-chip parallelism. In: Proc. of the 22 nd Ann. Int. Symp. on Comp. Arch., pp. 392–403 (1995)
2. Montanaro, J., Witek, R., Anne, K., Black, A., Cooper, E., Dobberpuhl, D., Donahue, P., Eno, J., Farell, A., Hoeppner, G., Kruckemyer, D., Lee, T., Lin, P., Madden, L., Murray, D., Pearce, M., Santhanam, S., Snyder, K., Stephany, R., Thierauf, S.: A 160 MHz 32 b 0.5 W CMOS RISC microprocessor. In: Proc. of 1996 IEEE Int. Solid-State Circuits Conference Digest of Technical Papers, pp. 214–215, 447 (1996)

3. Segars, S.: Low power design techniques for microprocessors. ISSCC Tutorial note (February 2001)
4. Gwennap, L.: What's inside the Krait. Microprocessor Report 26, 1–9 (2012)
5. Sundararajan, K.T., Jones, T.M., Topham, N.: Smart cache: A self adaptive cache architecture for energy efficiency. In: Proc. of the Int. Conference on Embedded Comp. Systems: Architectures, Modeling, and Simulation, pp. 41–50 (July 2011)
6. Zhang, C., Vahid, F., Najjar, W.: A highly configurable cache for low energy embedded systems. ACM Trans. Embed. Comput. Syst. 4, 363–387 (2005)
7. Bellas, N., Hajj, I., Polychronopoulos, C., Stamoulis, G.: Architectural and compiler techniques for energy reduction in high-performance microprocessors. IEEE Trans. on Very Large Scale Integration Systems 8, 317–326 (2000)
8. Kin, J., Gupta, M., Mangione-Smith, W.: The filter cache: an energy efficient memory structure. In: Proc. of the 30th Ann. IEEE/ACM Int. Symp. on Microarchitecture, pp. 184–193 (1997)
9. Suárez, D., Dimitrakopoulos, G., Monreal, T., Katevenis, M.G.H., Viñals, V.: LP-NUCA: Networks-in-cache for high- performance low-power embedded processors. IEEE Trans. on Very Large Scale Integration Systems 20, 1510–1523 (2012)
10. LSI Corporation: PowerPC^{TM} processor (476FP) embedded core product brief (January 2010),
    http://www.lsi.com/DistributionSystem/AssetDocument/PPC476FP-PB-v7.pdf
11. Halfhill, T.R.: Netlogic broadens XLP family. Microprocessor Report 24, 1–11 (2010)
12. Byrne, J.: Freescale drops quad-core threshold. Microprocessor Report 26, 10–12 (2012)
13. Austin, T., Burger, D.: The simplescalar tool set, version 2.0. Technical Report CS-TR-97-1342, University of Wisconsin Madison (1997)
14. Muralimanohar, N., Balasubramonian, R., Jouppi, N.: Optimizing NUCA Organizations and Wiring Alternatives for Large Caches with CACTI 6.0. In: Proc. of the 40th Ann. IEEE/ACM Int. Symp. on Microarchitecture, pp. 3–14 (2007)
15. Henning, J.L.: SPEC CPU2006 benchmark descriptions. SIGARCH Comput. Archit. News 34, 1–17 (2006)
16. Hamerly, G., Perelman, E., Lau, J., Calder, B.: SimPoint 3.0: Faster and more flexible program analysis. Journal of Instruction Level Parallelism (2005)
17. Suárez, D., Monreal, T., Viñals, V.: A comparison of cache hierarchies for SMT processors. In: Proc. of the 22nd Jornadas de Paralelismo (2011)
18. Wackerly, D., Mendenhall, W., Scheaffer, R.L.: Mathematical Statistics with Applications, 7th edn. Brooks/Cole Cengage Learning (2008)
19. Gabor, R., Weiss, S., Mendelson, A.: Fairness and throughput in switch on event multithreading. In: Proc. of the 39th Ann. IEEE/ACM Int. Symp. on Microarchitecture, pp. 149–160 (2006)
20. Li, Y., Brooks, D., Hu, Z., Skadron, K., Bose, P.: Understanding the energy efficiency of simultaneous multithreading. In: Proc. of the 2004 Int. Symp. on Low Power Electronics and Design, pp. 44–49 (2004)
21. Yang, C.L., Lee, C.H.: Hotspot cache: joint temporal and spatial locality exploitation for i-cache energy reduction. In: Proc. of the 2004 Int. Symp. on Low Power Electronics and Design, pp. 114–119 (2004)
22. Albonesi, D.H.: Selective cache ways: on-demand cache resource allocation. In: Proc. of the 32nd Ann. ACM/IEEE Int. Symp. on Microarchitecture, pp. 248–259 (1999)

Arithmetic Unit for Computations in GF(p) with the Left-Shifting Multiplicative Inverse Algorithm

Josef Hlaváč and Róbert Lórencz

Czech Technical University in Prague, Faculty of Information Technology,
Thákurova 9, 160 00 Praha, Czech Republic
{josef.hlavac,robert.lorencz}@fit.cvut.cz

Abstract We present the hardware architecture of an arithmetic unit intended for computing basic operations over a Galois field GF(p). The arithmetic unit supports addition, subtraction, multiplication, and multiplicative inverse modulo a prime p. To compute the multiplicative inverse, we use the promising left-shifting algorithm that is based on the extended Euclidean algorithm. We discuss the potential applications of the arithmetic unit, including elliptic curve cryptography.

Keywords: Galois field, multiplicative inverse, modular arithmetic, left-shift algorithm.

1 Introduction

Modular arithmetic is widely used in many areas of computer science, with cryptography being one of the most prominent ones. There is increasing demand for cryptographic devices that are small and consume little power, yet provide a high level of security. As a result, there is strong interest in hardware solutions that can perform cryptographic operations as efficiently as possible.

In this paper, we extend the hardware architecture for computing the modular multiplicative inverse using the left-shifting algorithm [14] into a complete modular arithmetic unit. The unit supports all the basic operations – addition, subtraction, multiplication, and the multiplicative inverse modulo a prime p. The use of the left-shifting algorithm is the primary difference from previous approaches.

2 Algorithms

2.1 Multiplicative Inverse

Modular multiplicative inverse is the most complicated operation that our arithmetic unit needs to support. Since our aim is to minimize hardware complexity and avoid dedicated units for each type of operation, the choice of algorithm for computing the inverse determines the overall datapath structure.

C. Hochberger et al. (Eds.): ARCS 2013, LNCS 7767, pp. 268–279, 2013.
© Springer-Verlag Berlin Heidelberg 2013

Algorithm 1. Left-shifting modular inverse

Input: $p, a \ (0 < a < p)$
Output: $y = \left|a^{-1}\right|_p$

1. $u \leftarrow p, v \leftarrow a, r \leftarrow 0, s \leftarrow 1, cu \leftarrow 0, cv \leftarrow 0$
2.   **while** $u \neq \pm 2^{cu} \wedge v \neq \pm 2^{cv}$ **do**
3.   **if** left shift of u possible **then**
4.   **if** $cu \geq cv$ **then** $u \leftarrow 2u, r \leftarrow 2r, cu \leftarrow cu + 1$
5.   **else** $u \leftarrow 2u, s \leftarrow s/2, cu \leftarrow cu + 1$
6.   **else if** left shift of v possible **then**
7.   **if** $cv \geq cu$ **then** $v \leftarrow 2v, s \leftarrow 2s, cv \leftarrow cv + 1$
8.   **else** $v \leftarrow 2v, r \leftarrow r/2, cv \leftarrow cv + 1$
9.   **else if** $v_n = u_n$ **then**
10.   **if** $cu \leq cv$ **then** $u \leftarrow u - v, r \leftarrow r - s$
11.   **else** $v \leftarrow v - u, s \leftarrow s - r$
12.   **else**
14.   **if** $cu \leq cv$ **then** $u \leftarrow u + v, r \leftarrow r + s$
15.   **else** $v \leftarrow v + u, s \leftarrow s + r$
16. **if** $v = \pm 2^{cv}$ **then** $r \leftarrow s, u_n \leftarrow v_n$
17. **if** $u_n = 1$ **then**
18.   **if** $r < 0$ **then** $r \leftarrow -r$
19.   **else** $r \leftarrow p - r$
20. **if** $r < 0$ **then** $r \leftarrow r + p$
21. **return** r

Algorithm 2. Modular multiplication

Input: $p, a, b \ (0 \leq a, b < p)$
Output: $y = \left|a \cdot b\right|_p$

1. $s \leftarrow 0, v \leftarrow a, r \leftarrow b$
2.   **while** $r \neq 0$ **do**
3.   **if** $r_0 = 1$ **then** $s \leftarrow s + v$
4.   **if** $s \geq p$ **then** $s \leftarrow s - p$
5. $r \leftarrow r/2$
6. $v \leftarrow 2 \cdot v$
7.   **if** $v \geq p$ **then** $v \leftarrow v - p$
8. $y \leftarrow s$
9.   **return** s

Algorithm 3. Modular addition

Input: $p, a, b\ (0 \leq a, b < p)$
Output: $y = |a + b|_p$

1. $s \leftarrow a,\ r \leftarrow b$
2. $s \leftarrow r + s$
3. **if** $s \geq p$ **then** $y \leftarrow s - p$ **else** $y \leftarrow s$
4. **return** y

Algorithm 4. Modular subtraction

Input: $p, a, b\ (0 \leq a, b < p)$
Output: $y = |a - b|_p$

1. $s \leftarrow a,\ r \leftarrow b$
2. $s \leftarrow s - r$
3. **if** $s < 0$ **then** $y \leftarrow s + p$ **else** $y \leftarrow s$
4. **return** y

Modular multiplicative inverse is usually computed using an algorithm derived from the Extended Euclidean Algorithm (EEA) [5,6,12,14]. A basic binary EEA version is attributed to M. Penk (Exercise 4.5.2.39 in [12]). Later, Kaliski described an algorithm [11] for computing the so-called Montgomery modular inverse, which computes the multiplicative inverse in the Montgomery domain [15]. With a simple modification, Kaliski's algorithm can be used to compute the inverse in the integer domain; this approach is shown e.g. in [14], with additional optimizations presented e.g. in [4,9,18].

In [14], another algorithm is shown. In this algorithm, the intermediate results are shifted to the left; hence the name "left-shifting algorithm". While still based on the EEA, this algorithm tries to avoid the drawbacks of the previous algorithms.

The qualities of this left-shifting algorithm are confirmed in [6], where a variant of the left-shifting algorithm is shown to be the least-complex algorithm as long as the shift operation does not cost anything (which is the case in a hardware implementation).

We based our design on the left-shifting algorithm, see Algorithm 1.

2.2   Multiplication

There are many algorithms for modular multiplication; however, most of them use special representations of numbers, such as the Montgomery domain, or special hardware elements [1]. Our choice of algorithms is limited because the left-shifting inverse algorithm works in the integer domain. We chose the simple algorithm of alternating addition and modular correction (Algorithm 2). This algorithm is simple and straightforward, yet reasonably efficient, and it can be easily added to the hardware architecture.

2.3 Addition and Subtraction

Addition and subtraction are the simplest operations. Compared to their integer counterparts, only one additional step is needed – correction of results greater than $p - 1$. Algorithm 3 and Algorithm 4 detail the operation.

3 Hardware Architecture

As already mentioned, the hardware structure is largely determined by the necessary datapath for the left-shifting inverse algorithm. An architecture for computing the multiplicative inverse alone is proposed in [13,14], and our design is somewhat similar. However, our architecture is more complex because it supports more operations, and we chose to use multiplexers instead of the implied tri-state outputs.

Our hardware architecture is shown in Figure 1. The control logic, implemented as a Finite State Machine, is described in the following sections, broken down by individual operations.

3.1 Multiplicative Inverse

When computing the multiplicative inverse, the data path can be seen as a combination of a "master" part (containing the work registers u, v, and the associated combinatorial logic), and a "slave" part (containing the work registers r, s, the output register y, and the associated combinatorial units).

Algorithm 1 internally allows negative values in the two's complement code. A sign bit is therefore needed in all internal registers, implying the width of $n + 1$ bits. In certain very rare cases, the register r can exceed the $[-p + 1, p - 1]$ range and has to be $n + 2$ bits wide.

Algorithm 1, as presented in the previous section, can be implemented in hardware in quite a straightforward way; however, significant optimizations are possible. Most of the optimizations shown in [13,14] can be applied to our design as well and are briefly mentioned below for the sake of completeness.

First, a shift by a constant number of bits needs zero time and logic resources. It is therefore advantageous to perform shifts together with add/subtract operations in one clock cycle whenever possible.

In line 2, there is no need to test both registers u, v since only one of them can change in each clock cycle. Thus, the test can be applied to the output of ADD1, checking for ± 1 shifted by $\min(cu, cv)$. In the special case of $a = 1$, the inverse still computes correctly, it just takes longer. The test results are stored in two 1-bit registers (t_pos, t_neg) for use in the next clock cycle.

In line 16, the result is moved to the register r if it is not already there. To avoid this test, a flip-flop (the wu signal) is used to "remember" which of the registers u, v was last updated.

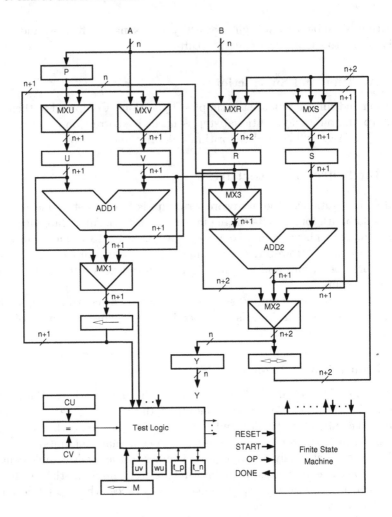

Fig. 1. Modular arithmetic unit – Hardware architecture

The tests in lines 4, 7, 10 and 14 imply an e-bit subtracter, where $e = \log_2 n$. However, the subtracter can be replaced with an e-bit equality comparator (that outputs the difference signal d) and one flip-flop (signal uv).

The ±1 tests are implemented using the register m, which contains a binary mask shifted by the appropriate number of bits+1, that is, $-2^{\min(cu,cv)+1}$ (-1 shifted to the left by $\min(cu, cv) + 1$). To test for $+1$, the mask is AND'ed with the value to be tested. To test for -1, the mask is XOR'ed with two times the value to be tested. In both cases, if the result is zero, ±1 is present. Test results are stored in the t_pos and t_neg flip-flops.

The tu, tv signals represent the "left shift is possible" conditions (more precisely "value can be doubled without causing an arithmetic overflow") in lines 3 and 4 of Algorithm 1. The t_cond test signal results from the implementation of the conditions in lines 17–20 of Algorithm 1; it is high whenever s has the same sign as the ± 1 that has caused the main loop to terminate. A summary of the test signals introduced in the preceding paragraphs follows:

$$t\_pos = (m_{n-1} \cdot a_n) + (m_{n-2} \cdot a_{n-1}) + \ldots + (m_0 \cdot a_1)$$
$$t\_neg = (m_n \oplus a_n) + (m_{n-1} \oplus a_{n-1}) + \ldots + (m_0 \oplus a_0)$$
$$tu = (u_n = u_{n-1} = 0) \vee ((u_n = u_{n-1} = 1) \wedge (u_{n-2} + u_{n-3} + \ldots + u_0 = 1))$$
$$tv = (v_n = v_{n-1} = 0) \vee ((v_n = v_{n-1} = 1) \wedge (v_{n-2} + v_{n-3} + \ldots + v_0 = 1))$$
$$t\_cond = (t\_neg = 0 \wedge s_n = 1) \vee (t\_pos = 0 \wedge s_n = 0)$$

The tests are rather complicated, and so is the associated test logic consisting of the $n+1$-bit register m, 1-bit registers uv, wu, t_pos, t_neg, and the counters cu, cv. Most of these are not found in the plain version of the algorithm (Algorithm 1) and result from implementing the optimizations.

Due to the number of optimizations that are not obvious from Algorithm 1, the FSM operation is detailed in an algorithmic form (Algorithm 5) with a simplified diagram of states and transitions (Figure 2).

Theoretically, the lowest number of clock cycles needed to compute one inverse is a constant – one such case is $a = p - 1$. In this case, the main loop exits after just one iteration, no matter what the n is. The theoretical maximum is $2n$, plus a few cycles for initialization etc, since in each iteration the number of significant bits in one of the variables u, v is decreased at least by one. The average number of clock cycles is near this maximum. There is a linear relationship between the word size in bits and the average number of clock cycles needed.

3.2 Multiplication

For multiplication, we used a straightforward implementation of Algorithm 2. The computation takes at most $2n + 1$ clock cycles including the initialization (line 1 of Algorithm 2), with the average around $2n$. Each iteration of the main loop (lines 2–7) takes two clock cycles: in the first one, operations in lines 3, 5, 6 are performed; in the second one, operations in lines 4 and 7 are performed. Figure 3 shows the corresponding portion of the FSM.

3.3 Addition and Subtraction

Again, a straightforward implementation of Algorithm 3 and Algorithm 4 is used. The calculation takes exactly 3 clock cycles – initialization, addition or subtraction, and modular correction. Figure 4 shows the portion of the FSM that controls these operations.

Algorithm 5. Multiplicative inverse – FSM operation

---

1. $u \leftarrow p, v \leftarrow a, s \leftarrow 1, m \leftarrow -2$;
    clear r, cu, cv; **set** uv, t_pos, t_neg $S\_INIT \rightarrow S\_ML$
2. **while** $(t\_neg = 1) \wedge (t\_pos = 1)$ **do** $S\_ML \rightarrow S\_ML$
3.   **if** $tu = 1$ **then**   ·
4.   **if** $(d = 0) \vee (uv = 0)$ **then**   ·
5. $u \leftarrow 2u, r \leftarrow 2r$; **inc** cu; **clear** uv ·
6.   **else**   ·
7. $u \leftarrow 2u, s \leftarrow s/2, m \leftarrow 2m$; **inc** cu ·
8.   **else if** $tv = 1$ **then**   ·
9.   **if** $(d = 0) \vee (uv = 1)$ **then**   ·
10. $v \leftarrow 2v, s \leftarrow 2s$; **inc** cv; **set** uv ·
11.   **else**   ·
12. $v \leftarrow 2v, r \leftarrow r/2, m \leftarrow 2m$; **inc** cv ·
13.   **else if** $u_n = v_n$ **then**   ·
14.   **if** $d = 0$ **then**   ·
15. $u \leftarrow 2(u - v), r \leftarrow 2(r - s)$ ·
16.   **inc** cu; **clear** uv; **set** wu; **update** t_pos, t_neg ·
17.   **else if** $uv = 1$ **then**   ·
18. $u \leftarrow 2(u - v), r \leftarrow r - s, s \leftarrow s/2, m \leftarrow 2m$ ·
19.   **inc** cu; **set** wu; **update** t_neg, t_pos ·
20.   **else**   ·
21. $v \leftarrow 2(v - u), s \leftarrow s - r, r \leftarrow r/2, m \leftarrow 2m$ ·
22.   **inc** cv; **clear** wu; **update** t_neg, t_pos ·
23.   **else**   ·
24.   **if** $d = 0$ **then**   ·
25. $u \leftarrow 2(u + v), r \leftarrow 2(r + s)$ ·
26.   **inc** cu; **clear** uv; **set** wu; **update** t_neg, t_pos ·
27.   **else if** $uv = 1$ **then**   ·
28. $u \leftarrow 2(u + v), r \leftarrow r + s, s \leftarrow s/2, m \leftarrow 2m$ ·
29.   **inc** cu; **set** wu; **update** t_neg, t_pos ·
30.   **else**   ·
31. $v \leftarrow 2(v + u), s \leftarrow s + r, r \leftarrow r/2, m \leftarrow 2m$ ·
32.   **inc** cv; **clear** wu; **update** t_neg, t_pos $S\_ML \rightarrow S\_ML$
33. **if** $wu = 1$ **then** $S\_INV \rightarrow S\_INV1$
34.   **if** $uv = 1$ **then** $s \leftarrow r$ ·
35.   **else** $s \leftarrow r/2$ ·
36. $r \leftarrow 0$ $S\_INV \rightarrow S\_INV1$
37. **if** $t\_cond = 1$ **then** $S\_INV1 \rightarrow S\_INIT$
38.   **if** $t\_neg = 0$ **then** $y \leftarrow r - s$ ·
39.   **else** $y \leftarrow r + s$ ·
40. **else**   ·
41.   **if** $t\_neg = 0$ **then** $y \leftarrow p - s$ ·
42.   **else** $y \leftarrow p + s$ $S\_INV1 \rightarrow S\_INIT$

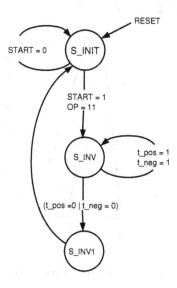

Fig. 2. Multiplicative inverse – FSM states and transitions

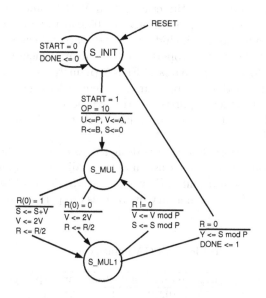

Fig. 3. Multiplication – FSM states and transitions

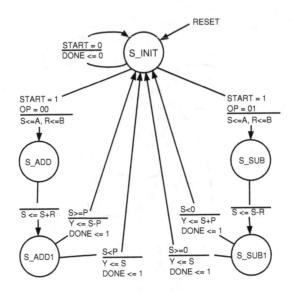

Fig. 4. Adddition and subtraction – FSM states and transitions

4   Results and Discussion

4.1   Implementation

We described the modular arithmetic unit in VHDL, and tested the correct operation of our design by applying about 500,000 random test vectors with various operands and moduli, including several marginal cases.

To get an idea about the properties of a real implementation, we synthesized the design into a Xilinx Spartan2 FPGA (namely "xc2s200-fg456-5"). The following table shows the occupied area (in equivalent gates) and maximum attainable clock frequency reported by the synthesis tool for various operand lengths in bits. The synthesis was optimized either for the smallest area or for the highest speed.

The left-shift inversion algorithm is designed to minimize the number of additions/subtractions. This is very useful if the additions and subtractions take more clock cycles than pure shifts. However, our unit does not take advantage of this property since all the elementary operations are performed in a single clock cycle.

Table 1. FPGA implementation

Bits	Eq. gates (area/spd opt.)	f_{CLK} (area/spd opt.)
32	7752 / 10222	28 / 44
64	14309 / 17205	22 / 26
80	17593 / 21020	20 / 24

4.2 Comparison with Other Approaches

In general, it is tricky to compare numbers given by various authors. To obtain comparable results, one should take the same target platform and use the same version of synthesis tools. For this reason, the following discussion may seem somewhat vague.

The dual-field arithmetic unit in [17] does not support the modular inverse directly; the calculation must be controlled from the outside and takes many clock cycles. Multiplication takes n cycles; however, one cycle includes both addition and correction. Our approach is significantly faster thanks to the directly implemented inverse.

The $GF(p)$ arithmetic unit in [3] is designed for operation in the Montgomery domain, while our unit operates in the integer domain. The unit in [3] utilizes the advantages of the Montgomery multiplication which is performed in n cycles. Inversion always takes $2n$ cycles. Our design is therefore slightly faster in the inverse calculation but slower in multiplication. However, this does not take into account the overhead of converting to/from the Montgomery domain and difference in complexity of one clock cycle (and therefore the maximum attainable frequency). The required area, based on the quoted number of equivalent gates, is roughly the same.

4.3 Applications

One of the possible application areas is elliptic curve cryptography (ECC) [10]. The operations supported by the arithmetic unit are sufficient to implement all operations over points on elliptic curves – point addition, point doubling, and scalar multiplication.

Another intended application of the modular arithmetic unit is in a system for solving sets of linear equations exactly. One such system is shown in [16]; it takes advantage of modular arithmetic with many prime moduli and the Chinese Remainder Theorem to avoid rounding errors during calculations. To use the proposed arithmetic unit in such a system, one would simply use many instances (possibly thousands) of this unit in parallel and let them perform the same sequence of operations for different moduli. In this application, the word size should stay small, let's say 16 to 32 bits, to avoid large propagation delays.

5 Conclusion

We presented a hardware implementation of a modular arithmetic unit that can add, subtract, multiply and invert modulo a prime number p. To compute the multiplicative inverse efficiently, the unit uses the promising left-shifting algorithm [13,14]. The arithmetic unit can be used whenever there is need to perform modular arithmetic operations efficiently in hardware, such as in elliptic curve cryptography, or for calculations that use a residual number system.

In comparison with the current state of the art, our arithmetic unit outperforms designs that do not directly implement the inversion. Other designs may have the upper edge thanks to faster multiplication. Future work should therefore focus on improving the multiplication performance, in addition to further optimizations of the left-shift inverse algorithm.

References

1. Bernal, A.: Conception et Etude d'une Architecture Numerique de Haute Performance pour le Calcul de la Fonction Exponentielle Modulaire. PhD thesis, Institut National Polytechnique de Grenoble (1999)
2. Ciet, M., Joye, M., Lauter, K., Montgomery, P.L.: Trading Inversions for Multiplications in Elliptic Curve Cryptography. Designs, Codes and Cryptography 39(2), 189–206 (2006)
3. Daly, A., Marmane, W., Kerins, T., Popovici, E.: An FPGA Implementation of a GF(p) ALU for Encryption Processors. Microprocessors and Microsystems 28(5-6), 253–260 (2004)
4. Meurice de Dormale, G., Bulens, P., Quisquater, J.-J.: An Improved Montgomery Modular Inversion Targeted for Efficient Implementation on FPGA. In: International Conference on Field-Programmable Technology, FPT 2004, pp. 441–444 (2004)
5. Gutub, A.: New Hardware Algorithms and Designs for Montgomery Modular Inverse Computation in Galois Fields GF(p) and GF(2^n). PhD Thesis, Department of Electrical & Computer Engineering, Oregon State University (2002)
6. Hars, L.: Modular Inverse Algorithms without Multiplications. EURASIP Journal on Embedded Systems 32192:2006, 1–13 (2006)
7. Hitchcock, Y., Dawson, E., Clark, A., Montague, P.: Implementing an Efficient Elliptic Curve Cryptosystem over $GF(p)$ on a Smart Card. In: Proc. of 10th Computational Techniques and Applications Conference, CTAC 2001. ANZIAM J., vol. 44, pp. C354–C377 (2003)
8. Hlaváč, J.: Hardware Implementation of Algorithms for Computations in Finite Fields. PhD thesis, Czech Technical University in Prague (2010)
9. Hlaváč, J., Lórencz, R.: Improved Hardware Architecture for Computing the Modular Inverse using AMI. In: International Conference on Computer, Communication and Control Technologies, CCCT 2003 and ISAS 2003, vol. III, pp. 255–260 (2003)
10. IEEE Computer Society: IEEE Standard Specifications for Public-Key Cryptography. Document No. IEEE 1363-2000 (2000) ISBN: 0-7381-1956-3
11. Kaliski Jr., B.S.: The Montgomery Inverse and Its Applications. IEEE Trans. on Computers 44(8), 1064–1065 (1995)
12. Knuth, D.E.: The Art of Computer Programming, 3rd edn. Seminumerical Algorithms, vol. 2. Addison-Wesley (1998)
13. Lórencz, R.: Method for Generating the Multiplicative Inverse in a Finite Field GF(p). U.S. Patent No. 7574469 (2009)
14. Lórencz, R.: New Algorithm for Classical Modular Inverse. In: Kaliski Jr., B.S., Koç, Ç.K., Paar, C. (eds.) CHES 2002. LNCS, vol. 2523, pp. 57–70. Springer, Heidelberg (2003)
15. Montgomery, P.L.: Modular Multiplication Without Trial Division. Mathematics of Computation 44(170), 519–521 (1985)

16. Morháč, M., Lórencz, R.: Modular System for Solving Linear Equations Exactly, I. Architecture and Numerical Algorithms. Computers and Artificial Intelligence 11(4), 351–361 (1992)
17. Wolkerstorfer, J.: Dual-Field Arithmetic Unit for $GF(p)$ and $GF(2^m)$. In: Kaliski Jr., B.S., Koç, Ç.K., Paar, C. (eds.) CHES 2002. LNCS, vol. 2523, pp. 500–514. Springer, Heidelberg (2003)
18. Yan, X.: Modified Modular Inversion Algorithm for VLSI Implementation. In: 7th International Conference on ASIC – ASICON 2007, pp. 90–93 (2007)

HW-OSQM: Reducing the Impact of Event Signaling by Hardware-Based Operating System Queue Manipulation

Stefan Wallentowitz, Thomas Wild, and Andreas Herkersdorf

Technische Universität München, Institute for Integrated Systems
Arcisstr. 21, D–80290 München
stefan.wallentowitz@tum.de

Abstract. System-on-chip integrate an increasing amount of processing elements and on-chip communication is of particular importance. Rising communication rates with varying delays require efficient techniques to signal events related to the on-chip communication to the application software. While latencies are commonly hidden by multithreading, the signaling of events is usually done by polling or interrupts. With rising rates of such events the classic techniques expose an increasing software overhead that becomes significantly important.

In this paper we present the concept of *hardware-based operating system queue manipulation (HW-OSQM)* to offload the process of event signaling. The concept is implemented as a flexible hardware accelerator which integrates with the communication hardware and autonomously manipulates the queue data structures of the operating system. It eliminates the associated software overhead and utilizes small additional resources while allowing for the required flexibility. The performance improvement shows that HW-OSQM can nearly eliminate any overhead in software.

1 Introduction

Modern multiprocessor system-on-chip integrate an increasing amount of programmable processing elements ranging from heterogeneous embedded systems to homogeneous massively parallel manycore platforms. The processing elements in such platforms become more powerful and also the operating systems can be complex. Multithreading can be found to some certain degree, so that at least concurrent application tasks share a processing node in such a platform. Communication of applications running on such platforms is an increasingly important factor. Future platforms have to deal with rising data rates and bandwidth demands, such as for example in mobile communication devices [1].

The communication among the processing and other elements is commonly performed as message passing or shared memory accesses. Usually threads are waiting for events that signal the completion of a transfer, the availability of data and other events. Multithreading allows to interleave the waiting time for events with other thread processing to increase efficiency. When a thread suspends to

C. Hochberger et al. (Eds.): ARCS 2013, LNCS 7767, pp. 280–291, 2013.

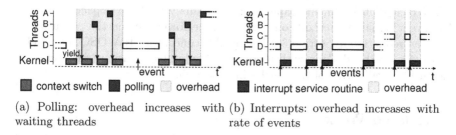

(a) Polling: overhead increases with waiting threads

(b) Interrupts: overhead increases with rate of events

Fig. 1. Scalability issues for the two common signaling methods

wait for an event, it has to be re-scheduled after its occurrence. Hence, the problem is how to efficiently signal such events to the thread.

Two techniques are commonly used to signal events to waiting threads: *Polling* is the repeated checking of a certain address by the thread itself and *interrupts* are signals from the corresponding hardware to the processor which trigger the operating system (see [2]). When polling is used, a thread yields (releases) the processor to the operating system. It is scheduled later again and repeatedly checks for the event. The operating system performs context switches and invokes the scheduler every time a threads yields. Multiple outstanding events have an increasing performance impact as sketched in Figure 1(a). It is possible to reduce the overhead of the polling operations by reducing the polling thread's priority. But this automatically leads to reduced re-activeness.

When interrupts are used, a thread suspends while waiting for an event. The scheduler will not select a suspended thread for execution again unless it is "woken up". In the occurrence of the event, the hardware raises an interrupt and the interrupt service routine (ISR) re-schedules the waiting thread. Compared to polling there is no overhead of checking for the completion, but the overhead of the ISR. Furthermore, this method is advantageous when the latency from an event to the notification needs to be low. But the overhead of the ISR becomes a significant factor with an increasing rate of events as depicted in Figure 1(b).

Two factors impact the performance of the two methods: the number of concurrently waiting threads and the event rate. To be independent of both factors, we propose to offload the processing related to event signaling to the hardware that generates such events, such as a DMA controller or a Network-on-Chip network interface. The proposed *hardware-based operating system queue manipulation (HW-OSQM)* assists such modules and appears to the application (or driver) similar to interrupting and therefore eliminates the problems of polling. HW-OSQM autonomously performs the central operation of the interrupt service routine: Waking up a thread by putting it back to the ready queue of the operating system's scheduler. The proposed method is scalable and easy to adapt to different scenarios as we will discuss in this paper. Contrary to existing approaches the proposed method does entirely remove any software overhead related to external events. On the other extreme, HW-OSQM does not offload the entire scheduler operation to hardware, but allows for flexible integration with existing operating systems, even without modifications to it.

The contributions of this paper are: (i) an analysis of the impact of the classical event signaling methods on computing performance and the potentials for overhead reduction in Section 3, (ii) a flexible concept for HW-OSQM that eliminates this overhead along with a configurable implementation (see Section 4), and (iii) the validation of the results in Section 5.

2 Related Work

The tradeoff between interrupts and polling has been researched for a long time. Langendoen et al. [2] for example investigated this tradeoff for cluster computing. During execution of software the choice for interrupts or polling is adapted depending on the question whether other threads are runnable. In many cases interrupt-based event notification is favored due to its minimal latency and the lack of influences on the software other than the ISR. To reduce the impact of the ISR on software performance *interrupt coalescing* has been introduced. Events are here "collected" and signaled with a single interrupt. In network interface cards several packets are stored in memory before raising an interrupt, such as discussed in [3]. MSIQ [4] is an on-chip message passing adapter that coalesces interrupts. Although this technique can achieve good results, the impact of interrupts can still be reduced by saving the ISR and execute its operations directly in hardware as proposed in this work.

Substituting parts of an operating system by much faster hardware elements has been proposed before. Approaches often focus on hard real-time systems and their specific demands. In change for the real-time behavior such hardware accelerators are often restricted in their flexibility, e.g., only allowing for a bound set of threads or events. The prior solutions vary in their set of operating system functionalities offloaded to hardware and their implementation style. One class of such hardware-assists for operation systems are programmable as separate (application-specific) processors or microcontrollers. OSIP [5] for example is an application-specific instruction set processor that replaces the entire scheduler. Scheler et al. [6] present an approach which utilizes a microcontroller to order interrupt requests and perform scheduling and processor interrupts for real-time systems. While those approaches are very flexible and can also perform the task addressed in this paper, they are complex to use and consume much resources. Other hardware offloads for operating systems implement specialized hardware. HW-RTOS [7] implements a scheduler and communication for a dual core system. Threads are woken up when communication events occur. Nevertheless, HW-RTOS as other hardware operating systems is restricted in the amount of buffers, threads, and events supported and lacks an external interface.

In microthreading platforms several threads execute in parallel and are dynamically scheduled [8]. Context switches are fast and special instructions allow for cycle-to-cycle thread switches. A waiting thread can be signaled using a specific instruction for efficient thread synchronization. For external events such as a data load this specific instruction is issued in the pipeline to signal the thread. In recent years this concept has been extended to multiprocessor environments such as the Microgrid architecture for the Self-adaptive Virtual Processor (SVP) model [9]. Families of threads run concurrently on one or more processors and synchronize with the means of microthreading. [10] extends this concepts to integrate I/O events. A general problem with this microthreaded approach is the specialization and overhead induced by having several contexts in hardware.

Transputers also work with a sleep and wake up mechanism controlled by the hardware [11, p. 32]. Two priority queues hold the active threads. Threads that are waiting for external or internal events are automatically notified by the hardware by putting them back to the active queue. The scheduler is microcoded hardware which is complex compared to our proposed module. Instructions for queue manipulation in software were provided by the (CISC) VAX instruction set, but the other overhead persists.

Summarized, contrary to interrupt coalescing and related techniques the goal of our work is to offload the essential task of the interrupt service routine – waking up a waiting task – entirely to hardware. Although running the entire scheduler in hardware might be favorable in some cases, our approach keeps the software data structures intact and keeps the full flexibility of the operating system by only doing the necessary operations in hardware.

3   Problem Analysis

The performance impact of the classical methods strongly depends on the characteristics of the application scenario and the operating system parameters. In the following we will analytically derive the overhead and evaluate the impact.

3.1   Performance Metric and Parameters

The basic performance metric is the *overhead* o that is the share of the total execution time the software spends in operations specific to the respective signaling mechanism. This overhead should be minimal and it is influenced by many parameters and characteristics. First of all, the execution times of the specific operations influence the overhead. They are approximately constant for each implementation: the time for polling T_{poll} and the time for the interrupt service routine T_{isr}. Similarly, the time for context switches T_{CS} is another constant factor. Contrary, the time slice length T_{slice} is a parameter of the kernel: Longer time slices reduce the impact of kernel context switches and the scheduler on the computational performance while shorter time slice lengths increase the reactiveness. Application characteristics also influence the overhead. The average event rate r_{event} is the number of generated events per second. In steady-state this is the rate applications start waiting for external events. T_{delay} is the average time from the start of the waiting of a thread until the event is signaled.

The *latency* between the event and the thread gets to know this similarly needs to be minimal. There are too many factors influencing the latency and a detailed analysis discussion goes beyond the scope this paper. Nevertheless it is important that a generic solution can still cope with this issue (see "Critical Events and Demand Interrupting" in Section 4.2).

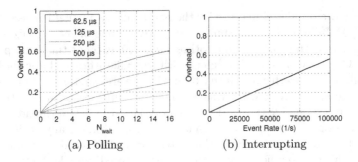

Fig. 2. Analytical result of overhead of polling and interrupting

3.2 Analysis

We calibrated the constant factors based on a minimalistic operating system and a simple off-the-shelf RISC processor assuming an operating frequency of 400 MHz. To research the impact of our proposed solution we did a steady-state analysis as such an analysis can capture different application scenarios. The overhead of polling can be derived from Figure 1(a). The rate of events r_{event} and the average delay T_{delay} together determine the average number of concurrently waiting threads $N_{wait} = r_{event} \cdot T_{delay}$ and the overhead is

$$o_{polling} = \frac{N_{wait} \cdot (T_{poll} + T_{CS})}{T_{slice} + N_{wait} \cdot (T_{poll} + T_{CS})}$$

Figure 2(a) shows the overhead for different typical time slice lengths T_{slice} and numbers of average waiting threads N_{wait}. Even for long time slice lengths, the overhead becomes around 10% for 8 waiting threads. At a short time slice length even two waiting threads already induce an overhead in that range.

In the interrupt scheme the number of waiting threads is not relevant, but instead only the event rate r_{event} determines the overhead. Furthermore, the time slice length T_{slice} does principally not influence the overhead, as there is one run of the interrupt service routine for each event, thus leading to the linear dependency

$$o_{interrupting} = r_{event} \cdot T_{isr}$$

Figure 2(b) shows the overhead when using interrupts. For event rates around 25kHz the overhead is already above 10%. As motivated before, in future many-core systems developers can easily face higher event rates. The analytical results show a good potential for improvements.

4   Operating System Queue Manipulation

The goal is to get rid of the overhead associated with the signaling of an event to a suspended thread. First of all, threads should not poll for events, but instead yield the processor while the event is pending. The events then need to

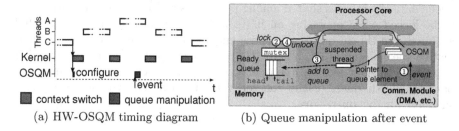

(a) HW-OSQM timing diagram   (b) Queue manipulation after event

Fig. 3. HW-OSQM: basic principle, integration and operation

be signaled to the thread by appending them to the *ready queue* of the operating system. In principal, this ready queue of an operating system resides in the memory. It usually points to head and tail of a linked list of queue elements. The scheduler dequeues an element from the head to select the next thread and enqueues threads that yield or which are preempted. When the event occurs, an interrupt service routine appends the thread queue element to the list.

The actual scheduling operation and context switches are not part of this manipulation, so that the approach is generic and can be integrated in more sophisticated systems.

4.1 HW-OSQM Operation

In *Hardware-based Operation System Queue Manipulation (HW-OSQM)* the queue operations are performed asynchronously by the assisted hardware (e.g., DMA controller or similar) as depicted in Figure 3(b). The principal functionality of HW-OSQM is sketched in Figure 3(a): When suspending a thread, the HW-OSQM is configured to wake up this thread on a certain event by appending it to the ready queue. Both phases and variations of HW-OSQM are described subsequently, followed by the implementation description.

Configuration Phase. In the beginning the pointer to the ready queue needs to be configured once. When a thread starts waiting for an event, e.g., the completion of a DMA transfer it initiated, it suspends. The respective queue element is thereby removed from the ready queue. As HW-OSQM has to find the element in the memory when the event occurs, it needs to be configured during the thread suspension. Therefore, HW-OSQM needs to store the pointer to the queue element for every tracked event. In Figure 3(b) the set of pointers associated to events are depicted as part of the HW-OSQM module.

Event Phase. The basic operations performed in hardware are depicted in Figure 3(b). After an event occurred (①) the thread queue element address as set during configuration is looked up and appended to the ready queue. As the queue data structure is shared among processors and the hardware assist it has to be locked when operating on it (②). After the lock has been successfully acquired, the thread queue element is enqueued to the ready queue by manipulating the pointers (③). Finally, the lock is released (④). In case atomicity is possible without locking, the operation does not need to lock the queue apparently. Furthermore, cache coherency needs to be ensured, for example by snooping for this operations.

4.2 HW-OSQM Variations

This basic scheme already matches many minimalistic operating systems. Nevertheless, it is not sufficient to handle more sophisticated cases that can also be handled with slight modifications of the basic concept.

Multiple Priority Queues. Above we described a scenario where one queue holds all runnable threads, while waiting threads are stored separately. In many operating systems, especially real-time operating systems, there are multiple queues for runnable threads that are ordered by thread priority. Such structures can be easily handled by extending the thread entry in HW-OSQM with the associated priority queue.

Critical Events & Demand Interrupting. The major advantage of HW-OSQM over interrupts is that the normal software execution is not interfered with the wake-up operation. But this interference might be desired. For example when the event is critical for the thread or additional actions might be required by the kernel when the event occurs. For using such critical events the HW-OSQM entry can be extended with a flag. Each of those events apparently reduces the performance gain of HW-OSQM, but cannot be avoided due to the application demands.

Signaling with Ready Flag. Sometimes bitmap schedulers are used. Those schedulers store threads in a table that holds a restricted number of them. Such a data structure is rarely used in standard operating systems but is sometimes chosen as alternative in real-time operating systems. This scheduler structure is can also be handled with HW-OSQM. Instead of modifying the ready queue, the HW-OSQM simply directly modifies the runnable flag.

This set of extensions to HW-OSQM allows to support most common simple operating systems, e.g., VxWorks, FreeRTOS, eCos etc. Even more complex scheduler implementations may use HW-OSQM by defining an additional queue, for example in Linux or similar. HW-OSQM then uses this queue to enqueue ready threads and the scheduler can then check this queue for threads and add them to its own data structures.

4.3 Implementation

A generic implementation of HW-OSQM is depicted in Figure 4(a) beside integration examples with the assisted modules in Figure 4(b). The implementation

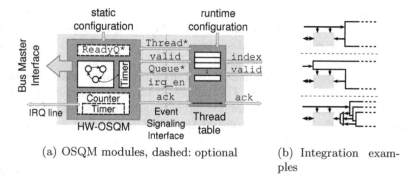

(a) OSQM modules, dashed: optional   (b) Integration examples

Fig. 4. HW-OSQM implementation and integration with the assisted modules

essentially consists of two parts: the logic that performs the queue operations via a bus interface and the table that holds the addresses of the thread queue elements associated with each event. The configuration ports of the modules can be accessed via a slave bus interface from the processor or integrated with the assisted modules. The configuration of the queues etc. (HW-OSQM module) is typically done by the software at start time. At runtime, the table is then configured to associate a thread queue element with each event. Assisted modules usually have a number of requests that it handles in parallel, e.g. multiple DMA transfers, messages or similar. It is important that the events can later be associated with the correct thread. The software therefore sets the thread queue element corresponding to the event that is created after transfer completion.

The event itself is signaled from the assisted modules, such as a DMA controller, by setting the `index` and signal the event with `valid`. HW-OSQM can also assist multiple modules when those signals are multiplexed (see Figure 4(b)). The HW-OSQM module acknowledges the completion with `ack`. The address of the corresponding thread queue element is picked from the table and handed to the state machine (`Thread*`). The pseudo code of the operations that the state machine executes are depicted in Figure 5. Depending on the different implementation configurations the execution flow is slightly different.

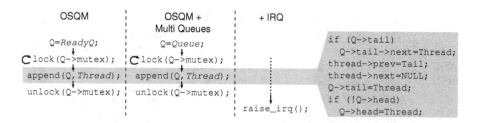

Fig. 5. Pseudo code of the HW-OSQM state machine functionality

If the queue (set either by internal register or external signal) cannot be locked a timer is used to wait. After locking the thread element is simply added to the end of queue. This is a normal linked list operation which consists of just a few reads and writes. Finally the lock is released.

For the extensions described in Section 4 some optional interface signals can be added (dashed in Figure 4(a)): The Queue* signal allows for multiple priority queues and irq_en triggers a demanded interrupt after completion of the queue manipulation. With demand interrupting the HW-OSQM raises an interrupt to the operating system. Finally, in case the assisted module can be extended it is also possible to directly interface the HW-OSQM queue manipulation. The transfer table of a DMA controller may for example be extended by the required entries.

5   Results

Based on the described implementation we will present the implementation results with respect to hardware overhead and the computational performance impact.

5.1   Resource Utilization

Figure 6 summarizes the resource utilization of HW-OSQM. The synthesis results for the HW-OSQM state machine logic are shown in Figure 6(a). Provided are the results of an FPGA (Xilinx Virtex6) and an ASIC process (TSMC 65nm). Beside the basic HW-OSQM implementation the three variants described in Section 4.2 are depicted. The requirement for registers in the basic HW-OSQM implementation stems from the state machine, the runtime configuration register and a counter that implements the timeout when acquiring a lock. In the variant where the queue is configured as an additional signal (Queues) there is no configuration register. Additional states are required for the interrupt configuration (IRQ). Finally, the version for flag manipulation (Flags) does not require a configuration register and locking at all. The frequencies of all modules are around

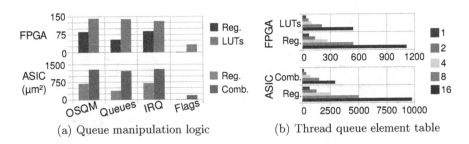

(a) Queue manipulation logic   (b) Thread queue element table

Fig. 6. Synthesis results for the basic module and the thread table

500 MHz for the FPGA and 1.5 GHz for the ASIC. Apparently, this frequency can be bound by other modules, such as the bus and the network adapter.

In Figure 6(b) the impact of the variation of the number of supported waiting threads, that is the number of HW-OSQM table entries, on the resource utilization is given. As expected, the variation of the entries is the direct determinant for the register part, plus muxing logic. Finally, we integrated the prototype with a remote DMA network adapter that can handle four different transfers concurrently. The additional resource utilization here varies from 3% to 25% depending on the HW-OSQM implementation variant.

5.2 Performance Impact

Finally, we compare the impact of HW-OSQM on the computational performance and compare the findings to the analysis in Section 3.2.

Methodology. The performance tests are executed with a subsystem of a multiprocessor system-on-chip. It consists of a 400 MHz processor core, a local memory and a DMA unit that fetches data from remote memory (compare Figure 3(b)). A minimalistic operating system that does not add much additional noise in the performance measurement runs on the processor core. We ran a synthetic test bed, that produces events depending on the characteristics described in Section 3. The data is gathered non-intrusively by directly observing the processor state and other signals in an accurate RTL simulation. To compare the polling and interrupting with HW-OSQM, we measure the computational performance with the average share of time that the user applications have of the total time. This is the time productive operations are executed by runnable threads that do not wait for events.

Polling vs. HW-OSQM. As discussed in Section 3.2 (cf. Figure 2(a)), the determining factors for the polling overhead are the number of waiting threads (N_{wait}) and the time slice length (T_{slice}). Figure 7 shows the impact of the variation of those parameters. In Figure 7(a) the average share of user time

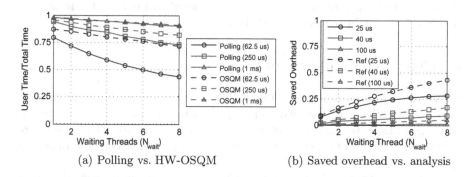

(a) Polling vs. HW-OSQM   (b) Saved overhead vs. analysis

Fig. 7. Polling improvement

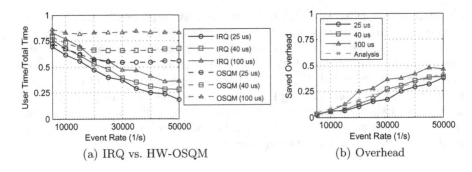

(a) IRQ vs. HW-OSQM   (b) Overhead

Fig. 8. Interrupting improvement

of the total time is depicted for polling and HW-OSQM. From the graph it is visible that with decreasing time slice length and increasing number of waiting threads the performance decreases for polling. With HW-OSQM there is also a slight loss that results from the additional overhead of the waiting threads that have to initiate another request via the kernel driver before yielding again. The improvement in terms of saved software overhead is plotted in Figure 7(b). It shows a very good improvement especially for decreasing time slice lengths. In many system-on-chip it is desirable that the time slice length is relatively short (here: 62.5μs ≙ 25000cycles), so that the delay for signaling is shorter. The graph compares the results with the analytically derived overhead (Ref.). The actual numbers are slightly reduced as a part of the polling is hidden in other kernel operations.

Interrupting vs. HW-OSQM. In Section 3.2 we analytically derived that the overhead of interrupting depends on the event rate and does not depend on the time slice length, but other kernel operations influence the share of the user execution time of the total time. Figure 8(a) compares this share for the variation of the event rate and the time slice length. The event rate was chosen in a range based on the consideration in the introduction. The improvement in terms of saved software overhead is again depicted in Figure 8(b). It shows a significant saving, in the range as predicted by the analysis.

6   Conclusion and Outlook

In today's and future system-on-chip the communication and data rates steadily increase. The trend of integrating more and more processing elements concentrates this high rates on the on-chip communication interfaces. The completion of transfers, arrival of external data etc. have to be signaled to the operating system and finally to the threads.

We have analytically derived that the signaling of those events using the classic methods polling and interrupting has a significant impact on the computational performance of the software with such increasing event rates. In this paper we presented the concept of HW-OSQM that directly modifies the data structures of the operating system on the occurrence of events.

The concept is flexible and can be used in different scenarios. The concept has been implemented and the resource utilization has been analyzed. The impact on computational performance was measured and shows that HW-OSQM delivers a significant improvement especially for increasing numbers of waiting threads and increasing event rates.

Future work will include more extensive studies of HW-OSQM in different multiprocessing platform scenarios. Furthermore we will investigate the performance impact on complete application scenarios. The analysis and synthetic measurements in this work support that HW-OSQM will increase the computational performance significantly.

References

1. van Berkel, C.H.K.: Multi-core for mobile phones. In: Proceedings of the Conference on Design, Automation and Test in Europe, DATE 2009, pp. 1260–1265. European Design and Automation Association, Leuven (2009)
2. Langendoen, K., et al.: Integrating Polling, Interrupts, and Thread Management. In: Proceedings of the 6th Symposium on the Frontiers of Massively Parallel Computation, pp. 13–22. IEEE Computer Society (1996)
3. Goglin, B., Furmento, N.: Finding a tradeoff between host interrupt load and MPI latency over Ethernet. In: IEEE International Conference on Cluster Computing and Workshops, CLUSTER 2009, August 31-September 4, pp. 1–9 (2009)
4. Kariniemi, H., Nurmi, J.: High-performance NoC Interface with interrupt batching for Micronmesh MPSoC prototype platform on FPGA. In: NORCHIP, pp. 1–6 (November 2010)
5. Castrillon, J., et al.: Task management in MPSoCs: an ASIP approach. In: Proceedings of the 2009 International Conference on Computer-Aided Design, ICCAD 2009, pp. 587–594. ACM, New York (2009)
6. Scheler, F., et al.: Parallel, hardware-supported interrupt handling in an event-triggered real-time operating system. In: Proceedings of the 2009 International Conference on Compilers, Architecture, and Synthesis for Embedded Systems, CASES 2009, pp. 167–174. ACM, New York (2009)
7. Nácul, A.C., Regazzoni, F., Lajolo, M.: Hardware scheduling support in SMP architectures. In: Proceedings of the Conference on Design, Automation and Test in Europe, DATE 2007, San Jose, CA, USA, EDA Consortium, pp. 642–647 (2007)
8. Bolychevsky, A., Jesshope, C., Muchnick, V.: Dynamic scheduling in RISC architectures. IEE Proceedings Computers and Digital Techniques 143(5), 309–317 (1996)
9. Bousias, K., et al.: Implementation and evaluation of a microthread architecture. J. Syst. Archit. 55, 149–161 (2009)
10. Hicks, M., van Tol, M., Jesshope, C.: Towards scalable I/O on a many-core architecture. In: 2010 International Conference on Embedded Computer Systems (SAMOS), pp. 341–348 (July 2010)
11. INMOS Limited: Transputer Reference Manual. Prentice Hall (1992)

Comparison of GPU and FPGA Implementation of SVM Algorithm for Fast Image Segmentation

Marcin Pietron, Maciej Wielgosz, Dominik Zurek,
Ernest Jamro, and Kazimierz Wiatr

AGH University of Science and Technology,
al. Mickiewicza 30, 30-059 Krakow
ACK Cyfronet AGH
ul. Nawojki 11, 30-950 Krakow
{pietron,wielgosz,jamro,wiatr}@agh.edu.pl
dominik.zurek1102@gmail.com

Abstract. This paper presents preliminary implementation results of the SVM (Support Vector Machine) algorithm. SVM is a dedicated mathematical formula which allows us to extract selective objects from a picture and assign them to an appropriate class. Consequently, a black and white images reflecting an occurrence of the desired feature is derived from an original picture fed into the classifier. This work is primarily focused on the FPGA and GPU implementations aspects of the algorithm as well as on comparison of the hardware and software performance. A human skin classifier was used as an example and implemented both on Intel Xeon E5645.40 GHz, Xilinx Virtex-5 LX220 and Nvidia Tesla m2090. It is worth emphasizing that in case of FPGA implementation the critical hardware components were designed using HDL (Hardware Description Language), whereas the less demanding or standard ones such as communication interfaces, FIFO, FSMs were implemented in Impulse C. Such an approach allowed us both to cut a design time and preserve a high performance of the hardware classification module. In case of GPU implementation whole algorithm is implemented in CUDA.

Keywords: SVM, image segmentation, FPGA, GPU, CUDA.

1 Introduction

This work is part of the Synat project embracing several initiatives aiming to create a repository of images which are assigned a descriptive name according to their contents. Such a database of tagged images will significantly reduce search time since only picture tags will be processed instead of images so the process will involve simple string operations rather than image recognition.

The project is a huge challenge due to an immense volume of data collected over the past years denoted today as the Internet resources. Therefore the core part of the undertaking is to design and implement a classification system which should be both reliable and fast. In order to achieve the high performance of a search engine the most computationally intensive operations are to be ported to

C. Hochberger et al. (Eds.): ARCS 2013, LNCS 7767, pp. 292–302, 2013.
© Springer-Verlag Berlin Heidelberg 2013

hardware. Thus FPGAs and GPUs due to their strongly parallel structure and growing processing speed [1] seem to be the best choice.

Image segmentation is a process which aims to separate a picture into several regions based on objects or features of interest. A single SVM system may embrace several modules trained to recognize different features so the unit as a whole is capable of tracing multidimensional objects in terms of a number of features.

It is worth emphasizing that a segmentation may also be regarded as a form of data compression, the classfier accepts images and yields information regarding objects which usually occupies much less memory resources than corresponding original data.

There are plantiful image segmentation algorithms [2,3,4] and their number is still growing to meet constantly rising demands of data analysis systems. However, reliability and data processing speed are the factors which are at a premium when it comes to a real life application of a given algorithm. SVM meets both those criterions and therefore was chosen as a classification algorithm for the project.

2   SVM Classifiers

Support vector machines were originally devised and described by Vapnik [5,6]. They are used for binary classification which means that there are exactly two classes of objects (e.g. black and white rectangles) and a classification formula is found in a training process of the classifier.

The SVM algorithm can be envisioned as a process of creating a hyperplane which separates data in an n-dimensional space. It is conducted in an iterative manner in which a selected plane is gradually adjusted to provide the optimal so-called generalization margin. The following cases may occur:

- Input data is linearly separable and the SVM method guaranties that at least one plane of the best separation margin exists and will be adopted
- A dimension incrementation is used to bring data to a space of more dimensions so a separation plane can be found

A feature space for 2D can be modeled as a sphere with its center and radius (see Fig. 1).

The sphere is build upon a set of supportive vectors which constitute its structure. A classification process of a priorly trained SVM maybe perceived as probing whether a given point (input data) belongs to the sphere or it's located outside of it. In the first case a point is positively classified whereas in the second one it's considered to be an outliner.

3   A Choice of a Hardware Platform

It is very important to choose a proper hardware units and appropriate data transfer protocol since it affects the overall performance of the computational

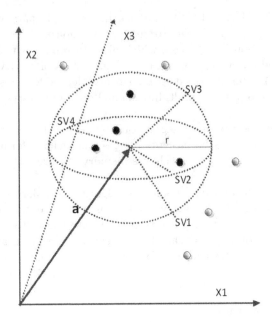

Fig. 1. N-sphere

system. It also may balk an effort invested in the development of the hardware algorithm. Therefore the authors decided to compare FPGA and GPU implementations in order to be able to choose the most appropriate solution for the complete system realization.

3.1 FPGA

FPGAs have been developed since late 1980s, and have a lot of advantages over processors. The most important ones are: massive parallel architecture, reconfigurability, low energy consumption, ability to shape freely its internal architecture.

Design and effective use of computing system based on FPGA is a difficult task, as evidenced by the long history of such trials. Existing HPRC (High Performance Reconfigurable Computing) solutions can be classified based on their integration with other computing nodes in the system. However, the authors have used DRC platform for the implementation of the SVM algorithm.

The architecture of Accelium (Xilinx Virtex-5) [12] is based on an idea of populating CPU sockets with FPGAs and the fast communication link between them. This architecture allows for equal access of processor and FPGA to the system resources.

3.2 GPU

The architecture of a GPU card is described in Fig. 2. The graphical processor unit has a multiprocessor structure. In Fig. 2 is shown N multiprocessor GPU with M cores each. The cores share an Instruction Unit with other cores in a multiprocessor. Multiprocessors have special memories which are much faster than global memory which is common for all multiprocessors. These memories are: read-only constant/texture memory and shared memory. The GPU cards are massive parallel devices. They enable thousands of parallel threads to run which are grouped in blocks with shared memory. The blocks are grouped in a grid (Fig. 3). CUDA is a software architecture that enables graphics processing unit (GPU), to be programmed using high-level languages such as C and C++. CUDA requires an NVIDIA GPU like Fermi, GeForce 8XXX/Tesla/Quadro, and so on. CUDA provides three key mechanisms to parallelize programs: thread group hierarchy, shared memories, and barrier synchronization. These mechanisms provide fine-grained parallelism nested within coarse-grained task parallelism.

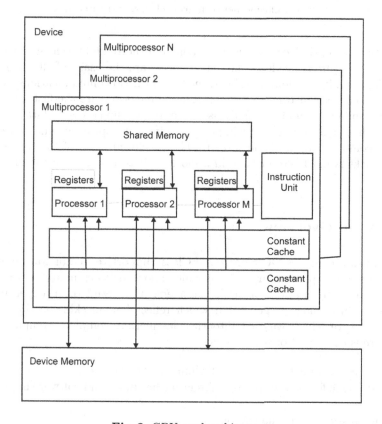

Fig. 2. GPU card architecture

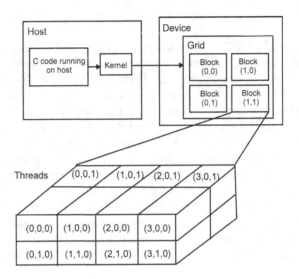

Fig. 3. Relation between grid, blocks, and threads

Creating the optimized code is not trivial and thorough knowledge about the GPUs architecture is needed. The main aspects are the usage of the memories, an efficient dividing code to parallel threads and thread communications. As was mentioned earlier constant/texture and shared memories are the fastest. Therefore programmers should optimally use them to speedup access to data on which an algorithm operates. Another important thing is to optimise synchronization and the communication of the threads. The synchronization of the threads between blocks is much slower than in a block. If it is not necessary it should be avoided.

4   System Overview

A human skin classifier OC-SVM (One Class Supportive Vector Machine) was implemented as a preliminary project which allows us to estimate performance and resource consumption for other classifiers. As a result of an experiment a black-and-white image is generated which reflect human skin location in the original picture which was fed into the classifier. A complete computational procedure is composed of several steps:

- SVM vectors and τ generation (training of the classifier)
- Input image fetch (the step is different for hardware and software implementation)
- Image resize and normalization
- Classification
- Noise and skin-like objects filtration

4.1   The Classification Algorithm

The classification algorithm is given by the following formula:

$$\sum_i \alpha_i K(X_x, X_i) \geq \sum_i \alpha_i K(X_s, X_i) = \tau \tag{1}$$

where τ is the sphere radius, X_s and α_i are supportive vectors derived in a training process, X_x is an input pixel.

Regardless of a choice of vectors in right side of the equation 1 the result is constant and equals τ. Each pixel fed into the classifier is compared against all the support vectors in order to determine if it is located inside the sphere (see Fig.1).

In this implementation a Gaussian computational kernel was used:

$$K = e^{-\gamma \|X_i - X_j\|^2} \tag{2}$$

where γ is a spread of the kernel.

If the (1) is met a given point is classified as belonging to the desired class. For SVM classifies the best results are achieved when input data is normalized (i.e. fall in the range [-1;1]).

4.2   Architecture of the Hardware Module in FPGA

The computationally intensive routines were ported to hardware to offload the GPP (General Purpose Processor) and to accelerate the computations. It was possible due to several features of the algorithm which makes it well suited for the FPGA implementation such as: fixed-point arithmetic, parallel structure (easy to pipeline), narrow-range input argument. Consequently a series of hardware units were designed which constitute the internal structure of computational module as presented in Fig.4. All the modules are parameterized and pipelined blocks which process a single input vector X every clock cycle. For a sake of the software compatibility the base data format employed in the application is 32 bit fixed-point (16 bits of both fractional and integer part) but it can be adjusted to meet different precision requirements in the future. Each module is equipped with the overflow signal which propagates across all the units composing the classification module. Such an approach allows us to avoid corruptions of the result just by simply examining the overflow output.

It is possible to connect several classification modules to form a parallel structure. Furthermore, it is worth noting that supportive vectors (denoted as SV in Fig. 5) are fetched from an external memory only once for the whole computations and therefore can be stored in the internal memory for all the computation. Moreover, the number of the supportive vectors as well as a is not large and usually not exceed tens, thus internal BRAM memory suffice to accommodate those coefficients (e.g. for the human skin classification only 16 supportive vectors are used). Increase of a number of supportive vectors improves the classifier accuracy at the expense of the accumulator throughput decrease (see Fig.4) which in turn affects an overall system performance.

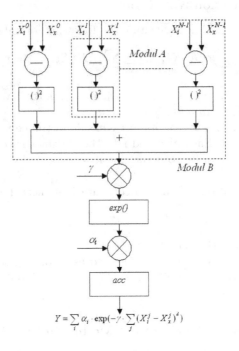

Fig. 4. Block diagram of the classification module

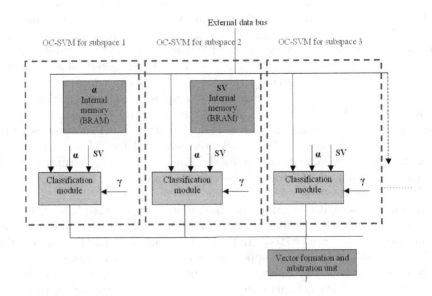

Fig. 5. Block diagram of the multimodule structure

The classifier (presented in Fig. 4) yields one bit results which reflects an occurrence of a feature of interest within an image. Therefore in order to take a full advantage of an external bus throughput, classification results are compacted into 32 bit bundles and sent to a host processor as such. Thereafter the GPP transforms those binary values into pixels to form a black-and-white image depicting the features of interest.

4.3   Architecture of the Implementation in GPU

In case of GPU implementation whole image is transfered to global memory. Each pixel is computed by single thread. Therefore as it is shown in Fig.6 in each block 512 pixels are processed. Each thread reads value of pixel form global memory, then computes SVM classifier formula (1) for one point of image and writes result back to shared memory (at the same location as pixel value). Apart from values of points of image shared memory stores sphere radius and supportive vectors derived from training process needed to classify each pixel. In this case each shared memory contains 512*3 bytes of image, 16*3 bytes of supportive vectors and 16 bytes of sphere radius (Fig.6). When the number of points exceeds 512 then they are divided to multiple blocks of GPU card.

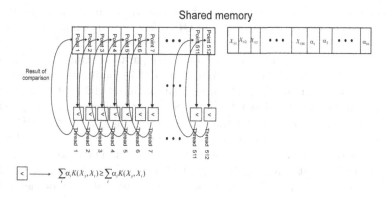

Fig. 6. Diagram of the SVM implementation in GPU

5   Implementation Results

The classification algorithm was initially implemented on GPP in C++ and the OpenCV library was used. A set of 16 support vectors was generated which described a human skin, each of which are 32bit RGB colors.

Fig. 7 and 8 represent experimental results for the randomly chosen images. It can be noticed that the system wrongly classified some parts of the image. Unfortunately the system often confuses bright objects with a human skin. One way to improve the accuracy is increasing the contrast between an object and a background. Similar result of accuracy improvement may be achieved when a

Fig. 7. Original image (before segmentation)

Fig. 8. Results of human skin segmentation

larger number of supportive vectors is employed but it is done at a expanse of a loss of classifier's generalization feature.

Time required to execute the following algorithm on GPP, FPGA and GPU is presented in Tab. 2 and Fig.9 . They show that in case of less number of pixels FPGA platform is faster than CPU and GPU. When more points are processed the GPU card is fastest and CPU is the slowest execution unit. In case of more points GPU cards takes advantage of its massive parallel architecture. Therefore it is faster than pipelined FPGA architecture. FPGA hardware implementation according to the formula (1) (assuming that no input data fetch delay is introduced) can be calculated as follows: $16(SVM) \times 480(pixels) \times 480(pixels) \cong 4 \times 10^6$ clock cycles. Consequently theoretical processing time for 200 MHz equals 0.02s. Due to a low resources consumption a single FPGA can accommodate several modules which boost a performance several times. The power consumption in case of FPGA (Virtex-5 LX220) is about 15 watts, GPU (Nvidia Tesla m2090) consumption is 250 watts. The implementation results of the module on DRC AC2020 [12] were presented in Tab. 1. Tranfer times are described in Tab. 3.

It is worth noting that a number of coefficients has a large impact on the resources occupation in case of FPGA. On the GPU platform coefficients occupied very small part of shared memory. In this particular implementation the number of the coefficient is three (R, G, B).

Table 1. Implementation results of the module building block in Impulse C (see Fig.4)

# 4-input LUT	# flip-flops	# BRAM
122,637[83%]	59,208[42%]	2,049[6%]

Table 2. Implementation results

Number of pixels	# GPU [ms]	# CPU [ms]	# FPGA [ms]
2048	0,6	1,82	0,16896
10240	0,74	36,1	0,8448
51200	1,58	180,7	4,224
204800	5,13	714	16,896
512000	12,15	1813,54	42,24

Table 3. Transfer time

Number of pixels	# GPU [ms]	# FPGA [ms]
2048	0,45	1,12
10240	0,49	1,22
51200	0,66	1,65
204800	1,3	3,25
512000	2,6	6,5

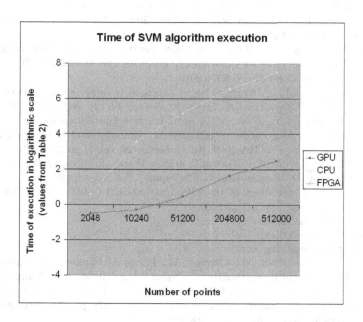

Fig. 9. Chart with implementation results

The classification module in case of FPGA is a fully pipelined structure and it is capable of working at the frequency of 200 MHz. Each module generates a single result every n clock cycles where n denotes number of the support vectors employed.

Support vectors along with α,γ,τ are generated on the host side (by GPP) and are sent to the FPGA and GPU only once for the whole computations. The both implementations perform the classification for all the X vectors and sends the results back to the host processor.

6   Summary

In this paper implementation results of the selected parts of the fast image segmentation were presented along with some performance analysis. Both FPGA and GPU implementation were discussed. GPU significantly surpasses FPGA and GPP in the high volume calculations. It is worth emphasizing that SVM can be easily parallelized due to its structure which makes it an ideal candidate for GPU implementation.

Acknowledgments. The work presented in this paper was financed through the research program - *Synat*.

References

1. Mueller, R., Teubner, J., Alonso, G.: Data Processing on FPGAs. In: Systems Group, Department of Computer Science, VLDB 2009, ETH Zurich, Switzerland, Lyon, France, August 24-28 (2009)
2. Jun, T.: A color image segmentation algorithm based on region growing. In: 2010 2nd International Conference on Computer Engineering and Technology (ICCET), April 16-18, vol. 6, pp.V6-634–V6-637 (2010)
3. Farmer, M.E., Jain, A.K.: A wrapper-based approach to image segmentation and classification. IEEE Transactions on Image Processing 14(12), 2060–2072 (2005)
4. Lan, Y., Li, C., Zhang, Y., Zhao, X.: A novel image segmentation method based on random walk. In: Asia-Pacific Conference on Computational Intelligence and Industrial Applications, PACIIA 2009, November 28-29, vol. 1, pp. 207–210 (2009)
5. Vapnik, V.N.: The Nature of Statistical Learning Theory. Springer (2000)
6. Ben-Hur, A., Horn, D., Siegelmann, H.T., Vapnik, V.N.: A support vector clustering method. In: Proceedings of the 15th International Conference on Pattern Recognition, vol. 2, pp. 724–727 (2000)
7. http://www.alpha-data.com/
8. http://www.nallatech.com/
9. http://www.picocomputing.com/
10. Baxter, R., Booth, S., Bull, M., Cawood, G., Perry, J., Parsons, M., Simpson, A., Trew, A., McCormick, A., Smart, G., Smart, R., Cantle, A., Chamberlain, R., Genest, G.: Maxwell - a 64 FPGA Supercomputer. In: Second NASA/ESA Conference on Adaptive Hardware and Systems (AHS 2007), pp. 287–294 (2007)
11. www.silicongraphics.ru/pdf/rasc_data.pdf
12. www.drccomputer.com/pdfs/DRC_Accelium_Overview.pdf
13. www.vhdl.org/fphdl/
14. Wielgosz, M., Jamro, E., Wiatr, K.: Hardware Implementation of the Exponent Based Computational Core for an Exchange-Correlation Potential Matrix Generation. In: Wyrzykowski, R., Dongarra, J., Karczewski, K., Wasniewski, J. (eds.) PPAM 2009, Part I. LNCS, vol. 6067, pp. 115–124. Springer, Heidelberg (2010)

Automatic Floorplanning and Interface Synthesis of Island Style Reconfigurable Systems with GOAHEAD

Christian Beckhoff[1], Dirk Koch[2], and Jim Torreson[2]

[1] ReCoBus
christian@recobus.de
[2] University of Oslo, Norway
{dirk,jimtoer}@ifi.uio.no

Abstract. When floorplanning a reconfigurable system on an FPGA, we have to identify the area of the device in which modules share resources over time. This process should minimize internal fragmentation without impacting the performance of the static and module routing. Floorplanning reconfigurable systems also comprises the layout of a reconfigurable areas interface around its borders. In this article, we introduce a novel floorplanning algorithms that is based on an initial placement proposal created by the Xilinx vendor placer. The algorithms are built-in in our tool GOAHEAD. We apply our algorithms in a case study where we automate the design of a reconfigurable system.

1 Introduction

When building static only systems, a user has at least to select a target device, constrain the clock frequency and define the I/O pinning. The further placement and routing is then carried out by the vendor tools. Manually floorplanning is usually not necessary. When building a reconfigurable system however, a designer *has to* manually first, assign a physical location to each reconfigurable area and second, manually place the interface of a reconfigurable area along its borders. This process is called floorplanning a reconfigurable area and is a crucial step as it influences the later placement and routing of both the static part of the system and the partial modules.

1.1 Related Work

Related work in the field of floorplanning reconfigurable systems can be categorized by two means: First, how is the placement of the reconfigurable area derived? Second, how is the layout of reconfigurable areas interface derived?

For fully manual floorplanning of reconfigurable areas, low level CAD tools have been developed (e.g. PlanAhead from Xilinx [1] or academic tools like [2–4]). The authors in [5] present a tool for building reconfigurable systems that is also capable of floorplanning. However, details about the implemented floorplaning algorithm are omitted. The approaches in [6, 7] apply simulated annealing (SA) for floorplanning, however they do not discuss the interface layout of the resulting floorplan. Reference [8] proposes *kernel tessellation*: First, all reconfigurable areas are clustered by the resource types they require. Then, starting with the most demanding area, an initial area on the chip (called kernel) is iteratively enlarged until all resource requirements are met. The

C. Hochberger et al. (Eds.): ARCS 2013, LNCS 7767, pp. 303–316, 2013.

allocated resources are then no longer available for subsequent areas. This process is repeated several times each starting with different initial kernels. The resulting floorplans are compared by wire length between regions and fragmentation. However, the interface layout and how this approach impacts the static and partial module routing is not discussed.

The approaches in [9, 10] use both SA for floorplanning. The authors in [9] place the interfaces at *predefined locations* around the reconfigurable area without further specifying how these locations are derived. In [10], a *covering heuristic* is introduced to layout the interface: The authors consider the placement of all modules that shall be executed in a reconfigurable area and sort the tiles in the reconfigurable area by the number of modules occupying a tile. Then, the heuristic distributes the interface over these tiles starting with the tile that is most frequently occupied by modules. Note that this heuristic does not favor routing to carry chains used for e.g. adders or comparators and therefore may result in routing congestion.

After a manual placement of the reconfigurable area, the authors in [11] use SA only to layout the interface. However, to evaluate the fitness of each SA iteration a complete place and route step is required rendering this approach time-consuming. In [12], both the placement of the reconfigurable area and the definition of the interface layout as SA based. Again, the the fitness evaluation requires time-consuming place and route steps. Table 1 summarizes the presented approaches:

Table 1. Classification of related work by their approach to place the reconfigurable area and to layout its interface

	Reconfigurable Area Placement	Interface Layout
PlanAhead [1]	manual	manual
Academic tools [2–4]	manual	manual
Göhringer et al.	not discussed	not discussed
Craven et al. [6]	SA	not discussed
He et al. [7]	SA	not discussed
Vipin et al. [8]	Kernel Tessellation	not discussed
Singhal et al. [9]	SA	predefined layout
Montone et al. [10]	SA	Covering heuristic
Carver et al. [11]	manual	SA
Yousuf et al. [12]	SA	SA

1.2 Paper Contribution

In this paper, we present novel algorithms for floorplanning a reconfigurable area and for layouting the interface of the reconfigurable area around its borders. Our work differs from the approaches [11, 12] in that we base on an initial placement carried out by the Xilinx placer taking advantage of all built-in placement optimizations. From this initial placement we derive the position and layout (i.e. the aspect ratio) of the reconfigurable region. Moreover, we determine an interface layout optimized for routing the static system and the partial modules. These results are used to physically implement the static system and the modules in separate implementation steps. Note that due to our algorithms, this is carried out without further manual interaction. We are removing iterative place and route steps of the simulated annealing approaches [11, 12] that can easily take more than a day.

Consider an FPGA-based system where different video processing modules are used mutually exclusively over time (see Figure 1 a)). Due to the different functionality of the modules, they require different number of resources in terms of look-up tables (LUTs), multiplier blocks (DSPs), or memory blocks (BRAMs). Moreover, the different modules might further have different interfaces. However, rather than using multiplexers to select a specific video function, we now assume that the system uses partial reconfiguration to use the FPGA more efficiently (see Figure 1 b)). The reconfigurable area must provide sufficient resources (e.g. CLBs, DSPs, and BRAMs) for hosting *any* of the partial modules. Furthermore the reconfigurable area must provide the *unioned* interface of all modules.

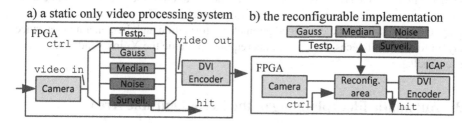

Fig. 1. a) Static only implementation of a video processing system. The video stream is demultiplexed into either one of the filters whose output is in turn multiplexed into a DVI encoder. The resource savings due to partial reconfiguration come at the expense of additional reconfiguration logic interfacing the Internal Configuration Access Port (ICAP) and corresponding drivers or their equivalent hardware implementation.

After deriving 1) the resource requirements and 2) the unioned interface, we have to 3) place the reconfigurable area on the FPGA such that static and module routing are optimized. As outlined in [2], the first two steps can be carried out with our tool GOA-HEAD. In this paper, we reveal how GOAHEAD automates the whole process of building a reconfigurable system from a high level system specification – over floorplanning the reconfigurable area – all the way down to the final bitstreams. The contributions of this paper are as follows:

- a design flow and corresponding system specification for automatically implementing island style reconfigurable systems with our tool GOAHEAD (Section 2)
- an algorithm for floorplanning reconfigurable areas (Section 3)
- an algorithm for layouting the interface of a reconfigurable area (Section 4)
- an evaluation and a case study applying our algorithms (Section 5)

2   Specifying an Island Style Reconfigurable System

The widely used hardware description languages VHDL and Verilog have been developed for *static* hardware designs and they provide no constructs required for automating the design of *dynamically* run-time reconfigurable systems. For example, there is no construct for dynamically instantiating a module into a system; or there is no construct to describe that a set of modules is executed mutually exclusive and that they can share FPGA resources with the help of reconfiguration.

Before building a reconfigurable system with GOAHEAD, a designer has to define groups of modules that can share resources in a reconfigurable region over time and those modules that are executed permanently and therefore become part of the static system. In this paper, we assume that only one module is hosted exclusively in a reconfigurable region at a point in time. In our flow, a designer provides the modules that will share a reconfigurable area as netlists. From these netlists, GOAHEAD computes the resource and interface requirements. The result is used to determine the geometry information (i.e. the placement and shape of a reconfigurable areas) and the interface layout. The interface layout is a user friendly specification of the wires the will be used to route signal across the border of a reconfigurable area. The wires act like pins in a plug. GOAHEAD uses the computed geometry information and the generated interface layout to create all necessary constraints required to guide the Xilinx vendor place and route tools.

3   Automatic Floorplanning of the Reconfigurable Area

At beginning of the floorplanning, GOAHEAD will parse in the module netlists and count for each module the resource consumption $r = (C, D, B)$; with C, D, and B denoting the number of CLBs, DSP tiles and Block RAMs for a module. The overall resource requirement r_{req} of the reconfigurable area is then the componentwise maximum over the resource requirements over all modules. Note that r_{req} may be selected larger in order to get less densely packed modules that can be routed more easily.

For building a union interface, GOAHEAD scans the entities of each module sharing a reconfigurable area. Here, the tool supports VHDL, XDL, and EDIF specifications of the module. Now, GOAHEAD creates an artificial HDL *union module* that does not carry out any functions but that during synthesis requires exactly the same amount of resources as calculated in r_{req} and provides the unioned interface of all partial modules. The primitives of the union module are densely intermeshed in order to create a clustering of the primitives in the union module. Consequently, the placed union module will represent an obstacle for the static system as the reconfigurable area would do. Note that GOAHEAD permits static signals to cross reconfigurable regions. GOAHEAD generates instantiation VHDL code for the union module that the designer uses to manually instantiate the union module as a placeholder for the reconfigurable area in the static design. We now let the placer place the static system together with the union module without applying further placement constraints. Therefore, we exploit the built-in optimizations of the vendor tools. GOAHEAD will then use the placement results of the union module to derive the placement of a reconfigurable area. For this reason,

GOAHEAD reads in the placed netlist (in the XDL format) and determines the *center of mass* of the union module by calculating the arithmetic mean of the position of all its primitives. Finding the best position for a reconfigurable area is however a hard combinatorial problem even if we only consider rectangular shaped reconfigurable areas. In an FPGA that provides $n \times m$ tiles, there are

$$\sum_{i=1}^{n}\sum_{j=1}^{m} i \cdot j = \sum_{i=1}^{n} i \cdot \sum_{j=1}^{m} j = \frac{n(n+1)}{2} \cdot \frac{m(m+1)}{2} \qquad (1)$$

possible different rectangles to enumerate the problem of finding a rectangle that provides the required resources with a minimal internal fragmentation and the best routing. Equation 1 shows that enumerating all rectangles has a complexity of $O(n^2 \times m^2)$. However, the solution space can be reduced significantly, as shown in the following.

Vertical Clustering due to Clock Regions: First of all, the tile grid is coarsely-grained in vertical direction due to the column-wise reconfiguration scheme. This means that in Xilinx FPGAs (Virtex-4, Spartan-6 and beyond), only larger portions of the resources can be atomically reconfigured without the risk of side effects. On these devices, the smallest atomic unit that can be reconfigured affects the resources in a single tile column (CLB, DSP, BRAM) that has the height of a clock region. For a Spartan-6 device, this means that a reconfigurable tile has a height of 4 BRAM or DSP tiles or 16 CLB primitives. In the following, the height h of a reconfigurable area will hence always be an integer multiple of the height of a clock region.

Resource Regularities along columns: Due to the column based layout of the primitives, the resources change only if we move sidewards, while the resources along a column are all equal. This observation allows us to represent a single row by a resource string R (also used in [13]). In a resource string, each character represents the resource type within its column (see Figure 3 for an example).

DSP Chaining: DSP and logic tiles are often chained to implement wider datapaths that consists of chains of multiple adjacent DSP or logic tiles. Consequently, we also have to consider the length of DSP and carry chains. With Algorithm 1, we can thus a priori compute 1) the minimal heights $h_{min}(d)$ as a function of the number of allocated DSP columns d and 2) feasible values of d that provide enough resources for all DSP chains.

Starting with $d = 1$ in each iteration, we allocate d DSP columns each spanning the full height of the FPGA. Then we bind each DSP chain from each module to the allocated d columns in a balanced manner, minimizing the difference between the filling levels of all columns. The resulting maximal filling level of all columns is rounded up to an integer multiple of a clock region h_d and stored: $h_{min}(d) = h_d$. If in an iteration the amount of allocated columns d does not provide sufficient resources for all DSP chains, the binding fails ($h_{min}(d) = \infty$). Consequently, allocations with less or equal d DSP columns are not further considered. In each following iteration, we allocate one more column, until the additionally allocated column does not yield in a further reduction (i.e until $h_{min}(d-1) = h_{min}(d)$) or until the number of allocated columns exceeds the number of available columns on the device.

Algorithm 1. Compute the array of minimal heights $h_{min}(d)$ for the number of allocated DSP columns d and all feasible values of d.

---

  if DSP_Chains $= \emptyset$ **then**
    return 0
  end if
  $h_{min} = \emptyset$ ▷ store results in this array
  $d = 1$ ▷ allocate the first column
  while $d \leq$ #columns on device **do**
    h_d = round(strip_pack(DSP_Chains, d))
    if strip_pack failed **then**
      $h_{min}(d) = \infty$ ▷ unfeasible, do not further consider d
    else
      $h_{min}(d) = h_d$ ▷ store minimal height of d
    end if
    if $h_{min}(d-1) = h_{min}(d)$ **then**   ▷ no further reduction
      break
    end if
    $d = d + 1$ ▷ allocate one more column
  end while
  return h_{min} ▷ return result

In general, binding DSP chains to columns states a strip packing of DSP chains into a variable number of columns. Note that we use a simple best fit heuristic (bind the longest chain to the currently least filled column) for solving the strip pack problem. This takes into account that also the vendor placer will not necessarily find an optimal fitting of DSP chains into the allocated columns.

Logic Chaining. In the last section, we considered that the technology mapping can result in chains of cascaded DSP blocks (e.g. when mapping wide multipliers). As a consequence, an individual DSP chain is always mapped atomically to a single DSP column of the FPGA. In addition to this, chaining is commonly used for logic primitives. Here, carry chain logic is used to cascade multiple logic primitives (i.e., slices on Xilinx FPGAs). In many cases (e.g., adders and counters), the Xilinx vendor tools (ISE 13.4) are able to automatically break a chain over multiple logic columns. This is not available for wide comparators that also use carry chain logic. However, as a module typically consists of more logic columns than DSP columns and because of the finer vertical placement grid for logic columns, mapping logic carry chains is far easier than mapping DSP chains. Moreover, logic chains are typically relatively short. For example, a 32-bit comparator is mapped to a chain with only three slices, when targeting Virtex-6 or Spartan-6 FPGAs. On the FPGA grid, this comparator is shorter than the height of a single multiplier block. Consequently, we are not further considering logic chaining in our placement algorithm.

With the representation of the heterogeneous FPGAs resource as a resource string, and the knowledge of $h_{min}(d)$, it is possible to fully enumerate the remaining solution space to find a rectangular reconfigurable area. This area has to provide the required resources at a minimal internal fragmentation. Let the set of all sub-resource strings of R be defined as $S(R)$. Let for any resource substring $s \in S(R)$ the function $\#(x,s)$ return the number of occurrences of x in s. We then define the following functions that return the number of CLBs, DSP, and BRAM tiles included in s: $CLB(s) = \#(C,s) \cdot \lambda_C$, $DSP(s) = \#(D,s) \cdot \lambda_D$, and $BRAM(s) = \#(B,s) \cdot \lambda_B$, whereby e.g. λ_C (λ_D, λ_B) denotes the number of CLBs (DSPs and BRAMs) in a single sub column that spans the height of a clock region. A resource triple $r = (C,D,B)$ for a resource substring $s \in S(R)$ and a height h is then calculated by the resource function:

$$r(s,h) = (CLB(s) \cdot h, DSP(s) \cdot h, BRAM(s) \cdot h)$$

Two resource triples can be compared componentwise, e.g the resource triple $r_r = (C_r, D_r, B_r)$ fulfills the resource requirements $r_{req} = (C_{req}, D_{req}, B_{req})$, iff for each resource type r_{req} requires less or equal resources: $r_r \geq r_{req} \Leftrightarrow C_r \geq C_{req} \wedge D_r \geq D_{req} \wedge B_r \geq B_{req}$. The required height h for a substring s is the maximum of all componentwise minimum resource requirements and is given in terms of clock regions heights:

$$h(s, r_{req}) = max \left\{ \left\lceil \frac{C_{req}}{CLB(s)} \right\rceil, h_{min}(\#(D,s)), \left\lceil \frac{B_{req}}{BRAM(s)} \right\rceil \right\}$$

The fragmentation denotes how many resources will be left unused, when selecting a reconfigurable region of height h over the resource string s: $fragmentation(s,h,r_{req}) = r_{req} - resources(s,h)$. Note that the fragmentation has multiple dimensions. Consequently, minimizing the internal fragmentation of a reconfigurable area is a multi objective problem.

3.1   Horizontal Placement of Reconfigurable Regions

Now, in order to find the horizontal position of the reconfigurable area on the FPGA, we consider all tuples (s,h) that provide minimal fragmentation:

$$min\{fragmentation(s,h(s,r_{req}),r_{req}) \mid h \leq h_{max} \wedge h_{min}(DSP(s)) \neq \infty \wedge$$
$$s \in S(R) \wedge r(s,h) \geq r_{req}\}$$

Note that, if the length of the resource string R is $l = |R|$, then the number of substrings in R is:

$$|S(R)| = \sum_{i=1}^{l} i = \frac{l(l+1)}{2}$$

However, there are a lot of duplicates among all substrings which reduce the number of necessary iterations to find the resource string height tuple with minimal fragmentation. For instance, the full resource string of even the large Virtex-6 SX475T FPGA is only 134 characters long and thus provides 9045 substrings (including 6764 unique strings). The device provides nine rows of clock regions. Consequently, an exhaustive search is a process taking only a few seconds on the largest available FPGA. Figure 2 shows examples for the available resources with in an assumed clock region for three different resource strings.

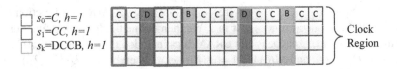

Fig. 2. Enumerating over all substrings of the resource string means horizontally sweeping a rectangle. Each rectangle s_0, s_1, and s_k provides different resources ($resources(s_0, 1) = (4, 0, 0), resources(s_1, 1) = (8, 0, 0), resources(s_k, 1) = (8, 1, 1)$).

In Figure 3, the substring *DCCB* with the minimal fragmentation occurs twice in the resource string and both occurrences result in the same fragmentation. If we end up with more than one tuple of resource string s and height h that yield in a minimal fragmentation, we calculate the center of mass of each tuple and pick the tuple that is the closest to the center of mass of the union module. If the whole system does not use all available resources on the FPGA (resource slack), we will alternatively take a higher fragmentation into account and use a placement that is closer to the union modules center of mass (see the center placement in Figure 3) to favor routability over area consumption. In other words, we allow a fragmentation of the reconfigurable area if there is sufficient resource slack available for improving the routing of the system. In a final step, we move the rectangle described by s and h in a vertical direction clock region-wise to the closest position of the union modules center of mass.

4   Interface Floorplanning

In our previous papers [2] and [14], we outlined that the fundamental task in implementing physical interfaces for reconfigurable areas is the allocation of physical routing resources and the binding of each module interface signal to an allocated wire. A wire can cross the boundary of the reconfigurable area in any cardinal direction (N, S, W, and E). In addition, our flow allows us to *interleave* signals and thus to connect double[1] the amount of wires per row (E and W) and column (S or N).

We define *interface floorplanning* as 1) the assignment of a cardinal direction, 2) the allocation of CLBs around the reconfigurable area, and 3) the binding of each interface signal to an allocated CLB. GOAHEAD generates an *interface placeholder module* that provides the same interface as the union module does, however the interface placeholder module does not consume any further resources. At the center of the interface placeholder module GOAHEAD places primitives that serve as dummy sinks and sources for input and output signals of the reconfigurable area. In addition, GOAHEAD generates placement constraints that exclusively assign the interface placeholder module at the position derived in Section 3. Finally, the static system is placed together with the interface placeholder module by the Xilinx placer.

---

[1] We may double the amount of wires using *double lines* that are available on all recent Xilinx FPGA. However, it is even possible to interleave *quad lines* that span the distance of four CLBs, consequently we connect four times the amount of wires. However, quad lines interleaving is currently not available in automatic mode.

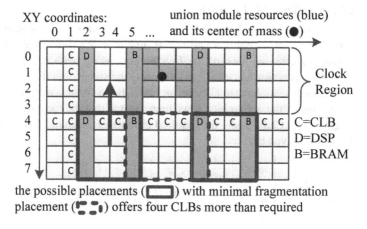

XY coordinates: union module resources (blue)
                         and its center of mass (●)

the possible placements (▭) with minimal fragmentation
placement (▞▞) offers four CLBs more than required

Fig. 3. An FGPA with different resources (C,D,B) and a placed module union (blue). The resources on the FPGA are identical in a given column. The resources along a row can be represented by the resource string CCDCCBCCCDCCBCC with one character for each column
abbreviating the resource type of the column [13]. Each DSP and Block-RAM spans the height
of four CLBs. For brevity we assume in figures that the height of a clock region is the height of
a DSP or Block-RAM. The floorplanning algorithm found two possible horizontal placements
with $s = DCCB$ and $h = 1$ that both provide enough resources and minimal fragmentation. The
left placement is however closer to the union modules center of mass. The placement has to be
moved upwards (indicated by the arrow) such that the placements center of mass gets closest to
the union modules center of mass. Note that with $s = BCCCD$ and $h = 1$ we could also place
the reconfigurable area in the very center. However, this option is only used if the system has a
resource slack of one extra CLB column.

4.1   Assigning a Cardinal Direction

The resulting XDL netlists provides full placement information for all primitives and all
outpins and inpins of each net. Based on this placement information, the GOAHEAD interface floorplanning algorithm views nets from the interface placeholder module point
of view and distinguishes between the following two types of nets:

1. *Outputs Nets:* The nets *outpin* is part of the interface placeholder module and the
   net has at least one inpin located on a primitive that is not part of the interface
   placeholder module.
2. *Input Nets:* At least one *inpin* of the net is part of the interface placeholder module
   and the nets outpin is not part of the interface placeholder module.

Now, we move the before derived rectangular shape r (see Section 3) of the reconfigurable area over the interface placeholder modules center of mass and determine for
each output and input net in which cardinal direction it crosses the border of the reconfigurable area. The naming scheme for nets in XDL allows GOAHEAD, to recompose
different input and output nets to a signal vector. GOAHEAD clusters all signal vectors
according to the cardinal direction where it crosses the border of the reconfigurable area
and thus assigns a cardinal direction to each complete input and output vector.

4.2 Allocating Configurable Logic Blocks

In our papers [2] and [14], we show, how we can connect up $n_i = 8$ input and $n_o = 8$ signal bits per CLB row or column and signal direction. We define the number of input and output bits crossing each of the four borders as ω_c^d with $c \in \{E, W, S, N\}$ denoting the cardinal direction and $d \in \{I, O\}$ denoting the signal direction (either input or output). Consequently, we have to allocate ω_c^I / n_i CLBs to connect the input bits and ω_c^O / n_o CLBs to connect the output bits. If we then assume that the reconfigurable area is h_c CLBs high and w_c CLBs wide, the required number of columns or rows n_c for a cardinal direction c is given by:

$$
n_c = \begin{cases} max\left\{ \left\lceil \frac{\omega_c^I}{h_c \cdot n_i} \right\rceil, \left\lceil \frac{\omega_c^O}{h_c \cdot n_o} \right\rceil \right\} & \text{if } c \in \{E, W\} \\ max\left\{ \left\lceil \frac{\omega_c^I}{w_c \cdot n_i} \right\rceil, \left\lceil \frac{\omega_c^O}{w_c \cdot n_o} \right\rceil \right\} & \text{if } c \in \{S, N\} \end{cases}
\tag{2}
$$

4.3 Binding Signals to Allocated Configurable Logic Blocks

After allocation, we bind each signal bit to wire of a CLB. The signal to wire binding is implemented by connecting signals to primitive inputs and outputs in the allocated CLB and by constraining the routing such that for each wire only one possible routing path exists to cross the boundary of the reconfigurable area. Starting with the widest signal vector, we partition each signal vector into slices of n_i bits for input and n_o bits for output signals. Then, we distribute the bit slices over the allocated columns in a row wise manner starting with the least significant bit and the button most CLB. This distribution scheme directly correlates with the mapping of operands to carry chains. The distribution of signals onto CLBs states physically layouting an interface of a reconfigurable area. We connect vector signals only in E, W cardinal direction as this fits best the vertical mapping of signal bits to primitives and operands. Table 2 gives examples of vertical wire densities for commonly used primitives and operands. According to that results, we connect up to 8 signal bits of a vector per CLB row. The vectors are placed into the rows by firstly considering the vector with the longest Manhattan distance for the connection to the interface placeholder module. The process is repeated, until all signal vectors are connected. If one cardinal direction $\{E, W\}$ is filled completely, the process continues with the entire other cardinal direction $\{W, E\}$. In this case, we force the router to either cross the reconfigurable region[2] or to route around it. However, this only done for the shortest nets.

4.4 Floorplanning Multiple Reconfigurable Areas

Our algorithms presented in Section 3 and 4 can floorplan a single island style reconfigurable area. However, both algorithms are also capable of floorplanning multi island style reconfigurable systems. In this case, we use an individual union module for each island. All union modules are then placed in a single initial placement step that is carried out by the vendor placer. Our floorplanning algorithms are applied iteratively to

---

[2] By default, GOAHEAD will allocate some wires within the reconfigurable region to be used for routing nets of the static system directly through the reconfigurable area.

Table 2. Vertical wire density of different operators and primitives per switch matrix row on two Xilinx FPGAs. For primitives spanning over multiple vertically aligned switch matrices, the peak and (average) wire density is listed. In case of the 1-bit BRAM, the values are for the address vector while for the other memory examples, the values are for the data vector.

primitive or function	ADD/ SUB	compare		single BRAM memory			single MAC				
		$A \geq B$	A=B	1-bit	32-bit	72-bit	A $\cdot$	B	+ C		= P
Spartan-6	4	8	12	13 (3.5)	16 (8)	18	13 (4.5)	9 (4.5)	12		13 (12)
Virtex-6	4	8	12	7 (3)	8 (6.4)	16 (14.4)	8 (6)	4 (3.6)	12 (9.6)		12 (9.6)

each different union module. In the first iteration, all resources on the FPGA are available. However, each iteration results in a placement of one island and thus reduces the available resources for following iterations. The implementation and evaluation of this approach are left for future research.

5   Case Study and Evaluation

We used our floorplanning approach to implement the system shown in Figure 1b). While some of the partial modules need only a few hundred logic slices (e.g., one video overlay module and the background module), a generic convolution filter uses the component-wise resource maximum, which is $r_{req} = (205CLBs, 15DSPs, 8BRAMs)$. Figure 4 show the different steps for an implementation on a Spartan-6 LX16 FPGA (Nexys 3 board). In this example, there exist only two possible regions with minimal fragmentation. While both alternatives were fully routable, only the one that was closer to the center of mass of the union module meet the 100 MHz timing requirement.

Figure 4 shows highlighted the video input and output modules. Based on the relative position of these modules with respect to the reconfigurable area, GOAHEAD derived the shown interface binding at the east border of the reconfigurable region.

For an evaluation experiment, we used a synthetic benchmark, as shown in Figure 5a). As a reference system, we took a Spartan-6 LX45 FPGA with five mostly identical modules. However, one of the modules was actually replaced by a reconfigurable region providing the same number of resources $r_{req} = (576CLBs, 12DSPs, 24BRAMs)$. We used identical modules, to get a strong impact of the placement on the clock frequency with less tool noise. For the same reason, we have used a very regular netlist (kind of a shifting network). The overall resource consumption was 75% for a relative densely meshed netlist. In this example, there exist 21 possible placement positions for the reconfigurable region. We used GOAHEAD to try out all of the 21 candidates in order to determine the achievable clock frequency for all of them. In addition, we used a union module in an initial placement run and determined the center of mass of the union, as depicted in Figure 5b).

Figure 5c) reveals that only four regions resulted in a complete routing, while all other experiments failed to route (within 4 hours). Our algorithm started to try the first reconfigurable region (i.e., the closest region to the center of mass), but failed with a few nets that were left unrouted. However, trying the second closest region resulted in

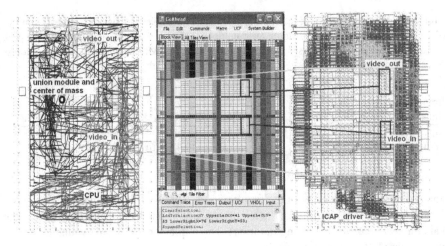

Fig. 4. Video system from Figure 1b). Left: placed system with union module, middle: automatically generated floorplan in GOAHEAD , right: the final routed static system with the reconfigurable region.

a successfully routed design. Note that the distance difference is very little between the first two cases. In this experiment, there were three sweet spots that result in (almost) successful routing. Only one sweet spot had two solutions and that was the one closest to the center of mass. Consequently our algorithm starts trying the most promising positions for the reconfigurable region first.

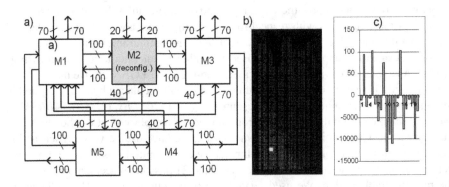

Fig. 5. Evaluation of the partial floorplanning algorithm. a) example system, b) placed system with union module, and c) pos: achieved clock frequency in MHz, neg: number of unrouted nets. The reconfigurable islands are listed from left to right in ascending order given by the distance from the unions' center of mass.

6 Conclusion

In this paper, we presented a flow with minimal user interaction from a system specification down to bitstreams with our tool GOAHEAD. The flow comprises two novel algorithms for floorplanning a island style reconfigurable area and for placing interface signals along the border of the reconfigurable area. Both algorithms are based on an initial placement of the Xilinx placer in order to remove the time-consuming iterations needed by related simulated annealing approaches. The algorithms are integrated in our tool GOAHEAD which is available at our project website [15].

References

1. Xilinx, Inc., PlanAhead User Guide 2009
2. Beckhoff, C., Koch, D., Torresen, J.: GoAhead: A Partial Reconfiguration Framework. In: Proceedings of the 20th IEEE Symposium Field-Programmable Custom Computing Machines (FCCM 2002) (April 2012)
3. Koch, D., Beckhoff, C., Teich, J.: ReCoBus-Builder– a Novel Tool and Technique to Build Statically and Dynamically Reconfigurable Systems for FPGAs. In: Proceedings of International Conference on Field-Programmable Logic and Applications (FPL 2008), Heidelberg, Germany, pp. 119–124 (September 2008)
4. Cancare, F., Santambrogio, M., Sciuto, D.: A Design Flow Tailored for Self Dynamic Reconfigurable Architecture. In: IEEE International Symposium on Parallel and Distributed Processing, IPDPS 2008, pp. 1–8 (April 2008)
5. Gohringer, D., Luhmann, J., Becker, J.: Generatercs: A high-level design tool for generating reconfigurable computing systems. In: 2009 17th IFIP International Conference on Very Large Scale Integration (VLSI-SoC), pp. 159–164 (October 2009)
6. Craven, S.D., Athanas, P.M.: Dynamic Hardware Development. Int. J. Reconfig. Comp. (2008) (2008)
7. He, R., Liang, G., Ma, Y., Wang, Y., Bian, J.: PDPR: Fine-Grained Placement for Dynamic Partially Reconfigurable FPGAs. In: Choy, O.C.S., Cheung, R.C.C., Athanas, P., Sano, K. (eds.) ARC 2012. LNCS, vol. 7199, pp. 350–356. Springer, Heidelberg (2012)
8. Vipin, K., Fahmy, S.: Architecture-Aware Reconfiguration-Centric Floorplanning for Partial Reconfiguration. Applied Reconfigurable Computing (2012)
9. Singhal, L., Bozorgzadeh, E.: SPECIAL SECTION ON FIELD PROGRAMMABLE LOGIC AND APPLICATIONS - Multi-layer floorplanning for reconfigurable designs. Computers Digital Techniques, IET 1(4), 276–294 (2007)
10. Montone, A., Santambrogio, M.D., Sciuto, D., Memik, S.O.: Placement and Floorplanning in Dynamically Reconfigurable FPGAs. ACM Trans. Reconfigurable Technol. Syst. 3(4), 24:1–24:34 (2010)
11. Carver, J.M., Pittman, R.N., Forin, A.: Automatic Bus Macro Placement for Partially Reconfigurable FPGA Designs. In: Proceedings of the ACM/SIGDA International Symposium on Field Programmable Gate Arrays, FPGA 2009, pp. 269–272. ACM, New York (2009)
12. Yousuf, S., Gordon-Ross, A.: DAPR: Design Automation for Partially Reconfigurable FPGAs. In: Proceedings of the International Conference on Engineering of Reconfigurable Systems and Algorithms (ERSA). CSREA Press (June 2010)

13. Fekete, S., Kamphans, T., Schweer, N., Tessars, C., van der Veen, J., Angermeier, J., Koch, D., Teich, J.: No-break Dnamic Defragmentation of Reconfigurable Devices. In: International Conference on Field Programmable Logic and Applications, FPL 2008, Heidelberg, Germany, pp. 113–118 (September 2008)
14. Koch, D., Beckhoff, C., Torresen, J.: Zero Logic Overhead Integration of Partially Reconfigurable Modules. In: 23rd Symposium on Integrated Circuits and Systems Design (SBCCI), pp. 103–108. ACM (September 2010)
15. CosReCos project website,
http://www.mn.uio.no/ifi/eng-lish/research/projects/cosrecos/

Separable 2D Convolution with Polymorphic Register Files

Cătălin B. Ciobanu[1,2] and Georgi N. Gaydadjiev[1,2]

[1] Computer Engineering Laboratory,
EEMCS, Delft University of Technology,
The Netherlands
{c.b.ciobanu,g.n.gaydadjiev}@tudelft.nl
[2] Department of Computer Science and Engineering
Chalmers University of Technology,
Sweden
{catalin,georgig}@chalmers.se

Abstract. This paper studies the performance of separable 2D convolution on multi-lane Polymorphic Register Files (PRFs). We present a matrix transposition algorithm optimized for PRFs, and a 2D vectorized convolution algorithm which avoids strided memory accesses. We compare the throughput of our PRF to the nVidia Tesla C2050 GPU. The results show that even in bandwidth constrained systems, multi-lane PRFs can outperform the GPU for 9×9 or larger mask sizes.

1 Introduction

Processor designers consider various options to utilize the steadily increasing number of transistors of each new semiconductor technology generation [1]. Further increases of processor clock frequencies are infeasible, as current technology faces severe thermal and power constraints. In recent years, Chip Multiprocessor (CMP) designs became mainstream, along with accelerators targeting specific workloads (e.g., hardware support for encryption algorithms [2] and various Single Instruction Multiple Data Extensions (SIMD) [3] to exploit data level parallelism). Best performance is typically obtained by balancing single threaded performance and multi-processor scalability. When determining the characteristics of a new processor, the potential workloads are carefully examined. However, new, yet unknown workloads will appear in the future, making it close to impossible to provide a single solution. One possibility is to use reconfigurable hardware and runtime partial reconfiguration; ASIC solutions, however, are typically used to obtain the best performance.

When targeting vector architectures such as IBM 370 [4], General Purpose Processors (GPPs) with SIMD extensions such as Altivec [5] or Heterogeneous Multicores as the Cell Broadband Engine [6], the programs need to be optimized according to the width and number of the Vector Registers. In all these systems, the available register file storage is divided in a fixed number of equally sized registers. When a new design changes either the number or the width of the

C. Hochberger et al. (Eds.): ARCS 2013, LNCS 7767, pp. 317–328, 2013.
© Springer-Verlag Berlin Heidelberg 2013

registers, software compatibility is broken and costly software adaptation effort is usually required. As part of the Scalable computer ARChitecture (SARC) [7], the Polymorphic Register File (PRF) [8] has been proposed to provide a relaxed way of programming high performance vector applications, compatible with both FPGA [9] and ASIC [10] technologies. The PRF is designed to be customizable to the various data structures, enabling the programmer to focus on the code functionality instead of describing complex, platform specific, data operations and transfers, while maintaining high performance levels. Contrary to the approach used in previous vector architectures, the PRF is able to dynamically divide the available register storage into multidimensional registers of arbitrary shapes and sizes at runtime. PRFs have been shown to be suitable for computationally intensive workloads such as the Conjugate Gradient (CG) method, Floyd, and dense matrix multiplication [8,7]. It was also suggested that PRFs can potentially save area and power in state of the art many-core systems [11]. The benefits of two-dimensional (2D) PRFs are: i) improved storage efficiency, as the number of registers, as well as their dimensions and sizes are dynamically customized to the workload requirements, and ii) performance gain, by greatly reducing the number of committed instructions.

This paper studies the implementation of separable 2D convolutions using PRFs. More specifically, the main contributions of this paper are:

– A vectorized matrix transposition algorithm, optimized for PRFs;
– A vectorized separable 2D convolution algorithm utilizing our transposition, avoiding strided memory accesses while accessing column-wise input data;
– Performance evaluation of the separable 2D convolution kernel, comparing the throughput with the nVidia Tesla C2050 Graphics Processing Unit (GPU). Starting from mask sizes of 9×9 elements, the multi-lane PRFs outperform the GPU.

The remainder of this paper is organized as follows: the background information and related work are presented in Section 2. The experimental setup is introduced in Section 3. The 2D separable convolution kernel is introduced in Section 4. Our vectorized transposition and 2D convolution algorithms are described in Section 5, and the experimental results are studied in Section 6. Finally, Section 7 concludes the paper.

2   Background and Related Work

A PRF is a parameterizable register file, logically reorganized under software control, by the system / application programmer or by the runtime system, to support multiple register dimensions and sizes simultaneously [8]. Figure 1 provides an example of a 2D PRF of $N = 9$ by $M = 12$ elements, containing 14 registers defined by the Special Purpose Registers (SPR) contents. For each vector register it is necessary to specify the location of the upper left corner (BASE), the shape of the register (REctangular, Main Diagonal or Secondary Diagonal), the dimensions (Horizontal and Vertical Lengths) and the data type

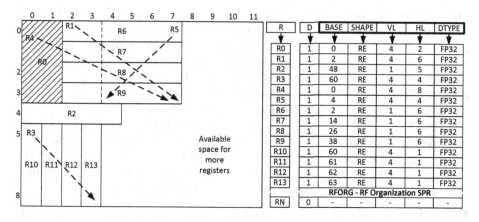

Fig. 1. The Polymorphic Register File (First iteration), N=9, M=12

(DTYPE) - INTeger 8/16/32/64 bit or Floating Point 32/64 bit. The benefits of the PRF are:

- Potential performance gain, by greatly reducing the number of committed instructions, and increasing the number of data elements processed with a single instruction using multi-axis vectorization;
- Improved storage efficiency, as the number of vector registers, their dimensions and sizes are dynamically adjusted during runtime according to the workload requirements, optimizing the use of the available register storage;
- Reduced static code footprint, as fewer, higher level instructions are used to describe the data processing. The same binary instructions may be used regardless of the shapes, dimensions and data types of the vector registers.

Previous works indicate that by employing PRFs, the number of committed instructions may be reduced by up to three orders of magnitude [8]. Compared to the Cell processor, PRFs decrease the number of instructions for a customized, high performance dense matrix multiplication by up to 35 times [7] and improve performance for Floyd and sparse matrix vector multiplication [8]. A CG case study [11] evaluated the scalability of up to 256 PRF based accelerators in a heterogenous multi-core architecture, with two orders of magnitude performance improvements. Furthermore, potential power and area savings were shown by employing fewer PRF cores compared to a Cell processors system.

The mathematical foundations for multi-lane PRF hardware implementations, as well as synthesis results for FPGA and ASIC technologies have been presented in [9] and [10]. The PRF data is stored using a 2D matrix of memory modules with p rows and q columns, enabling the efficient use of up to $p \cdot q$ parallel vector lanes [12]. As in those papers, here we will use "×" to refer to a 2D matrix, and "." to denote multiplication. Five parallel access schemes have been considered for the hardware implementation of the PRF: the single-view Rectangle Only (**ReO**) scheme, which supports conflict free accesses shaped as $p \times q$ rectangles, suggested in [13], and a set of four multi-view schemes, supporting conflict free access to the most common vector operations for scientific and multimedia applications [9]: 1) Rectangle Row (**ReRo**): $p \times q$ rectangle, $p \cdot q$ row, $p \cdot q$ main diagonals if p and $q + 1$ and co-prime, $p \cdot q$ secondary diagonals if p and $q - 1$ are co-prime; 2) Rectangle Column (**ReCo**): $p \times q$ rectangle, $p \cdot q$ column, $p \cdot q$ main diagonals if $p + 1$ and q are co-prime, $p \cdot q$ secondary diagonals if $p - 1$ and q are co-prime; 3) Row Column (**RoCo**): $p \cdot q$ row, $p \cdot q$ column, aligned ($i\%q = 0$ or $j\%q = 0$) $p \times q$ rectangle; 4) Rectangle Transposed Rectangle (**ReTr**): $p \times q$, $q \times p$ rectangles if $p\%q = 0$ or $q\%p = 0$. Using 90nm ASIC technology, the PRF clock frequency varies between 500MHz and 970MHz for storage sizes of up to 512KB and up to 64 vector lanes. Estimated power consumption is also within reasonable limits, up to 8.7W dynamic and 276mW leakage [10].

Related Work: The efficient processing of multidimensional matrices has been targeted by other architectures as well. One approach is to use a memory to memory architecture, such as the Burrows Scientific Processor (BSP) [14]. Being optimized for executing Fortran code, the ISA composed of high level vector instructions with a large number of parameters. The arithmetic units were equipped with 10 registers which are not directly accessible by the programmer. The Polymorphic register file also creates the premises for a high level ISA, but can reuse data directly within the register file. The Complex Streamed Instructions (CSI) [15] approach did not make use of data registers. CSI allows the processing of 2D data streams of arbitrary length, but requires data caches to benefit from data locality. Our approach suggests the register file as a cost-effective alternative of high speed data caches.

The Vector Register Windows (VRW) [16] concept allows grouping of consecutive vector registers in a 2D window. However, one of the dimensions is fixed, contrary to our proposal. The Matrix Oriented Multimedia (MOM) [17] also uses a 2D register file, but with a fixed number of registers which used subword parallelism in order to store up to 16x8 elements. The PRF also supports sub-word level parallelism, but doesn't restrict the number or shapes of the two dimensional registers. A Modified MMX (MMMX) [18] supports 8 multimedia registers, each 96 bits wide, with matrix operations limited to only loads and stores.

The Register Pointer Architecture(RPA) [19] extends scalar processors by adding two additional register files - Dereferencible Register File (DRF) and the Register Pointers (RP). The DRF provides the storage space, while the RP provide indirect access to the DRF. The PRF also uses indirect accessing to a dedicated register file, but the RPA maps scalar registers, while in our proposal each indirection register points to a matrix, being more suitable for vectors.

In order to adjust the number of registers and the total size of the physical register file in a VLIW, FPGA partial reconfiguration is used in [20]. Our approach assumes fixed physical register file size, but at a higher level logical view, offers variable fragmentation of the storage space, eliminating many overhead instructions and costly partial reconfigurations, potentially improving performance. While partial reconfiguration is only available in FPGAs, the PRF does not rely on any specific hardware technology, therefore it can be successfully implemented in both ASICs and FPGAs.

Accelerators for 2D convolutions have been previously implemented in reconfigurable technology [21], as well as bit level [22] and defect tolerant [23] systolic arrays in ASIC.

3   Experimental Setup

We use the simulation infrastructure introduced in [8], which consists of a cycle accurate simulator written in Unisim [24], an extension of SystemC. The PRF is implemented as part of the SARC Scientific Vector Accelerator (SVA), a loosely coupled processor, controlled by a General Purpose Processor (GPP). The experimental results take into consideration the communication between the GPP and the SVA, which is performed by using a number of exchange registers, similar to the Molen processor [25]. We also consider the overhead instructions required to reconfigure the Polymorphic Registers. The separable 2D convolutions are executed entirely on the SVA. Parallel execution between the GPP and the SVA is not considered. The SVA cannot directly accesses the main memory - it can only process data from its Local Store (LS), similar to the Cell Synergistic Processor Units (SPU) [6]. We assume that all input data is present in the Local Store when the SVA starts processing, a situation that can be practically achieved by using DMA transfers and double buffering. Furthermore, we assume that all PRF configurations have the same clock frequency, regardless of the number of vector lanes. Therefore, the experimental results represent an upper bound with respect to performance. A detailed description of the simulation environment is available in [8].

The SVA sends the load and store requests to a Local Store Controller (LSC). While in [8], the LSC was able to handle complex memory requests such as 2D and strided accesses, in this work we assume a more realistic scenario: only 1D contiguous vector loads and stores are supported. Therefore, a simple multi-banked Local Store which uses low order interleaving can provide sufficient bandwidth to the PRF. In our experiments, we set the latency of the LS to 11 cycles, taking into account the overhead incurred by the 1D vector memory accesses, and the bandwidth between the SVA and the LS to 16 bytes, equal to the bus width used in the Cell processor between the SPU and the LS.

4   Separable 2D Convolution

In digital signal processing, each output of the convolution is computed as a weighted sum of neighbouring data items. The coefficients of the products are defined by a mask (also known as the convolution kernel), which is used for all elements of the input array. Intuitively, convolution can be viewed as a blending operation between the input signal and the mask. Because there are no data dependencies, all output elements can be computed in parallel.

The dimensions of a convolution mask are usually odd, making it possible to position the output element in the middle of the mask. For example, considering a 6 element 1D input $I = [\,20\ 21\ 22\ 23\ 24\ 25\,]$ and a 5 element mask $M = [\,1\ 2\ 3\ 4\ 5\,]$. The 1D convolution output corresponding to the 3rd input (22) is $1 \cdot 20 + 2 \cdot 21 + \mathbf{3 \cdot 22} + 4 \cdot 23 + 5 \cdot 24 = 340$. Similarly, the output corresponding to the 4th input (23) is obtained by shifting the mask by one position to the right: $1 \cdot 21 + 2 \cdot 21 + \mathbf{3 \cdot 23} + 4 \cdot 24 + 5 \cdot 25 = 355$.

If the same convolution algorithm is used to for the elements close to the edges of the input, the mask should be applied to elements outside the input array (to the left of the first element, and to the right of the last element of the input). For the rest of this paper we will refer to those elements as "halo" elements. In practice, a convention is made for a default value for halo elements. If we consider the halo elements to be 0, the output corresponding to the 5th input (24) is $1 \cdot 22 + 2 \cdot 23 + \mathbf{3 \cdot 24} + 4 \cdot 25 + 4 \cdot 25 + \mathit{5 \cdot 0} = 240$.

In the case of 2D convolutions, both the input data as well as the mask are 2D matrices. Assuming the 2D mask has **MASK_V** rows and **MASK_H** columns, the number of multiplications required to compute one output element using for 2D convolution is **MASK_V · MASK_H**. Separable 2D convolutions (e.g., the Sobel operator) can be computed as two 1D convolutions on the same data, requiring only **MASK_V + MASK_H** multiplications for each output element. For example [26], the 2D convolution $\begin{bmatrix} -1 & 0 & 1 \\ -2 & 0 & 2 \\ -1 & 0 & 1 \end{bmatrix}$ is equivalent to first applying $\begin{bmatrix} 1 \\ 2 \\ 1 \end{bmatrix}$ and then $[\,-1\ 0\ 1\,]$. In this work, we will focus on accelerating separable 2D convolutions.

Separable 2D convolutions consist of two data dependent steps: a row-wise 1D convolution on the input matrix followed by a column-wise 1D convolution. The column-wise access involves strided memory accesses, which may degrade performance due to bank conflicts in multi-bank memory systems. In order to avoid the strided memory accesses, we propose to transpose outputs of the 1D transpositions while processing the data. This can be performed conflict free by using our **RoCo** memory scheme introduced in Section 2.

5 Vectorizing the 2D Convolution

In this Section, we first introduce the conflict free transposition algorithm. Then, we propose a 2D vectorized separable convolution algorithm for PRFs.

5.1 Conflict Free Transposition

In Figure 1, the dotted angled arrow is used to highlight the size of overlapping registers: R1, R4 and R5 overlap with R 6,7,8, 9, and R3 with R 10,11,12, 13. A block of input data of **VSIZE** = 4 rows and **HSIZE** = 6 columns is loaded from the LS in register R1, and the convolution result is stored in R3.

In order to perform the transposition, the data is loaded in the PRF into row registers, and stored from column registers. The input data consists of **VSIZE**

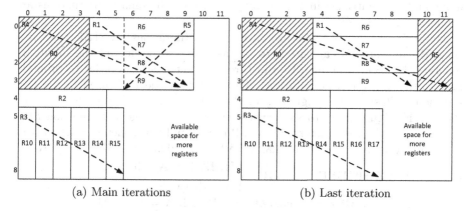

(a) Main iterations   (b) Last iteration

Fig. 2. PRF configurations for the Separable 2D Convolution algorithm

rows containing **HSIZE** elements each - R 6,7,8 and 9, which are loaded from the
LS as 1D accesses. R 10 - 13 single column registers are then stored using regular
1D accesses, effectively transposing the result. The Local Store will only send
and receive data in consecutive addresses, fully utilizing the available bandwidth.
For this example, if the PRF has at least 6 lanes and is implemented using the
RoCo scheme introduced in Section 2, that allows conflict free accesses for both
rows and columns, all the loads and stores used in the transposition can be
performed conflict free. The input data matrix is processed in **VSIZE** × **HSIZE**
blocks, and is stored transposed.

An additional requirement for the PRF is a modified auto-sectioning mechanism which stores the transposed output blocks in a top-to-bottom, left-to-right
(column-wise). The regular auto sectioning instruction loads the input matrices
in a left-to-right, top-to-bottom (row-wise) order. This is trivial to implement
by slightly modifying the regular auto sectioning instruction **update2d**, which
is described in detail [8]. Since two auto sectioning instructions are required,
the one which handles the transposition must not perform a branch to the first
instruction of the sectioning loop.

5.2   Our Implementation

The input matrix contains **MAX_V** × **MAX_H** elements. The two masks
used for row-wise and column-wise convolutions have **MASK_H** and **MASK_V**
elements respectively. We will refer to both as **MASK_H**, since both convolution
steps are handled identically by the PRF. The PRF algorithm processes the input
in blocks of **VSIZE** × **HSIZE** elements, vectorizing the computation both the
horizontal and vertical axes. For clarity, we only present the code required to
execute one convolution step. The code needs to be executed twice, once for the
row-wise convolution and the second time for the column-wise one. However,
only a small number of parameters needs to be updated (e.g., the pointer to the

input and out matrixes) in the exchange registers, the binary instructions are similar for both passes.

The data will be processed in multiple steps (iterations), **VSIZE** rows at a time. Because special care needs to be taken at the borders of the input, we separate the vectorized algorithm in three distinct phases in order to properly process the first and last iterations. The layout for the PRF used in the first iteration is illustrated in Figure 1, for the last iteration in Figure 2(b) and for the rest in Figure 2(a) (to save space, we only show the first iteration SPR content). The shaded registers (R0 and R5) contain halo elements. Without loss of generality, we assume that **MAX_V%VSIZE** = 0 and **MASK_H** = $2 \cdot \mathbf{R} + 1$.

Let $\mathbf{A} = \mathbf{MAX\_H\%HSIZE}$ and $\mathbf{B} = \begin{cases} \textbf{HSIZE, if } \mathbf{A} = 0 \\ \mathbf{A}, \text{ otherwise} \end{cases}$

In all figures, **VSIZE** = 4, **HSIZE** = 6, **R** = 2, **A** = 0, and **B** = 6.

For both Figure 1 and 2, the vector registers assignment is as follows:

- R0 contains the left hallo cells;
- R1 contains the input data which needs to be processed, and overlaps with R6-R9 which are used to load the data from the LS;
- R2 contains the mask;
- R3 stores the result of the convolution, and overlaps with R10-R17 which are used to transpose the result;
- R4 holds the halo elements as well as the loaded data;
- R5 holds the data which will become the halo of the next iteration, or the right halo cells for the last iteration.

The first iteration of the convolution takes into consideration the **R** halo elements to the left of the first input element. The algorithm performs the following steps:

```
f01. Define R2 as 1x(2*R+1), base=VSIZE
f02. Load R2
f03s.Define R0 as VSIZExR, base=0
f04. Initialize R0 with the default values for halos (e.g., 0)
f05. Resize R0 as VSIZEx2*R, base=0
f06. Define R4 as VSIZEx(HSIZE+R), base=0
f07. Define R1 as VSIZExHSIZE, base=R
f08. Define R6, R7,... R(6+VSIZE-1),as 1xHSIZE,
     base=R, R+M, ... R + (VSIZE-1)*M
f09. Define R(6+VSIZE),...R(6+VSIZE+HSIZE-R-1), as VSIZEx1,
     base=(VSIZE+1)*M, (VSIZE+1)*M+1, ... (VSIZE+1)*M + HSIZE-R-1
f10. Define R5 as VSIZEx2*R, base=HSIZE-R
f11. Define R3 as VSIZEx(HSIZE-R), base=VSIZE+1
f12. Load R6, R7,... R(6+VSIZE-1)
f13. Row-wise convolution: input=R4, Mask=R2, Output=R3
f14. Store R(6+VSIZE),...R(6+VSIZE+HSIZE-R-1)
f15. Move R5 to R0
f16. Update pointers to the input data and output data
```

The halo elements complicate the algorithm when processing the input data in blocks, as each new section of the data will require $2 \cdot \mathbf{R}$ elements from the previous iteration (R0 in Figure 2(a)). Our solution is to keep the halo elements in the PRF, and just move them to the left (from R5 to R0) before loading new data. This way, each input element is only loaded once for the horizontal pass and once for the vertical pass. The main iterations execute the following operations:

```
m01. Define R5 as VSIZEx2*R, base=HSIZE
m02. Define R1 as VSIZExHSIZE, base=2*R
m03. Define R4 as VSIZEx(HSIZE + 2*R), base=0
m04. Define R3 as VSIZExHSIZE, base=VSIZE+1
m05. Define R(6+VSIZE+HSIZE - R),...R(6+VSIZE+HSIZE - 1), as VSIZEx1,
     base=(VSIZE+1)*M+HSIZE-R, ... (VSIZE+1)*M + HSIZE-1
m06. Redefine R6, R7,... R(6+VSIZE-1),as 1xHSIZE, new base=2*R
m07s.Load R6, R7,... R(6+VSIZE-1)
m08. Row-wise convolution: input=R4, Mask=R2, Output=R3
m09. Store R(6+VSIZE),...R(6+VSIZE+HSIZE-1)
m10. Move R5 to R0
m11. Update pointers, continue if the last iteration follows
     or jump to instr. m07s otherwise
```

The last iteration needs to add the halo elements to the right of the last input element(Figure 2(b)). The width of the loads in the last iteration is $\mathbf{A}$, and the number of stores is $\mathbf{A+R}$. The pseudo-code for the last iteration is:

```
l01. Define R5 as VSIZExR, base=A+2*R
l02. Initialize R5 with the default values for halos (e.g., 0)
l03. Define R1 as VSIZExA, base=2*R
l04. Define R4 as VSIZEx(A+3*R), base=2*R
l05. Define R3 as VSIZEx(A+R), base=(VSIZE+1)
l06. Redefine R6, R7,... R(6+VSIZE-1),new size 1xA, new base=2*R
l07. Define R(6+VSIZE),...R(6+VSIZE+A+R-1) as VSIZEx1,
     base=(VSIZE+1)*M, ... (VSIZE+1)*M+A+R-1
l08. Load R6, R7,... R(6+VSIZE-1)
l09. Row-wise convolution: input=R4, Mask=R2, Output=R3
l10. Store R(6+VSIZE),...R(6+VSIZE+A+R-1),
l11. Update pointers and finish execution if last row
     or jump to instr. f03s otherwise
```

The algorithm also has two special cases, depending on the size of the input $\mathbf{MAX\_H}$ and $\mathbf{HSIZE}$. If $\mathbf{HSIZE} < \mathbf{MAX\_H} \leq 2 \cdot \mathbf{HSIZE}$, only the first and last iterations are executed. If $\mathbf{MAX\_H} \leq \mathbf{HSIZE}$, a single iteration is executed which processes full rows. Because of lack of space, we didn't include the corresponding pseudo-code and PRF configurations in this paper.

6   Experimental Results

The nVidia c2050 GPU [27] is running at 1.15 GHz, a frequency comparable to our ASIC synthesis results for the PRF presented in Section 2. Therefore,

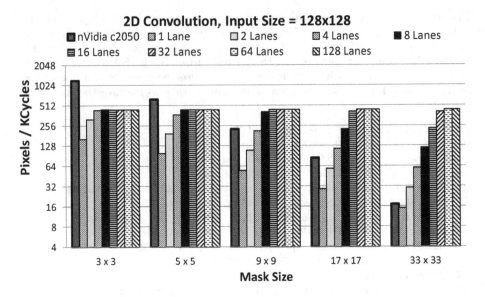

Fig. 3. 2D Convolution Algorithm Throughput

we measure the throughput for both the PRF and the nVidia c2050 in terms of pixels / 1000 cycles. Figure 3 compares the throughput of the c2050 card with multiple PRF configurations, ranging from 1 to 128 vector lanes. The peak throughput for the c2050 was obtained for an image size of 2048 × 2048 elements, which we will use for the comparison below. The input data for the PRF was set at 128 × 128 elements, as larger inputs did not improve performance. The mask sizes are varied between 3 × 3 and 33 × 33 elements, representing realistic scenarios. For the PRF experiments, we set **HSIZE = VSIZE** = 32.

The results suggest that for small masks of 3 × 3 or 5 × 5, the GPU is faster than the PRF, which is limited by the bandwidth to the Local Store when using more than 8 lanes.

However, as the masks increase in size, the convolution becomes more expensive in terms of computations, and the throughput of the GPU decreases. However, the PRF scales to a higher number of lanes, and starting from a mask size of 9 × 9, outperforms the GPU. For the largest mask size of 33 × 33, all but the slowest PRF configurations gain higher throughput than the GPU.

7   Conclusions and Future Work

We presented a matrix transposition algorithm optimized for PRFs, and a 2D vectorized separable convolution algorithm avoiding strided memory accesses when accesing the input data column-wise. We evaluated the performance of the vectorized algorithm executing on multi-lane PRFs, and compared the throughput with an nVidia Tesla C2050 GPU. The results show that even in a bandwidth constrained system, the PRF is able to outperform the GPU for 9×9 or larger mask sizes. As future work, we will evaluate the performance of the PRF with other computationally intensive workloads.

Acknowledgments. We thank Wen-mei W. Hwu and Nasser Salim Anssari for providing the nVidia Tesla C2050 GPU results.

This work was supported by the European Commission in the context of FP7 FASTER project (#287804).

References

1. ITRS: International Technology Roadmap for Semiconductors. Online, 2011 edn., http://www.itrs.net/
2. Akdemir, K., et al.: Breakthrough AES Performance with Intel AES New Instructions. White paper, 12 pages (June 2010), http://communities.intel.com/docs/DOC-5003
3. Gwennap, L.: Digital, MIPS Add Multimedia Extensions. Microdesign Resources 10(15), 1–5 (1996)
4. Buchholz, W.: The IBM System/370 vector architecture. IBM Systems Journal, 51–62 (1986)
5. Gwennap, L.: AltiVec Vectorizes PowerPC. Microprocessor Report 12(6), 1–5 (1998)
6. IBM. Cell BE Programming Handbook Including the PowerXCell 8i Processor, 1.11 edn. (May 2008)
7. Ramirez, A., Cabarcas, F., Juurlink, B., Alvarez Mesa, M., Sanchez, F., Azevedo, A., Meenderinck, C., Ciobanu, C., Isaza, S., Gaydadjiev, G.: The SARC Architecture. IEEE Micro 30(5), 16–29 (2010); ISSN 0272-1732
8. Ciobanu, C., Kuzmanov, G.K., Ramirez, A., Gaydadjiev, G.N.: A Polymorphic Register File for Matrix Operations. In: Proceedings of the 2010 International Conference on Embedded Computer Systems: Architectures, Modeling and Simulation (SAMOS 2010), pp. 241–249 (July 2010)
9. Ciobanu, C., Kuzmanov, G.K., Gaydadjiev, G.N.: On Implementability of Polymorphic Register Files. In: Proceedings of the 7th Int. Workshop on Reconfigurable Communication-centric Systems-on-Chip (ReCoSoC 2012), pp. 1–6 (2012)
10. Ciobanu, C., Kuzmanov, G.K., Gaydadjiev, G.N.: Scalability Study of Polymorphic Register Files. In: Proceedings of the 15th Euromicro Conference on Digital System Design (DSD 2012), pp. 803–808 (2012)
11. Ciobanu, C.B., Martorell, X., Kuzmanov, G.K., Ramirez, A., Gaydadjiev, G.N.: Scalability Evaluation of a Polymorphic Register File: A CG Case Study. In: Berekovic, M., Fornaciari, W., Brinkschulte, U., Silvano, C. (eds.) ARCS 2011. LNCS, vol. 6566, pp. 13–25. Springer, Heidelberg (2011)
12. Asanović, K.: Vector Microprocessors. PhD thesis, University of California at Berkeley (1998)
13. Kuzmanov, G., Gaydadjiev, G., Vassiliadis, S.: Multimedia rectangularly addressable memory. IEEE Transactions on Multimedia, 315–322 (2006)
14. Kuck, D.J., Stokes, R.A.: The Burroughs Scientific Processor (BSP). IEEE Transactions on Computers C-31(5), 363–376 (1982); ISSN 0018-9340

15. Juurlink, B.H.H., Cheresiz, D., Vassiliadis, S., Wijshoff, H.A.G.: Implementation and Evaluation of the Complex Streamed Instruction Set. In: Int. Conf. on Parallel Architectures and Compilation Techniques (PACT), pp. 73–82 (2001)
16. Panda, D.K., Hwang, K.: Reconfigurable Vector Register Windows for Fast Matrix Computation on the Orthogonal Multiprocessor. In: Proc. of the Int. Conference on Application Specific Array Processors, September 5-7, pp. 202–213 (1990)
17. Corbal, J., Espasa, R., Valero, M.: MOM: a Matrix SIMD Instruction Set Architecture for Multimedia Applications. In: Proceedings of the ACM/IEEE SC 1999 Conference, pp. 1–12 (1999)
18. Shahbahrami, A., Juurlink, B.H.H., Vassiliadis, S.: Matrix Register File and Extended Subwords: Two Techniques for Embedded Media Processors. In: Proc. of the 2nd ACM Int. Conf. on Computing Frontiers, pp. 171–180 (May 2005)
19. Park, J., Park, S.-B., Balfour, J.D., Black-Schaffer, D., Kozyrakis, C., Dally, W.J.: Register Pointer Architecture for Efficient Embedded Processors. In: Proceedings of on Design, Automation and Test in Europe, DATE 2007, San Jose, CA, USA, pp. 978–973. EDA Consortium (2007) ISBN 978-3-9810801-2-4
20. Wong, S., Anjam, F., Nadeem, M.F.: Dynamically Reconfigurable Register File for a Softcore VLIW Processor. In: Proceedings of the Design, Automation and Test in Europe Conference (DATE 2010), pp. 969–972 (March 2010)
21. Wong, S.C., Jasiunas, M., Kearney, D.: Fast 2D Convolution Using Reconfigurable Computing. In: Proceedings of the Eighth International Symposium on Signal Processing and Its Applications, August 28-31, vol. 2, pp. 791–794 (2005)
22. Lee, J.-J., Song, G.-Y.: Super-Systolic Array for 2D Convolution. In: 2006 IEEE Region 10 Conference on TENCON 2006, pp. 1–4 (November 2006)
23. Hecht, V., Ronner, K.: An Advanced Programmable 2D-Convolution Chip for Real Time Image Processing. In: IEEE International Sympoisum on Circuits and Systems, vol. 4, pp. 1897–1900 (June 1991)
24. August, D., Chang, J., et al.: UNISIM: An Open Simulation Environment and Library for Complex Architecture Design and Collaborative Development. IEEE Comput. Archit. Lett. 6(2), 45–48 (2007); ISSN 1556-6056
25. Vassiliadis, S., Wong, S., Gaydadjiev, G., Bertels, K., Kuzmanov, G., Panainte, E.M.: The molen polymorphic processor. IEEE Transactions on Computers 53(11), 1363–1375 (2004); ISSN 0018-9340.
26. Podlozhnyuk, V.: Image Convolution with CUDA. Online (June 2007), http://developer.download.nvidia.com/compute/cuda/1.1-Beta/x86_64_website/projects/convolutionSeparable/doc/convolutionSeparable.pdf
27. TESLA C2050 / C2070 GPU Computing Processor. Supercomputing at 1/10th of the Cost. Online, www.nvidia.com/docs/IO/43395/NV_DS_Tesla_C2050_C2070_jul10_lores.pdf

Architecture of a Parallel
MOSFET Parameter Extraction System

Tomáš Zahradnický and Róbert Lórencz

Department of Computer Systems,
Faculty of Information Technology,
Czech Technical University in Prague,
Thákurova 9, Prague 6, 160 00, Czech Republic
{zahradt,lorencz}@fit.cvut.cz

Abstract. The paper first describes an existing parameter estimation approach used to estimate MOSFET mathematical model parameters. Next, all of the presented algorithms are analyzed with respect to the current multiple core processor architecture design. The parallel equivalents of the presented algorithms are given, including their computational complexities. The presented approach is specific that is uses the multiple-modulus arithmetic of the Residue Number System for solution of sets of linear equations. Finally, the paper shows the scalability of the presented approach and compares the obtained results to the original approach.

1 Introduction

The process of parameter extraction is today an indispensable portion of modeling and simulation, and is used to find and verify parameters of a mathematical model describing some physical reality. Modeling processes utilize parameter extraction with theoretical mathematical models to verify predicted behavior of a studied experimental object or reality and also to create reliable mathematical descriptions that model the object's behavior as close as possible. Simulation utilizes the already verified mathematical models, and replaces the object by its mathematical description allowing to virtualize the object or a system of objects and to perform virtual experiments on a computer.

Parameter extraction uses statistical methods such as the method of maximum likelihood or weighted least squares and these methods end up with solution of a set of linear equations (SLE)s. Problems may occur in floating point arithmetic since it is not associative, higher precision arithmetic is needed, or if rounding errors committed during the solution process are undesirable. If we use the arithmetic of the Residue Number System (RNS) [2,3], we address parallel processing, error free computation, and associativity at once.

SLE solution in residue arithmetic happens as a solution of a number of sets of linear congruences (SLC)s, each with its own unique modulus. Since there are no relations in between the individual SLCs their solution can safely occur in parallel. Once the SLC solutions are available, the result is transformed into the

C. Hochberger et al. (Eds.): ARCS 2013, LNCS 7767, pp. 329–340, 2013.
© Springer-Verlag Berlin Heidelberg 2013

rational number set either with the backward transformation based on Chinese Remainder Theorem (CRT) or Mixed Radix Conversion (MRC) [2,3].

The purpose of this paper is to present an architecture of a parallel parameter extraction system capable of extracting several to many mathematical model parameters simultaneously. The extraction system is special in a way that it uses residue arithmetic, which is especially suitable for parallel processing. The system originates in [4], and is able to extract several to many parameters with the all-at-once approach. After a recapitulation of the method [4], the paper provides a scalable equivalent including its complexity.

The structure of the paper is as follows: Section 2, *Related Work*, provides the state-of-the-art in MOSFET parameter extraction, classifies our method, and discusses possible alternative approaches. Section 3, *The Original Method*, recapitulates the original method [4] along with its computational complexity. Section 4, *The Parallel Method*, presents a scalable version of the original method, which is the main contribution of the paper. Section 5, *Conclusions*, summarizes the contributions of the the paper and concludes it.

2   Related Work

Since the paper is related to a MOSFET [5], we restrict the related work to the recent electronic component parameter estimations that generally consist of a determination of a set of relevant parameters and their initial values, followed by the optimization efforts.

The parameter set and the initial values for the parameters within it are determined by the technologist. Some parameter values can determined directly from the data sheet, some of them can be measured, while others have to be determined experimentally with a significant amount of experience.

Next, relevant parameters are determined (ranked). Lórencz et al. [4] suggest to use statistic evaluation methods to remove parameters that strongly intercorrelate and those with high measures of uncertainty. Ben Hadj Slama [6] suggests a sensitivity survey method to determine relevant parameters. It is also possible to use neural networks. Other possible ranking methods are discussed in [7].

The current MOSFET parameter extraction approaches define an objective function[1] as a function expressing the overall distance in between the observed values and the values predicted by the mathematical model. The goal of the optimization is to find such parameter values that minimize the objective function. Since the parameter space can be extremely large, there are global and local approaches to finding the minimum of the objective function.

Global optimization techniques search the entire parameter space searching for a region containing the global minimum. The methods currently used often include evolutionary algorithms. There are methods based on genetic algorithms

---

[1] The naming of the objective function varies across the literature. Genetic algorithms usually use fitness function, we call this function a goodness of the fit function, while methods based on simulated annealing calculate with an energy function.

[8,9,10,11,12], simulated annealing [13,14], or fuzzy logic [15]. Recently, there are appearing global approaches using particle swarm optimization [16,17].

Local optimization techniques are preferred when we expect that the sought global minimum of the objective function lies near to the current solution. We can see Levenberg-Marquardt's algorithm [18,19] (LMA) in [8,9], and the steepest descent methods, often combined with heuristics. Bryant [20] suggests to use Tabu search [21] to avoid exploring the already explored portions of the parameter space. The use of other gradient methods such as the conjugated gradients method [22] was not observed in MOSFET parameter extraction. The approach presented in this paper can be classified as a static parallel local parameter extraction approach using steepest descent methods (LMA).

The interesting point about the above papers is that they often do not discuss computer arithmetic and plainly assume the IEEE 754 [1] arithmetic.

3   The Original Method

The section briefly describes the original parameter extraction method [4]. Technological and mathematical backgrounds and evaluation of the results are discussed in [4,23] and were left out of the paper. It is also assumed that all relevant parameters have already been determined, all data measurements conducted, including their standard deviation estimates. The paper focuses on the process of searching for a minimum of the objective function.

The parameter extraction system [4,23] uses the Levenberg-Marquardt's algorithm (LMA) [18,19] to find mathematical model parameter values from the input data being MOSFET's drain current, base-source, drain-source, and gate-source voltages. The original paper deals with a Bipolar Junction Transistor (BJT), but we are using the same approach for a MOSFET.

First, it is necessary to calculate the goodness of the fit (the objective function). The goodness of the fit tells how the current parameter set is far from the measured data parameter set and is calculated as follows [4]:

$$\chi^2(\mathbf{X}, \mathbf{p}^{(k)}) = \mathbf{f}(\mathbf{X}, \mathbf{p}^{(k)})^T \mathbf{f}(\mathbf{X}, \mathbf{p}^{(k)}) = \sum_{i=1}^{N} f_i(\mathbf{X}_i, \mathbf{p}^{(k)})^2, \tag{1}$$

where $\mathbf{X} \in \mathbb{R}^{N \times I}$ is a matrix of independent variables (input voltages). There are I measured input voltages for N data points. $\mathbf{X}_i$ denotes the ith row of $\mathbf{X}$ and is a vector of measured input voltages at the ith data point, while $\mathbf{p}$ resp. $\mathbf{p}^{(k)}$ denotes the parameter vector resp. the parameter vector at the kth iteration step. $\mathbf{f}(\mathbf{X}, \mathbf{p}^{(k)})$ is a vector error function containing weighted differences in between the measured and calculated values of the mathematical model so $f_i(\mathbf{X}, \mathbf{p}^{(k)}) = [I_{DS_i} - m_i(\mathbf{X}_i, \mathbf{p}^{(k)})]\sigma_i^{-1}$. IDS_i, σ_i, and $m_i(\mathbf{X}_i, \mathbf{p})$ are a drain current, its standard deviation, and the value of the math. model at the ith data point.

Then we need to find Jacobi's matrix $\mathbf{J}^{(k)} = \left(\nabla_{\mathbf{p}}\left(\mathbf{f}(\mathbf{X}_i, \mathbf{p})^T\right)\right)^T \big|_{\mathbf{p}=\mathbf{p}^{(k)}} \in \mathbb{R}^{N \times P}$, where P is a number of parameters. The derivatives are evaluated either with a parabolic approximation [4] or with Neville's algorithm [24,23].

Finally we solve a set of linear equations (for more information refer to [4,23]):

$$\left[\left(\mathbf{J}^{(k)}\right)^{T}\mathbf{J}^{(k)} + \lambda^{(k)}\mathbf{D}^{(k)}\right]\varDelta\mathbf{p}^{(k)} = \left(\mathbf{J}^{(k)}\right)^{T}\mathbf{f}\left(\mathbf{X}, \mathbf{p}^{(k)}\right), \tag{2}$$

where $\mathbf{J}^{(k)} \in \mathbb{R}^{N \times P}$ is Jacobi's matrix at the kth iteration step. $\mathbf{D}^{(k)} \in \mathbb{R}^{P \times P}$ and $\lambda^{(k)} \in \mathbb{R}$ are the LMA's diagonal matrix and the damping factor at the kth iteration step, for $\varDelta\mathbf{p}^{(k)}$ being the kth parameter vector adjustment.

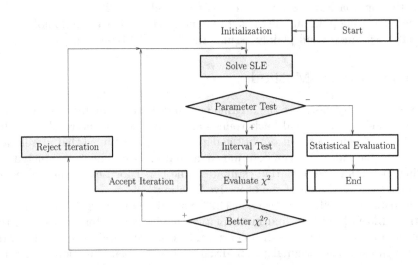

Fig. 1. The parameter extraction algorithm. The algorithm starts in the **Start** block, where the relevant parameters are selected forming the parameter set, the default parameter values $\mathbf{p}^{(0)}$ assigned, and the initial goodness of the fit calculated. **Initialization** sets the initial values for the damping coefficient, and the iteration step counter $k = 0$. The **Solve SLE** block finds a new par. vector $\mathbf{p}^{(k+1)}$ and passes it to the **Parameter Test** for decision whether to continue or stop, based on the relative change in each $\mathbf{p}^{(k+1)}$'s component. If the change is insignificant $(-)$, the algorithm stops, and the results are statistically evaluated; otherwise $(+)$ the new par. vector is passed to the **Interval Test** checking $\mathbf{p}^{(k+1)}$'s physical constraints and resetting all non-conforming elements to their default values. The **Evaluate** χ^2 block computes a new goodness of the fit, followed by comparing of the last two values of the goodness of the fit. If there is a better goodness than in the previous step $(+)$, the computed parameter set is retained in the **Accept Iteration** block, the iteration number k increased, and the damping coefficient divided by 10; otherwise $(-)$ the algorithm goes to the **Reject Iteration** block, where the damping coefficient is multiplied by 10, and the new par. vector $\mathbf{p}^{(k+1)}$ discarded. Finally, the algorithm starts over in the **Solve SLE** block.

The extraction algorithm can be described with the following scheme:
The extraction algorithm is described in detail in [4,23]. The following section
will discuss the SLE solution in arithmetic of the Residue Number System.

3.1 Residue Number System Arithmetic

We use the multiple-modulus residue arithmetic [25,2] with Q distinct prime
number moduli, which is equivalent to a single modulus arithmetic with joint
module $M = \prod_{i=1}^{Q} m_i$ $\forall_{i=1, i \neq j}^{Q} \gcd(m_i, m_j) = 1$. CRT guarantees that each
integer $x \in [0, M)$ can be uniquely represented as $|x|_M = \{x_1, \ldots, x_Q\}$, where
$x_i = x \bmod m_i \equiv |x|_{m_i}$. For integers $x, y \in [0, M)$ and $\square \in \{+, -, \cdot\}$

$$|x \square y|_M \equiv \left\{ |x_1 \square y_1|_{m_1}, \ldots, |x_Q \square y_Q|_{m_Q} \right\}, \quad \text{and} \tag{3}$$

$$\left| \frac{x}{y} \right|_M \equiv \left\{ \left| x_1 \cdot |y_1^{-1}|_{m_1} \right|_{m_1}, \ldots, \left| x_Q \cdot |y_Q^{-1}|_{m_Q} \right|_{m_Q} \right\} \quad \text{for } y \neq 0, \tag{4}$$

where $|y_i^{-1}|_{m_i}$ denotes a multiplicative inverse of $y_i \bmod m_i$.

Relations (3) and (4) are particularly important since individual prime number moduli m_i are chosen small enough to perfectly fit into a CPU register as well
as products of addition, subtraction, multiplication, and multiplicative inverse
modulo m_i. Since there are no relations in between calculations across different moduli in (3) and (4), the computation in single big modulus is replaced
by a computation in multiple smaller moduli and can occur in parallel and is
naturally scalable. Note that since we are using integers only, the operations are
associative, commutative, distributive, and there is no rounding at all in contrary
to the floating point arithmetic which rounds after every operation.

3.2 Solving Sets of Linear Equations in Residue Arithmetic

Residue arithmetic can be also used to solve an SLE and a typical SLE solution
is accomplished in 4 steps [26]:

1. Scaling Transformation. The input extended SLE matrix is scaled, as it ensures that the elements of the SLE matrix have proper magnitude for the
   remainder after division (modulo) operation performed in the next step.
2. Forward Transformation. The remainder mod m_i operation is applied at the
   scaled matrix and an entirely integral matrix is obtained. This step repeats
   Q times and we obtain Q sets of linear congruences (SLC)s.
3. SLCs Solution. SLCs are independently solved e.g. by Gauss-Jordan elimination with pivoting and all singular solutions are discarded along with their
   corresponding moduli and Q decreased by 1 for any singular SLC.
4. Backward Transformation [3,26]. The results from step 3 are recombined
   back into a rational number SLE solution with MRC.

Table 1. Complexities of a solution of a set of linear equations in the multiple-modulus residue arithmetic. P stands for the number of parameters (unknowns) and Q a number of prime number moduli. The set is solved with Gauss-Jordan elimination with nonzero residual pivoting [26] and Mixed Radix Conversion used for the Backward transformation.

Operation	Complexity	Times Repeated	Total
Scaling Transformation	$O(P^2)$	1	$O(P^2)$
Forward Transformation	$O(P^2)$	Q	$O(P^2Q)$
Solution of an SLC	$O(P^3)$	Q	$O(P^3Q)$
Backward Transformation	$O(Q^2)$	P	$O(PQ^2)$
Total			$C = O(P^3Q + PQ^2)$

Table 1 provides a summary of the computational complexities (derived precisely in [23]) for each of the above 4 SLE solution steps:

3.3 Summary

When we summarize the complexities of the original parameter extraction system, we obtain the following [23]:

Table 2. Iteration step complexity overview. N stands for a number of data points, P a number of parameters, Q a number of moduli, and α resp. δ for a number of flops required to evaluate a single value of the mathematical model resp. a derivative of it.

Iteration Step Name	Complexity
Goodness of the Fit Evaluation with (1)	$O(N\alpha)$
Jacobi's Matrix Evaluation	$O(NP\delta)$
$(\mathbf{J}^{(k)})^T\mathbf{J}^{(k)}$ Matrix Multiplication in (2)	$O(NP^2)$
$(\mathbf{J}^{(k)})^T\mathbf{f}(\mathbf{X}, \mathbf{p}^{(k)})$ Matrix Multiplication in (2)	$O(N)$
Application of $\lambda^{(k)}$ in (2)	$O(P)$
SLE Solution with (2) in RNS	$O(P^3Q + PQ^2)$
Interval Test	$O(P)$
Parameter Test	$O(P)$

When expressed in big-O notation, the joint complexity of 1 iteration is:
$$C = O\left(P^3Q + PQ^2 + NP^2 + NP\delta + N\alpha\right).$$

The presented method was described in [4] and could be used to estimate MOS-FET parameters, but hence is was not designed to be scalable. The following section offers a scalable equivalent of the method.

4   The Parallel Method

The purpose of the paper is to present an improvement to the original parameter extraction method presented in sec. 3 of the paper. The improvement provided is for a computer with one or more processors, each with one or more processor cores, and a shared memory system big enough to carry out the calculation. The parallel method is designed for run at a thread level and all work is partitioned in a way so that the load balance of the individual threads is about the same, where possible. The method is designed to provide the same result regardless of a number of threads p used for the computation. We assume that the number of data points N is greater than the number of threads p ($N > p$), and that the number of flops required to evaluate a value of the mathematical model $\alpha \gg 1$.

The following sections analyze the algorithm depicted at Fig. 1 step by step and present changes to the individual steps in Table 2 that make the algorithm scalable along with complexities of the approach.

4.1   Parallel Goodness of the Fit Evaluation

The value of the goodness of the fit $\chi^2(\mathbf{X}, \mathbf{p}^{(k)})$ function is evaluated with (1), and since it evaluates a sum of independent data quantities, we can evaluate each $f_i(\mathbf{X}_i, \mathbf{p}^{(k)})^2$ independently, and then perform a parallel summation of the obtained results. This approach does not work in floating point arithmetic since the addition *is not* associative because of rounding. For this reason, we assign N/p elements to each thread and let it calculate $f_i(\mathbf{X}_i, \mathbf{p}^{(k)})^2$ values independently, gathering the sum sequentially afterwards. If α is the number of flops required to evaluate a single value of the mathematical model and since $\alpha \gg 1$ then $O\left(f_i(\mathbf{X}_i, \mathbf{p}^{(k)})\right) = O(\alpha)$. We have to perform N additions sequentially and calculate N/p times $f_i(\mathbf{X}_i, \mathbf{p}^{(k)})^2$ in parallel. When expressed in big-O notation, the parallel goodness of the fit is evaluated in:

$$C = O\left(N + N\alpha/p\right).$$

4.2   Parallel Jacobi's Matrix Evaluation

The Jacobi's matrix $\mathbf{J}^{(k)} \in \mathbb{R}^{N \times P}$ elements are calculated independently and there are NP elements to be calculated. We assume $N > p$ or even $N \gg p$ and if $\delta \gg 1$ is a number of flops required to evaluate a derivative, it is sufficient to partition the evaluation of the matrix such that each thread gets assigned a set of approximately N/p rows. The complexity directly follows as:

$$C = O(NP\delta/p).$$

4.3 Parallel Matrix Multiplication

Parallel matrix multiplication is a well explored topic. The extraction algorithm performs optimizations, based on whether the multiplication result is: i) a non-symmetric matrix, such as $\mathbf{J}(\mathbf{X}, \mathbf{p}^{(k)})^T \mathbf{f}(\mathbf{X}, \mathbf{p}^{(k)})$, and ii) symmetric matrix such as $\mathbf{J}(\mathbf{X}, \mathbf{p}^{(k)})^T \mathbf{J}(\mathbf{X}, \mathbf{p}^{(k)})$, where only a half of the elements needs to be calculated. We consider the complexity for $\mathbf{C} = \mathbf{AB}$, where $\mathbf{A} \in \mathbb{R}^{R \times S}$, $\mathbf{B} \in \mathbb{R}^{S \times T}$, and $\mathbf{C} \in \mathbb{R}^{R \times T}$ to be:

$$C = O(RST/p) \text{ for non-symmetric matrices,}$$
$$C = O(R^2 S/p) \text{ for symmetric matrices,}$$

where R, S, $T \in \mathbb{N}$.

4.4 Solving Sets of Linear Equations in Parallel

The sequential version of the SLE solving process in RNS got already briefly discussed in sec. 3.2. The parallel solution process comprises of the same 4 steps; a scaling transformation, a forward transformation, solution of Q SLCs, and a backward transformation.

Parallel Scaling Transformation. prepares the SLE to take a remainder modulo m_q operations, for m_q being the qth unique prime number modulus for $q = 1 : Q$. The scaling transformation takes each row of the extended SLE matrix $\mathbf{W} \in \mathbb{R}^{P \times (P+1)}$, finds the element with the smallest nonzero magnitude, and scales the entire row in a way so that all nonzero elements of the row $|w_{i,*}| \geq 1$. The algorithm uses matrix row partitioning so each processor core processes an assigned interval of rows I_c of $\mathbf{W}$. There are $P + 1$ columns in $\mathbf{W}$ and each processor core processes $L_c = 1 + \max I_c - \min I_c$ rows. Since $L_c \approx P/p$, the complexity expressed in terms of big-O notation yields:

$$C = O(P^2/p).$$

Parallel Forward Transformation. gets the scaled extended SLE matrix and calculates $|\mathbf{W}|_q = \mathbf{W} \bmod m_q$, for $q = 1 : Q$, producing Q independent sets of linear congruencies. This process is made parallel by assigning each processor core c approximately Q/p moduli in form of an interval I_c and having the core compute the standard forward transformation for $L_c = 1 + \max I_c - \min I_c$ moduli. There are $P(P+1)L_c$ modular reductions per processor and since $L_c \approx Q/p$ the complexity expressed in terms of big-O notation is:

$$C = O(P^2 Q/p).$$

Parallel SLC Solutions. In this step, we solve Q sets of linear congruencies. Since SLCs have small to moderate number of equations, it is better to solve them as a whole, dividing the whole Q sets among the p processor cores so that each processor core gets approximately Q/p SLCs, each represented by an extended SLC matrix $|\mathbf{W}|_q$. SLCs are solved with Gauss-Jordan elimination with pivoting. The complexity of Gauss-Jordan elimination is $O(P^3)$ and since each core solves approximate Q/p SLCs, the overall complexity of this step is:

$$C = O\left(P^3 Q/p\right).$$

Parallel Backward Transformation. recombines the partial SLC solutions into an SLE solution with the MRC algorithm [3,26]. There are at most Q SLC solutions, each with a determinant value. The backward transformation needs to be run for each element of the solution vector $\mathbf{x}$. Since the complexity of Garner's algorithm is $O(Q^2)$, and since each processor core evaluates approximately P/p elements of the solution vector, the asymptotic complexity is:

$$C = O\left(PQ^2/p\right).$$

The complexity of a parallel SLE solution in residue arithmetic:

Table 3. The complexities of parallel solution of a set of P linear equations (SLE)s in the multiple-modulus arithmetic of the Residue Number System with Q distinct prime number moduli. The SLE solution consists of a scaling transformation performed once for the entire set followed by a forward transformation performed once for each module. Then Q sets of linear congruencies (SLC)s are solved providing up to Q solutions that get combined into an SLE solution with the backward transformation. The algorithms are run on p processor cores.

Operation	Complexity	Times Repeated	Total
Scaling Transformation	$O(P^2/p)$	1	$O(P^2/p)$
Forward Transformation	$O(P^2)$	Q/p	$O(P^2Q/p)$
SLC Solution	$O(P^3)$	Q/p	$O(P^3Q/p)$
Backward Transformation	$O(Q^2)$	P/p	$O(PQ^2/p)$
Total			$C = O\left(P^3Q/p + PQ^2/p\right)$

4.5   Summary

The previous section described a parallel SLE solution in residue arithmetic. Table 4 summarizes the complexities of each step of the extraction algorithm while Fig. 2 compares the sequential and parallel run times of both algorithms:

Table 4. The complexities of each portion of an iteration step of the parallel algorithm. The complexities are presented for the shaded portions of Fig. 1 on page 332. N stands for the number of data points, Q a number of RNS prime number moduli, P a number of equations, α resp. δ for a number of flops required to evaluate a value of the mathematical model resp. a derivative of it.

Operation	Parallel Complexity
Goodness of the Fit Evaluation	$O(N\alpha/p)$
Jacobi's Matrix Evaluation	$O(NP\delta/p)$
$\mathbf{J}^T\mathbf{J}$ Matrix Multiplication	$O(NP^2/p)$
$\mathbf{J}^T\mathbf{f}$ Matrix Multiplication	$O(N/p)$
Application of $\lambda^{(k)}$	$O(P)$
SLE Solution	$O(P^3Q/p + PQ^2/p)$
Interval Test	$O(P)$
Parameter Test	$O(P)$

The overall complexity of the parallel algorithm is:

$$C = O\left(P^3Q/p + PQ^2/p + NP^2 + NP\delta/p + N\alpha/p + 3P\right).$$

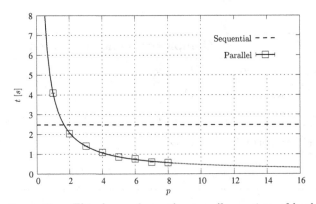

Fig. 2. Overall run time. This figure shows the overall run time of both methods for $P = 13$, $Q = 250$, and $N = 1350$. The horizontal line denotes run time of the serial extraction system, the RNS curve presents results obtained with the parallel system calculating in Residue Number System.

5   Conclusions

The purpose of parameter extraction is to find the unknown parameters of a mathematical model that models some kind of physical reality, so that the behavior of the mathematical model matches the physical reality as closely as possible. With the model, one can simulate processes, pose what-if questions, and verify the validity of experiments.

The paper first describes an existing parameter extraction method [4]. The method is analyzed within sec. 3 and scalable equivalents to all algorithms are offered in sec. 4, including complexities.

The original method in sec. 3 uses the maximum likelihood estimator to find a maximum likelihood fit of a mathematical model with the data set so that the value of goodness of the fit function is minimal with the Levenberg-Marquardt's method is used. Since a linearization of the mathematical model is necessary, the minimization is turned into an iterative process with a necessity to solve a set of linear equations. A multiple-modulus arithmetic of the Residue Number System is used to solve the set, as the solution may be sensitive to rounding errors.

All algorithms of the presented method are analyzed, and their scalable equivalents are provided in sec. 4, including computational complexities. We start with a parallel goodness of the fit evaluation, matrix partitioning and multiplication, Jacobi's matrix evaluation, and finish with a solution of a set of linear equations. All of the algorithms are scalable and their complexity given. At the end we compare the original and parallel approach and find that the parallel system scales well with the number of processors. The scalability got also verified with a case study which results are presented in Fig. 2.

References

1. IEEE Computer Society Standards Committee.: IEEE Standard for Floating-Point Arithmetic. ANSI/IEEE STD 754-2008. The Institute of Electrical and Electronics Engineers, Inc. (2008)
2. Young, D.M., Gregory, R.T.: A Survey of Numerical Mathematics. Addison-Wesley Series in Mathematics, vol. 2. Addison-Wesley Pub. Company, Inc. (1973)
3. Gregory, R.T., Krishnamurthy, E.V.: Methods and Application of Error-free Computation. Springer (1984)
4. Lórencz, R., Reckleben, C., Hansen, K.: A Novel Extraction Method for BJT-Parameters. J. Elec. E. 51, 21–29 (2000)
5. Cheng, Y., Hu, C.: MOSFET Modeling & BSIM3 User's Guide. Kluwer Academic Publishers (2002)
6. Slama, B.H., et al.: Relevant Parameters of SPICE3 MOSFET Model for EMC Analysis. In: Proceedings of the IEEE International Symposium on Electromagnetic Compatibility, Austin, Texas, USA, pp. 319–323 (September 2009)
7. Guyon, I., Elisseeff, A.: An introduction to variable and feature selection. J. Mach. Learn. Res. 3, 1157–1182 (2003)
8. Zhou, Q., et al.: Parameter extraction for the PSP MOSFET model by the combination of genetic and Levenberg-Marquardt algorithms. In: Proceeding of the International IEEE Conference on Microelectronic Test Structures, pp. 137–142 (2009)

9. Murakawa, M., et al.: Instruction tables: Lists of instruction latencies, throughputs and micro-operation breakdowns for Intel and AMD CPU's Towards Automatic Parameter Extraction for Surface-Potential-Based MOSFET Models with the Genetic Algorithm. In: Proceedings of the 2005 Asia South Pacific Design Automation Conference (ASP-DAC 2005), vol. 1, pp. 204–207. IEEE, Shanghai (2005)

10. Antoun, G., El-Nozahi, M., Fikry, W., Abbas, H.: A hybrid genetic algorithm for MOSFET parameter extraction. In: Proceeding of the IEEE Canadian Conference on Electical and Computer Engineering, vol. 2, pp. 1111–1114 (2003)

11. Keser, M., Joardar, K.: Genetic Algorithm Based MOSFET Model Parameter Extraction. Technical Proceedings of the 2000 International Conference on Modeling and Simulation of Microsystems, pp. 341–344 (2000)

12. Li, Y., Cho, Y.Y.: Parallel genetic algorithm for SPICE model parameter extraction. In: 20th Intl. Symposium on Parallel and Distributed Processing (April 2006)

13. Abbasian, A., et al.: Modeling of MOS Transistors Based on Genetic Algorithm and Simulated Annealing. In: Proceedings of the IEEE International Symposium on Circuits and Systems, vol. 6, pp. 6218–6221 (May 2005)

14. Ruizhen, L., et al.: Model Parameters Extraction of SOI MOSFETs. In: Proceedings of Intl. Workshop on Junction Technology, Shanghai, China, pp. 240–243 (August 2006)

15. Picos, R., et al.: MOSFET Parameters Extraction Using Fuzzy Logic Techniques. In: Proceedings of the 6th International Caribbean Conference on Devices, Circuits and Systems, Playa del Carmen, Mexico, pp. 17–21 (April 2006)

16. Chopde, A., Khandelwal, S., Thakker, R., Patil, M., Anil, K.: Parameter extraction for MOS model 11 using Particle Swarm Optimization. In: Proceedings of International Workshop on Physics of Semiconductor Devices, pp. 253–256 (December 2007)

17. Thakker, R., Gandhi, N., Patil, M., Anil, K.: Parameter extraction for PSP MOSFET model using particle swarm optimization. In: Proceedings of International Workshop on Physics of Semiconductor Devices, pp. 130–133 (December 2007)

18. Levenberg, K.: A Method for the Solution of Certain Problems in Least-Squares. Quarterly Applied Mathematics 2, 164–168 (1944)

19. Marquardt, D.W.: An algorithm for least-squares estimation of nonlinear parameters. Journal of Applied Mathematics 11(2), 431–441 (1963)

20. Bryant, A.T., et al.: The Use of a Formal Optimisation Procedure in Automatic Parameter Extraction of Power Semiconductor Devices. In: Proceedings of the 34th Annual IEEE Power Electronics Specialists Conference, Acapulco, Mexico, vol. 2, pp. 822–827 (July 2003)

21. Connor, A.M., Tilley, D.G.: A Tabu search for the optimization of fluid power circuits. Journal of Systems and Control 212(5), 373–381 (1998)

22. Hestenes, M.R., et al.: Methods of Conjugate Gradients for Solving Linear Systems. Journal of Research of the National Bureau of Standards 49(6), 409–436 (1952)

23. Zahradnický, T.: MOSFET Parameter Extraction Optimization. PhD thesis, Department of Computer Science and Engineering, Faculty of Electrical Engineering, The Czech Technical University in Prague (February 2010)

24. Press, W.H., et al.: Numerical Recipes in C, The Art of Scientific Computing, 2nd edn. Cambridge University Press (1999)

25. Gregory, R.T.: Error-free computation: Why It Is Needed and Methods For Doing It. Robert E. Krieger Publishing Company, Inc. (January 1980)

26. Morháč, M., Lórencz, R.: A modular system for solving linear equations exactly, I. Architecture and numerical algorithms. Computers and Artificial Intelligence 11, 351–361 (1992)

Predictable Two-Level Bus Arbitration
for Heterogeneous Task Sets

Roman Bourgade, Christine Rochange, and Pascal Sainrat

IRIT - University of Toulouse, France
{bourgade,rochange,sainrat}@irit.fr

Abstract. In a multicore processor, arbitrating the shared resources so as to ensure predictable latencies for hard real-time tasks is challenging. In [1], we have introduced a two-level bus arbitration scheme that fits the needs of heterogeneous task sets, when some tasks have a higher demand to memory than others. In this paper, we show how this scheme can be used to optimise the overall utilisation of the cores while enforcing the schedulability of the whole task set. Our approach both configures the bus arbiter and maps the tasks onto the cores. Experimental results show that it reduces the global utilisation of the cores compared to the traditional round-robin scheme.

Keywords: Real-time, multicore, bus arbitration, task mapping, task scheduling.

1 Introduction

Multicore processors (CMP or chip multiprocessors) are becoming essential in the design of constrained embedded systems due to their high performance and efficiency in terms of power consumption, thermal dissipation, cost. This efficiency is reached by sharing resources among the cores. For example, in a typical medium-scale multicore, the cores share a bus to the highest levels of the memory hierarchy.

Resource sharing engenders conflicts between cores trying to accessing the same resource simultaneously. A consequence is that the resource latency seen by each core is higher than it would have been in a single-core processor. In real-time systems, this can be acceptable if and only if a safe upper-bound of the latency is known: this bound is required to determine the worst-case execution times (WCETs) of critical tasks.

In this paper, we focus on shared buses. Several schemes have been studied in the past to perform time-predictable bus arbitration, i.e. arbitration that makes it possible to predict the worst-case bus latency seen by a core [2][3][4]. In a recent paper, we have introduced a two-level scheme that was specially designed to support heterogeneous task sets, in which tasks exhibit various levels of demands to the shared bus [1]. With this scheme, the cores undergo different latencies, and the ones that see the shortest latencies should host the highest demanding tasks. In this paper, we propose an approach to exploit such a scheme,

C. Hochberger et al. (Eds.): ARCS 2013, LNCS 7767, pp. 341–351, 2013.
© Springer-Verlag Berlin Heidelberg 2013

i.e. to select the best arbiter configuration and to map the tasks onto the cores, so that the overall core utilisation is minimised.

We report a reduction of the global utilisation of up to 29.1% compared to a solution with the traditional round-robin algorithm. In addition, we show that our two-level bus arbiter combined to our mapping approach may allow mapping a given task set on a smaller number of cores compared to round-robin.

The paper is organised as follows. Section 2 gives an overview of related work. Our bus arbiter is described in Section 3 and the mapping approach is introduced in Section 4. Section 5 reports experimental results. We conclude the paper in Section 6.

2   Related Work

A real-time aware bus arbiter allows computing the worst-case latency for a given core to be granted the bus. Several such schemes have been proposed in the last years. In [2], a round-robin algorithm is considered. Each core is granted the bus in turn, then the maximum delay it can undergo when requesting the bus is a linear function of the total number of cores. The worst-case latency is predictable and identical for all the cores. This approach fits homogeneous workloads. However, for heterogeneous task sets, it may be desirable to fasten the execution of high demanding tasks by granting them the bus more often than less demanding tasks. For parallel applications with inter-task dependencies, it may also be needed to accelerate the tasks on the critical path.

Time-Division Multiple Access (TDMA) policies allocate time slots for bus access to the cores. The bus schedule is determined off-line [3][4]. However, it may be hard to determine with enough accuracy whether an access to the bus falls within a slot allocated to the hosting core or not, at WCET analysis time. To predict latencies, the alignment of basic block time-stamps to the allocated bus slots may be analyzed [5]. However, it makes the WCET analysis of one task dependent on the bus scheduling and thus on the co-running tasks. We instead aim at keeping the worst-case bus latencies for any task independent of the other tasks. This simplifies the analysis and favours timing composition.

3   Time-Predictable Bus Arbitration

A round-robin bus arbiter generates the same worst-case latency for each core in a shared-bus multicore: $N \times L$, where N is the number of cores and L the latency of the longest bus transaction. This latency, computed by considering that each core is permanently requesting the bus, is generally overestimated but safe. This may be acceptable when all the tasks exhibit homogeneous bus demands. Otherwise, its impact might be negligible for low-demanding tasks but disastrous for high-demanding tasks. For this reason, we have introduced a new bus arbitration scheme that enforces different worst-case latencies for the cores: some cores see a low latency and should host the most-demanding tasks, while other cores undergo longer latencies and should run low-demanding tasks [1].

Figure 1 gives an overview of our two-level arbiter. The cores are organised into groups, and the L1 arbiter grants permission to one group. Then the L2 arbiter selects one core in this group. The worst-case latency to be considered for the tasks running on a given core depends on: (a) the number of groups and the L1 arbitration policy; and (b) the number of cores in each group and the L2 arbitration policy.

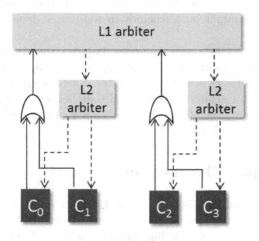

Fig. 1. Two-level bus arbiter

For the sake of simplicity, we consider a round-robin algorithm in level L2. This means that the cores that belong to the same group see the same latency, which can be computed as: $L_c = n_c \times L_g$, where n_c is the number of cores in the group and L_g is the worst-case delay for the group to be selected by the L1 arbiter.

We consider two possible policies for the L1 arbiter: (a) the round-robin algorithm, and (b) an original scheme which we call *Geometric Latencies*. The resulting two-level schemes are denoted *GRR* and *GGL*, respectively.

For *GRR*, the worst-case bus latency for a group is given by $L_g = n_g \times L$, where n_g is the number of groups. As a result, the worst-case latency seen by one core is $L_c = n_c \times n_g \times L$.

The *Geometric Latencies* arbitration policy generates worst-case latencies that follow a geometric series: group G_0 sees a latency of $2 \times L$, group G_1 a latency of $4 \times L$, group G_2 a latency of $8 \times L$, etc. The two last groups have the same latency. In [1], we provide a formal specification of the scheme that also describes its possible implementation in logic. The worst case latency of group G_i ($\forall i < n_g - 1$) is given by $L_{g_i} = 2^{i+1} \times L$, and $L_{g_{(n_g-1)}} = 2^{n_g-1} \times L$ (see proof in [6]).

With the GGL scheme, the latency to be considered for a task running on one core in group G_i is then:

$$\begin{cases} L_c = n_{c_i} \times 2^{i+1} \times L & for\ 0 \leq i < n_g - 1 \\ L_c = n_{c_i} \times 2^{n_g - 1} \times L & if\ i = n_g - 1 \end{cases} \tag{1}$$

where n_{c_i} is the number of cores in group G_i.

To summarise, the worst-case latency seen by one core depends on the number of cores in the same group in both schemes. In addition, it depends on the group's rank in GGL.

Configuring our two-level arbiter means mapping the cores to groups. The arbiter configuration impacts the bus latency seen by each core, and then the worst-case execution times of the tasks it runs. In next section, we introduce an algorithm to select an arbiter configuration together with a mapping of tasks to cores that both minimise the overall utilisation of cores while ensuring the schedulability of the whole task set.

4   Task Mapping Optimisation

The problem addressed in this section breaks down into: (a) determining the best configuration of our bus arbiter for a given task set; (b) finding out the best mapping of tasks to cores considering this configuration. Both should be solved simultaneously.

Algorithm 1. Computation of time/utilisation vectors

```
 1  for n ← 1 to num_cores do
 2      Γ_n ← PossibleConfigurations(n);
 3      Λ_n ← ∅;
 4      foreach γ ∈ Γ_n do
 5          Λ_n ← Λ_n ∪ PossibleLatencies(γ);
 6      end
 7      foreach task τ ∈ T do
 8          foreach λ ∈ Λ_n do
 9              t_τ^λ ← WCET(τ, λ);
10              u_τ^λ ← t_τ^λ / P_τ;
11          end
12      end
13  end
```

4.1   Preliminary Computations

The WCET of a task, and thus its core utilisation, depends on the bus latency seen by the core that hosts it, which in turn depends on the arbiter configuration. Algorithm 1 computes the WCET and utilisation of each task, considering each possible value of the bus latency (the possible values result from the various possible arbiter configurations). These results are later used to analyse the schedulability of the task set.

4.2   General Approach to Task Mapping

The problem of mapping tasks together with configuring the two-level arbiter exhibits several degrees of liberty: L1 arbitration policy (*GRR* or *GGL*), number of groups, number of cores, number of cores in each group, assignment of each task to a core. Only schedulable solutions should be retained.

Our approach is shown in Algorithm 2. To keep the problem resolution tractable, the problem is split into several sub-problems. Each sub-problem consists in finding out the best task mapping for a given arbiter configuration (*line 5*): our approach is explained in Section 4.3. If one solution is found, it is added to the set of possible solutions (*line 7*). The set of possible configurations is exhaustively scanned in the two outer loops (*lines 2 and 4*). As we will see, splitting the whole problem into sub-problems allows using Integer Linear Programming (ILP) techniques.

Algorithm 2. General approach to task mapping

---

1 $\mathcal{M} \leftarrow \emptyset$;
2 **for** $n \leftarrow 1$ **to** num_cores **do**
3 $\quad$ $\Gamma_n \leftarrow PossibleConfigurations(n)$;
4 $\quad$ **foreach** $\gamma \in \Gamma_n$ **do**
5 $\quad\quad$ $(schedulable, m) \leftarrow FindSolution(\gamma, T)$;
6 $\quad\quad$ **if** $(schedulable)$ **then**
7 $\quad\quad\quad$ $\mathcal{M} \leftarrow \mathcal{M} \cup \{\gamma, m\}$;
8 $\quad\quad$ **end**
9 $\quad$ **end**
10 **end**

4.3   Task Mapping for a Given Arbiter Configuration

Overview. Algorithm 3 describes the process of searching the best task mapping for a given arbiter configuration. We consider the aggregated utilisation of the cores (i.e. the sum of the individual utilisations) as the primary criterion to estimate the quality of a particular mapping. A lower global utilisation leaves computing resources to run additional tasks.

Now, to be acceptable, a task mapping must also be globally schedulable. In this paper, we consider a partitioned scheduling strategy. Then each subset of tasks assigned to one core must be shown schedulable on this core. In the following, we assume non-preemptive EDF scheduling and we use the related schedulability test [7].

In Algorithm 3, a loop (*line 5*) iterates until a schedulable solution has been found or no other task mapping exists. In each iteration, an integer linear program is used to find a task mapping (*line 6*). If a solution is found, it is tested for schedulability on each core (*line 10*). When a subset assigned to one core is found schedulable, it is locked to this core (*line 11*). Otherwise, it is appended to the black list and the task mapping is invalidated (*lines 13-14*). In the next iteration, the integer linear program is enriched with information about the locked and black-listed subsets to search for another task mapping. Locking task subsets is a way to accelerate the mapping process, as we will see in Section 5.

Algorithm 3. Mapping of tasks for a given arbiter configuration ($FindSolution(\gamma, T)$)

---

1 **foreach** $k \in [1..n]$ **do**
2 | $\mathcal{B}_k \leftarrow \emptyset; \mathcal{L}_k \leftarrow \emptyset;$
3 **end**
4 $mappable \leftarrow true; schedulable \leftarrow false;$
5 **while** $mappable$ && $!schedulable$ **do**
6 | $(mappable, m) \leftarrow Map(n, T, \mathcal{B}, \mathcal{L});$
7 | **if** $mappable$ **then**
8 | | $schedulable \leftarrow true;$
9 | | **foreach** $k \in [1..n]$ **do**
10 | | | **if** $IsSchedulable(m_k)$ **then**
11 | | | | $\mathcal{L}_k \leftarrow m_k;$
12 | | | **else**
13 | | | | $\mathcal{B}_k \leftarrow \mathcal{B}_k \cup m_k;$
14 | | | | $schedulable \leftarrow false;$
15 | | | **end**
16 | | **end**
17 | **end**
18 **end**
19 **return** $(schedulable, m);$

Basic ILP Formulation of the Task Mapping Problem. The mapping of a task set onto cores for a given arbiter configuration γ is described by the following set:

$$\{\mu_{\tau,k} | \tau \in T, 0 \leq k < n\}$$

with: $\mu_{\tau,k} = \begin{cases} 1 \text{ if task } \tau \text{ is mapped to core } k \\ 0 \text{ otherwise} \end{cases}$

Let $\lambda_{k,\gamma}$ be the bus latency for core k considering configuration γ. The ILP formulation is the following:

$$min : \mathcal{U} = \sum_{k=0}^{n} \mathcal{U}_k \quad \text{/* objective: minimising the global utilisation */}$$

$$\forall k | 0 \le k < n, \quad \mathcal{U}_k = \sum_{\tau \in T} \mu_{\tau,k} . u_\tau^{\lambda_{k,\gamma}} \quad \text{/* utilisation of one core is the sum of the utilisations of the tasks it runs */}$$

$$\forall k | 0 \le k < n, \quad \mathcal{U}_k \le 1 \quad \text{/* utilisation of one core cannot exceed 1*/}$$

$$\forall \tau \in T, \quad \sum_{k=0}^{n-1} \mu_{\tau,k} = 1 \quad \text{/* a task cannot be mapped on several cores */}$$

Additional Constraints for Locked Task Subsets and Black Lists. These constraints are used to accelerate the search for a schedulable task mapping. They avoid exploring new possible tasks subsets when one schedulable subset has been found for a given core. In addition, they avoid considering subsets that have already been shown unschedulable.

$$\forall k | 0 \le k < n, \forall \tau \in \mathcal{L}_k, \quad \mu_{\tau,k} = 1 \quad \text{/* locked task } \tau \text{ is mapped onto core } k \text{ */}$$

$$\forall k | 0 \le k < n, \forall \tau \notin \mathcal{L}_k, \quad \mu_{\tau,k} = 0 \quad \text{/* locked task } \tau \text{ is not mapped onto core } k \text{ */}$$

$$\forall k | 0 \le k < n, \quad \sum_{\tau \in \mathcal{B}_k} \mu_{\tau,k} < |\mathcal{B}_k| \quad \text{/* tasks in the blacklist for core } k \text{ cannot be mapped together on core } k \text{ */}$$

5 Experimental Results

5.1 Methodology

In the following, we consider an 8-core architecture, with in-order 2-way superscalar cores supporting the PowerPC ISA. Each core has a 2-Kbyte 2-way associative level-1 instruction cache with 16-byte cache lines. We consider a perfect level-1 data cache [1].

We consider a 32-bit bus, with a bus latency of 1 cycle. The memory latency is 5 cycles for the first word of a cache line and one additional cycle for each subsequent word.

Our task set includes 32 tasks, that is four instances of each of the tasks described in Table 1. They belong to the Mälardalen Benchmark Suite [8] (nsischneu and statemate), the SPEC95 suite[2] (compress) and the MiBench

---

[1] This assumption is only due to the fact that our WCET analysis does not completely handle data caches. We also have performed experiments considering no data cache, which are not reported here for the sake of clarity, and we have found similar conclusions to the ones drawn with perfect caches.

[2] www.spec.org

suite [9] (susan). These tasks have been selected because of their heterogeneous demands to the bus. Figure 2 show the variability of the WCET for each of these tasks as a function of the bus latency. The reference value is the WCET found considering the 8-core round-robin scheme (that gives a 73-cycle latency). The latency values are those observed in various configurations of our arbiter, as will be shown later.

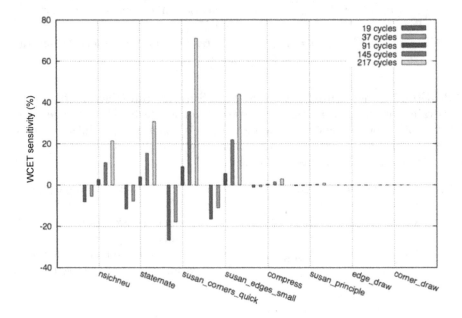

Fig. 2. Sensitivity of the tasks WCETs to the bus latency

For each task, considered as a real-time task, a period must be specified. In this paper, we consider a uniform core utilisation among the tasks. The utilisation of a task is computed as the ratio of its (worst-case) execution time to its period. To choose its value, we have performed some experiments considering a round-robin bus arbiter. We have observed that our task set is schedulable if the utilisation of tasks is not higher than 0.21. Since the schemes we propose aim at performing better than the round-robin algorithm, we have decided to use this value for the rest of the experiments. Then, the period of each task (used to decide on the task set schedulability) is computed as the ratio of its WCET to 0.21.

The worst-case execution times are analysed using our OTAWA/oRange toolset [10][11]. It implements static analysis techniques to build a representation of the binary code of the application (a Control Flow Graph), to determine flow facts (e.g. loop bounds), to derive the worst-case execution costs of basic blocks, and to determine the global WCET with the IPET technique [12].

Table 1. Benchmark tasks

Task name	Function
nsischneu	Simulation of an extended Petri net
statemate	Automatically generated code (STARC tool)
compress	Data compression
susan_corners_quick susan_edges_small susan_principle edge_draw corner_draw	Image processing (SUSAN)

The algorithms presented in this paper are implemented in Perl and the integer linear programs are solved with the CPLEX tool[3].

5.2 Results

Quantitative results for eight cores are provided in Table 2. For each configuration, described by the number of cores in each group (limited to three groups), it gives:

- the latency seen by any core in each group;
- the minimum global utilisation and the number of iterations needed to find it (see Algorithm 3), for both schemes (GRR and GGL).

When several configurations enforce the same values for bus latencies, only one of them has been considered. Doubles do not appear in the table, or with their latencies italicised. Configurations for which no schedulable mapping could be found are marked *n.s.*

Reference Value. The first configuration (all the eight cores in group G_0) enforces the same latency for each core; it is equivalent to the traditional round-robin scheme. The corresponding minimum utilisation (6.72) will then be considered as our reference value.

Performance of the GRR and GGL Schemes. Our two-level schemes both help in lowering the global utilisation of the cores compared to the round-robin algorithm: GRR can reduce it by 25.1% and GGL by 29.1%. GGL configurations that have a low number of cores in the highest priority group (G_0) perform better than GRR.

In addition, our schemes may be able to map and schedule the task set on a smaller number of cores. For example, the task set considered in these experiments cannot be scheduled on six or seven cores with the round-robin scheme. But we can find schedulable mappings considering both GRR and GGL. They

---

[3] www.ibm.com/software/integration/optimization/cplex-optimizer/

Table 2. Minimum utilisation obtained for all the possible configurations (8 cores)

Configuration			GRR					GGL				
N_0	N_1	N_2	L_{c_0}	L_{c_1}	L_{c_2}	U_{min}	#iter	L_{c_0}	L_{c_1}	L_{c_0}	U_{min}	#iter
8	-	-	73	-	-	6.72	101	73	-	-	-	-
1	7	-	19	127	-	5.30	28	19	127	-	-	-
2	6	-	37	127	-	5.86	9	37	127	-	-	-
3	5	-	55	91	-	6.15	13	55	91	-	-	-
1	1	6	28	28	163	5.03	18	19	27	217	4.76	62
1	2	5	28	55	136	5.30	75	19	73	181	4.86	7
1	3	4	28	82	109	5.46	5	19	109	145	5.05	32
2	1	5	55	28	136	-	-	37	37	181	n.s.	
2	2	4	55	55	109	6.15	10	37	73	145	5.61	111
3	1	4	82	28	109	-	-	55	37	145	5.72	20
3	2	3	82	55	82	6.35	19	55	73	109	6.42	18
4	1	3	109	28	82	-	-	73	37	109	5.95	28
5	1	2	136	28	55	-	-	91	37	73	5.86	10

even exhibit slightly lower utilisations: 5.01 and 4.70, respectively, for seven cores.

Finally, both GRR and GGL have solutions for this task set considering an utilisation of up to 0.27 for each task. The global utilisation then reaches 6.8 for eight cores. On the contrary, the task set cannot be mapped and scheduled with the round-robin scheme if the individual task utilisation exceeds 0.21.

Impact of Locking Schedulable Task Subsets. In Algorithm3, we have introduced task subsets locking as a way of making the computation faster: as soon as the mapping algorithm finds a solution with some of the task subsets being schedulable on their assigned core, these task subsets are locked on their core. Subsequent iterations of the loop, that may be necessary if some subsets are still not schedulable, consider the locked task subsets as a starting point and focus on mapping the remaining tasks only. Our experiments have shown that this drastically limits the number of needed iterations: without this feature, as many as 7 290 iterations are needed for some configurations; the maximum number of iterations with subsets locking is lowered down to 111.

6   Conclusion

Time-predictable resource sharing is a key feature that will allow using multicore architectures for hard real-time systems. In this paper, we propose an approach to efficiently use a time-predictable bus arbiter which was introduced in a recent paper [1]. This arbiter enforces different worst-case bus latencies for the different cores in order to meet the requirements of heterogeneous workloads. The approach presented here determines the best arbiter configuration and mapping of the tasks to the cores. Experimental results show a reduction of the multicore utilisation by more than 29% compared to a round-robin bus arbiter.

References

1. Bourgade, R., Rochange, C., Sainrat, P.: Predictable Bus Arbitration Schemes for Heterogeneous Time-Critical Workloads Running on Multicore Processors. In: Emerging Technologies and Factory Automation (ETFA). IEEE (September 2011)
2. Paolieri, M., Quiñones, E., Cazorla, F.J., Bernat, G., Valero, M.: Hardware support for wcet analysis of hard real-time multicore systems. In: Proc. 36th Annual International Symposium on Computer Architecture, ISCA 2009, pp. 57–68 (2009)
3. Andrei, A., Eles, P., Peng, Z., Rosen, J.: Predictable implementation of real-time applications on multiprocessor system-on-chip. In: International Conference on VLSI Design, pp. 103–110 (2008)
4. Wandeler, E., Thiele, L.: Optimal tdma time slot and cycle length allocation for hard real-time systems. In: Proceedings of the 2006 Asia and South Pacific Design Automation Conference, pp. 479–484 (2006)
5. Chattopadhyay, S., Roychoudhury, A., Mitra, T.: Modeling shared cache and bus in multi-cores for timing analysis. In: Proc. 13th Int'l Workshop on Software & Compilers for Embedded Systems, SCOPES 2010, pp. 6:1–6:10 (2010)
6. Bourgade, R., Rochange, C., Sainrat, P.: Predictable bus arbitration schemes for heterogeneous time-critical workloads running on multicore processors. Technical Report 2011-19, IRIT (2011)
7. Jeffay, K., Stanat, D.F.: On non-preemptive scheduling of periodic and sporadic tasks. In: Real-Time Systems Symposium (1991)
8. Gustafsson, J., Betts, A., Ermedahl, A., Lisper, B.: The Mälardalen WCET benchmarks – past, present and future. In: Int'l Workshop on WCET Analysis (2010)
9. Guthaus, M.R., Ringenberg, J.S., Ernst, D., Austin, T.M., Mudge, T., Brown, R.B.: Mibench: A free, commercially representative embedded benchmark suite. In: Int'l Workshop on Workload Characterization (2001)
10. Ballabriga, C., Cassé, H., Rochange, C., Sainrat, P.: Otawa: An open toolbox for adaptive wcet analysis. In: IFIP WG 10.2 International Workshop on Software Technologies for Embedded and Ubiquitous Systems (2010)
11. Michiel, M.D., Bonenfant, A., Cassé, H., Sainrat, P.: Static loop bound analysis of c programs based on flow analysis and abstract interpretation. In: Int'l Conf. on Embedded and Real-Time Computing Systems and Applications (2008)
12. Li, Y.T.S., Malik, S.: Performance analysis of embedded software using implicit path enumeration. In: ACM/IEEE Design Automation Conf., pp. 456–461 (June 1995)

Author Index